Rethinking Ethics in the Midst of Violence

New Feminist Perspectives Series

General Editor: Rosemarie Tong, Davidson College

Rethinking Ethics in the Midst of Violence

A Feminist Approach to Freedom

Linda A. Bell

with a Foreword by Claudia Card

Rowman & Littlefield Publishers, Inc.

ROWMAN & LITTLEFIELD PUBLISHERS, INC.

Published in the United States of America
by Rowman & Littlefield Publishers, Inc.
4720 Boston Way, Lanham, Maryland 20706

British Cataloging in Publication Information Available

Library of Congress Cataloging-in-Publication Data

Bell, Linda A.
Rethinking ethics in the midst of violence : a feminist approach
to freedom / Linda A. Bell.
p.   cm — (New feminist perspectives series).
Includes bibliographical references and index.
1. Feminist ethics. 2. Violence—Moral and ethical aspects.
I. Title. II. Series.
BJ1395.B45   1993   170'.82—dc20   93-2697   CIP

ISBN 0-8476-7844-X (cloth : alk. paper)
ISBN 0-8476-7845-8 (paper : alk. paper)

Printed in the United States of America

The paper used in this publication meets the minimum requirements of
American National Standard for Information Sciences—Permanence of
Paper for Printed Library Materials, ANSI Z39.48–1984.

For Liberty and Jennifer
and a better world in which to grow up,
a world in which all oppression and all hate crimes,
including those against women and girls,
will be viewed as crimes against real people.

Contents

Foreword

by Claudia Card

On December 6, 1989, Marc Lepine, angry at "fucking feminists," walked into a classroom at the University of Montreal's school of engineering and shot to death fourteen women.[1] What made this murder of women unusual was that it was done publicly and the victims were concentrated in one place. It received more publicity than murders of women usually receive. However, it is not unusual for women to be murdered because they are women. Although statistics indicate that more men than women are murdered annually, few men are murdered because they are men.[2] Law enforcement experts agree that the vast majority of victims of serial murderers are female.[3] Of female murder victims, it is primarily prostitutes and homeless women who are killed by strangers. For women generally, the place where they are most at risk is home "when that home is shared by a man, be he husband, male lover, father, or brother."[4] *The War at Home* is a documentary film about 1960s campus political unrest in Madison, Wisconsin regarding Vietnam.[5] However, for women, that title is apt to suggest a more intimate scenario of domestic rape, harassment, incest, battering and stalking—much unreported, much reported only to women's crisis centers in confidence, for fear of reprisals.[6]

The law has been far better at protecting men against women's accusations of assault than at protecting women from assault.[7] Women who strike back, even in clear self-defense, commonly receive heavy prison sentences in otherwise similar cases where men defending themselves would be charged with no crime at all.[8] Feminist ethics needs to center such facts and confront the questions: how should women (and men) meet misogynist violence, much of which is socially sanctioned? how are we to recognize its forms, in others and in ourselves?

xi

to shield ourselves, and heal ourselves, from its damage? to create
environments in which we are not so totally shaped by it and by daily
needs to do something about it? when, and how, are we justified in
meeting violence with violence? what values help structure sane answers to such questions?

Professor Linda Bell's work is motivated by this concern and by
analogous and interlocking concerns regarding the violence of racism,
classism, heterosexism, and hate crimes in all their many forms. In this
book she offers a feminist approach to ethics based on freedom, love,
and play, which she presents as having the potentiality to recognize
and respond to misogynist violence better than popular contemporary
alternatives, both the historically great moral philosophies taught in
the schools and recent "care ethics" favored by some feminists. To
highlight her contribution, it may be helpful to place this book, briefly,
in the context of some of this work, contrasting it with other feminist
approaches to ethics that are critical of some of the same historical
traditions that she criticizes. Linda Bell's work innovatively develops
ideas and themes from the philosophy of Jean-Paul Sartre in the service of feminist goals. Other feminist philosophers have drawn upon
the philosophy of nineteenth-century pro-feminists John Stuart Mill
and Friedrich Engels, and some have even been inspired by Immanuel
Kant and Friedrich Wilhelm Nietzsche, who were not feminists of any
kind.[9] Sartre was no feminist either, but he did nevertheless take seriously oppression and resistance to it, theorizing against the back-
ground of World War II and the French Resistance, and he explicitly
addressed such phenomena as anti-Semitism.

I see Linda Bell's work as continuing, in important ways, certain
traditions in the feminist writings of Mary Daly, Marilyn Frye, Sarah
Hoagland, and María Lugones. These traditions include taking seriously violence against women, seeking to understand and expose in-
terconnections of racism and sexism, not being preoccupied with the
concepts of family or law, centering freedom rather than care-taking,
and looking to playfulness as an alternative to current obsessions with
control. Of the feminist philosophers mentioned, the one whose work
is most naturally compared with that of Linda Bell is Professor Sarah
Hoagland of Northeastern Illinois University. The works of Linda Bell
and Sarah Hoagland not only have interesting themes in common but
also complement each other in audience, scope, and emphasis. Sarah
Hoagland's theorizing in *Lesbian Ethics: Toward New Value* (1988),
like Linda Bell's in the present work, has roots in the existentialisms
of Sartre and Simone de Beauvoir.[10] However, Linda Bell develops, in
a more systematic and self-conscious way, what is worth attending to

and exploiting, from a feminist perspective, in specific ideas and concepts from Sartre's ethical writings. Sarah Hoagland's ethic of agency is addressed to lesbians in community with each other. Linda Bell's ethic of freedom addresses members of a misogynist society who interact in mixed communities of women and men. Sarah Hoagland was moved by her concern to address the problem of lesbian community organizations falling apart from internal failures of interaction. Linda Bell's theorizing grows out of reflection on misogynist violence and women's resistance to it. Yet both are troubled by the idea that resistance to oppression requires us to be able to gain control of our situations. Both are dissatisfied with utilitarian, Kantian, and Aristotelian ethics standardly taught in college courses. And both exhibit qualified skepticism regarding recently developed "care ethics." Mother-child relationships are frequently taken as paradigms of caring in care ethics, and women's mothering capacities are often the inspiration for such ethics. Disturbed by the inequality of mother-child relationships, Sarah Hoagland took instead as her paradigms of caring adult lesbian relationships. Likewise concerned about the quality of caring relationships, Linda Bell acknowledges that although a care ethic has valuable insights for a nonviolent, nonoppressive society, by itself it is naive as a response to the society we live in. Rather, women's care-taking of those who benefit from sex oppression is part of the problem that a feminist ethic needs to address.

The most popular conception of feminist ethics in the nonfeminist media today is "care ethics."[11] Harvard professor of education Carol Gilligan contrasts an ethic of care, which she finds almost exclusively among women, with an ethic of justice that she finds more characteristic of men's than of women's thinking on moral issues.[12] Critics have pointed out the potentialities of care ethics, unqualified by justice, for reinforcing dominance and subordinance.[13] Rather than entering the "justice versus care" debates, Linda Bell begins anew. She agrees, however, that the value of caring is qualified by its context and by the values that caring supports, maintains, and helps to implement. When caring is valued in total independence of the values espoused and enacted by those cared for and independently of the presence or absence of genuine reciprocity and respect, it is easily exploited in the service of oppression. Women's socializations as care-takers have kept many locked into abusive relationships, giving abusers confidence that women will not turn on them, no matter what, but will always be there to pick up the pieces and knit together once again the fabric of life. An ethic of freedom challenges that assumption.

A difficulty less widely discussed is that care ethics tends easily toward pacifism, or to a centering of nonviolence in conflict resolution. At least, it has done so historically.[14] The paradigms of violence typically discussed by pacifists are overt and public or publicly accessible: street crime, capital punishment, war—the kinds of violence that, notoriously, men have done to one another. Women are, of course, victims of such violence as well, although less visibly so. Violence against women goes severely underreported and remains underattended to when reported. Ida B. Wells-Barnett reported lynchings of women and children as well as of men. Yet the general public remains ignorant of those facts.[15] Much of the violence men do *systematically to women*, however, remains unreportable, for it is done in *private*, and survivors are terrorized into silence. Pacifist ethics, with its appeals to moral conscience, requires a *public* setting. Pacifists attempt to shame perpetrators before witnesses. But there are characteristically no (other) witnesses to the private violence men do daily to women. In this context, women's socialization to pacifism seems also part of the problem rather than the solution. Attending to the kinds of violence women have suffered historically is thus important for identifying limitations of care ethics, especially in its pacifist incarnations.

Also easily overlooked, if one's paradigms of violence are war, street crime, and capital punishment, are many very mundane forms of institutionalized racism and sexism—in education, health care, and law enforcement, for example. As Linda Bell argues, disruptions of institutionalized racism and sexism are more liable than nondisruptions to be *experienced* or *felt* as violent by those who have been benefiting from current practices. Those who *resist* such practices may be thus more liable than those who cooperate to being identified by those in power as *perpetrators* of violence—as women who kill batterers are commonly treated as criminals—particularly if the standards or values applied are those of peace, happiness, pleasure, or nurturance. The inability of many traditional approaches to ethics, as well as of some contemporary forms of care ethics, to distinguish resistance to oppression from oppression itself is among the specific motivating concerns of Linda Bell's development of an alternative.

Aristotle's self-realization ethic and Kant's ethic of freedom both seem more promising than either hedonistic utilitarianism or recent care ethics with respect to articulating a standard or set of values that could identify oppression and justify resistance to it. And yet, in this book, Linda Bell identifies serious limitations in each of these approaches as well. Neither, she argues, is as well equipped as Sartrean ethics to recognize and respond to *institutionalized* oppression. For Aristotle, the difficulty is that the "self" whose "nature" is realized may be to a great extent socially constructed by institutions themselves severely in need of criticism and evaluation. In the case of Kant, a major difficulty is his reliance upon the presence of an *intention* in the agent for the possibility of moral or ethical evaluation of that agent's conduct. The intention becomes the "maxim of the action," which the Categorical Imperative then directs the agent to imagine to be a universal law. If, however, an agent is unaware of participating in oppressive practices, is not paying attention, is doing harm inadvertently, there is no relevant intention to evaluate. There would be such an intention if the agent were *as a matter of principle* not paying attention. But often this is not the case. The case is, rather, that those who have been raised to participate in oppressive institutions have been taught from childhood that those institutions are natural or beneficial or both. They have been trained not to see the oppressiveness of those institutions, and participants who benefit may have had no motive to examine them critically. For assessing the conduct of unreflective agents in an oppressive society, the Categorical Imperative may be of no help. And yet Kant's emphasis on freedom as what gives a worth beyond price to rational agents suggests a value by which even such an agent's conduct might ultimately be assessed. For freedom need not be measured in a simple manner by way of intentions. Freedom, for Linda Bell, is a far more embodied affair than it appears to have been for Kant. Freedom from oppression is *situated*, not freedom from the physical world, which Kant appears to have sought.

Although Nietzsche does not figure in this work, Linda Bell's emphasis upon play and playfulness calls to mind the child who plays, the highest stage of the development of the human spirit in the "Three Metamorphoses" of *Thus Spoke Zarathustra*.[16] Play, here, suggests creativity, a polar opposite of violence. Violence tears down, mutilates, destroys; creativity constructs, gives a new beginning. Play turns up in Sarah Hoagland's ethics in the form of the "trickster," borrowed from Native American traditions, who offers advice and criticism through humor.[17] It turns up in María Lugones' "'world'-travelling" as the appropriately animating spirit of one who would travel to the "worlds" of others for the sake of understanding and love.[18] It turns up in Marilyn Frye's recent "willful virgin" and, earlier, in her lesbian seer who disrupts the patriarchal play by attending to the (female) "stage hands" instead of to the (male) "players."[19] It turns up in Mary Daly's vision of roaring hags, dances throughout her *Pure Lust* and *Wickedary*, and, most recently, animates her autobiographical voyage, *Outercourse*.[20] Linda Bell's rethinking of ethics in the midst of violence is in a tradition that values creativity over the security of utilitarian benefits and interprets creativity not, as so many do when thinking of women, in terms of biological reproduction but, rather, as a capacity for spiritual renewal and joy. This tradition does not assume that women have the ability to prevent misogynist violence or that ethics requires as the justifying end of action the production of a less violent or even less oppressive world. It does, however, offer inspiration for communities of resistance and guidance for creating worthwhile lives in the midst of violence and threats of violence that we may be powerless to prevent.

NOTES

1. *Femicide: The Politics of Woman Killing*, ed. Jill Radford and Diana E.H. Russell (New York: Twayne Publishers, 1992), pp. 5-6. See, also, *The Montreal Massacre*, ed. Louise Mallette and Marie Chalouh, trans. Marlene Wildemen (Charlotte Town, Prince Edward Island: Gynergy Books, 1991).

2. *Femicide*, p. 10.

3. Jane Caputi, *The Age of Sex Crime* (Bowling Green, Ohio: Bowling Green State University, 1987), p. 203. This came as a surprise to me. For, if my own recollections are reliable, it would seem that serial murders of men and boys receive more publicity.

4. Diana E.H. Russell, Preface to *Femicide*, p. xi.

5. Produced/directed by Glenn Silber and Barry Alexander Brown. Madison, Wisc.: Madison Film Production Co., 1974.

6. Donna Ferrato, *Living with the Enemy* (New York: Aperture, 1991), offers an extraordinary photographic documentary of domestic assault.

A growing source of information on the domestic assaults of children is the literature on multiple personality. See Eugene L. Bliss, *Multiple Personality, Allied Disorders and Hypnosis* (New York: Oxford University Press, 1987); *Childhood Antecedents of Multiple Personality*, ed. Richard Kluft (Washington, D.C.: American Psychiatric Press, 1985); Frank W. Putnam, *Diagnosis and Treatment of Multiple Personality Disorder* (New York: Guilford Press, 1989); and Colin A. Ross, *Multiple Personality Disorder: Diagnosis, Clinical Features, and Treatment* (New York: Wiley, 1989). See, also, *Lasting Effects of Child Sexual Abuse*, ed. Gail Elizabeth Wyatt and Gloria Johnson Powell (Newbury Park, Calif.: Sage, 1989).

7. On rape as the center of a protection racket, see my "Rape as a Terrorist Institution" in *Violence, Terrorism, and Justice*, ed. R.G. Frey and Christopher W. Morris (Cambridge, Eng.: Cambridge University Press, 1991), pp. 296-319.

8. See Angela Browne, *When Battered Women Kill* (New York: Free Press, 1987) and Cynthia K. Gillespie, *Justifiable Homicide: Battered Women, Self-Defense, and the Law* (Columbus: Ohio State University Press, 1989).

9. See John Stuart Mill, *The Subjection of Women* (London 1869; written in 1861) and *On Liberty* (London 1859); Friedrich Engels, *On the Origin of*

the Family, Private Property, and the State (Zurich 1884; trans. E. Undermann, 1902).

10. Sarah Lucia Hoagland, *Lesbian Ethics: Toward New Value* (Palo Alto, Calif.: Institute for Lesbian Studies, 1988). For relevant work by Simone de Beauvoir, see *The Ethics of Ambiguity*, trans. Bernard Frechtman (Secaucus, N.J.: Citadel, 1975), as well as *The Second Sex*, trans. H.M. Parshley (New York: Knopf, 1952).

11. An excellent collection of articles on this topic is *An Ethic of Care*, ed. Mary Jeanne Larrabee (New York: Routledge, 1993).

12. Carol Gilligan, *In a Different Voice: Psychological Theory and Women's Development* (Cambridge, Mass.: Harvard University Press, 1982) and *Mapping the Moral Domain*, with Janie Victoria Ward, Jill McLean Taylor, and Betty Bardige (Cambridge, Mass.: Harvard University Graduate School of Education, 1988). For sympathetic development and discussion, see *Women and Moral Theory*, ed. Eva Feder Kittay and Diana T. Meyers (Totowa, N.J.: Rowman and Littlefield, 1987). Unlike Nel Noddings in *Caring: A Feminine Approach to Ethics and Moral Education* (Berkeley: University of California Press, 1984), Carol Gilligan does not claim the superiority of a care ethic to an ethic of justice.

For a wider range of conceptions of feminist ethics, see *Explorations in Feminist Ethics: Theory and Practice*, ed. Eve Browning Cole and Susan Coultrap-McQuin (Bloomington: Indiana University Press, 1992) and *Feminist Ethics*, ed. Claudia Card (Lawrence: University Press of Kansas, 1991).

13. See, e.g., Owen Flanagan and Kathryn Jackson, "Justice, Care, and Gender: The Kohlberg-Gilligan Debate Revisited" and Marilyn Friedman, "Beyond Caring: The De-Moralization of Gender," both in *An Ethic of Care*, and Claudia Card, "Caring and Evil," *Hypatia* 5:1 (Spring 1990), 101-8.

14. See, especially, Sara Ruddick, *Maternal Thinking: Toward a Politics of Peace* (Boston: Beacon, 1989).

For a nonpacifist view of mothering, see Jeffner Allen, "Motherhood: The Annihilation of Women" in *Mothering: Essays in Feminist Theory*, ed. Joyce Trebilcot (Totowa, N.J.: Rowman & Allanheld, 1983).

15. Ida B. Wells-Barnette, *On Lynchings* (Salem, N.H.: Ayer Publishers, reprint edition 1987).

16. Friedrich Nietzsche, *Thus Spoke Zarathustra*, trans. Walter Kaufmann, in *The Portable Nietzsche*, ed. Walter Kaufmann (New York: Viking Press, 1954), pp. 137-39.

17. Hoagland, pp. 243-46.

18. María Lugones, "Playfulness, 'World'-Travelling, and Loving Perception," *Hypatia* 2:2 (Summer 1987), 3-19, esp. 9-17

19. See Marilyn Frye, "Willful Virgin *or* Do You Have to Be a Lesbian to Be a Feminist" in *Willful Virgin: Essays in Feminism 1976-1992* (Freedom, Calif.: Crossing Press, 1992) and "To See and Be Seen: The Politics of Reality" in *The Politics of Reality: Essays in Feminist Theory* (Trumansburg, N.Y.: Crossing Press, 1983).

20. On roaring hags, see Mary Daly, *Gyn/Ecology: The Metaethics of Radical*

Feminism (Boston: Beacon, 1978), p. 17. The *Wickedary* is her *Webster's First New Intergalactic Wickedary of the English Language*, conjured in cahoots with Jane Caputi (Boston: Beacon, 1987). The autobiography is her *Outercourse: The Be-Dazzling Voyage* (San Francisco: Harper, 1992). See, also, her *Pure Lust: Elemental Feminist Philosophy* (Boston: Beacon, 1984).

Acknowledgments

This book is a product of so many forces and individuals that it is difficult to begin to name all of them, much less to give each proper credit.

First, years of living in, thinking about, and reacting to a racist and sexist society were probably necessary. Perhaps it even helps to view the society from the point of view of a Southerner, since, until fairly recently, the South's more explicit racism and sexism made racist and sexist actions and social structures more readily apparent and more difficult to ignore, for whites certainly and probably even for blacks, than seems to have been the case in other parts of the country. Unfortunately, the particular virulence of racism and sexism in the South offered many in other parts of the country a rationale to dismiss these as uniquely Southern problems. For those familiar with the history of lynching, job discrimination, the use of capital punishment and other penalties by the so-called criminal justice system, and legal treatment of rape and of spouse and child abuse, though, it is quite clear that racism and sexism are not and never have been uniquely or even predominantly Southern problems.

As painful as some of my own experiences, particularly in academe, have been, they, too, have increased my awareness and fueled my recognition that things are not as they ought to be and must be changed. In fact, those experiences were a major catalyst in undermining the hold exerted on me by society's various ways of maintaining the status quo. Even teaching for many years in a university with a very backward, racist, and sexist administration gave me valuable insight into the necessity of constant vigilance and struggle. Of course, until I could gain some perspective on and distance from them, those personal experiences also for quite a while prevented me from writing about the issues discussed in the following pages.

Both for helping me through many difficult experiences and struggles and for encouraging me in my academic endeavors, I owe much to my sisters, Mary L. Law and Susan B. Bostwick, my mother, Marjorie W. Law, and my many friends without whose continuing love and concern this would not have been written. Without them, I would have been lost.

The idea for this book resulted from my contact with Alison M. Jaggar. When she came to Atlanta a number of years ago as a visiting scholar in philosophy for the University Center in Georgia, she quite courteously asked what my interests were. When she learned that I was working in feminist theory as well as Sartrean ethics, she enthusiastically suggested that I combine these interests and write a book on feminist ethics from the perspective of existentialism.

Many have made significant contributions to the specific ideas and arguments found in the following pages. Although it would be pointless to name here as well as in the Bibliography all the feminist theorists from whose work I have drawn inspiration, I must name one to whose work and example I find myself continually returning. In my experience, Gloria Watkins, aka bell hooks, shines like a beacon for those who want to correct problems we see in the world but without excluding and harming some who are worse off. I have been challenged by her ideas and by her loving and inclusive revolutionary zeal.

Faculty and students of Women's Studies at Georgia State University have been particularly helpful, especially Paula Dressel, Valerie Fennell, and Diane Fowlkes. Their often courageous attempts to live according to feminist insights and principles have inspired some of my thinking, perhaps even more than have their thoughtful analyses of ideas, arguments, actions, and political and social structures.

For their careful and helpful readings of my entire manuscript, albeit at very different stages, I am grateful to Diane L. Fowlkes, Albert C. Skaggs, an unidentified reader for a university press, and Claudia Card.

I was particularly fortunate that Claudia Card was asked by Rowman & Littlefield to read my manuscript. Her response was thorough, critical, and extremely generous in pointing out strengths as well as weaknesses, in suggesting more careful wordings, and in bringing to my attention at numerous points other work with which I should have been but was not familiar. The manuscript is much improved as the result of her effort, an effort far in excess of the time and energy many readers would have put into it. So many of her suggestions were incorporated into the text that I made no attempt to credit them individually. As the result of my incorporation of her criticisms, questions, and suggestions, Chapter 4 in particular is substantially different from the original version she read. In many respects, it is almost as much her chapter as mine, although, given that I exercised ultimate control over the chapter's direction and over the final construction of arguments, I would not want her to be seen as sharing any responsibility for remaining blunders or for arguments that fail. After all her generous labor to make this a better book, though, it was singularly appropriate that she be asked to write the Foreword. I thank her for accepting that additional task.

For selecting Claudia Card to read and critique my manuscript, I thank the publisher, Rowman & Littlefield. Jennifer Dudley, assistant editor, has been especially helpful and supportive.

Moreover, a reading group at the First Existentialist Congregation of Atlanta, formed specifically to read my manuscript toward the end of its development, was very supportive, encouraging, and insightful. For the opportunity to discuss more deeply many of the issues, ideas, and arguments in the manuscript, I thank the congregation for sponsoring the group, Marcia Mitchiner for setting it up, Rev. R. Lanier Clance for encouraging and participating in it, and all the participants whose discussion of the issues raised by my manuscript often supported and endorsed my own thinking but always gave me more to think about.

Others read and commented on individual sections, often giving me much needed feedback on aspects I found particularly troubling. For their assistance, I am indebted to Susan Fox Beversluis, Dorothy P. Gray, C. Grant Luckhardt, Theresa C. Singletary, and Olga Skorapa. Yet others were of enormous help with my earlier work on Sartre and ethics, the foundation on which the present work was developed. They include some I have already mentioned as well as John Beversluis and Dieter Turck. When I needed help in documenting my claims about the press, Marion Meyers and Celeste Tibbets were extremely helpful.

Finally, for their patience and the generosity with which they shared their computer skills with a stumbling beginner, I thank William Bechtel and Henri Madigan. Sometimes my questions and problems were silly and merely the result of carelessness or technophobia; sometimes they were quite serious; but always Bill and Henri treated me with great respect and, when necessary, performed their computer wizardry to get me "unstuck."

Many of my ideas and arguments were developed in previously published work. That work includes the following:

Visions of Women (Clifton, N.J.: Humana Press, Inc., 1983);

Sartre's Ethics of Authenticity (Tuscaloosa: University of Alabama Press, 1989);

"Sartre: Alienation and Society," *Philosophy and Social Criticism*, Vol. 6, No. 4 (Winter 1979), pp. 409-22;

"Loser Wins: The Importance of Play in a Sartrean Ethics of Authenticity," *Phenomenology in a Pluralistic Context*, ed. William L. McBride and Calvin O. Schrag, *Selected Studies in Phenomenology and Existential Philosophy*, Vol. 9 (Albany: State University of New York Press, 1983), pp. 5-13;

"Love and Perfect Coincidence in a Sartrean Ethics," *Writing the Politics of Difference*, ed. Hugh J. Silverman and Donn Welton, *Selected Studies in Phenomenology and Existential Philosophy*, Vol. 14 (Albany: State University of New York Press, 1991), pp. 89-97, 313-15;

"Gallantry: What It Is and Why It Should Not Survive," *Southern Journal of Philosophy*, Vol. XXII, No. 2 (Summer 1984), pp. 165-73;

"Does Marriage Require a 'Head'? Some Historical Arguments," *Hypatia*, Vol. 4, No. 1 (Spring 1989), pp. 139-54;

"Play in a Sartrean Feminist Ethics," *Bulletin de la Société Américaine de Philosophie de Langue Française* (special Sartre issue), Vol IV, Nos. 2-3 (Summer-Fall 1992), pp. 281-301.

Introduction

Teaching and thinking about ethics over the years, I have frequently despaired over my inability to find within traditional ethics of Western culture a satisfactory position. Whatever the plausibility of an Aristotelian ethics of self-realization, I remain enormously wary of any talk of an essence or nature each individual ought to realize. Utilitarian ethics, with its claim that right actions maximize good consequences, also becomes problematic even though I admire its egalitarian emphasis on the effects of our acts upon each and every human being and even, as some have argued, every sentient being. Still, though, I doubt that a utilitarian calculus of consequences can give human freedom the consideration it deserves, particularly if considerable pain and suffering are necessary to secure or to preserve that freedom. Even Kantian ethics runs into difficulties in spite of its emphasis on universalizability and treating others and oneself as ends, not merely as means. When pressed, Kantian ethics allows as morally permissible either too much or too little, makes morality too much a matter of intention with too little attention paid to the effects of our actions, and secures the status quo by condemning effective resistance.

For feminist thinkers, the problems in these positions become especially acute. As a group, women have been affected adversely, though admittedly in diverse ways, by claims about "woman" and "the feminine." Given the various historical attempts to decipher what this nature is, self-realization for women, realization of their alleged nature, has usually meant their development into roles that complement or serve males and that sustain privileges and prerogatives, at least for males in the dominant race and class. Essentialist claims have also been used to shore up racism, white dominance, and even class hierarchies.

1

Though potentially far more favorable to oppressed groups, utilitarianism offers serious obstacles. Carol Gilligan[1] has discussed and documented the fact that girls and women tend to concern themselves, in a fairly utilitarian manner, with the ways actions will affect others. In societies where most girls but not many boys are raised to be sensitive to the needs, wishes, and sufferings of at least some others, a utilitarian ethics is likely simply to reinforce the societal expectations and to bind girls and women more tightly into their socially ordained roles of service to males. Moreover, changing the status quo is always difficult; and utilitarianism reinforces existing oppressive structures by requiring that the suffering caused by change be warranted by the anticipated improvement in the general happiness. Utilitarian ethics cannot simply and unequivocally condemn oppression as oppression and urge its overthrow. Rather, the burden of proof is on the revolutionary to show that society would be better off with less or no oppression, that the less oppressive state is achievable, and that its achievement would warrant the pain and suffering caused by the transition.

On the other hand, Kantian ethics seems to offer a paradigm of a gender- and race-neutral ethics, universalizing as it does over all rational beings and instructing us to treat every one of these beings as an end in itself, not merely as a means. Although this might seem to be a feminist ethics par excellence, it, too, leaves much to be desired. First, in order to know which individuals to treat as ends in themselves, one must be able to recognize rationality wherever it occurs; and this is certainly not as easy as it may sound. Numerous scholars have called attention to the considerable difficulty men have had recognizing women as rational beings, and male philosophers are not exempt from this difficulty. While there are important exceptions, Immanuel Kant, quite definitely, is not one. In his aesthetic and anthropological writings, he portrays women as primarily creatures of feelings and rather nastily dismisses those who do not conform to this allegedly descriptive claim, mocking them as women who might as well have beards.[2] Even worse, by affirming that women's virtues are virtues of feeling rather than of reason, he excludes them—whether he means to or not—from the rational demands of morality, particularly the demand of universalizability—the Categorical Imperative—imposed by reason on itself.

Second, Kantian ethics is concerned with intentions rather than consequences. It thereby too glibly dismisses Sharon D. Welch's concern that *"well-intentioned people are responsible for the nuclear arms race,"* a consideration that leads her to conclude that "such 'good' intentions are beside the point."[3] It ignores the way existing social institutions curtail the options of certain individuals. Moreover, focusing on intentions, Kantian ethicists neglect, because irrelevant, the radically different ways different individuals are affected by a given behavior as the result of their diverse situations in society.

Not just the consequences but also the social *meaning* of the behavior, which is not reducible to intentions, will differ from society to society and even from situation to situation within a particular society. For example, white women campaigning for abortion rights sometimes find themselves at odds with black women, not because the latter are opposed to such rights but rather because the black but not the white women are aware of the numerous racist attempts in this country, including forced sterilization, to limit the fertility of black women and of third world women generally. Because of the false but still prevalent myth of the black rapist and the appalling history of lynching in the United States, similar difficulties arise for black and white women who try to work together to combat rape.[4] Kantian attempts to universalize fail, both as a result of their neglect of crucial social differences but also because any such recognition is likely to undermine the whole project of universalizing.

Finally, Kantian ethics is inadequate in dealing with oppression. It too often ignores it or allows little opportunity to confront, challenge, and remove oppressive social structures, particularly where there are no individuals who can be held responsible. Whenever individuals are not implicated in the oppression, they are recognized as having no responsibility whatsoever to do anything about it. In addition, even when implicated, individuals are given mixed—contradictory—messages by this ethics which fails to acknowledge the way oppression manipulates the options of the oppressed. Again, women and other oppressed groups are caught in a bind. The rights of some are likely to be violated by any attempt to resist, undermine, or overthrow the oppressive structures. As we shall see in Chapter 4, any such attempt is apt to be condemned on Kantian grounds and regarded as morally impermissible. Yet this means that individuals of various groups will continue to encounter, without the slightest demurral from such a moralist, "barriers and forces which reduce, immobilize and mold [them] . . . and effect their subordination to another group."[5]

What feminist ethics requires is a theoretical structure that allows for (1) affirmation of individual freedom against the determinism of nature and natures, but with clear recognition that freedom can be curtailed by systems of oppression, (2) affirmation of the worth and value of individual freedom against those who would concern themselves only with overall happiness or the meeting of needs, and (3) postulation of *ideals* of gender- and race-neutrality and a kingdom of ends in such a way that they do not too easily become co-opted as supports for an oppressive order that neither is gender- and race-neutral nor treats all individuals as ends in themselves. Given our current political rhetoric, neutrality is likely to suggest gender- and race-"blindness" and the same legal treatment for everyone. This "equal" treatment of unequals will not and cannot be just. Moreover, in a society like ours, the standard for determining what is proper legal treatment very likely will be set by considering the needs of able-bodied, straight, well-off, white males. Though all might eventually be treated the same under such a system of justice, their needs would receive quite different and unequal consideration. This is not neutrality, and it is what we must avoid in our ideals. Instead, we need to formulate ideals in which gender and race are not set up as handicaps to individual freedom and in which the freedom of all is affirmed.

Welch sketches some of the theoretical structure needed by feminist ethics in what she calls "a feminist ethic of risk": "a definition of responsible action within the limits of bounded power . . . [describing] the nature of responsible action when control is impossible and . . . [naming] the resources that evoke persistent defiance and resistance in the face of repeated defeats."[6] While her contribution to feminist ethics is important and especially evocative in its use of the writings of black women, it draws inspiration from theology and recasts central Christian affirmations in feminist terms. What I seek is different—an ethics independent of religion and theology, that has neither a loving nor an authoritarian deity as its base, as its support, or even playing any important role in its actual development. Thus, I turn to the work of Jean-Paul Sartre, where I find at least an outline of an ethics incorporating affirmations of freedom and the requisite analyses of the role of ideals. I shall use that outline and those analyses in the remainder of this book.

In the following pages, I draw heavily on the ethics suggested by Sartre in his various writings, an ethics to which I have devoted attention previously in *Sartre's Ethics of Authenticity*.[7] There I argued that Sartre develops a notion of authenticity and an ethics based on it that, at least implicitly, provide solutions to various problems recognized by other ethicists in the Western tradition. For Sartre, the authentic individual is one who wills her or his own freedom and the freedom of others. Whatever values are chosen by this individual, those values inevitably implicate others. Thus, I proposed, Sartre offers a way of affirming universalizability in moral judgments without either adopting a Kantian view of human reason or importing an unsupported and insupportable "absolute" value (such as consistency) into his ethics.

Second, I indicated how Sartre's ethics affirms a way of avoiding and overcoming a particular kind of alienation. Admittedly, not all alienation can be overcome; some alienation is fundamental to the human condition. Still, the alienation resulting from bad faith or self-deception—self-alienation—is not fundamental and is avoidable. Such avoidable alienation can and should be overcome. Moreover, on the level of societies, two similar forms of alienation exist, one being fundamental and inescapable, the other, not fundamental, which can and should be eliminated. Thus, Sartre can criticize oppressive societies for the alienations they impose or fail to remove, just as he criticizes individuals who fail to recognize and affirm their own freedom and that of others.

Third, I developed playfulness as Sartre's alternative to seriousness. Individuals are serious who refuse to recognize freedom and who pretend that values exist prior to and independently of their creation by human beings. Cognizant of freedom and of responsibility for values, the authentic individual is playful rather than serious, acting out of freedom rather than an alleged determinism. Given the recognition of choice as the origin of values, relativism, and futility present special problems; but these problems, I argued, are resolved by play.

Finally, I explored the possibilities of a nonappropriative love that approaches the other with confidence in freedom and with trust and generosity. Although sequestration and individualism play a major role in Sartre's writings, there are nevertheless indications of a kind of love that affirms freedom and respects the other as an end. Once again, Sartre can affirm an aspect of Kantian ethics—the kingdom of ends— without at the same time affirming the Kantian view of human reason.

With these analyses, I concluded, against Sartre's critics, that an ethics based on freedom is indeed possible and coherent. I showed how an emphasis on a freedom vitally connected with embodiment allows commitment and avoids the heartless and ludicrous conclusion that the individual can be and do absolutely anything and is responsible for whatever happens to her or him.

The present work differs from that earlier one in a number of ways. First, I am in many instances presupposing rather than developing the ethics I previously teased from Sartre's writings. I do not view it as necessary here to answer the same critics. In fact, I now am trying to answer an almost completely different set of critics since I am addressing primarily feminists and others concerned to resist oppression rather than Sartre scholars. Second, in using Sartre's ethics to resolve problems presented by feminist theory and practice, I frequently and deliberately take his ethics in directions that he did not, sometimes applying it to examples quite unlike his own, but generally in ways that seem to me consistent with the spirit of his ethics. Some problems lead to resolutions with no analogues in the work of Sartre. Even where this is the case, though, those resolutions seem to me quite consistent with others that are connected.

While much of the following is Sartre-inspired, it is not centered in Sartre's work. Sartre's (or Sartrean) answers to problems enter the text where appropriate and needed, largely in opposition to other ethics and when they have been found wanting. Although I give an overview of this ethics of freedom in Chapter 1, the ethics of freedom being proposed for consideration is expanded with each later chapter.

After proposing resolutions to some issues confronting ethics in general and feminist ethics in particular—concerning violence, the personal, co-optation, objectivity, separatism, equality, and power—the book moves on to examine traditional theories of ethics from the perspective of feminism and a focus on violence and oppression. Aristotelian ethics is examined and rejected on the basis of the unacceptable aspects of an appeal to essences or natures. From a similar perspective, an ethics based on needs is also challenged. These rejections are balanced by recognition of the high costs of simply rejecting essences or natures—and needs—out of hand and by argument that an adequate ethics must take into account the role of social constructions. An ethics of freedom rejects the naturalness of natures and needs but nonetheless is able to recognize the ways they are socially constructed and affect the lives of everyone in oppressive societies. It thereby avoids both the unacceptable appeal to the "natural" to settle moral issues and the risks incurred by individuals who fail to realize that a rejection of the "natural" as arbiter of moral issues nonetheless leaves in place the realities of class, gender, race, and sexuality.

Later chapters examine the theories of ethical egoism, utilitarianism, and Kantian ethics, and a more recently developed ethics of caring. The difficulties confronting these ethics are seen to center largely around issues of violence—in particular, the relation of violence to the feminine and the relation of women to violence—and the intricate connections among violence, pleasure, protection, domination, privacy, and revolution. I conclude that the traditional ethical theories are less adequate than an ethics of freedom and that even an ethics of caring is inadequate in its analysis of caring and its proposal that ideals emerging from this analysis can be adequate guides to action in situations premised on and maintained by violence.

Since an ethics requires a vision of the way things should be, different possibilities of love and friendship are probed to discover whether any captures a feminist ideal of human relations. Here, the ethics of caring and various claims about family, friendship, and love are sifted for what they might contribute to the formulation of such an ideal. An ethics of caring is reinterpreted as a profound and helpful attempt at characterizing an ideal society although its proposals were previously rejected as inadequate—and even dangerous—as guides to action in society as presently constituted.

Finally, in the last chapter, an attitude of playfulness is proposed not just as the alternative to the rejected attitude of seriousness but also as a resolution to challenges posed to an ethics of freedom by relativism and futility. In addition, this last chapter examines the revolutionary potential of play, a potential suggested by several feminist theorists as well as by others.

In turning for inspiration and guidance to work written by and often attributed solely to Sartre, I realize that I fit, along with many others, into a long tradition in which the oppressed, the dispossessed, and those constituted as "others" by their society have looked to theorists more comfortably ensconced both in society and in the philosophical tradition for analyses and theories to critique the status quo and to recognize the legitimacy of the concerns of the marginal and oppressed. Andrea Nye, in her book *Feminist Theory and the Philosophies of Man*, has challenged such attempts, demonstrating the problematic aspects of past efforts to weave feminist theory from the strands offered by the traditional "philosophies of man." However promising the strands, she argues that the misogynist and patriarchal assumptions of the different philosophical positions remain an inextricable part of those strands and contaminate any feminist tapestry into which they may be woven.[8]

Adequately warned by Nye's analyses, any who see Sartre's work as useful in providing the underpinning necessary for critiquing the status quo must scrutinize his work for sexist assumptions. We must see as clearly as possible how these assumptions relate to his philosophical position as a whole so we can determine whether and how it is possible to avoid using contaminated "threads" that ultimately will undermine our analyses. Most important, we must be able to meet Nye's challenge that contamination permeates the views of Sartre and destroys their utilizability by feminist theorists.

A sufficient case has already been made for the claim that serious sexism exists in Sartre's writings. For example, in a 1973 article, "Holes and Slime: Sexism in Sartre's Psychoanalysis," Margery L. Collins and Christine Pierce call attention to the sexist way that Sartre depicts human activity and non-human reality, referring not only to his discussions of "holes" and "slime" but also to such statements as "The obscenity of the feminine sex is that of everything which gapes open."[9] In addition, Carole Pateman and Elizabeth Gross have observed that what Sartre says of the look simply does not apply to a case of street harassment where a woman is dehumanized and made into a thing with no possibility of reciprocity. They point out that Sartre's analysis is from the point of view of men and not even all of them.[10] More recently, Hazel E. Barnes has added to these challenges by pointing to his linkage of "female with notions of treacherous receptivity" and of knowledge with "penetration and conquest."[11]

Interestingly enough, Sartre himself gives an analysis that can be used to make the strongest case against him. In *Anti-Semite and Jew*, he observes that an individual's anti-Semitism cannot be seen as limited, as just an unfortunate characteristic, as merely an idiosyncracy, completely consistent with the individual's being in every other respect a fine person. As a choice to live in passion, he claims, this choice cannot be circumscribed; rather, it affects every aspect of the individual's life—and presumably, as Nye might add, every aspect of a writer's thought.[12] Thus, Sartre himself seems to prohibit our saying, for example, that a philosopher's anti-Semitism affects only limited aspects of his or her thought while the rest is acceptable.

Sartre's uncompromising appraisal of anti-Semites thus appears to place all of his own philosophy under indictment once we acknowledge the compelling evidence of sexism in his work. Thus, if we grant Sartre's indictment of anti-Semites, we must conclude that sexism like anti-Semitism affects all of a philosopher's work and hence that the remainder of Sartre's work is itself tainted by sexism and should be avoided by any of us who might wish to use such a philosophy as a grounding for feminist ethics. Without any further analysis of specifics, Sartre's own analysis appears to lead to Nye's conclusion.

This argument, however, is a bit too glib, even, I think, in Sartre's use of it against the anti-Semite. When applied to Sartre's philosophy, it ignores the ambiguities to which he himself constantly draws our attention and of which he was amazingly cognizant. Moreover, it ignores some important ways in which our embodiment reflects the institutionalization of racism and sexism in our societies.

The analysis of racism and sexism I have in mind utilizes an important discussion from another part of *Anti-Semite and Jew* as well as his treatment of institutions and other social structures in *The Critique of Dialectical Reason*. In referring to the Jew as "overdetermined" by anti-Semitic society, Sartre indicates the ways the actions of the Jew can be restricted and limited by the behavior of others. The Jew is in effect given a nature—Jewishness—by anti-Semitic society, a nature through which all of the Jew's actions will be interpreted and on the basis of which certain activities will be prescribed as appropriate whereas others will be proscribed.[13] When what Sartre says about such overdetermination is added to his survey of social structures and the oppressions perpetuated by many of them, it becomes evident that anti-Semitism, other forms of racism, and sexism can and should be discussed on two levels, the level of individual anti-Semitism, racism, and sexism and the level of institutionalized anti-Semitism, racism, and sexism.

If these two levels are kept as distinct as possible, then individual anti-Semitism can be distinguished from an aspect of society that looks rather like it and with which it might otherwise be confused. That aspect of society—societal or institutionalized anti-Semitism—is reflected in institutions, is sedimented in language and folklore, and is part of patterns of behavior and of the very atmosphere in which individuals live and move. Such anti-Semitism is not the same as that of individuals in bad faith. Society is not a conscious individual, and thus there is no social consciousness maintaining these social structures through a duplicity parallel to that of the individual anti-Semite who passionately justifies himself and his mediocrity with a Manichaean move attaching all evil to "the Jew." Such duplicity is what Sartre calls the bad faith of anti-Semitism, but this bad faith is present only in the case of individual anti-Semitism, not in institutional anti-Semitism, there being no institutional consciousness to effect the requisite duplicity.

The fact that racism and sexism are embedded in social institutions means that individuals growing up in a racist and sexist society will absorb the racism and sexism of the society much as they absorb the toxic chemicals in the air they breathe, in the food they eat, and in the water they drink. Such aspects of the society become part of every individual's embeddedness; and to that extent, everyone in such a society will be racist and sexist. This does not mean all members of the society will reflect these social characteristics in the same ways nor does it mean there is nothing an individual can or should do about them. Just as we try to alter other aspects of our embodiment, we can and should come to see, for example, that certain expressions in the language are objectionable and to be avoided no matter how difficult such avoidance might be. Failure to try will indicate the individual racism or sexism Sartre discusses. However, to shed all vestiges of objectionable and oppressive aspects of one's society is likely to be very difficult or even impossible.

With this distinction between individual and societal racism and sexism, we can reexamine Sartre's sexism, as well as the sexism of others, from a much more sophisticated perspective. In fact, this new perspective enables us to see exactly what was too glib about Sartre's previous argument. By failing to recognize institutional structures of anti-Semitism, other forms of racism, and sexism, the argument simply makes it both too easy to dismiss individuals in bad faith and too difficult

to challenge the forms of racism and sexism that structure the milieu
in which individuals come into awareness and make their decisions.

Once we make the distinction between individual and institutional
racism or sexism, we see that it is possible to find racism and sexism
in a thinker without concluding that the thinker is thereby exemplifying a racist or sexist bad faith. Of course, just saying this is possible
does not mean it is the case in any particular case, such as Sartre's. It
does mean, however, that we should continue to examine the thinker
closely in order to determine exactly where the racism or sexism lies.
It means, too, that individuals are likely to constitute a rather broad
spectrum of awareness of and success in eliminating the racism and
sexism by which their thinking, feeling, and acting are constituted by
society.

As Barnes and others have demonstrated, a close examination of
Sartre's thought reveals much to make even a half-hearted feminist
cringe. His claim that to see is to deflower[14] certainly suggests the
arrogant perceiver quite properly rejected by Marilyn Frye and replaced
by her with the loving eye.[15] While this arrogance must be acknowledged and challenged, though, Sartre's own discussion of embodiment
conflicts with and undermines the arrogance of his epistemological
claim. In addition, much of his philosophy explicitly challenges the
further arrogance of which he is perhaps implicitly guilty here, namely, taking the male perspective as the only legitimate one, neglecting
the fact that women are also perceivers, and treating them as "other."
This is why, as Barnes observes, Simone de Beauvoir was able to write
The Second Sex on the foundation delineated in Sartre's works,[16] a
foundation to which, incidentally, she herself was apparently an important contributor both in the original formulation, in conversations,
of the ideas and arguments, and in additional suggestions as she read,
carefully edited, and apparently sometimes even completed Sartre's
drafts.

Sartre himself may have been somewhat uncomfortable with his
own physical embodiment, a lack of comfort evinced by his horror of
the sticky and slimy as well as by his sense that his "natural place" was
a "sixth floor in Paris with a view overlooking the roofs," with "the
Universe" rising "in tiers" at his feet, all things "humbly beg[ging] for
a name," begging to be created and taken.[17] Even though he may have
been more comfortable identifying himself as a disembodied look, Sartre
avoided the bad faith move of such identification by acknowledging
his embodiment, for example, in experiencing (and later writing about)
his facticity and its social dimensions as he watched two laborers at
work on either side of a wall.[18] Thus, even though there seems to be

evidence of individual and not just institutional bad faith in Sartre's identification of himself, it does not seem to be a bad faith that colors and contaminates his philosophical analyses of even his own situation.

As we learn more about Sartre's relationships with women, particularly with de Beauvoir,[19] we find his bad faith to be complex and extensive. His and even de Beauvoir's descriptions of his seemingly cruel and arrogant relations with her and with others manifest hints and sometimes glaring testimonies of both individual and institutionalized bad faith. Even so, he developed a philosophical point of view a central function of which is to critique this very sort of bad faith, even if it happens to be his own; and he himself was sometimes able to apply this critique to himself, as, for example, in the confessions quoted above from *The Words*.

Although he was indeed a child of his culture, and in many ways not a particularly admirable one, Sartre recognized and endorsed too much of what is essential to feminist theory for us easily to dismiss him. For one thing, the very distinction between individual and institutional racism and sexism is vital to feminist theory. Since a focus on the personal is a way of buttressing the status quo with all of its oppressions, we simply cannot allow such pervasive structures of society as racism and sexism to be regarded as nothing more than the result of the bad faith of a few or even of many individuals. This is not to say, of course, that we cannot or should not recognize and hold individuals accountable for their racist and sexist behavior and for the ways such behavior may strengthen or add new dimensions to the racism and sexism already embedded in the status quo. It is, however, to recognize that racism and sexism in the society cannot be abolished simply by converting such individuals one by one or by changing their words and actions. It is also to recognize that racism and sexism are likely to be present in every theorist, a recognition requiring constant vigilance on our part no matter how pure of heart a particular theorist may seem or even be.

Similarly, feminists must applaud Sartre's rejection of the "democrat's" naive claim that all should be recognized and should see themselves as equal, even in situations where some (in his study, Jews) are "overdetermined" as the result of racist and other oppressions. In this rejection is an early recognition of the tragic facts that equality can be a dangerous veneer covering over vicious systems of inequality and that equal treatment often holds in place past injustices, a recognition developed more thoroughly in the posthumously published *Notebooks for an Ethics*. This rejection also implicitly acknowledges that such equality masks the way some (in our society, these are white, financially well-off, able-bodied, heterosexual males) are taken as the norm while differences are sometimes magnified, sometimes ignored, depending on the situation, and any appeal by oppressed others to their different needs or situations is seen as a matter of special pleading, no matter how much these differences may be constituted by the society as limitations of freedom and opportunities.

In addition, Sartre's analyses of violence, love, and play can be immensely important to feminists and feminist theory. These analyses enable us to round out an ethics in ways that acknowledge both ideals and present realities and that prevent as far as possible its being co-opted in support of the status quo.

On the basis of my study of Sartre, I conclude that although serious sexism is present in Sartre's life and in his writings and that the latter must be acknowledged and expunged, this sexism should be put in perspective. Once this is done, we see that, rather than being a consistent thread running through Sartre's thought, sexism is explicitly challenged and undermined by key aspects of that very work. The sexism in his thought thus seems not to be structural and, consequently, not quite as likely to contaminate every aspect of his work as might be the case with other individuals in bad faith.

In point of fact, Sartre's distinction between institutional and individual racism and sexism, though important in directing us to an awareness of the extent to which racism and sexism are a part of each and every individual reared in racist and sexist societies, may not be much help in enabling us to distinguish less integral from more integral racism and sexism in philosophical and other work. Actually, it seems quite likely that institutional sexism and racism may be potentially as detrimental as individual racism and sexism to a theory's favorable use by feminists, since institutional racism and sexism will permeate every theory to some extent, no matter how hard we try to escape such negative aspects of our society. Just because it is so much a part of the writer's milieu—and to the extent that it is part of the reader's—it will be even more difficult to detect.

Thus, we must proceed with caution, but proceed nonetheless, in our use of a theory like Sartre's. To require feminist theorists to draw only from theories uncontaminated by *any* sexism—or classism, heterosexism, racism, etc.—is to require that each theorist in effect reinvent the wheel and then be discarded in turn by later theorists who find sexism, etc., in her or his theory. Instead of looking for a pure theory, uncontaminated even in serious ways, we need rather to seek constantly to expunge such contamination both in the theories from which we draw inspiration or guidance and in the theories we develop.

Besides beginning with a recognition of and a commitment to difference, the best way to learn to spot classism, heterosexism, racism, sexism, etc., in the theories we use as well as in those we create is to proceed in a way María Lugones calls "interactive."[20] Those of us who are privileged in some way or other (and, of course, almost all who construct theory are) would no longer talk about those who are not, cite a few individuals we select as their spokespersons, and give perfunctory nods to how they might differ (perhaps from ourselves, if we substitute the privileged female for the privileged male who generally serves as the cultural standard against which "differences" are to be judged). We would actively try to learn about the particularities of the endlessly diverse ways individual women are located in and affected by the various oppressions that organize the lives of people worldwide. As Elizabeth V. Spelman acknowledges, "[t]his leads us to the paradox at the heart of feminism: Any attempt to talk about all women in terms of something we have in common undermines attempts to talk about the differences among us, and vice versa."[21]

Recognizing differences in an interactive way seems far more difficult than merely discarding and distancing ourselves from the "impure," thereby leaving unexamined and unchallenged our present insights into what constitutes classism, heterosexism, racism, and sexism. Though considerably harder to accomplish, a more active and interactive stance vis-à-vis differences is also more likely to avoid what Spelman refers to as "boomerang perception": "I look at you and come right back to myself," the tolerance that "leaves me the same" while it expresses rather than undermines privilege.[22]

In using the work of a continental philosopher like Sartre to develop a feminist ethics, I am confronting feminist issues with the work of a thinker and a philosophical framework infrequently encountered in feminist theory. Alison M. Jaggar no doubt expresses the sentiments of many feminist theorists when she confesses, in her preface to *Feminist Politics and Human Nature*, that she has omitted existentialist conceptions of women's liberation from her book primarily because she "find[s] them implausible." Moreover, she is correct when she adds that such conceptions "are outside the mainstream of contemporary feminist theorizing."[23] However, when she learned of my work on Sartrean ethics and my interest in feminist theory, she encouraged me to try to bring the two together. What follows is my attempt to do so and to demonstrate that such an ethics is indeed plausible and that it provides a better ethics for feminists than alternatives do.

By this effort, I hope, at least, to bring an existentialist conception of liberation into the discussion of those in the recognized mainstream or mainstreams of feminist theorizing in this country and Europe. Ideally, though, through my efforts to engage as many different theorists from as many perspectives as possible, I hope to contribute to the expansion of what is understood as feminist theory so that it ultimately will be seen as an ongoing and very inclusive dialogue, without a "mainstream" that contributes to the continuing marginalization of many.[24] Admittedly, this is a task fraught with hazards. There are, unfortunately, many ways of co-opting the voices and work of those in the margin while solidifying the margin and perhaps even their place in it. As Gayatri Chakravorty Spivak notes, "The putative center welcomes selective inhabitants of the margin in order better to exclude the margin."[25]

NOTES

1. Carol Gilligan, *In a Different Voice: Psychological Theory and Women's Development* (Cambridge, MA: Harvard University Press, 1982).

2. Immanuel Kant, "From *Observations on the Feeling of the Beautiful and Sublime*," in *Visions of Women*, ed. Linda A. Bell (Clifton, NJ: Humana Press, 1983), p. 242.

3. Sharon D. Welch, *A Feminist Ethic of Risk* (Minneapolis: Fortress Press, 1990), p. 2.

4. See Chapters 11 and 12, "Rape, Racism and the Myth of the Black Rapist" and "Racism, Birth Control and Reproductive Rights," in Angela Y. Davis, *Women, Race & Class* (New York: Vintage Books: 1983), pp. 172-201.

5. Marilyn Frye, *The Politics of Reality: Essays in Feminist Theory* (Trumansburg, NY: Crossing Press, 1983), p. 33.

6. Welch, p. 19.

7. Linda A. Bell, *Sartre's Ethics of Authenticity* (Tuscaloosa: University of Alabama Press, 1989).

8. Andrea Nye, *Feminist Theory and the Philosophies of Man* (New York: Croom Helm, 1988).

9. Margery L. Collins and Christine Pierce, "Holes and Slime: Sexism in Sartre's Psychoanalysis," in *Women and Philosophy: Toward a Theory of Liberation*, ed. Carol C. Gould and Marx W. Wartofsky (New York: G. P. Putnam's Sons, 1980), pp. 117-18.

10. Carole Pateman and Elizabeth Gross, *Feminist Challenges: Social and Political Theory* (Boston: Northeastern University Press, 1987), p. 19.

11. Hazel E. Barnes, "Sartre and Sexism," *Philosophy and Literature*, Vol. 14 (1990), p. 340. This is a reworking of her paper "Sartre's Sexism: Contingent or Essential?" delivered at the December 28, 1989, meeting of the Society for Women in Philosophy honoring her as Woman of the Year. The meeting was held in Atlanta, Georgia, in conjunction with the meeting of the Eastern Division of the American Philosophical Association.

12. Jean-Paul Sartre, *Anti-Semite and Jew*, trans. George J. Becker (New York: Schocken Books, 1965), p. 8.

13. *Ibid.*, p. 79.

14. Barnes, *op. cit.* She is quoting Sartre, *Being and Nothingness*, trans. Hazel E. Barnes (New York: Philosophical Library, 1956), p. 578.

15. See Frye, pp. 52-83.

16. Barnes, p. 341.

17. Sartre, *The Words*, trans. Bernard Frechtman (New York: Fawcett World Library, 1966), p. 38.

18. Sartre, *Critique of Dialectical Reason*, trans. Alan Sheridan-Smith (Atlantic Highlands, NJ: Humanities Press, 1976), pp. 100-102.

19. See Deidre Bair, *Simone de Beauvoir: A Biography* (New York: Summit Books, 1990).

20. María Lugones, "On the Logic of Pluralist Feminism," *Feminist Ethics*, ed. Claudia Card (Lawrence: University of Kansas Press, 1991), p. 38.

21. Elizabeth V. Spelman, *The Inessential Woman: Problems of Exclusion in Feminist Thought* (Boston: Beacon Press, 1988), p. 2.

22. *Ibid.*, pp. 12, 182.

23. Alison Jaggar, *Feminist Politics and Human Nature* (Totowa, NJ: Rowman & Allanheld, 1983), p. 10.

24. I owe this insight into the way talk of "mainstream" perpetuates marginalization to Diane Fowlkes, who was, in turn, influenced by bell hooks.

25. Gayatri Chakravorty Spivak, *In Other Worlds: Essays in Cultural Politics* (New York: Routledge, 1988), p. 107.

Chapter One

Feminist Ethics

A feminist ethics must be guided by and reflect the central concerns of feminism. Minimally, feminism demands the admission to full human status of women—*all* women—along with all others who have been excluded. It recognizes that this can be achieved only by the abolition of all forms of oppression. Thus, although feminism begins with a focus on women, it quickly becomes a movement to abolish all systemic and systematic injustice.

Since feminist ethics develops out of a concern to abolish injustice and oppression, it must be cognizant of the fact that it is developed within a context of violence and that all action takes place within this context. It, therefore, requires a clarity concerning violence and the relation to violence of any action it prescribes, permits, or prohibits.

In any ethics, but particularly in a feminist and freedom-centered one, it is especially important to be clear about goals while being very careful to distinguish ideals both from the reality in which we live and from what is possible in this reality. This requires, as Janice G. Raymond says, a dual vision. This vision includes both near- and far-sightedness, a clear perception of "the world as men have fabricated it . . . illuminated by a vision of a feminist imagination that acts."[1]

Moreover, partly because of the extent of violence and the ways efforts to combat it are co-opted, partly because of the ideals guiding our ethics and the ways they serve as regulative but never realizable ideals, problems of living with futility propel ethical theory into an analysis of play. In an ethics of freedom, a spirit of play contrasts with the "seriousness" of those who try to convince themselves and others that values are somehow given rather than created by human choices. A recognition of playfulness is part of what must be developed as a response to those who question how individuals can act on chosen values, values that have no warrant or justification or bindingness beyond the fact that they and not other values have been chosen by the agent.

Finally, by opposing itself to the seriousness of those who deny freedom—both their own and that of others—play suggests itself and has been proposed by various thinkers as a strategy for change. Whatever possibilities play may have as an instrument for effecting change in oppressive societies, a feminist ethics focused on violence can ill afford to ignore them.

FEMINISM AND ETHICAL THEORY

Narrow understandings of feminism are simply unworkable. To restrict feminism to a rejection of a specific form of oppression, namely, so-called gender oppression, ignores and thus fails to address the subtle and not so subtle shifts in the ways gender oppression affects individuals of different racial and ethnic groups and even of different classes within those groups. To consider gender oppression apart from all other forms of oppression is to ignore these differences and to privilege the specific gender oppression of certain racial or ethnic groups, and only particular class segments of those.

Moreover, besides ignoring the often quite different ways women of different groups are affected by gender oppression, to disregard other oppressions is to ignore the needs and concerns of women who are seriously and adversely oppressed, not just because of gender, but also because of their race, class, sexuality, or non-able-bodiedness. Because of this, we must agree with Alison Jaggar that women's issues, politically speaking, encompass virtually all issues: women are affected by not only "'domestic' issues of racism, homophobia or class privilege but also such international issues as environmental destruction, war, and the current grotesque inequality in access to world resources."[2] As Pat Parker says, "We as women face a particular oppression, not in a vacuum but as a part of this corrupt system. . . . By not having this understanding, the women's movement has allowed itself to be co-opted and mis-directed."[3]

In "A Black Feminist Statement," the Combahee River Collective proposes that there is only one group of women capable of fighting for itself alone without ignoring other forms of oppression. Members of this group are affected by every kind of oppression: "If Black women were free, it would mean that everyone else would have to be free since our freedom would necessitate the destruction of all the systems of oppression."[4] Of course, even black women are likely to find themselves differently oppressed because of their differences along the lines of class, able-bodiedness, and sexuality. Even differences in skin shade sometimes result in very different treatment under racism of those who identify themselves and are identified by others as black. While not all black women are affected by all forms of oppression, certainly *some* are; and their freedom would indeed mean the end of all systems of oppression. Recognizing this, Angela Y. Davis proposes that only those at the bottom of the social pyramid will improve the status of others as they improve their lot. Since "[t]he forward movement of women of color almost always initiates progressive change for all women," her reminder that "[w]e must always lift as we climb"[5] seems necessary even when she is addressing women of color (not all of whom are at the "bottom of the social pyramid"). Admittedly, though, it is most needed when directed toward others, particularly when we acknowledge the history of black women in the United States, indicating as it does a remarkable degree of social and political solidarity as well as keen awareness of their differences along class and other lines.[6]

Although "ethics" and "morality" may be used as synonyms in everyday parlance as well as in philosophy, a distinction between a morality and theoretical ethics will be useful. A morality may be thought of as a set of prescriptions and proscriptions, a practical list of dos and don'ts, or a principle or set of principles that would allow an adherent to determine what should or should not be done in any given circumstances. Though ultimately most who think and write about feminist ethics are seeking some practical guides to action and to the overall structuring of our lives, what I envision as feminist ethics is more than this. It will examine different moralities and explore problems generated by them, question their internal consistency, their reasoning, and their adequacy, and debate whether and how any morality can be shown to be superior to any other. Though it focuses on developing a morality that would be adequate given feminist insights into and opposition to oppression, it must do so in a critical and even self-critical way. In other words, it will be a theoretical ethics

Thus, feminist ethics not only must be concerned with what *ought to be* and how to bring what *is* more in line with what ought to be, but also must ask "Why?" and critically examine each normative claim. It will propose moral principles or precepts founded on and consistent with feminist insights and commitments. It will weigh these principles and precepts for consistency with each other; and it will examine their adequacy in terms of various considerations, such as how they relate to the way things are, whether they undermine themselves or those who use them, and how they measure up when compared to alternative principles. It will not fall victim to the "dogmatism of tolerance," a dogmatism so fearful of imposing values on others that it strips its adherents of the capacity for moral judgment, a danger of which Janice Raymond warns: "When women do not take responsibility for generating and representing their agreed-upon values, they become pushovers for the tyranny of others' values. It is the tyranny of tolerance that fosters a loss of feminist will—the will to shape history in a value-defined way."[7] Feminist ethics must guide us in resisting oppression and give us ways to defend ourselves from such tyranny. As such, it will be, as Ruth Ginzberg argues, a vital survival tool.[8]

A feminist ethics is concerned with what is as well as with what ought to be. While every ethics recognizes a gap between what is and what ought to be, most ethics do not recognize, as feminist ethics must, the way this gap makes even ethical theorizing itself problematic. This is so partly because any ethics can be co-opted and used by those in control to maintain the status quo. Thus, a feminist ethics, given its central opposition to oppression, must begin and proceed with a constantly watchful eye on the way things are, lest the ensuing theorizing exacerbate current problems and undermine the emancipatory force of its analyses and ideals.

Also damaging and dangerous to ethical theory, though, is the tendency of moral visionaries to discuss principles and issues in a vacuum. This tendency probably has many causes. These include: a single-minded focus, on the part of many visionaries, on the goal to be achieved while everything else is ignored, particularly the ways efforts on behalf of the ideal perpetuate negative and oppressive realities in certain circumstances; lack of practical experience and factual research skills on the part of both visionaries who strive for social change and philosophers who do ethical analysis; and the embeddedness in the status quo of all who would critique or change it.

The last of these is no doubt the most serious. Because of our embeddedness in the social fabric, those of us who would critique and change the status quo confront and find ourselves needing to challenge the very social systems to which we belong and by which we are likely to be privileged in many ways. Along with all others raised in and by their respective societies, we have been shaped to accept the status quo; and many of us have considerable interest at stake in its continuation. Not surprisingly, then, moral issues are frequently dealt with in ways that limit the consideration of context and that are unlikely to lead to much more than superficial analysis and criticism of the institutions and structures of the society.

When moral problems are discussed in a vacuum, the resulting analyses and resolutions will obscure much that should be clarified and may, in fact, perpetuate very real oppressions that could not be condoned were they directly and honestly confronted. For example, discussions of the morality of abortion begin to have a hollow ring once we become aware of the sexual violence that too often passes as normal in our society. Although parties to the dispute individually may acknowledge somewhat ruefully the reality of rape and sexual child abuse, the discussion of abortion too frequently proceeds as though women and girls are almost always full and equal participants in the activities that led to the pregnancies.

If, on the other hand, the discussants begin, as they should, with a recognition of the horrifying statistics concerning various forms of male violence against women and girls, they simply cannot make the naive and erroneous assumption that female human beings are generally the arbiters of their own sexual activity. These statistics turn attention away from individuals who seek abortions and toward a social system that not only encourages girls and women to be sexually available to males and punishes in multifarious—and nefarious—ways those who are not, but also allows and even encourages others to determine by force when and where this sexual availability will be accessed.

RECOGNITION OF THE REALITY OF VIOLENCE

Violence pervades our society. Sexual child abuse, rape, sexual harassment, and other hate crimes are common occurrences. Women are beaten by their lovers and husbands on a regular basis; many are murdered. Children are abused by parents, relatives, family friends, teachers, and strangers. In fact, since female children[9] are the victims of sexual attacks in such large numbers, Andrea Dworkin concludes, "incest is increasingly the sadism of choice, the intercourse itself wounding the female child and socializing her to her female status—early; perhaps a sexual response to the political rebellion of adult women; a tyranny to destroy the potential for rebellion."[10] Though other forms of violence against women and girls are so common that it would be difficult to determine which is truly "the sadism of choice," the legal system is notoriously lax in protecting the victims of such violence and in punishing the perpetrators. For women of color even more than for white women, as Gloria Anzaldúa observes, "The world is not a safe place to live in . . . when males of all races hunt her as prey."[11] Barbara Cameron eloquently and poetically describes the situation: our society, she says, is "a society with arrogance rising, moon in oppression, and sun in destruction."[12]

Michèle Le Doeuff objects to beginning a discussion like this with "an array of shocking images and other horrors," claiming that "the immediate effect of intellectual terrorism is to block intelligence, starting with that of the writer."[13] She is quite right to be suspicious of such moves. They are likely to obscure and hide as much as they illuminate, particularly factors such as race and class. Moreover, they frequently focus our attention on individual victims and perpetrators and away from the fact that although violence toward women involves identifiable agents and victims, it is, nonetheless, a larger issue, requiring analysis of structures of society not generally thought relevant.

In spite of the hazards, though, I choose to begin by calling attention to the horrors and to deal with blocks to intelligence as they may arise. It is, after all, the horrors that tend to give rise to and fuel feminist thinking, while so much that goes on in society counters this thinking by dismissing it, by disparaging it, by co-opting it, and even by denying the very existence of the horrors themselves. Not just the significance and truth of feminist thought come under challenge but also the sanity of those who dare to credit their sense, arising out of their experiences, that things are not what they are affirmed to be and certainly not what they should be.

For instance, the official social "line" seems to be that cases of sexual abuse and rape are rare, "exceptions to the rule."[14] However, statistics indicate that this is false. Statistics indicate, on the contrary, that women who are raped or who were sexually abused as children are in fact quite common in our society and not at all exceptional. Citing a study by the Los Angeles Commission on Assaults Against Women and "statistical calculations combining FBI figures as modified with a projection of rising rape rates through the year 2000," *The New Our Bodies, Ourselves: A Book By and For Women* predicts that "[o]ne out of three women will be raped (forced to have sex without her consent) during her lifetime." The percentage of girls who will have been sexually abused by the age of 18 is generally placed around 25 percent.[15] Catharine A. MacKinnon, using a 1983 study, puts the figures much higher—at 44 percent for women who are raped[16] and at 43 percent for girls who are sexually abused by the time they reach the age of eighteen. She estimates that only 7.8 percent of women will *not* be sexually assaulted or harassed in their lifetimes.[17]

Given the statistics and the depiction throughout the culture—in advertisements, in novels and stories written for the mass market (including pornography), in movies and on TV, even in supposedly objective research in colleges and universities—of violence against women (and girls) as natural, normal, and desirable, the claim that sexual abuse of girls and rape of women is exceptional clearly is ideological. It is part of a complicated system of reinforcing myths, supported by many forces in the society, which in turn supports a system giving virtually all men power over at least some women and a certain group of men power over everyone else in the society.[18]

The official line does not stop with denying the existence and the number of such women and girls. The denial is also used to reinforce racism since statistics indicate that 90 percent of all rapes are intraracial, not interracial; and, as Angela Davis says, "proportionately more white men rape Black women than Black men rape white women."[19] The racist myth that the typical rapist is a stranger and black—another part of that complex ideology—hides from all women the truth concerning those at greatest risk of rape and displaces white women's fears from their acquaintances, dates, husbands/lovers, and former husbands/lovers who are far likelier to be their rapists.[20] The implicit assumption that the victim is white suggests that women of color either are not or cannot be raped and perhaps helps to explain why black women, though statistically more likely to be raped than white women, are "less likely to report their rapes, less likely to have their cases come to trial, less likely to have their trials result in convictions, and, most disturbing, less likely to seek counseling and other support services."[21]

Moreover, with the help of all media, from television to magazines to tabloids to newspapers, personal and workplace problems of women who have been or are being abused, sexually and otherwise, are presented as individual "failures," responsibility for which rests with the women themselves, not with others and certainly not with society as a whole. The competition, whether for jobs or for lovers (necessarily men, according to this line) or for custody of children, is presented as inherently fair, unproblematic, and, of course, healthy. Seldom, if ever, is the imbalance of male over female power in personal relationships mentioned, much less seriously questioned or challenged. Even less frequently does anyone ask how minimally functioning, much less truly competitive, women manage to emerge from the abuse of such power by males, particularly when the abuse begun in the so-called private realm is likely to continue in different forms in the public arena. In fact, "private" abuse is made virtually invisible by the official line and is consigned by theorist after theorist to the hidden recesses of the so-called "private sphere."

Even when violence directed at women is quite clearly in the public sphere, the private is often used to subvert this public aspect and to undermine awareness of the violence. When something having sexual overtones—such as sexual harassment—occurs in the workplace, it is often referred to as a private matter between two adults simply because of the sexual overtones. Thus, the public abuse of power is hidden from view. Even when it is brought to light, the sexual overtones result in our blaming the messenger who, after all, speaks publicly of what is decreed private and must, therefore, do so out of some animosity. Thus, for example, the motives of Anita Hill become more suspect than the behavior of Clarence Thomas when her accusations of sexual harassment against Thomas come to light.

Even very public killings of women often are treated with ambivalence, as though people are not quite sure whether this is properly a private or a public matter. For example, on December 6, 1989, Marc Lépine, an angry young man with a list of women who allegedly had "wronged" him, killed 14 female students in an engineering class at the University of Montreal. Though the misogyny manifest in this killing spree was noted and actually worried over in some reports,[22] others tended to diminish the seriousness of the massacre by downplaying the story, wondering what "feminists" had done to the gunman, or presenting him as simply "crazed."[23] Even such a prestigious U.S. newspaper as the *New York Times* only briefly mentioned the story on its December 7 front page[24] and thereby, for the most part, consigned the news of this horrendous bloodbath to an inside page (p. A23), although the massacre was noted by the *Los Angeles Times* as "the worst mass shooting ever in Canada . . . and the third-worst in North America."[25] Thus, the deaths of women are trivialized, sometimes as accidents by the presumption that the killer is crazy, or they are obscured by the hint of personal involvement with the killer.

The Montreal massacre, by virtue of being so prominent, is likely to receive more serious treatment than more local cases. Several recent accounts of the murder of women have been particularly unsettling. In these instances, Atlanta reporters and headline writers presented women's murders as sad but seemingly expected results of "love gone sour." In one, journalists sympathetically noted and recounted the murderer's "obsession" with his victim (who happened to have been a child and his stepdaughter when this "obsession" began) and almost failed in the headlines to give any indication that she had been murdered. In the first of the two stories, her death was not even mentioned until the third paragraph.[26]

A second case was reported under the headline "Slaying, suicide end 'lovers' quarrel.'" This account begins "A romance 'gone sour' . . ." and concerned an administrator in a local school who killed a department head in the same school and then himself. The medical examiner was quoted as saying: "'We understand that these two individuals had been having a relationship that recently had gone sour for reasons we don't know. You could call it a lovers' quarrel.'"[27] In yet another account, this one on TV, a reporter simply ended a TV report of a woman's death with the observation that no one had been able to determine what triggered the man's violence. Whether this reporter intended to suggest that perhaps she did something to provoke and thereby justify the violence or that other circumstances could have been to blame, his off-the-cuff remark nevertheless takes seriously and endorses men's rage and violence. His remark exemplifies the cultural treatment of male violence, a treatment that accepts as natural, inevitable, and possibly justified activity frequently deadly for women.

Most recently, two stories in the same column of "News Briefs" described murders, one of a man by his brother, the other of a woman by her husband from whom she had separated several weeks earlier and who fatally stabbed himself after killing her. The headlines for the two stories once again reveal how differently the writers treat murders of women by their partners or former partners: "Man charged with murder in brother's death" and "Husband, wife die in *dispute* (italics added)."[28]

Feminists are tearing down the curtains that have so successfully hidden from view and from critical assessment not only the homes and "private" areas in which devastating abuse has been inflicted but also even public violence against women. Feminist theorists are pointing to the larger pattern of male domination of females in society, some referring to this as patriarchy, others, like bell hooks,[29] arguing that patriarchy is itself part of a more complex system of oppression.[30] Feminist ethics must continue in this vein, illuminating the real situations of domination and offering a moral critique based on the physical, emotional, financial, and psychological effects on the individuals, both male and female, touched by such situations, as well as the effects on the institutions and structures of society as a whole.

Feminist ethics must anchor itself in the reality of violence, oppression, and colonization in order to offer adequate moral critiques. An ethics so anchored will inevitably develop a perspective on moral issues quite different from that of other ethics, a critical perspective not likely to arise for those who do not begin with such awareness. This perspective will make moral issues of matters not recognized as such in other theories. Even moral problems recognized in other theories will appear differently to one who is immersed in this awareness and who does not approach the issues in ways tantamount to asking, "should there be, e.g., 'abortion on demand,' in the best of all possible worlds?"

Even those of us who recognize a fetus in its earliest development as
no more a full human being than a sprouting acorn is an oak tree may
bemoan the numbers of abortions, particularly when we recognize the
pain experienced by those who undergo them. Nevertheless, we can
affirm that access to abortion is essential, given that girls and women
do not control either access to their own sexuality or the development
and use of contraception and given the additional injustice as well as
the great pain that denial of abortion would create. At the same time,
we can agree with Catharine MacKinnon that this availability has done
little to extend that control: "[v]irtually every ounce of control that
women won out of this legalization has gone directly into the hands of
men—husbands, doctors, or fathers—or is now in the process of attempts to reclaim it through regulation." Rather, as she observes, legalization of abortion has facilitated women's "heterosexual availability."[31]

THE PERSONAL IS POLITICAL:
REJECTING INDIVIDUAL SOLUTIONS

Feminist ethics must give new life to the claim of feminist theorists
and activists that the personal is political. It must be used to focus
attention on the way in which objective institutions and political forces structure even the most personal aspects of each individual's existence and personality.

It must be freed from the interpretation it is sometimes given in
feminist circles, an interpretation Ruth Ginzberg connects with pressure to conform to what one's moral community deems "politically
correct." In that interpretation, "[a]ny decision, by virtue of being political,
is fair game for being held accountable by and to my moral community. It is also fair game for becoming grounds for my exclusion from
a moral community." As she notes, the resultant pressure to conform
to one's moral community is incompatible not only with liberal individualism but also with moral courage since the latter alienates one
from the community as much as does moral irresponsibility and "indeed, in some ways the two begin to look quite indistinguishable."[32]
Although, as Marilyn Frye says, it is important to get things right
politically, thus, in fact to be politically correct, this means something
quite different from conforming one's life and thinking to others. To
actually "get it right" requires not only an individual's "aligning, al-
lying, and engaging" with others "in the making of value" but also her
or his obtaining "a sound working understanding of the politics of a
situation."[33] This requires constant critique and criticism, not adhering
thoughtlessly to formulas specified by others, however well intentioned,
and treated as unchallengeable.

The claim that the personal is political has also been used to deflect attention to issues of individual identity and relationship and, as bell hooks says, away "from the larger cultural framework wherein focus on identity was already legitimized within structures of domination."[34] Constant vigilance is required to keep the claim that the personal is political from being turned into an identity, which then can be properly—and with disastrous consequences—converted to read, "The political is personal."

There are a number of reasons why we need to keep attention focused on the larger cultural framework, the ways it impacts individuals, and the ways it in turn can be impacted by individual and group action. First, a focus only on self and individual relationships leaves the larger systems of oppression intact and leaves at their mercy all who do not have the wherewithal to protect themselves effectively. Often individual solutions turn attention away from the larger systems of oppression and leave many women—along with many men—firmly in the grip of the oppressions. Even changing the views and behavior of individual members of society one at a time is not sufficient to effect social change since society is a complex network of institutions and power relations, not simply "an amalgam of independent and solitary individuals."[35]

Second, individual solutions may, in fact, ultimately undermine themselves by strengthening the status quo to such an extent that solutions, even of this sort, become more problematic and difficult. For example, individual women frequently attempt to gain their own freedom and recognition by first meeting men's needs. This strategy seems unlikely to accomplish the women's goals and far likelier to undermine, if not their own efforts, at least future efforts of others using the same strategy. As Dorothy E. Smith observes, the harder a woman works in "an external order which oppresses her," the more she strengthens it:

> The more successful women are in mediating the world of concrete particulars so that men do not have to become engaged with (and therefore conscious of) that world as a condition to their abstract activities, the more complete man's absorption in it, the more effective the authority of that world and the more total women's subservience to it. And also the more complete the dichotomy between the two worlds, and the estrangement between them.[36]

Similarly, by themselves, individual and even group experiments will not bring social change and may even strengthen the status quo.

In discussing the hope, entertained by John Stuart Mill and Harriet Taylor, that their own example of a feminist, egalitarian relationship would inspire others by "show[ing] what a feminist utopia could be," Andrea Nye notes the improbability of such exceptional experiments leading to significant change. Furthermore, she observes, "Utopian experiments could even function as useful safety valves, creating comforting conduits for the moral uneasiness of a middle class sufficiently well off to dabble in a socialism that in no way threatened real power relationships."[37]

Third, the individuals who strive to create new patterns within their lives and relationships are more likely than not to require the support of the very structures of dominance and oppression to which they are opposed. For example, at the beginning of the so-called "second phase" of the white women's movement in the United States,[38] middle- and upper-class white women, seeking to make more egalitarian their intimate relationships with men, frequently thought in terms of freeing themselves from total responsibility for house and child care by employing other—usually poor—women as maids and nannies. Thinking along such lines was, of course, far easier than trying to envision—and create—a more egalitarian dispersion of responsibilities between women and men.

Unfortunately, though, such thinking and acting did nothing to challenge the assumption that such responsibilities ultimately belong to women nor did it question the class hierarchy in which poor women are expected to clean the homes and care for the children of others (as well their own), and to do so generally for very low wages and few if any benefits. Such thinking led to divisions among women of different socioeconomic groups and to serious exclusions both in theorizing and in practice. The exclusions had more and more negative impact as predominantly white middle- and upper-class theorists and groups managed to secure their work and activities as "mainstream." Neither did such thinking question, much less challenge, the fundamental indifference or hostility of most workplaces to individuals with child or home responsibilities. Nor, of course, did it address the important issue of care for the children of poor women. Thus, these "solutions" are elitist inasmuch as they are not and cannot be options for most women. Even worse, they presuppose and perpetuate the oppression of others.

Fourth, such solutions are simplistic. In focusing on the individuals and their relationships, they are likely to recognize only one form of oppression—sexism—at work in the larger society, and very limited aspects of that. By assuming that they can escape the oppressive structures of their society, they are likely not to realize how thoroughly gender is constructed by society and how they take their sexualities, constructed under conditions of male supremacy, into sexually intimate relationships, heterosexual or homosexual.[39] Moreover, by not recognizing other forms of oppression such as racism, classism, and heterosexism and the ways these moderate, exacerbate, or simply change the effects of sexism on women in differently oppressed groups, personal solutions leave unacknowledged and unaddressed other manifestations of sexism along with other forms of oppression.

Finally, individual solutions to oppression fail even as individual solutions. The larger society will inevitably impinge on those involved, and the unaddressed forms of oppression will undermine the most valiant attempts of individuals to overcome oppression in their intimate relationships. This is what we should expect, since, after all, as Andrea Dworkin observes, "The principle that 'the personal is political' belongs to patriarchal law itself, originating there in a virtual synthesis of intimacy and state policy, the private and the public."[40] Thus, not only are individual solutions inextricably a part of the larger society and thereby tied into whatever oppressions exist therein,[41] but also they fail since, as Sartre recognizes in *What Is Literature?*, "it is quite impossible to treat concrete men as ends in contemporary society." This is because, as he illustrates in the lives of various characters in his fiction, the injustices of the age—class divisions, racism, etc.— inevitably intervene and vitiate "at the roots" the good one strives to accomplish.[42]

Sartre's analysis begins, as we must, with the political and then shows how existing political structures contaminate and undermine all our efforts, even the most personal and intimate. He would thus agree with bell hooks that it is a fundamental error to focus on the personal with the assumption that this realm can be reconstructed without changing the social/political context in which it exists.

THE PROBLEM OF CO-OPTATION

The status quo is not easily unsettled. Even the most serious threats to it are often co-opted and defused. As Michèle Le Doeuff says, "no government does anything for women unless it is pushed very hard. When it is pushed, there is always a great loss of energy and a blunting of ideas. When it is not pushed, the clock starts going back."[43]

Even when government is pushed and important gains are made, those very gains are likely to be co-opted and placed in the service of reactionary forces or of preserving the status quo from any further such gains. We have watched while the symbols and rhetoric of the Civil Rights and Women's Movements were robbed of their revolutionary import and turned into marketing tools. We have seen those for whose rights and dignity these movements worked once again turned into objects and manipulated for capitalistic purposes. Consider, for example, the insidiousness of the advertising slogans "You've come a long way, Baby" and "Black is beautiful." Incorporation of revolutionary demands into mass media slogans like these helps to mask, mystify, and thus strengthen oppressive structures. Recognizing the way society marshals the smallest of gains in defense against any others, significant or not, Mary Daly has expressed concern that relatively minor reform, such as the linguistic reform exemplified by the use of words like "chairperson," is more dangerous than leaving the sexism visible.[44]

The potentially revolutionary impact of movements is constantly undermined by their incorporation, in a harmless and nonthreatening way, into the status quo. When, for example, revolutionary demands are taken up by marketing strategies and treated as accomplished facts, any remaining problems in the society (if such stubbornly continue to exist in spite of the presumed corrections by the society!) are thereby placed quite firmly at the feet of individuals: if, given such optimal or at least fair circumstances, particular individuals still cannot succeed or find happiness, then it must be because of *their* inadequacies. As Susan Faludi relentlessly documents the process in *Backlash*,[45] forces of backlash, nostalgic for the way things were—and for the most part still are (the lamented changes are generally rather small)—will even blame those failures on the demands for social change themselves rather than on the continuing resistance to the demands. Thus, feminism, rather than low pay, glass ceilings, sexual harassment, and a second work shift when they get home, is to blame for any unhappiness of women in the work force. The social institutions are thus reinforced and critics are encouraged to find—and correct—the source of the problems within themselves.

Given that even revolutionary demands are undercut by society's tendency to regard them as personal problems or failings, surely demands initially stated in terms of personal dissatisfactions undercut themselves from the outset. Consequently, bell hooks realizes, an apolitical focus on self and on "finding an identity" fits neatly into the processes of co-optation rather than offering a means for resisting them.[46] Andrea Dworkin, too, argues that problems with oppression are undercut and obscured by individualizing the problems and working with the victims. Focus on victims is easily turned into analysis of what is wrong with them and thus subsumed under the "Catch 22" set up by male sexual domination, dismissing as "repression" a woman's refusal to engage in "combat on the world's tiniest battlefield" and diagnosing as "penis envy" an attempt, like that of Joan of Arc, to fight on the large one.[47]

While individual solutions and resistance are likely to accomplish little in terms of unsettling the status quo, they are nonetheless very important to the agents themselves. Thus, as Sarah Lucia Hoagland recognizes, individual resistance must not be seen simply as self-defeating: without choices like these through which an individual establishes herself as separate, "there would be no self to defeat." Yet, while admitting that such actions are often necessary, she notes that they may *also* be self-defeating: they can be subsumed under the feminine stereotype and will not constitute serious challenges to it. Moreover, if there are others with whom to act in concert in ways that would be perceived as resistance and would threaten the status quo, individual, isolated action is woefully self-defeating.[48]

The cult of the individual is even fostered at the expense of the development of revolutionary critical consciousness by something as positive as the belated but nonetheless welcome cultural honoring of the civil rights work of Dr. Martin Luther King, Jr. As King is made a social and mass media hero, however, more and more is heard of his dreams, less and less mention is made of his actual struggles for human rights, and nothing is said of his keen social and political critique of the United States and its worldwide practices of domination. Basking in the humane and humanitarian glow of King's dreams, the society retreats from small gains in antidiscrimination enforcement and affirmative action, made as the result of the courageous work and enormous sacrifices of King and other civil rights workers. At the same time, ironically enough, this elevation of a black man, though dead as the result of white hostility, to larger-than-life proportions no doubt helps confirm the view of reactionary whites that blacks have it made or have taken over.[49]

In his *Critique of Dialectical Reason*, Sartre analyzes the tendency of society to resist change and to co-opt even small gains made by revolutionary forces. Moreover, in *Notebooks for an Ethics*, he discusses the ways the revolutionary will be condemned by the accepted morality, a morality that condemns violence and affirms "justice," "duty," "equality," and "obligation," all the while supporting the prior violence on which the status quo is based. In fact, Sartre says, "right" arises only in periods of injustice; it would disappear in a harmonious,

egalitarian society: "a right is an absolute denial of violence that can
only serve the oppressor because the violence from which the right
came is prior to the establishment of the right and because the concrete
inequality is entirely outside the juridical realm."[50]

If Sartre is correct about the condemnation and co-opting of revolutionary gains, liberal reformers should certainly expect their more
modest reforms to suffer similar or worse condemnation, corruption,
and reversals. This is clearly something Sarah Hoagland anticipates
with her assessment of the way the state, depending on its size, uses
"virtue" and "merit" or "justice," "duty," and "obligation," not to make
sure that all groups are protected from the excesses of other groups,
but rather "to maintain the existing power structure." Even arguing for
women's rights, she notes, reinforces the status quo by treating wom-
en's rights, but not men's, as debatable, but particularly by affirming,
at least implicitly, the arrogantly assumed "right" of some men to
determine who is to be part of the human community and to have rights.[51]

It should not, then, surprise us when those gains for which the hardest
battles are fought turn out not only to be quite different from what was
hoped but also, sometimes, to make bad situations even worse. Catharine MacKinnon gives two examples:

> The law of rape divides the world of women into spheres of consent according
> to how much say we are legally presumed to have over sexual access to
> us by various categories of men. . . . The age line under which girls are
> presumed disabled from withholding consent to sex rationalizes a condi-
> tion of sexual coercion women never outgrow. As with protective labor
> laws for women only, dividing and protecting the most vulnerable be-
> comes a device for not protecting everyone. Risking loss of even so little
> cannot be afforded. Yet the protection is denigrating and limiting (girls
> may not choose to be sexual) as well as perverse (girls are eroticized as
> untouchable; now reconsider the data on incest).[52]

In *Toward a Feminist Theory of the State*, MacKinnon makes her
point about the eroticization of girls even more convincingly: "Taboo
and crime may serve to eroticize what would otherwise feel about as
much like dominance as taking candy from a baby. Assimilating actual
powerlessness to male prohibition, to male power, provides the appearance of resistance, which makes overcoming possible, while never
undermining the reality of power, or its dignity, by giving the powerless actual power." At best, she says, these laws and taboos tell men
"who is open season and who is off limits, not how to listen to wom-
en."[53]

THE IMPORTANCE OF STRUGGLE

The oppressed, in general, and all who recognize the immorality of oppression are in an untenable situation. They find themselves in circumstances such that if they do not revolt, they acquiesce in and perpetuate their own and others' oppression; yet if they do revolt, they are condemned by the laws and morality that buttress the status quo. Particularly if the revolt is violent, it conflicts with the ideal in the name of which it might operate (an ideal Sartre calls, with Kant, "the city of ends," according to which the freedom of all human beings would be recognized and respected). Condemned by both the morality of the status quo and that of the city of ends, revolt nonetheless may be necessary (the only recourse freedom has "[w]hen the Good is alienated, that is, when it is in the hands of the Other") and even "a progress toward freedom." Though the slave's revolt, for example, may do violence to the master and cannot be said to be "*a Good* because the master's values block any view toward constituting another Good, it is at least the claim not to make one's own an Other's Good" particularly not when the other's good conflicts with the slave's very freedom. While acting in an unambiguously moral way is possible only if everyone is moral, still the very negativity of revolt "implies unthematically the unity of a human world where Others would be the same in the other, a world of intersubjectivity where man would renounce seeing himself from the outside, that is, seeing other men as though he himself were outside humanity."[54]

This is a problem of dirty hands. Michael Stocker analyzes dirty hands in a way that seems to me exactly what Sartre means by "ethics is not possible unless everyone is ethical."[55] According to Stocker, "The demand that it must be possible for us to be good and also innocent, and also to retain emotional wholeness, is . . . a demand for . . . a morally good world or at least not an evil or bad world." Because we live in an evil or bad world, we are confronted by what Stocker calls "impossible oughts—oughts we are unable to obey." He gives the choice of Sophie from William Styron's *Sophie's Choice* as an example: "Upon entering a Nazi concentration camp with her two children, she is told by an officer that only one of the children will be allowed to live, that she must choose which of them this will be, and that if she does not choose, both will be killed. She picks one. And does so with dirty hands." Often, he thinks, dirty hands will involve being coerced, as was Sophie, into implementing or helping to implement the evil project of someone else.[56]

While Sophie's freedom is violated along with the freedom(s) of the child or children (depending on what Sophie does and whether the officer keeps the bargain), it does matter—very much—to both Stocker and Sartre what she does. The major difference between them, though largely verbal, is that Stocker sees one choice as possibly "justified,"[57] while for Sartre all choices must be regarded as "unjustified" though one should be chosen if it is "the only way to liberate oneself from the Good of others."[58] Thus, Sartre ultimately makes the same point as Stocker, but with different language, when he says some violence is "necessary," though always morally unacceptable. Sartre's different choice of language, I believe, results from his greater realization—and fear—that ethical affirmation of violence as justified may support violence and thus undermine attempts to overthrow oppression.

Michèle Le Doeuff recognizes this problem of "impossible oughts" and dirty hands in connection with a hypothetical debate in which a woman constantly takes a man's view into account while he never considers anything but his own. Although the woman is morally right to place herself "at the intersubjective level," what results is that "he does what he likes with her." In this way, women become "victims of their own qualities, indeed of their virtues." As she later says, "Perfect intersubjectivity is a fine ideal, but unfortunately it is easily perverted, as happens when there is no reciprocity."[59]

What one says about morality thus can make the already untenable position of the revolutionary all the more untenable. Oppression stands in the way of moral action that would create even a slightly better society, much less the city of ends in which the freedom of all is respected. It stands in the way of developing an ethics, too, since its ideals and its principles all too easily can be used and co-opted by systems of oppression to support the status quo. Upholders of the status quo and thus of oppression will use the revolutionary's ethics to condemn any opposing violence. Conflating inaction with not acting and thereby placing it beyond the purview of ethics, they ignore individual responsibility for perpetuating through inaction the prior violence on which the status quo is founded. They thus place much existing oppression, certainly that which is institutionalized, beyond the purview of moral judgment. Other oppression may be condemned because there are actual and identifiable oppressors engaging in concrete acts of oppression; but even so, the oppression is protected from effective resistance by reminders that violent resistance is unacceptable and by reiteration of the claim accepted even by the revolutionaries themselves: two wrongs do not make a right.

To combat the conflation of inaction with not acting, we must make very clear that inaction generally is tantamount to action, that *to do none of the acts we could do to oppose oppression is to act on the side of the oppressors*, that is, to collaborate in the oppression. Only if our ethics makes this clear will it become apparent that inaction supporting the status quo—and thereby tacitly endorsing the violence that underlies it—is subject to moral condemnation. Only then can ethics acknowledge the impossibility in which some are placed—that violence is sometimes an inevitable aspect of their choice, no matter which way they turn. In this way, a feminist ethics can, with Sartre, acknowledge that sometimes violence is inescapable, while condemning all violence as morally unacceptable. This paradoxical recognition of violence as sometimes necessary but always morally unacceptable will be elaborated further in Chapter 5.

VIOLENCE, THE FEMININE, AND AN ETHICS OF CARING

Some feminists have, in fact, tried to create substantially "new tools" for dealing with violence by developing ethical systems in which the legitimacy of violence is either totally denied or limited to acts of desperation, literally last resorts. Nel Noddings provides an important example of this. In her provocative book *Caring: A Feminine Approach to Ethics & Moral Education*, she envisions, as her subtitle indicates, a "feminine" approach to ethics. She proposes to speak with the voice of the long-silent mother who is unwilling to sacrifice individuals to principles or even to abstract "greater goods." This ethics emphasizes caring and challenges ethical systems that reflect the voice of the father. In resisting the sacrifice of individuals either to principles or to allegedly greater goods, Noddings opposes the conclusions of many traditional ethics, allegedly from the perspective of the mother. To most violence and sacrifice, this voice consistently responds, "Let us find some other way."[60] Particularly important in her opposition is the reminder that there often *is* "some other way," a way, however, the actors in the moral drama simply do not or perhaps will not entertain.

Noddings acknowledges times when violence—even killing—is necessary. She cites the example of the mother who kills her abusive husband in order to save herself and her children. She suggests that although such action results from a "degraded" and "sadly diminished ethical ideal," the one who performs the action may have been "driven to it by unscrupulous others who made caring impossible to sustain" and thus would herself be blameless.[61]

While recognition of the necessity of some acts of violence is significant, that recognition, like her notion of caring, nonetheless seems too limited, too personal, and ultimately too apolitical. It is an individual abuser who may be subjected, understandably and apparently legitimately, to violence just as it is individuals who are the focus of care. Individual relationships so dominate Noddings's caring perspective, though, that she recognizes, for example, no moral obligation on the part of those in the United States to care for starving children in Africa.[62] Her focus on individual relationships obscures and allows her not to worry about responsibility for and obligations to do something about complicity in systems of oppression resulting in starvation throughout the world.

This, according to Le Doeuff, is "[t]he sinister thing about the structure of altruism (when it excludes the problem of justice)": "not only that it prevents people from including themselves in the projected good, but that it also surreptitiously particularizes the other person to which I am being sacrificed by self-denial. The morality which is usually inculcated into women leads them to leave out two elements: themselves and humanity outside the family sphere."[63] They may not ask themselves questions Elizabeth V. Spelman finds morally essential, such as who is worthy of their care, "whose situation demands attention to details and whose does not," and are some forms of care "crucial to the maintenance of systematic inequalities among women" or between men and women.[64] Listening only to such altruistic voices, Noddings, along with Carol Gilligan, has indeed failed, as Michele M. Moody-Adams argues, to hear the voices of other women as they protest rape, sexual abuse, and sexual harassment (a protest not based on interconnection with others but recognizing "the perpetrator's refusal to respect the integrity and *separateness* of the victim") or as they protest or defend the legality of pornography or as they choose lives of principled celibacy.[65]

It is certainly clear that if the social system obscures from view many who are starving and oppressed, they will never enter into the frame of reference of Noddings's caring individuals and thus will make no demands on them. Claudia Card makes a similar point when she observes that a "society plagued by racism, ethnocentrism, and xenophobia" will make interracial caring relationships "not what they should be" and will thus leave those whose "ethical repertoire is exhausted by caring . . . [with] nothing left to operate with respect to many of the interracial consequences of one's conduct."[66] It may even leave them unaware of these consequences since those affected are often prevented by the consequences and other aspects of oppression from appearing at the front or back door of the caring individual.

Moreover, in many of the circumstances in which human beings find themselves, we cannot so easily and neatly identify individuals in the position of the abuser who forces the hands, as it were, of those he abuses. Those caught in such situations will have no abuser to attack, and even "sadly diminished" ethical ideals would probably not warrant, for Noddings, an attack on others. Nor must the ethical ideal from which we act in opposing violence and oppression always be "sadly diminished" as the result of the oppression.[67] At least, if there is any diminishment, it will be, in many cases, little noticed by the culture in which we live inasmuch as oppression affects our lives and our relationships in often subtle and insidious ways. Whatever diminishment exists in those not directly and adversely affected by oppression, it certainly is not the same as that of the mother, envisioned by Noddings, who sees no other alternatives if she is to save her own life and those of her children.

A feminist ethics simply cannot condone others turning their backs and leaving victims of oppression and violence to improve their own lot. Rather, the violence, the oppression, and the indifference that support them must be challenged by appealing to an ideal of a world in which, for example, no individuals starve so that the greed of others can be satisfied, or even to make possible for them a better lifestyle. The moral ideal is part of an ethical framework requiring individuals to accept responsibility for their own actions and lifestyles and for the ways actions and lifestyles involve virtually everyone in the complexities of oppressive systems.

This responsibility extends to the support even inaction may give to the violence of others and goes far beyond caring for neighbors or for Noddings's dreaded "proximate stranger"—a teenager, a cat, any "stranger" with whom there is the possibility of reciprocity, who shows up at the front or back door of the caring individual and thereby makes an "enormous claim" on her.[68] In addition to such caring for proximate strangers, a feminist ethics must affirm the unacceptability not just of being an oppressor but also of inaction in the face of oppression by and of others; even though oppressors may be operating in other countries continents away, inaction may be and often is tantamount to complicity in their behavior. Once one becomes aware of it, one often faces an unavoidable choice: do nothing about it or do something to stop it. Not doing what one can to stop the oppression affirms its acceptability and makes one an accomplice of a sort. Refusing to become aware makes one an accomplice of a different sort.

In the systems of oppression confronting us daily, individual responsibility for oppression may be quite diluted. There may be no central core of "bad guys"; or, if there is, those individuals may have died long ago. With no clear-cut guilty parties against whom to take action, any attempted disruption of the status quo may do violence (in the sense of violation spelled out later in Chapter 5) to some undeserving individuals, even if our action is far less extreme than the killing entertained by Noddings.

Reconstructing the example of an individual who finds herself in a dilemma as the result of another's threat to kill ten innocent individuals unless she chooses and kills one of them herself, Noddings suggests clean hands are generally possible. As the hypothetical individual placed in such an untenable position, she refuses the offer and claims all ten must be willing to die rather than have her do the bidding of the one who threatens to kill them.[69] In some cases, particularly in cases like this where one is asked, as it were, to "bargain with the devil," we may be able to keep our hands clean and not participate in the evil being done. After all, those who propose such bargains are obviously quite indifferent to morality; this indifference gives us reason to question whether they should be trusted to keep bargains like these. Unfortunately, though, clean hands often are not possible. I for one would be quite exasperated with Noddings, were she placed in the situation she describes and continued to refuse the offer while individual after individual, particularly those not able to participate in the refusal of the offer, is systematically slaughtered. At some point, I, along with the remaining individuals scheduled for execution, would be begging her to reconsider and to do what she can to save others. Neither Noddings's examples nor her more theoretical analyses give us any way to acknowledge this or to choose actions reflecting such awareness.

By not looking beyond the relationships to the institutions and structures in which they occur, Noddings's caring traps women in the immediacy of individual relationships and is thus a "feminine" ethics, as suggested by her subtitle, but not a feminist one. Traditionally, in most societies, women's horizons have been restricted to intimate relationships: a truly "feminine" woman devoted herself to the welfare of her family and perhaps a few friends. While both rearing and public opinion have tended thus to limit women's moral vision and concerns, these must be expanded beyond the realm of immediate relations—even with "proximate strangers." Central to this expansion is a feminist awareness of the political, an awareness vitally connected with a revolutionary stance against the status quo. This is quite opposed to the generally receptive stance of Noddings's caring individuals who, she says, "are not attempting to transform the world, but . . . are allowing . . . [themselves] to be transformed." While, according to Noddings, "we cannot remain perpetually in the receptive mode," she nonetheless sees this mode as "at the heart of human existence" and even the activity that replaces this receptivity is to remain focused on the relation.[70]

Noddings's fundamentally receptive stance places women in a relatively helpless position vis-à-vis the prevailing systems of power, a position in which their activity will be either supportive of the status quo or at best reactive against it (but on an individual level). While this is a danger for any ethics, it is the undoing of Noddings's inasmuch as caring by the subordinate for the dominant supports the status quo and disempowers carers in an especially problematic way. As Sandra Bartky shows, the caring subordinate constantly affirms the values of the dominant without a reciprocal affirmation of the caring subordinate's values. Tending and sympathizing with his injuries and fears, her understanding of the power relations between them and in the world is likely to be mystified and she to be demoralized.[71]

This is not to dispute that adherence to an ethics of caring very like Noddings's may have been and may even continue to be enormously useful to many women. As in the earlier domesticity movement, adherence to and affirmation of such an ethics may have given at least some women a way to seize a bit of control over their own lives and perhaps even a modicum of respect in otherwise enormously oppressive circumstances. Thus, Sarah Hoagland is right that women have used the notion of "the feminine" to develop "the 'giving' expected of women into survival skills, strategies for gaining some control in situations where their energy and attention are focused on others." Unfortunately, though, "the feminine" is a construction within a system in which women are to be dominated by men. It is a way of recognizing and praising a woman who supports men, "her man" in particular. As a part of heterosexual virtue, it "has its origin in masculinist ideology and does not represent a break from it."[72] Jeffner Allen observes: "The ideology of heterosexual virtue entitles men to terrorize—possess, humiliate, violate, objectify—women and forecloses the possibility of women's active response to men's sexual terrorization. . . . The moral imperative established by heterosexual virtue, that women are to be nonviolent, established a male-defined good that is beneficial to men and harmful to women."[73]

Thus, we must conclude, with Eléanor Kuykendall, that "no ethic, and certainly no ethic of nurturance, can be realized without a supporting politic."[74] Clearly, without such political analysis, Noddings's ethics proves inadequate.

Perhaps, though, Rita C. Manning is right that Noddings's own criteria, if taken seriously, lead to a less limited understanding of care. Heeding Noddings's emphasis on her ideal caring self, Manning asks, "Won't this ideal caring self feel some obligation toward animals and starving children in Africa?" She answers, "I'm convinced that it would, for much the same reasons that Hume thinks that the demands of justice will assert themselves after some reflection. We can come to recognize that the starving children in Africa share crucial characteristics with the children we know and love; we can see that animals share important characteristics as well. Surely, our ideal caring selves will not ignore this."[75]

Indeed, according to Manning, political consciousness is necessary for adequate caring. First, since individuals "must navigate through an uncaring world without falling into total caring burnout," they should work "for institutions, cultures, and practices that would reduce subsistence needs by redistributing resources and increasing the supply of caretakers, and they should encourage social change toward a culture of reciprocity in meeting psychological needs." Second, since we come to see that others with whom we are not directly related are "worthy of care," we must, if we are to care for them, understand political realities and even the additional obligations that may be ours because of the ways we have profited from the exploitation of the world's poor. Finally, we need political awareness in order to rank conflicting needs that cannot all be met. This consciousness allows Manning to side, for example, with the exploited and against capitalists who exploit in order to satisfy their need for profit.[76]

Surely Manning is right that many of the worst problems in Noddings's ethics of caring are self-correcting if her own criteria are taken more seriously and if her ethical analyses are supplemented with Humean insight and political consciousness, although I am less sanguine about the corrective power of a political consciousness that arises out of a concern to meet needs. After all, as I shall argue in Chapter 3, needs are problematic appeals, not just because we live in a culture that systematically trains us to distort or not to see some needs but also because oppression may create needs that, if satisfied, will only perpetuate oppression.

In addition, Manning readily admits that "[w]omen who adopt an ethic of care will be at a distinct disadvantage in conflicts with men." Claiming that the adoption of *any* moral perspective results in a disadvantage vis-à-vis those who refuse altogether to take the moral point of view, she finds some grounds for optimism in her survey, which indicated that "men are becoming more and more sensitive to the demands of care." Even so, she confesses that she is "not counting on this [reapportionment of the burdens of care] happening without a great deal of struggle, both personal and political." In the final analysis, though, she is so "terrified about a future in which no one cares about anything but his or her own projects" that she is willing to "run the risk of rationalizing the status quo by proselytizing for an ethic of care."[77]

I am less willing to take this risk, especially since it involves the oppression of others. Oppression must not be strengthened even if our caring and our proselytizing in behalf of care makes the world *seem* kinder and gentler. In fact, if our efforts help to disguise oppression or to make it more tolerable, I conclude, on the contrary, that we should channel our efforts in a different direction.

Moreover, I am convinced that Manning has offered what amounts to a false alternative. We must not stop our moral deliberations with advocacy that supports the status quo. We must find an alternative between advocacy of an ethics of care (with its strengthening of an oppressive status quo) and allowing an even more uncaring world to come into being. But in order to avoid both disastrous alternatives, we must move beyond simply affirming an ethics of care. This means analyzing violence, its relationship to women and ways it is woven through ideologies of protection, domination, and privacy. In this analysis, we discover both that violence is unavoidable in an oppressive society and that violence against oppression must be cautiously selected and carefully limited, lest it not only add to the level of unacceptable violence in the society but also undermine the very effort to overthrow oppression. These issues are examined and argued in Chapter 5.

THE CITY OF ENDS

In *Caring: A Feminine Approach to Ethics & Moral Education*, Nel Noddings does more of interest to feminists than the foregoing account of her ethics suggests. By carefully and consistently elaborating an ethics of care, stressing receptivity, relatedness, and responsiveness, she does indeed turn attention away from all ethics focusing on justification, fairness, and justice. Such ethics, she claims, have been discussed largely in the "language of the fathers." In a strategy familiar by now in feminist circles, she proposes that the "mother's voice," a voice previously silent in the development of ethical theory would center on relations with others and would be rooted in feeling.[78]

The ethics developed to give voice to this long-silent perspective is, as we have seen, an ethics of care, a care that is a "displacement of interest from my own reality to the reality of the other." She continues: "[w]hen we see the other's reality as a possibility for us, we

must act to eliminate the intolerable, to reduce the pain, to fill the
need, to actualize the dream." The attitude of care is warm, accepting,
trusting, and resistant to sacrifice for principles or for allegedly greater goods. In caring, "[w]e are not attempting to transform the world,
but we are allowing ourselves to be transformed." The possibility of
reciprocity is central to care.[79]

Although I have faulted Noddings's ethics for its lack of political
content and for the way it feeds into and supports the status quo,
nevertheless her development of caring as an ideal for human relationships has much to recommend it, particularly if we can supplement this
ideal with the needed feminist political analysis. This involves underpinning it with a recognition that violence will sometimes be inescapable (that whichever way we turn, we either do nothing to stop or prevent
the violence of others or we actively engage in violence ourselves),
hence, necessary—that there is no way to keep our hands clean, morally speaking. If we recognize the unavoidability of violence, we can,
without diminishing the moral agency either of the revolutionary or of
the one who kills her abuser, still acknowledge with Noddings that the
use of violence is highly problematic, that it is not to be considered an
acceptable part of the repertoire of a moral individual. Thus, the use
of violence remains immoral whether or not one's moral horizon has
been severely restricted by the individual(s) against whom the violence is directed.

With such a recognition, we can both avoid what Sartre calls the
maxim of violence—the end justifies the means—and affirm, with Sartre and Noddings, the necessity of violence in some situations. In opposition to Noddings, though, a political grounding coupled with an
ethics emphasizing freedom rather than caring requires us to choose
acts of violence with great care and with a clear awareness that they
are directed against the prior violence of others or the violence embedded in the status quo. Thus, a feminist ethics so grounded must not
limit violence, as does Noddings, to acts of desperation of those who,
surrounded by the violence of others, see no other way to save themselves or their loved ones.

In what she says about the way care should operate in human relations, Noddings sounds in fact rather like Sartre in his account of the
relationship of appeal and help. In *Notebooks for an Ethics*, Sartre
discusses how in helping another one not only comprehends the other's
end but makes it one's own. "The other's end," he says, "can appear
to me as an end only in and through the indication of my adopting that
end."[80] In choosing to help someone, I engage myself but nonetheless
recognize the end is not mine. To will this end authentically, I must

will "the end to be realized by the other"—"To want a value to be realized not because it is mine, not because it is a value, but because it is a value for someone on earth."[81]

Sartre's example of the "human relation of helping" illuminates both the appeal and the help and offers further insight into the ideal society for which we are to strive. His example concerns a man helped by another onto a moving bus: "A runs toward the bus, B, on the platform, extends his hand. . . . In grasping it as an instrument, [A] contributes to realizing his own project." But A becomes instrument for B, since A serves as a means to realizing B's end (in this case, that of himself serving as an instrument). A's hand is grasped and pulled; and A becomes an object seen, appraised, and pulled, a passivity. Yet A does not become an object against his own freedom since he becomes an instrument precisely in pursuing his own end. He discovers the other's freedom, not as opposed to and threatening his freedom, but *in* his own freedom: "he unveils it at the heart of his own freedom as a free movement accompanying him toward his ends. . . . Each freedom is wholly in the other one."[82]

In the relation of appeal/help, the one who assists adopts the other's end in such a way that *it remains the end of the other and to be realized by the other*. This is quite different from having a common project or fighting the same enemy.[83] One who helps responds to the appeal not because the helper happens to share the other's end but rather just because the other has this end.

This means that there is gratuity in the appeal; and gratuity, according to Sartre, is at the heart of morality: "But at the start, I recognize that my end has to be conditional for the other as it is for me. That is, that it must always be possible for the other to refuse to help if the means used in such help alter his own ends." In appealing to others, one adheres to the others' ends: "I uphold them in their concrete content through my approbation." This is why the appeal is a "promise of reciprocity" and why one does not demand help from those whose ends one cannot approve, from those whom one would not oneself aid.[84]

Even in a better world, this critical stance toward the ends of the other seems preferable to Noddings's seemingly uncritical "displacement of interest from . . . [the carer's] own reality to the reality of the other," a displacement tantamount, according to Claudia Card, to the "motivational displacement" of interest on the part of the good servant or slave. What Card desires and what Sartre's critical stance offers is a caring that not only values individuals for themselves but also preserves in itself and values in others "a certain spiritual integrity."[85] Such critical but caring individuals will cease caring for and aiding the abuser in the realization of his goals long before the point of "diminished ideals" discussed by Noddings.[86] The maintenance of a critical stance by the care giver no doubt means, as Sandra Bartky acknowledges, the quality of care will often suffer;[87] but such seems absolutely necessary if women are not to be further disempowered by their care giving, particularly in relationships with men.[88]

In the relation appeal/help, each discovers and wills the other's freedom and each is totally in the other. This is why Sartre sees in the appeal a sketch of a utopian world ("where each person treats the other as an end—that is, takes the other person's undertaking as end")—"a world where each person can call upon all the others." It is why Sartre sees an authentic appeal as necessarily "conscious of being a surpassing of every inequality of condition toward a human world where any appeal of anyone to anyone will always be possible."[89]

Sartre envisions authentic human relationships and a utopian future in which such relationships would be possible with no qualifications and with no interference from opposing and oppressive structures in society. This is an ideal of reciprocity and genuine cooperation, two features central to any feminist vision. Incidentally, the requisite reciprocity would be far more than mere "acknowledgment of the other's caring," which is all Sarah Hoagland can find of reciprocity in Noddings.[90] In fact, Noddings herself demands more than such acknowledgment when, in her response to Hoagland, she rejects unidirectional caring. If an act, supposedly of caring, induces noncaring or exploitative responses from the cared-for, then, she says, it is a perversion of genuine caring: "Properly, caring applies to a relation, and parties in both roles contribute to its maintenance."[91] Problems remain for Noddings, though, given that her concern with exploitation is focused on individuals and is not a part of a broader analysis of systems of oppression and their impact on individual relationships.

Authentic human relationships also go beyond the caring relationships depicted by Noddings by providing a basis for a new understanding of autonomy. Feminists have argued that autonomy is important and not simply to be discarded once we recognize its connection with liberal theory and with an outmoded conception of property. As Jennifer Nedelsky says, "We must develop and sustain the capacity for finding our own law, and the task is to understand what social forms, relationships, and personal practices foster that capacity." Since relationships, not isolation, enable people to be autonomous, she suggests that childrearing replace property as "the most promising model, symbol, or metaphor for autonomy."[92]

While childrearing is certainly a more promising model or meta-

phor than property, Sartre's relation of appeal/help and his notion of
a city of ends seem even more promising since, unlike childrearing,
they cannot be misread to support paternalism and unidirectional care
giving or as implicit support for the view of relationships as central for
children but not for adults. Similarly, unlike childrearing and even
Noddings's response to a "proximate stranger," the notion of a city of
ends leaves sufficient room for both distance and difference, something denied, as Iris Marion Young recognizes, by both liberal individualism and proponents of community.[93] In other words, Sartre's notion
of a city of ends denies the independent, self-sufficient individual of
liberalism as well as avoids postulating fusion in a community as the
social ideal. Chapter 6 will include further exploration of caring, friendship, sexual love, mothering, paternalism, and possibilities of nonappropriative, nonhierarchical relationships.

THE SPIRIT OF PLAY

Admittedly, it can be demoralizing to be engaged in a struggle in
which goals are perceived as unreachable and accomplishments acknowledged as constantly mutating into the very opposite of what was
sought. These recognitions are particularly likely to demoralize in a
society in which success seems to be all that matters and in which there
already is what Sharon Welch describes as an ideological "cultured
despair" that

> masks the bad faith of abandoning social justice work for others when one
> is already the beneficiary of partial social change. It masks the ideological
> definition of moral action that leads to despair when easy solutions cannot
> be found. Becoming so easily discouraged is the privilege of those accus-
> tomed to too much power, accustomed to having needs met without ne-
> gotiation and work, accustomed to having a political and economic system
> that responds to their needs.

What such despair hides from view is the "vital recognition that to stop
resisting, even when success is unimaginable, is to die. The death that
accompanies acquiescence to overwhelming problems is multidimen-
sional: the threat of physical death, the death of the imagination, the
death of the ability to care."[94]

An ethics focused on liberation must recognize this danger and, if
possible, offer practitioners a way to avoid demoralization while pursuing unreachable goals and watching their accomplishments used against
them. Sartre proposes play as a resolution to similar problems in his

ethics, and his development and use of this notion will be explored in
Chapter 7. I shall argue there that Sartre's analyses of ambiguity and
of the playful yet dedicated struggle for impossible goals offer a way
to adhere to crucial feminist insights *and* continue our struggle for
human liberation.

Finally, the revolutionary possibilities of play must not be ignored.
Virginia Woolf hinted at these when she observed the revolutionary
potential of women's laughter and turning away from the all-too-seri-
ous pomp and circumstance of those in positions of power. Play, like
laughter and turning away, involves a disconnection from the seriousness of those for whom values are given and not created. The playful
individual makes light of those values, indeed of all values, by recognizing and affirming freedom as their ultimate foundation. This playful iconoclasm differs greatly from the often cruel laughter of the serious,
a laughter that affirms hierarchy and presumes the permanence of values
rather than their origin in human freedom.

Woolf offers a delightful illustration of the way a mocking laughter
can undermine the seriousness of displays of dominance. Mockingly,
she describes how the "dazzling" public attire of the dominant "makes
us gape with astonishment." Connecting the "love of dress" with the
"hypnotic power of dominance" and seeing a causal link between the
competition and jealousy thus promoted and a "disposition towards
war," she urges women to "refuse all such distinctions and all such
uniforms for ourselves." But first she satirizes and shows the ludicrousness
of such displays:

> [This elaborate ceremonial dress where "each button, rosette and stripe
> seems to have some symbolical meaning"] not only covers nakedness,
> gratifies vanity, and creates pleasure for the eye, but it serves to advertise
> the social, professional, or intellectual standing of the wearer. If you will
> excuse the humble illustration, your dress fulfills the same function as the
> tickets in a grocer's shop. But, here, instead of saying, "This is margarine;
> this pure butter; this is the finest butter in the market," it says, "This man
> is a clever man—he is Master of Arts; this man is a very clever man—
> he is Doctor of Letters; this man is a most clever man—he is a Member
> of the Order of Merit."

In case the grocery analogy is not enough in the way of ridicule, she
imaginatively transposes such ostentatious behavior to the subordinate
group: "A woman who advertised her motherhood by a tuft of horse-
hair on the left shoulder would scarcely, you will agree, be a venerable
object."[95]

Such playfulness, like anger, requires what Marilyn Frye calls "uptake," though perhaps not in quite the same way. At least, play, like anger, requires uptake or recognition by others if it is to be revolutionary, if it is to make any difference vis-à-vis the structures and activities of oppression. Just as Frye recognizes that a woman's anger at a car mechanic may simply be dismissed as "crazy,"[96] so, too, may the playful treatment of serious and oppressive values by the oppressed be regarded by oppressors as well as by many of the oppressed themselves as mad or childlike. Or it may just be ignored. In such cases, it will accomplish nothing along the lines of undermining power.

Even when play is noticed and recognized as play, it is all too likely to be only momentarily unsettling, a fleeting dis-ease for the serious, a discomfort quickly replaced by the familiar and, for them, comfortable values and order of the ordinary. In fact, and far more dangerous, this temporary unsettling may be used by the forces of oppression as a safety valve for the purpose of releasing tensions in the oppressed and even as a means of relieving misgivings in the oppressors themselves. If everyone leaves the playful activity with a sense of distance from and moral superiority to the oppressive values embedded in the social structures, then those structures have been reinforced rather than challenged by the play. Such play is clearly part and parcel of the status quo and not a revolutionary force against it.

Guided by Mikhail Bakhtin and various feminist theorists, in Chapter 7 I explore the possibilities of revolutionary play. On the basis of this exploration, I conclude that, while playful activities may unsettle and disrupt the status quo, this is more likely than not to be temporary. However, the effect that such activities can have on the revolutionaries or would-be revolutionaries themselves is far from negligible. A spirit of play, coupled with a critical and political awareness, can be used by those who are oppressed to expunge from themselves internalized aspects of oppression and to open a space in which they may begin to relate nonoppressively to themselves and to one another.

CONCLUSION

Although a feminist ethics begins with a recognition and rejection of injustice and oppression, specifically against and of women, it cannot stop there. Since women are affected by different oppressions according to class, ethnicity, race, and sexual orientation, and, depending on these factors, are even affected differently by gender oppression, any restriction of feminist ethics to concern with gender oppression is impossible. Efforts to insist on such restriction, whether by the culture or by the well meaning, must be resisted.

Similarly, feminist ethics must insist on acknowledging the violence of its context and indeed the context of all the action it would guide. Although vision of a better society is necessary and important to those who would act morally as well as to those who would create ethical theory, feminist ethics recognizes that moral agents—even those who develop ethical theory—are situated in a society in which violence is both endemic and systemic. The ethicist condemns this violence and urges vigilance to prevent herself or himself from adding to or in some way encouraging such violence whether by ethical analysis, by inaction, or by the violent opposition to oppression that is acknowledged as sometimes necessary.

Love and caring are all too often valorized in oppressive societies, particularly as values for the oppressed, and centered in ethics in ways that support oppression and undermine the efforts of those who try to overthrow it. This is an effective strategy for those who support the status quo precisely because love and caring are crucial aspects of a feminist ideal. Thus, a feminist ethics must develop this ideal in such a way that it does not aid and abet oppression. An ethics of freedom, but not an ethics of caring, develops ideals of love and caring in such a way that they do not support a violent and oppressive status quo.

Relativism and futility are particularly vexing problems confronting such an ethics. A spirit of play serves to resolve both of those problems and to offer other possibilities as a strategy for those who confront oppression.

Other dangers await both those who develop ethical theory and those who try to act morally; and the ethicist must work slowly and cautiously through what is tantamount to a minefield. The next chapter examines some of these dangers.

NOTES

1. Janice G. Raymond, *A Passion for Friends: Toward a Philosophy of Female Affection* (Boston: Beacon Press, 1986), pp. 207-8.

2. Alison Jaggar, "Feminist Ethics: Projects, Problems, Prospects," in *Feminist Ethics*, ed. Claudia Card, pp. 85-86, 98.

3. Pat Parker, "Revolution: It's Not Neat or Pretty or Quick,"in *This Bridge Called My Back: Writings by Radical Women of Color*, ed. Cherríe Moraga and Gloria Anzaldúa (New York: Kitchen Table: Women of Color Press, 1983), p. 240.

4. The Combahee River Collective, "A Black Feminist Statement," in *But Some of Us Are Brave: Black Women's Studies*, ed. Gloria T. Hull, Patricia Bell Scott, and Barbara Smith (Old Westbury, NY: Feminist Press, 1982), p. 18.

5. Angela Y. Davis, *Women, Culture, & Politics* (New York: Vintage Books, 1990), pp. 31, 12.

6. See Paula Giddings, *When and Where I Enter: The Impact of Black Women on Race and Sex in America* (New York: Bantam Books, 1985).

7. Raymond, p. 169.

8. Ruth Ginzberg, "Philosophy Is Not a Luxury," *Feminist Ethics*, ed. Claudia Card, p. 130.

9. Admittedly many of these children who are sexually molested are boys, a fact that complicates our theories but that we cannot afford to ignore, particularly inasmuch as many of these grow up to abuse their own children.

10. Andrea Dworkin, *Intercourse* (New York: Free Press, 1987), p. 194.

11. Gloria Anzaldúa, *Borderlands/La Frontera: The New Mestiza* (San Francisco: Spinsters/Aunt Lute, 1987), p. 20.

12. Barbara Cameron, "Gee, You Don't Seem Like an Indian from the Reservation," in *The Bridge Called My Back: Writings by Radical Women of Color*, p. 49.

13. Michèle Le Doeuff, *Hipparchia's Choice: An Essay Concerning Women, Philosophy, etc.*, trans. Trista Selous (Cambridge, MA: Blackwell, 1991), p. 4.

14. Susan Faludi, *Backlash: The Undeclared War against American Women* (New York: Crown Publishers, 1991), p. 292, cites an article in *Commentary* by Allan Bloom, famous for his widely discussed book *The Closing of the American Mind*, in which he writes "in a tone of high skepticism" about violence against women. She quotes him thus: "'Women, it is said, . . . are raped by their husbands as well as by strangers, they are sexually harassed by professors and employers at school and work.'" "With mounting irritation," she says, he notes that feminists want "all these so-called crimes 'legislated against and punished.'" Bloom can intimate that such crimes against women are bogus without having to deal with outraged cries from all quarters, I think, simply because he is doing little more than lending an admittedly prestigious voice (albeit one with no recognized expertise, as far as I can see, on any issues of violence) to myths that are embedded in various ways in the ideology that supports the power imbalance between men and women. One of those myths, cited by The Boston Women's Health Collective, *The New Our Bodies, Ourselves: A Book By and For Women* (New York: Simon & Schuster, 1984), p. 102, denies the frequency of rape by claiming, "It's only done by perverts leaping from bushes."

15. The Boston Women's Health Book Collective, *The New Our Bodies, Ourselves: A Book By and For Women*, pp. 99, 114.

16. Andrea Dworkin, *Mercy* (New York: Four Walls Eight Windows, 1991), p. 343, elaborates on the source of this figure in her "Author's Note" at the end of the book. She cites a 1978 study, funded by the National Institute for Mental Health and conducted by Diana Russell, in which 930 adult women in San Francisco were questioned. Russell, according to Dworkin, "found that forty-four percent of the women had experienced rape or attempted rape as defined by California state law at least once . . . fully half [of those] had experienced more than one such attack."

17. Catharine A. MacKinnon, *Feminism Unmodified: Discourses on Life and Law* (Cambridge, MA: Harvard University Press, 1987), pp. 169, 51; *Toward a Feminist Theory of the State* (Cambridge, MA: Harvard University Press, 1989), p. 127.

18. My presentation of aspects of this system suggests that it is riddled with inconsistency. In some ways, this is so; feminists can and should present this system of myths so as to unmask apparent contradictions. Yet we need to recognize the ways that even the most glaring—to us—of contradictions appear able to coexist in this system. For example, the assumption that sexual child abuse of girls and rape of women are natural, normal, and desirable appears inconsistent with the claim that they are exceptional. But it is feminists, not the culture, who characterize the all too frequent acts in question as "sexual child abuse" and "rape." Depicting these acts of violence as natural, normal, and desirable, the culture does not view them as sexual child abuse or rape, both of which are seen as unacceptable and undesirable. Since the former are natural, normal, and desirable activities, according to the culture, they are not abuse or rape; and those involved should accept both these activities and their roles in causing them. Those who do not and who protest their treatment are viewed as perverse and unnatural themselves. Hence, the phenomenon we have recognized as "blaming the victim."

19. Davis, *Women, Culture, & Politics*, p. 43.

20. The Boston Women's Health Book Collective, *The New Our Bodies, Ourselves: A Book By and For Women*, p. 103.

21. Patricia Hill Collins, *Black Feminist Thought: Knowledge, Consciousness, and the Politics of Empowerment* (New York: Routledge, 1990), pp. 178-79.

22. See William R. Doerner, "The Man Who Hated Women: A sick obsession ignites the country's worst mass killing," *Time* (December 18, 1989), p. 30; Barry Came, with Dan Burke, George Ferzoco, Brenda O'Farrell, and Bruce Wallace, "Montreal Massacre: Railing against feminists, a gunman kills 14 women on a Montreal campus, then shoots himself," *Maclean's* (December 18, 1989), pp. 14-17; "Coping with Femicide," *off our backs* (March 1990), pp. 24-27.

23. Reuters News Service, "Angry Canadians Demand Stricter Gun Laws," *Los Angeles Times*, (December 8, 1989), p. A24, simply describes the killer, without mention of his name, as "a crazed gunman."

24. Ironically, it was given less prominence on the front page of the December 7 *New York Times* than a story about a Supreme Court hearing of a right-to-die case on behalf of a comatose woman (the latter given about three times more space and placed above the Montreal story in the same column).

25. Reuters News Service, p. A24.

26. The first story reporting the murder of Wanda Walters was by Katie Long, *The Atlanta Constitution* (August 11, 1990), pp. D1, D6, under the headline "Cyclorama chief tries to end life of battles." The battles to which the headline referred were the murderer's own—his widely publicized fight to secure his position at the Atlanta Cyclorama and his reported fight with his

obsession with his victim—but the choice of the word "battles" seems designed to conjure up images of the Civil War Battle of Atlanta portrayed in the Cyclorama.

This story was followed by one by Gary Pomerantz, *The Atlanta Journal and Constitution* (September 9, 1990), pp. A1, A8. Here the major headline read: "Walters family affair: a fatal attraction." Under that appeared a subordinate headline (journalists, I am told by Marian Meyers who was my source for the exact wordings and locations of the quoted material, call this a deck), purporting to quote the murderer and child molester, Dennis Walters: "'I never loved anybody like that girl . . . never like this.'" A reader who continued reading this story when it resumed on A8 was greeted by another headline: "Walters: in the end, his love consumed them both." At least, this last gives some indication, though still not a major one, that Dennis Walters was not the only one to suffer in this struggle. Such a serious omission together with the lighthearted word play—even about incestuous child abuse—in all of the headlines should be sufficient to shock even the most jaded. Seldom do we see murderers' suffering and obsessions given such serious attention except when men kill their female lovers and wives and particularly when the men kill themselves as well.

As Gus Kaufman, Jr., Richard Bathrick, and Marian Meyers, all of whom are connected with Men Stopping Violence, say in a response piece published in *The Atlanta Journal and Constitution* (September 16, 1990), p. G2:

> [I]t isn't "love" or "attraction" when an adult male sexually abuses a female minor and then, in an attempt to control her, adopts her, marries her and systematically dominates and terrorizes her—finally murdering her when he realizes that she will not longer be his possession. A more accurate characterization of that relationship is victimization, incest, rape, misogyny, abuse of power. Love has nothing to do with it.

They also challenge the way the reporters' depiction of Walters as "obsessed" "lets Walters off the hook for his actions." If he was obsessed and "a nut" (a description of Walters attributed to a former mayor of Atlanta), then he obviously could not help himself and cannot be held accountable for his action. To compound the problem, the victim's provocative actions are enumerated as though they explain—perhaps even justify—his action.

27. "Slaying, suicide end 'lovers' quarrel,'" *The Atlanta Constitution* (February 18, 1992), p. D2.

28. "Man charged with murder in brother's death" and "Husband, wife die in dispute," *The Atlanta Journal and Constitution* (December 6, 1992), p. E2.

29. This is a pseudonym under which Gloria Watkins publishes. Since she does not capitalize either part of this pseudonym, I shall respect her choice and only capitalize her name if I would capitalize any other lower-case word in that position, e.g., at the beginning of a sentence. Since, by itself, the uncapitalized last name "hooks" is likely to be confusing in many sentences, I shall generally use her full name when referring to her whereas with others I shall sometimes use just their last names even though feminists like Claudia Card caution against such use of patronyms in a patriarchal culture.

30. For example, in her book *White Political Women: Paths from Privilege to Empowerment* (Knoxville: University of Tennessee Press, 1992), Diane L. Fowlkes refers to this system as "complex domination."

31. MacKinnon, *Feminism Unmodified*, pp. 99, 101.

32. Ginzberg, p. 137.

33. Marilyn Frye, "Getting It Right," *Willful Virgin: Essays in Feminism*, ed. Frye, (Freedom, CA: Crossing Press, 1992), p. 16.

34. bell hooks, *Talking Back* (Boston: South End Press, 1989), p. 106.

35. MacKinnon, *Toward a Feminist Theory of the State*, p. 52.

36. Dorothy E. Smith, "Women's Perspective as a Radical Critique of Sociology," *Feminism & Methodology*, ed. Sandra Harding (Bloomington: Indiana University Press, 1987), p. 90.

37. Nye, p. 35.

38. I fear the designation "women's movement," if unqualified, takes predominantly white women's movements as exhaustive of women's movements in this country. It seems to ignore the work of black women for women's rights, work that began at least as early as white women's work for their own suffrage, that joined in the suffrage battle, and that continued when suffrage was accomplished by law but not in reality.

39. MacKinnon, *Toward a Feminist Theory of the State*, pp. 141-42.

40. Dworkin, *Intercourse*, p. 158.

41. Sara Ruddick, "Maternal Thinking," *Mothering: Essays in Feminist Theory*, ed. Joyce Trebilcot (Totowa, NJ: Rowman & Allanheld, 1983), p. 227, comments on the difficulties faced by an individual mother and father determined to be egalitarian in their child rearing only to lose any hard-won achievements of equality and mutual respect as the result of the derogation and subordination of the mother outside the home with its effect on the children who "feel angry, confused, and 'wildly unmothered.'"

42. Sartre, *What Is Literature?* trans. Bernard Frechtman (New York: Harper & Row, 1965), p. 269.

43. Le Doeuff, p. 247.

44. Nye, p, 177.

45. Susan Faludi, *Backlash: The Undeclared War Against American Women*.

46. bell hooks, *Talking Back*, pp. 105-9.

47. Dworkin, *Intercourse* p. 108.

48. Sarah Lucia Hoagland, *Lesbian Ethics: Toward New Value* (Palo Alto, CA: Institute of Lesbian Studies, 1988), pp. 47-49.

49. Although real-life suffering should not be confused with that of imaginary characters in movies, the movie *Thelma and Louise* has been described in a parallel way as one in which women win and men clearly don't have a chance. Such statements ignore the end of the movie—in which Thelma and Louise lose to men in a big way—just as racists conveniently ignore King's violent death at the hands of a racist.

50. Sartre, *Notebooks for an Ethics*, trans. David Pellauer (Chicago: University of Chicago Press, 1992), p. 142.

51. Hoagland, *Lesbian Ethics*, pp. 254-55, 26.

52. MacKinnon, "Feminism, Marxism, Method, and the State: Toward Feminist Jurisprudence," *Feminism & Methodology*, p. 142.

53. MacKinnon, *Toward a Feminist Theory of the State*, pp. 133, 175.

54. Sartre, *Notebooks for an Ethics*, pp. 9, 161, 402-5.

55. *Ibid.*, p. 9.

56. Michael Stocker, *Plural and Conflicting Values* (Oxford: Clarendon Press, 1990), pp. 34, 19, 25.

57. *Ibid.*, p. 10.

58. Sartre, *Notebooks for an Ethics*, p. 404.

59. Le Doeuff, pp. 174-75, 278.

60. Nel Noddings, *Caring: A Feminine Approach to Ethics & Moral Education* (Berkeley: University of California Press, 1984), p. 44.

61. *Ibid.*, p. 102.

62. *Ibid.*, p. 86.

63. Le Doeuff, p. 280.

64. Spelman, "The Virtue of Feeling and the Feeling of Virtue," in *Feminist Ethics*, ed. Claudia Card, pp. 216-19.

65. Michele M. Moody-Adams, "Gender and the Complexity of Moral Voices," *ibid.*, pp. 203-5.

66. Claudia Card, "Caring and Evil," *Hypatia*, Vol. 5, No. 1 (Spring 1990), p. 105.

67. Some victims of abuse will choose to leave the abusive relationships long before they reach the desperation of the woman in Noddings's example. In such cases, surely something besides caring drives the individual and presumably enables her to understand that she should leave. As Card, *ibid.*, p. 106, says, "I should have thought the richness of our ethical ideals *enabled* us to reject bad relationships and freed us up for ethically fuller ones. After all, it is by contrasting abusive relationships with such ideals that we are finally able to see the abuse for what it is."

68. Noddings, *Caring*, p. 47.

69. *Ibid.*, pp. 105-6.

70. *Ibid.*, pp. 34-36.

71. For a perceptive analysis of this support and disempowerment, see Sandra Lee Bartky, "Feeding Egos and Tending Wounds: Deference and Disaffection in Women's Emotional Labor," *Femininity and Domination: Studies in the Phenomenology of Oppression* (New York: Routledge, 1990), pp. 99-119.

72. Hoagland, *Lesbian Ethics*, p. 85.

73. Jeffner Allen, *Lesbian Philosophy: Explorations* (Palo Alto, CA: Institute of Lesbian Studies, 1986), p. 35.

74. Eléanor H. Kuykendall, "Toward an Ethic of Nurturance: Luce Irigaray on Mothering and Power," *Mothering: Essays in Feminist Theory*, p. 269.

75. Rita C. Manning, *Speaking from the Heart: A Feminist Perspective on Ethics* (Lanham, MD: Rowman & Littlefield, 1992), p. 72.

76. *Ibid.*, pp. 77, 145-47, 156.

77. *Ibid.*, pp. 138-39.

78. Noddings, *Caring*, pp. 1-2.

79. *Ibid.*, pp. 14, 65, 44, 34, 149.

80. I prefer my own translation of the last part of this sentence: "by the outlining of the adoption of this end by myself."

81. Sartre, *Notebooks for an Ethics*, pp. 277-80.

82. *Ibid.*, pp. 287-88.

83. In Chapter 6, authentic love will be distinguished from having the same enemy or sharing the same project.

84. Sartre, *Notebooks for an Ethics*, pp. 283-84.

85. Card, p. 107.

86. This is a point of emphatic disagreement by Noddings, "A Response," *Hypatia*, Vol. 5, No. 1 (Spring 1990), p. 124, since she rejects "withdrawing from relationships in which a partner is guilty of gross wrong-doing or wrong-thinking." She reminds the reader of an earlier work (*Women and Evil*) in which she "argued that such withdrawal often tends to make us feel righteous without doing much to alleviate the evil."

87. Bartky, "Feeding Egos and Tending Wounds: Deference and Disaffection in Women's Emotional Labor," in *Feminity and Domination*, p. 111.

88. For analysis of ways uncritical caring disempowers women in heterosexual relationships, see Bartky, *ibid.*, pp. 109-16.

89. Sartre, *Notebooks for an Ethics*, pp. 49, 285.

90. Hoagland, "Some Concerns about Nel Noddings' *Caring*," *Hypatia*, Vol 5, No. 1 (Spring 1990), p. 109.

91. Noddings, "A Response," p. 123.

92. Jennifer Nedelsky, "Reconceiving Autonomy: Sources, Thoughts and Possibilities," *Yale Journal of Law and Feminism*, Vol. 1, No. 1 (Spring 1989), pp. 10-12, 19.

93. Iris Marion Young, *Justice and the Politics of Difference* (Princeton, NJ: Princeton University Press, 1990), p. 229.

94. Welch, pp. 15, 20.

95. Virginia Woolf, *Three Guineas* (New York: Harcourt Brace Jovanovich, 1938), pp. 19, 150, 20-21.

96. Frye, *The Politics of Reality: Essays in Feminist Theory*, pp. 88-89.

Chapter Two

Rethinking Some Fundamental Concepts

A feminist ethics must be both critical of what is and ever mindful of what might be. It must work out consistent ideals for which humanity should strive. History is strewn with examples of ideals that have been used to justify rather than to condemn oppression, dehumanization, and violation of individuals. Bloody crusades have been undertaken to "save" nonbelievers, wars of aggression and territorial acquisition fought in the name of "freedom" and "democracy," atomic bombs dropped on cities to "save" lives, Vietnamese villages destroyed in line with some allegedly utilitarian calculation of benefit. Ideals advocated by a feminist ethics must be spelled out clearly so that they will not remain abstractions to be used to justify even worse atrocities than they are meant to critique. But most of all, a feminist ethics must be continually critical of itself, lest it repeat the mistakes it condemns in its opponents. This means that any attempt to construct a feminist ethics is and necessarily remains only partial, a step in an ongoing process of dialogue, struggle, and increasing awareness.

Since a feminist ethics must develop its ideals in a situation largely resistant and even antagonistic to them, some preliminary discussion of this task is in order. This discussion includes some of those ideals as well as cautions concerning the pitfalls awaiting such an ethics. Some of these await any ethics; some are specifically connected with feminist ethics because of its ideals or methodology. In rethinking those ideals and cautions, this chapter will elaborate some general parameters for a feminist ethics.

55

THE IDEAL OF OBJECTIVITY

Unmasking and rejecting the biased claims presented as objective by male anthropologists, biologists, historians, philosophers, sociologists, and others, many feminists despair of objectivity altogether and concur with Sarah Hoagland that "'objectivity' is nothing but a collection of perceptions which agree." This means, of course, as Hoagland recognizes, that "subjectivity" must be challenged as well inasmuch as it "implies we have private, totally separate perceptions which need the mediation of a judge (someone 'objective')."[1]

Few would disagree that objectivity has been used—speaking more properly, misused—by what Marilyn Frye describes as arrogant male perceivers to characterize the way *they* see the world *in terms of their interests.*[2] As Catharine MacKinnon observes:

> The male perspective is systemic and hegemonic. . . . In this context, objectivity—the nonsituated, universal standpoint, whether claimed or aspired to—is a denial of the existence or potency of sex inequality that tacitly participates in constructing reality from the dominant point of view. Objectivity, as the epistemological stance of which objectification is the social process, creates the reality it apprehends by defining as knowledge the reality it creates through its way of apprehending it.[3]

The creation of the world from this particular point of view reflects, as MacKinnon says later, power in its male form. This male point of view "does not comprehend its own perspectivity," but rather sees itself as "objectivity: the ostensibly noninvolved stance, the view from a distance and from no particular perspective, apparently transparent to its reality."[4] Given the hegemony and claims to objectivity and impartiality of this perspective, a particular perspective masking itself as a "view from nowhere,"[5] it is not surprising that many women, even against their own interests, reflect and help to perpetrate this arrogance.

Arrogance has not been limited to privileging male perspectives over those of females. Objectivity has been invoked frequently in other situations, for similar reasons and with similar effects. Thus, Frantz Fanon observes how Western reporters justify as "objective" their use of ambiguous terms in describing the struggles of colonized peoples such as those in Algeria. As Fanon says, "For the native, objectivity is always directed against us."[6]

It is precisely such problems with an uncritical—and nonpolitical— assumption of objectivity that should lead us to question claims made by someone like John Rawls about principles that would be chosen "behind a veil of ignorance." Rawls assumes that placing individuals behind such a veil (not allowing any to know "his place in society, his class position or social status," or "his fortune in the distributions of natural assets and abilities" or "his" own conception of the good or "special psychological propensities") would result in fair agreements. A society based on such hypothetical agreements would, he says, "come as close as a society can to being a voluntary scheme, for it meets the principles which free and equal persons would assent to under circumstances that are fair. In this sense its members are autonomous and the obligations they recognize self-imposed." While he believes "the outcome is not conditioned by arbitrary contingencies or the relative balance of social forces,"[7] he fails sufficiently to recognize that even the most minimal assumptions about human beings and what they want are strongly influenced by the actual gendered and culturally specific perspectives we bring with us to his thought experiment. Simply by virtue of being part of this culture, individuals, though hypothetically placed behind a veil of ignorance, will continue to reflect their arrogance as dominant white, Western, financially well-off males. Rawls should not speak so confidently about what individuals without privilege would choose if they in turn were place behind the veil. They may be considerably less averse to risk and are likely to assess present arrangements differently, partly because they have not been protected by privilege from experiencing and seeing the negative aspects of existing arrangements.

No doubt, arrogant—and false—claims should make us wary of any and all aspirations to objectivity. In addition, if objectivity and subjectivity require, as Hoagland believes, a judge to mediate between them, we would do well to be extremely suspicious of both; otherwise, we will inadvertently perpetuate rather than overthrow structures of domination and submission. However, we should hesitate before we dispense with everything co-optable and potentially capable of supporting the status quo since, indeed, we would be forced to dismiss far too much. Thus, objectivity, like morality, should not be dismissed just because it is so easily co-optable by those who wish to maintain their power over others and whatever advantages accompany such power.

In fact, although objectivity is a cry of which androcentrists[8] have been especially fond, feminists do themselves and human freedom a disservice by accepting the androcentric claim that women are incapable of objectivity. Even if feminists go on to deny that men can be any more objective than women, something vital is lost in the process. True, at least theoretically, a universal rejection of objectivity undermines androcentrists' allegedly objective claims about nature, history, humankind, about women's "nature," desires, needs, and even about men's "nature," desires, and needs. However, while these claims thereby lose their allegedly objective status, they unfortunately assume a new status: that of being unchallengeable. Although they reflect reality from a male perspective, they cannot be shown to be distortions and manipulations of reality since the feminist claims and revelations that might demonstrate this are themselves, according to this hypothesis, no more than reflections of reality from a *different* perspective. Unfortunately, a blanket rejection of objectivity makes all intersubjective claims and arguments equal.

Thus, if objectivity is too quickly dismissed, then the most ridiculous antifeminist claims, some with devastating consequences, are left on a footing that makes them as acceptable as the most careful and best documented claims of feminist researchers. Admittedly, dismissing the objectivity of androcentrist and misogynist claims by males takes away some of their clout; but, alas, the dismissal has a similar effect on the feminist challenges. Thus, for example, Joan Kelly-Gadol's ground-breaking reexamination of history and discovery of "a fairly regular pattern of relative loss of status for women precisely in periods of so-called progressive change," such as the Renaissance,[9] is on a par with androcentric histories that present these periods as positive for everyone.

Similarly, Angela Davis can be seen as no less—though, of course, no more—arrogant than the Western feminists who claim, without asking those affected, that female genital mutilation is the "pivotal issue in the quest for women's liberation in such countries as Egypt, the Sudan, and Somalia." The latter arrogance is called to Davis's attention by an Egyptian woman who notes that she would not dream of talking about women in the Egyptian countryside without conducting field research.[10] If, though, research only reflects the researcher's own point of view, how can anyone be said to be more arrogant or to have less adequate research than anyone else? This is why Jean Grimshaw, in *Philosophy and Feminist Thinking*, encourages feminists to find some way through all the talk of "shifting scientific paradigms" and "the social construction of reality" in order to note objective facts, for example, about the structure of capitalism (that "[i]t is in the *interests* of . . . corporations to maintain women's obsession with food") and about some Victorian medical conceptions of female nature (that "such theories were not *simply* a matter of beliefs about women, they were also a means of ensuring male control over women, of legitimating female dependence").[11]

Catharine MacKinnon's analyses of rape, sexual harassment, pornography, and obscenity proceed, as she says, "from the point of view of women." From that point of view, she demonstrates that rape is not sharply distinguishable from sexual intercourse in this society, that sexual harassment does not differ very much from ordinary sexual initiation, and that pornography and obscenity cannot be clearly separated from what passes as eroticism or, for that matter, from many of the images of women ordinarily used to sell products. Although her analyses explicitly take the point of view of women, refuse to countenance the androcentrist assumption that the knowing subject must be distinct from the known object,[12] and are quite clearly different from the traditional analyses offered from the point of view of dominant males, to understand this as meaning that these two sets of analyses simply represent two different points of view is to undermine the force of her arguments. Male assumptions of objectivity have been a camouflage covering male dominance and hiding the way male interests and desires are imposed on females. Feminist critics who dismantle that camouflage and reveal the dominance for what it is can hardly be said simply to be imposing "different" interests and desires on others and on the world. Surely we are not left with two equally valid but diametrically opposed views of the relations between males and females, of rape, sexual harassment, pornography, and obscenity.

Surely, too, we cannot simply accept—and thereby dismiss—as just another point of view either Marie-Aimée Helie-Lucas's challenge to the claim (she calls it "myth"), made by Fanon and others, that "the Algerian woman was liberated along with her country" or her contention that "tradition serves the purposes of those in power" (by which she opposes Fanon's praise for the "revolutionary virtue" of the veil for women).[13] Class and gender biases may indeed arise even in the work of those who challenge the distortions and omissions in Western accounts of the way things are; for example, Nabawiya Musa observes that Farid Effendi Wajdi "was distressed when he saw women in America standing in front of furnaces in factories . . . but does not see Egyptian women peddlars [*sic*] groaning under the heavy weight of their baskets of fruit and vegetables as they make their way down the streets enduring the bold stares and hands of insolent men."[14] Such biases must be noted and corrected just as bourgeois and Western distortions must be admitted when Gayatri Spivak calls attention to the way U.S. feminists have concentrated their attention—and praise—on corporations' treatments of women in the United States while ignoring the "*multi*national theater" in which the same corporations' actions are anything but worthy of praise.[15]

If, however, we simply dismiss objectivity, we concede intellectual defeat. After all, the views against which we wish to argue are firmly entrenched in social institutions and structures, in patterns of behavior, and in each and every individual's conscious and subconscious awareness. We are not likely to make much progress in a competition for hearts and minds in these circumstances if we concede at the outset that, no matter how careful and cautious the research by feminists, the resulting claims can be no closer to truth, can no more clearly reflect the way things are, than even the most outlandish and unsupported claims underpinning patriarchy and other forms of oppression.

MacKinnon's caution against affirming mere difference holds for such research as well as in law and ethics. In her discussions of the affirmation of difference in law and ethics, she points out that such affirmation "adopts the point of view of male supremacy on the status of the sexes" by leaving unchallenged and even unrecognized the fact that maleness is taken as the standard. To say that women and men simply see differently what goes on between them appears similarly to buttress the hegemony of the male (and therefore standard) point of view. Thus, even though the point of view of the disinterested observer should be rejected as epistemologically naive and politically disastrous, feminists cannot afford to reject all evaluation of objectivity, especially in a relative sense. Rather than claim that women experience and talk about a completely different social reality from that of men, we must, as MacKinnon says, presume women "able to have access to society and its structure because they live in it and have been formed by it, not in spite of those facts." In other words, "Women can know society because consciousness is part of it, not because of any capacity to stand outside it or oneself."[16] This means that claims can be disputed and some can quite properly be said to be more objective (that is, less distorted) than others.

This is not to say, of course, that we should make the same pompous claims for our research that androcentrists, racists, and others have made and are making for theirs. On the contrary, we can and should agree with Sandra Harding that "a problem is always a problem *for* someone or other."[17] Moreover, we must admit that our research, like theirs, reflects our cultural, racial, class, gender, and heterosexist biases, no matter how aware we try to be of the biases and no matter how strenuously we work to rid ourselves of them. Although Patricia Hill Collins sees "subjugated knowledge" such as Afrocentric feminist thought as "less likely than the specialized knowledge produced by dominant groups to deny the connection between ideas and the vested interests of their creators," she nonetheless admits that "a Black women's standpoint is only one angle of vision. Thus Black feminist thought represents a partial perspective. The overarching matrix of domination houses multiple groups, each with varying experiences with penalty and privilege that produce corresponding partial perspectives. . . . No one group has a clear angle of vision."[18] This is what Sharon Welch calls "[a]n epistemology of solidarity."[19]

We can acknowledge all of this, however, without giving up the ideal of objectivity. Just because we recognize our own and others' limitations and the fact that our analyses do not embody the "whole truth" does not mean that we give up objectivity as a goal. We may, for example, develop, as does Iris Young, an alternative notion of objectivity, quite unlike the hegemonic notion with which we are familiar and which is so fearful of difference. Rejecting the existence of an impartial point of view, Young requires that all perspectives and participants contribute to the discussion of an issue in order to arrive at an understanding as complete and objective as possible.[20] In this way, we would have as our goal a true "philosophical universalism," such as that urged by Michèle Le Doeuff, "a community in thought which includes everyone," according to which we can contrast—and reject the adequacy of—the "masculinism" and "particularism" of "work which, while claiming to be exhaustive, forgets about women's existence and concerns itself only with the position of men"[21] (and, we might add, not even of all men). Recognizing that the privileged must manifest more than just a willingness to talk in order to enable the oppressed to speak more honestly, Sharon Welch uses men as an example: "Men who work against rape or domestic violence, who are involved in challenging the value systems that lead to such violence, are able to hear the voices of women, and women are able to trust them in a way that would be impossible if the only form of relation is that of dialogue."[22]

Even if objectivity is an unachievable ideal, we can and should continue to aspire toward this ideal and to use it in evaluating our own and others' research. And we should continue to criticize theories and individual claims to the extent that they reflect distortions arising out of partiality and "particularism."

Impossible ideals are thought by many to be a serious problem for ethics, but such ideals are integral to the ethics of Sartre. For Sartre, impossible ideals are an inescapable ingredient in the human situation. They become morally problematic (as we shall see in Chapter 6) only when they are pursued in a particular kind of way, a way Sartre calls "seriousness." Those who are serious take ideals as "given," as somehow preexisting all choices and actions, perhaps as unreachable, and are unlikely to gauge correctly how far from the mark their own behavior falls. Even those who are not serious, though, inevitably set standards that cannot be reached. A move away from seriousness will not be sufficient by itself to enable one to cope with futility, with the sense that one's actions never quite measure up. In answer to this, Sartre proposes that certain goals be taken as "regulative ideals" and that they be pursued playfully.

If objectivity is approached in this fashion, it will be seen as guiding our behavior, behavior occasionally evincing little glimmers of the ideal even while always bogged down in the distortions of limitations and biases. We can tentatively accept claims that are less biased and less distorting than their rivals; and we can advance our own hypotheses in the same spirit of tentativeness, hoping that, as these are subjected to rigorous critical scrutiny and debate, their major distortions, omissions, and unexamined assumptions will be illuminated and, where necessary, corrected. As Sandra Harding says:

> [If we] . . . avoid the "objectivist" stance that attempts to make the researcher's cultural beliefs and practices invisible while simultaneously skewering the research objects [sic] beliefs and practices to the display board . . . [then] the beliefs and behaviors of the researcher are part of the empirical evidence for (or against) the claims advanced in the results of research. *This* evidence too must be open to critical scrutiny no less than what is traditionally defined as relevant evidence. Introducing this "subjective" element into the analysis in fact increases the objectivity of the research and decreases the "objectivism" which hides this kind of evidence from the public.[23]

Carol Anne Douglas affirms a similar approach when she says: "To conceal or repress one's assumptions will not remove them. Trying to formulate and make public as many of one's assumptions as possible at least allows others to evaluate them."[24]

In this way, we avoid the arrogance of the "arrogant eye" so aptly named and well described by Marilyn Frye.[25] The arrogant eye is an observer who unapologetically and unabashedly falsifies. We avoid such arrogance by examining questioningly and critically, always endeavoring to correct our inadvertent falsifications. The arrogant eye coerces what it sees in order to make those things or individuals satisfy the conditions it imposes. We avoid such coercion by recognizing and respecting the independence of the other, heeding the conditions this other imposes, and placing ourselves in a reciprocity with her or him or with it. While we work to get all human beings recognized and respected as such, we do not arrogate to ourselves or to others the right to include and exclude as we or they see fit or to respect freedom only when so inclined. Nor do we try to speak for others. We recognize that our ideal of objectivity requires us to acknowledge perspectives other than our own and to listen to those who speak from those perspectives. Patricia Collins states this as a requirement of community: "everyone has a voice, but everyone must listen and respond to other voices in order to be allowed to remain the community."[26]

As we form our conclusions, we do so in a way that reflects as adequately as possible the variety of voices we have heard and that affirms the tentativeness of our conclusions, given voices we may yet hear as well as our distortions and misunderstandings of those we have heard. In this way, we avoid the Kantian tone of much that has been written about race, class, and gender, a tone that has assimilated specifics and particularities "to a false universal that imposed agreement, submerged specificity, and silenced particularity."[27]

THE ROLE OF SEPARATISM

In any discussion of responses to oppression, separatism is likely to be suggested as an option. Sometimes a separatism is proposed that carries to an extreme the assumption that the personal realm can be reconstructed without restructuring the larger context. Not all separatist proposals, however, have done this. Thus, it is important to distinguish kinds of separatism. Bell hooks makes a helpful distinction between merely tactical separatism and what she calls "reactionary separatism," the latter viewing separation as an ultimate goal.[28]

Tactical separatism affirms separation as a limited strategy, as a temporary expedient, necessary if certain ends are to be achieved. Such separatism is regarded as absolutely unavoidable by most feminist theorists. Representative of these is Luce Irigaray when she states,

> For women to undertake tactical strikes, to keep themselves apart from men long enough to learn to defend their desire, especially through speech, to discover the love of other women while sheltered from men's imperious choices that put them in the position of rival commodities, to forge for themselves a social status that compels recognition, to earn their living in order to escape from the condition of prostitute . . . these are certainly indispensable stages in the escape from their proletarization on the exchange market.[29]

Even more basically, as Marilyn Frye argues, the creation of separate spaces "somewhat sheltered from the prevailing winds of patriarchal culture" is necessary for an individual's sense of body and self: "[O]ne needs space to *practice* an erect posture; one cannot just will it to happen. To retrain one's body one needs physical freedom from what are, in the last analysis, physical forces misshaping it to the contours of the subordinate."[30]

Separation is necessary, too, "to avoid being demoralized." As Sarah Hoagland says, at least separation dispels "the illusion that we are equal participants in these events, [thus] we can avoid claiming responsibility for something over which we have no control." This seems particularly important to recognize in a society that has developed into a fine art the technique of distorting power relations by blaming the victim, the one who is relatively powerless. Separation may be necessary if one is to understand what is going on, since it offers "a way of pulling back from the existing conceptual framework, noting its patterns, and understanding their function regardless of the mythology espoused within the framework."[31] Perhaps, too, only with some pulling away from the systems of oppression surrounding us can we begin to free our thinking and our imaginations to devise practical strategies and alternatives.

However necessary such tactical separatism, bell hooks warns against "reactionary separatism," a form of separatism that assumes that women must either accept the male supremacy of our culture or withdraw from the culture and try to create their own subculture. The problem she sees with this withdrawal is that it is "rooted in the conviction that male supremacy is an absolute aspect of our culture." As she says, such separatism "eliminates any need for revolutionary struggle and it is in no way a threat to the status quo."[32] This kind of separatism flees the public and has recourse to the private without recognizing just how invidious to women that very distinction is.

Such separatism not only buys into the public/private distinction but is itself in jeopardy as it hides behind a "protection," namely, "privacy," which has never been applied in any serious way to women. As Catharine MacKinnon says:

> Conceptually, this private is hermetic. It *means* that which is inaccessible to, unaccountable to, unconstructed by anything beyond itself. By definition, it is not part of or conditioned by anything systematic or outside of it. It is personal, intimate, autonomous, particular, individual, the original source and final outpost of the self, gender neutral. It is, in short, defined by everything that feminism reveals women have never been allowed to be or to have, and everything that women have been equated with and defined in terms of *men's* ability to have.[33]

To hide behind privacy is not only to hide behind a protection that does not apply to women; it is also, according to Andrea Dworkin's analysis, to hide behind a sham. As she says, sexual activity, an activity generally thought to be paradigmatic of the private, has been controlled by the state, particularly as far as women are concerned, and thus cannot be legitimately regarded as private.[34]

Bell hooks is correct in observing that separatists who simply advocate and maintain separation in order to avoid dealing with existing social structures are probably no threat to those structures, any more than other social drop-outs pose serious threats to a society. This is, of course, true only if the numbers in each group are relatively small and if others can easily replace them in whatever roles they play in society. Such drop-outs assume, as Janice Raymond says, the status of outcasts from the world rather than that of rebels "on the 'boundary' of it." This dissociation is particularly serious for women: "In a world that views women as superfluous, that is, as not needed, marginal, unimportant, and to be dispensed with, women add to this superfluousness by dissociating themselves from the world. The more women dissociate, the more catastrophic the effect can be."[35] Though it may be seen as a way to cease active participation in and positive support of institutions that oppress, such withdrawal of participation and support is quite problematic.

Maybe hooks is wrong, though, to dismiss all forms of nontemporary separation as reactionary; and perhaps, on the contrary, some quite permanent forms of separation do constitute a real threat to the status quo. As Janice Raymond reminds us, not every "chosen, organized, and public separation from marriage" and creative attempt to construct "a woman-identified existence" is an "apolitical dissociation from the world."[36] Where the separatism involves genuine and moral opposition to the oppressions embedded in the social structures of the society it opposes and where the opposition and the act of separating have at least some minimum degree of visibility, separatism may accomplish something quite significant. It at least confronts the upholders of the status quo with a genuine alternative and with the fact that if separation is a choice, then participation is equally a choice. This is Sarah Hoagland's point when she says, "the tradition tends not to recognize separation as a choice among those considered moral agents because it cannot afford to acknowledge that participation is a choice."[37]

Andrea Nye sees the "subversive power" of women-oriented communities as measurable "by the anger they often provoke in men and man-identified women."[38] This anger may reflect, for example, as Audre Lorde says, "a very real fear that openly women-identified Black women who are no longer dependent upon men for their self-definition may well reorder our whole concept of social relationships." A similar fear is likely to be felt concerning other women-identified women. Another source of this fear is recognized by Lorde when she discusses the fear of difference. Although, according to Lorde, other differences may be necessary in a profit economy as it creates the "surplus people" it needs to function, only one difference—that of gender—is regarded as legitimate in our society. Other differences are feared, a fear reflected in racism, sexism, and homophobia. This fear ascribes a false power to difference, as though, for example, "the presence of one [lesbian] can contaminate the whole sex."[39]

Challenging these fears and making visible the fact that participation is itself a choice, and a very important one, is an invaluable and revolutionary service. Too often the status quo is presented and accepted as just the way things are and must be. This presumption of inevitability is a serious obstacle to change. Any effective challenge to this presumption is therefore itself revolutionary: it weakens a key support of the status quo, the assumption that there are no alternatives, hence that present social structures are unchangeable. Sartre acknowledged the importance of such an unsettling affirmation when he wrote in "The Republic of Silence," published just after France was freed from the Nazis, "Never were we freer than under the German occupation."[40] What he meant by this enigmatic statement was that the occupation was so odious that the very presence and activities of the Nazis were constant reminders—at least to people like himself[41]—that individuals in the invaded population could not avoid choosing either to go along (hence, to collaborate) or to resist.

Those who have tried to create feminist separatist communities have found that pulling away from the patriarchy by refusing association with men—or even with men *and* nonlesbian women—does not magically cure all the ills of oppression. Because each individual and her ways of relating have been constructed by the society in which she was raised, creating nonoppressive relationships is not simple; it requires, after all, the re-creation of each and every individual. Problems of racism, classism, and even sexism and homophobia will quickly surface since these permeate the larger society which has molded the character, the language, and the ways of relating for each and every member, even in lesbian communities. Some of the problems are likely to impinge from the outside, given continued and probably ineradicable connections with the larger society; but many will result from the internalized structures of oppression within the separatists themselves.

It is surely difficult for many women to acknowledge, as does Audre Lorde, that a woman, too, may leave "her heelprint upon another woman's face" and that Paulo Freire has correctly seen that "the true focus of revolutionary change is never merely the oppressive situations which we seek to escape, but that piece of the oppressor which is planted deep within each of us, and which knows only the oppressors' tactics, the oppressors' relationships."[42] It is even more difficult to overcome these aspects of our situation. Clearly, they will not be overcome merely by seeking moral purity outside the oppressive structures of one's society. As Carole Pateman and Elizabeth Gross argue: "There is no 'outside' in the material and discursive system that structures our subjectivity."[43]

The most serious problem with separatist women's communities is that such a reaction to oppression is inevitably elitist in that it is not and cannot be an option for many women. What makes it an option for certain women is that women of privilege, e.g., white women with class privilege, "don't share oppression with white men." Women of color, who do share oppression with men of their race, are not in the same simple relation of antagonism to those men.[44] The realities of class, of colonialism, and of racism link these women—including the lesbians among them—tightly to males of their own race or social and economic class and link the lesbian to the nonlesbian women in these groups. Even the connection to male children is likely to be different than for women of privilege; for example, although Lorde is a lesbian, her son represents to her "as much hope for our future world" as does her daughter.[45] Yet males are excluded—even male children after a certain age—and the ties often unacknowledged by nonlesbian feminist separatists. As Alison Jaggar says: "On the most fundamental level, . . . total separatism is classist and racist because it denies the importance of class and racial divisions. It assumes that these can be overcome without the full participation of the groups who suffer from them."[46]

Though elitist and consequently not a solution to the oppression of the larger society, separatism, even allegedly nontactical separatism, recommends itself as a strategy that can be utilized at least to some extent against some forms of oppression. Sarah Hoagland suggests this use when she observes that separatism can render another's game plan "meaningless, at least to some extent, ceasing to exist for lack of acknowledgment."[47]

The importance of acknowledgment to many game plans allows us to recognize and utilize the unique power that at least some women have by virtue of being necessary audience for the dominant, in other words, by virtue of the fact that, as Richard A. Wasserstrom says, "their approval and admiration is sought [even though] . . . they are at the same time regarded as less competent than men and less able to live fully developed, fully human lives." Wasserstrom does not see such power in other oppressed groups where the ideology affecting their status is not as "complex and confusing."[48] Like Wasserstrom, Sara Ann Ketchum and Christine Pierce caution that revolutionary potential is lost to the extent that the group's separation is consistent with and even required by, e.g., racist doctrine, as in the case of Afro-Americans' familial relationships.[49]

Whether other groups have such power, at least some women do. They are women whose power to approve and admire is not undercut by ideologies of race or class. Their laughter and their turning away may significantly undermine the seriousness of the rituals and other activities of the dominant, even those done primarily to impress other men. After all, as Sartre would remind us, the "serious" pretense of the dominant that their values are "given," natural, inevitable, and not chosen, is rather difficult to maintain, since it is, after all, false and at some level known by almost everyone to be so.

Jaggar is no doubt right when she challenges, as "a form of idealism," the belief that "a separate women's culture" by itself can "effect the changes in the material base of society that are required to bring down patriarchy." As long as relatively few women separate, their denial of support even to a culture that depends on women's support is not likely to be felt as a very serious blow. "Patriarchy," she says, "will not fall to words, spells or songs."[50] To the extent, though, that words, spells, and songs are important supports of patriarchy, clear-sighted feminist analyses (words), withdrawal from and nonparticipation in the rituals and prescribed activities (spells), and even songs may do their bit to weaken those supports. Most crucial, however, in a perspective emphasizing freedom, is the fact that awareness of alternatives is not idealism but rather a necessary ingredient in a meaningful freedom. Highlighting the status quo with all its oppressions as itself a choice or a complex series of choices can be a significant part of revolutionary strategy if others thereby become more concretely aware of the choices available to them.

Thus, given the social and legal disparity between male and female power, Virginia Held may be right that "mutual concern and respect" are likely not to be as significant accomplishments in relationships between women as in those between individual women and individual men. Still, she is wrong if she believes that such accomplishments by themselves, whether between men and women or between women, will contribute substantially to "the transformation of society into a *community* of equals"[51] and also wrong if she thinks the two relationships have the same *potential* for unsettling the status quo.

THE IDEAL OF EQUALITY

The problem of co-optation is compounded by the fact that some goals are touted by society as essential to any emancipatory movement. One such goal is equality. Given the generally unquestioning praise of equality by those who have worked against oppression and given the fact that most hostility to equality comes from those who favor oppression, this goal will no doubt continue to attract the attention of feminists. In fact, it should. Certainly, where people have been subjected to such grossly unfair treatment as refusal to consider, much less to hire or admit to important positions, regardless of qualifications, anyone from certain ethnic or racial groups or even women from the dominant group, equal treatment of all contenders may indeed go a long way toward correcting some of the worst aspects of the society.

For feminists, though, equality is double edged. For one thing, equality is often used ideologically to mystify oppression. As Janet Radcliffe Richards recognizes, equality is praised in sentimental ways, such as when men laud the work women do "behind the scenes" while not admitting either that this was the only way the women were *allowed* to contribute or that, without the restrictions, the same women could have contributed much more to the general welfare in other and more visible ways. As she says: "Under all the assertions of equality the facts of inequality can go unexamined, to the advantage of any group which has the upper hand."[52]

Because of its connection with ideology, equality is a tricky notion to unpack. In a society where domination along lines of gender, race, and class is taught in a variety of ways as the way things are and ought to be and where indeed this *is* largely the way things are, more likely than not "equality" will reflect this dominance. Catharine MacKinnon shows how this notion is defined so as to buttress and perpetuate the status quo and the dominance therein. In discussing pornography, she says:

> Pornography constructs what a woman is in terms of its view of what men want sexually, such that acts of rape, battery, sexual harassment, prostitution, and sexual abuse of children become acts of sexual equality. Pornography's world of equality is a harmonious and balanced place. Men and women are perfectly complementary and bipolar. Women's desire to be fucked by men is equal to men's desire to fuck women. All the ways men love to take and violate women, women love to be taken and violated.[53]

Janice Raymond raises a different problem with equality. Her objection is that defining feminism in terms of a concern that women be equal with men "places feminism at a false starting point" by continuing to give women's relation to men paramount importance.[54] This could be stated a bit differently and more in line with feminist theorists like MacKinnon by noting that such a definition of feminism continues, inadvertently to be sure, to acknowledge men, at least some men, as the norm.

Marilyn Frye, too, sees equality as problematic, but for yet another reason: it accepts and reinforces dominance. If liberal white feminists simply desire that white women share equality with their white brothers, then, as Frye says, "what we [white women] want is, among other things, our own firsthand participation in racial dominance rather than the secondhand ersatz dominance we get as the dominant group's women." This is clearly objectionable since it means that the woman desiring such equality "simply wants to be in there *too*, as one of the men for whom men's God made everything 'for meat.'"[55] It is a desire simply to be allowed to become one of the dominant; it does not change the quality, degree, or wrongness of the domination. Unfortunately, according to MacKinnon, "much of what has passed for feminism in law has been the attempt to get for men what little has been reserved for women or to get for some women some of the plunder that some men have previously divided (unequally) among themselves."[56]

Bell hooks sees that equality blurs a complex situation, in which many ambiguities need to be clarified and about which some hard questions must be answered. Existing systems of oppression, exploitation, and discrimination are complex enough to allow that the same individual may be, in different ways, both victim and oppressor. For example, white women have been and continue to be victimized by sexism; but because of racism they, too, are in a position to exploit and oppress people of color. Similarly, black men have been and continue to be victimized by racism, but sexism allows them in turn to exploit and oppress black women. Even black women, victimized by multiple oppressions, may engage in homophobia, thus, as Patricia Collins says, "maintaining 'straightness' . . . [as] our last resort." There are, as she notes, "few pure oppressors or victims."[57]

Consequently, we must object, with bell hooks, to any group defining "liberation" in terms of "social equality with ruling class white men," since this leaves the group with "a vested interest in the continued exploitation and oppression of others." Thus, the liberal feminist demand for equality is problematic inasmuch as it leaves open the important question"—To which men do women wish to be equal?"—a question that makes apparent the domination and elitism in human relationships in the culture.[58]

Instead of working for equality, feminists must work, with bell hooks, to eradicate domination and elitism in all human relationships. Feminism, defined as "a struggle to end sexist oppression," thus becomes "necessarily a struggle to eradicate the ideology of domination that permeates Western culture on various levels as well as a commitment to reorganizing society so that the self-development of people can take precedence over imperialism, economic expansion, and material desires."[59]

This requires that those who join the struggle "leave behind the apolitical stance sexism decrees is . . . [women's] lot and develop political consciousness." The requisite political consciousness enables us to see that the enemy is not men, that, for example, while a lower class man may perpetuate sexism, "[t]he ruling class male power structure that promotes his sexist abuse of women reaps the real material benefits and privileges from his actions." "As long as he is attacking women and not sexism or capitalism, he helps to maintain a system that allows him few, if any, benefits or privileges."[60]

Bell hooks concludes from all this that men victimized by oppression, even those men who in turn victimize some women, may be natural allies in the struggle—if, that is, a developed political consciousness allows feminists to see and to help such apparently antifeminist men to look beyond the personal level to the larger systems of oppression. This political awareness allows her to acknowledge those men who truly are victimized by oppression while avoiding the "meaninglessness," to which Marilyn Frye also objects, of those who stretch the word "oppression" to include "the stresses and frustration of being a man."[61] Labeling all stresses and frustrations "oppression" leads to absurd claims, e.g., that both slaveholders and slaves were oppressed by slavery, a claim that obscures their actual relations to each other, to the system of slavery, and to its profits. To avoid such absurdities, we must follow bell hooks's lead in meticulously examining the actual workings of the systems of oppression in which we are enmeshed.

Finally, political consciousness will disclose to us, as it does to bell hooks, the "primary importance" of sexist oppression, not, as Friedrich Engels would claim, because it is the basis of all other oppression, but because "[i]t is the practice of domination most people are socialized to accept before they even know that other forms of group oppression exist." This does not mean that sexist oppression is the only form of oppression to be fought, but only that it is an extremely important one.[62] Surely it is one that no women can afford to ignore.[63] We simply do not need to determine which form of oppression is the most serious, important, or fundamental; indeed, it is foolish to waste our time and energy in such disputes and counterproductive to try to limit our work against oppression to any one type. With Patricia Collins, we must realize that resistance can and should take place on each of the three levels on which oppression works: "the level of personal biography; the group or community level of the cultural context created by race, class, and gender; and the systemic level of social institutions."[64]

This does mean, however, that the traditional family and the sex roles and identities it inculcates and perpetuates must be brought under extremely critical scrutiny. Thus, as Andrea Nye indicates, feminist theory must take seriously what Freud recognized, namely, the family's role in forming masculine and feminine selves.[65] Fundamental changes in relationships and in child-rearing practices are called for so that individuals, from the cradle on, do not learn the practice of domination and are not taught to see themselves and others in terms of those extra identities to which Sartre refers as "overdeterminations."

Legal equality also is problematic, as many men as well as women have occasion to discover. To equalize the treatment of individuals under the law is to treat unequals equally and thereby to act unjustly. Long ago, Aristotle recognized such treatment as a paradigm of injustice. Today, many are rediscovering this truth in a particularly compelling fashion as they learn first-hand how equal treatment by law of economically and socially unequal individuals results in unequal representation by lawyers and unequal chances of winning contested child custody cases[66] or criminal cases involving accusations of child abuse, rape, battery, and even murder.

Quite apart from the social and economic inequality between various litigants and accusers and those against whom they proceed, equal treatment before the law results in injustice if individuals have radically different needs. Women have found this to be so when their medical needs are denied coverage, for example, by corporate insurance programs. It is of little comfort and certainly no help in paying the bills for women to be told by those in control of these programs and perhaps even by the courts that men and women are *both* being denied pregnancy benefits—obviously, affecting women—and are *both* being granted, for example, benefits to cover hair implants—a procedure designed primarily for men.

As Catharine MacKinnon observes, the liberal view of equality, insisting on color blindness and sex-blindness in a society that is neither color- nor sex-blind, effectively discounts color and sex differences. Since the white and at least middle-class male constitutes the standard, those who are not white and middle class and male are recognized as meriting equal treatment to the extent they are *like* the white, middle class male.[67] For example, as Rosemarie Tong notes, as long as the test of offense is whether "a person of ordinary sensibilities" (generally—and appropriately—termed "the ordinary man") would have been offended—and as long as men find the offensiveness of sexual harassment very difficult to understand—courts are bound to find much sexual harassment problematic.[68] After all, men frequently are encouraged to regard such behavior toward women as normal and appropriate; many even profess (mistakenly, I believe) that they would feel flattered were a woman to engage in comparable behavior toward them.

Even Tong's remedy of "a supplemental ordinary *woman* test"[69] is not likely to work as a remedy as long as the courts, men, and women themselves find male dominance acceptable and are indoctrinated with its assumptions almost every moment of every day.[70] Indeed, the very commonplaceness of images and activities of dominance may be used, as it was in one case cited by Catharine MacKinnon,[71] as evidence that no offense should be taken and, consequently, that no discrimination exists. She sees this as meaning that if the abuse is pervasive enough, it is not actionable. Nor will it remove "the threat of making the sexual abuse public knowledge," a power held by perpetrators, which "functions like blackmail in silencing the victim and allowing the abuse to continue." Victims shun publicity since "[i]t is a fact that public knowledge of sexual abuse is often worse for the abused than the abuser, and victims who choose to complain have the courage to take that on."[72]

Moreover, Tong's "ordinary *woman* test" would be inadequate as a corrective inasmuch as sexism is not the only hegemonic oppression in the legal system in need of eradication. Racism and other systematic oppressions very likely would enter into the selection of the women who are thought to be "ordinary," that is, representative, and into the judgments of those women. Fortunately or unfortunately, all women are neither treated the same nor affected in the same way and with the same consequences even by activities specifically directed at them as women. Black women like Alice Walker have noted that black and white women are not even demeaned in the same way in pornography.[73]

When individuals who are not white and male demand that their differences receive the same attention as do those of white males, this is denounced as asking for special treatment. Thus, women find themselves caught in the legal double bind described by MacKinnon. They are "not receiving the benefits of the social change that would qualify them to assert rights on the same terms as men," while more and more they are losing the few benefits of the earlier "protection racket" in which at least some women were able to acquiesce to male prescriptions of "femininity" in exchange for so-called "benign discrimination" under the law. She points out: "Almost every sex discrimination case that has been won at the Supreme Court level has been brought by a man." Although the state's "protections" of women have not applied to all women, have been woefully inadequate, and more often than not have worked to women's disadvantage, MacKinnon sees this, not as grounds for quiescence, but rather as reason "to demand that the promise of 'equal protection of the laws' be *delivered upon* for us, as it is when real people are violated." This is why she urges "a further step," which she calls "the women's rights amendment": decreeing that "the subordination of women to men is hereby abolished."[74]

Even when the special needs of new parents are recognized by companies and leave is granted regardless of the gender of the parent, this superficially equal treatment leaves much to be desired if hidden costs of taking such leave make it exceedingly unlikely that men will use the leave and if the women who use it are passed over for promotions, losing their competitive edge to others who do not exercise their "right" to such leave. Moreover, in this as well as in other cases of supposedly equal treatment, it is not questioned, as it should be, "whether equality before the moral or positive law may not be rendered empty because of the dominant-subordinate structures in the economic or social (e.g., family) spheres."[75] As Friedrich Engels observed, contracts are not necessarily freely entered into just because the law has made the parties "equal on *paper.*"[76]

According to MacKinnon, even constitutional equality guarantees cannot correct the position of women since such guarantees can be invoked only where the state has *acted*. The state has *not acted* vis-à-vis many of the ways women are coerced, violated, and silenced; rather, much of this activity takes place in private and for the most part in areas ignored by law. Furthermore, the state does not need to act, e.g., by enacting laws giving men the right to rape women, to abuse their daughters sexually and otherwise, to batter their wives, to silence women, and to infringe the privacy of women. What she means is that such laws are totally unnecessary: given that no laws have seriously undermined men's sexual access to women and girls, there is nothing to stop men from raping, battering, and silencing women; and most women have no privacy to take from them. In summation, she says: "No law guarantees that women will forever remain the social unequals of men. This is not necessary, because the law guaranteeing sex equality requires, in an unequal society, that before one can be equal legally, one must be equal socially. . . . So long as men dominate women effectively enough in society without the support of positive law, nothing constitutional can be done about it."[77]

Equal treatment, either by law or in the workplace, leaves unexamined and unchallenged the demands and assumptions built into both. In *Three Guineas*, Virginia Woolf observes and critiques the demands and assumptions built into the workplace, at least as far as the professions are concerned. She cautions:

> [I]f you [women] are going to make the same incomes from the same professions that those men make you will have to accept the same conditions that they accept. . . . You will have to leave the house at nine and come back to it at six. . . . You will have to do this daily from the age of twenty-one or so to the age of about sixty-five. . . . You will have to perform some duties that are very arduous, others that are very barbarous. You will have to wear certain uniforms and profess certain loyalties.[78]

Her conclusion is that, though the cash value and prestige of these professions is admittedly great, their spiritual, moral, and intellectual value is not only questionable but indeed quite negative:

> They make us of the opinion that if people are highly successful in their professions they lose their senses. Sight goes. They have no time to look at pictures. Sound goes. They have no time to listen to music. Speech goes. They have no time for conversation. They lose their sense of proportion—the relations between one thing and another. Humanity goes. Money making becomes so important that they must work by night as well as by day. Health goes. And so competitive do they become that they will not share their work with others though they have more than they can do themselves.

What remains, she says, is "[o]nly a cripple in a cave."[79]

RETHINKING THE MEANING OF POWER

Like "equality," "power" requires rethinking. That feminism must address issues of power is beyond dispute; less obvious is the fact that the prevailing sense of power (in bell hooks's words, "domination and control over people or things") should be examined and rejected as too hierarchical and too narrow. Not doing so leaves us stuck in oppressive power relations. As long as men and women are taught from childhood "that domination and controlling others is *the* basic expression of power," women will not substantially change things as they move into positions where they can affect political and social policies. Rather, if oppression remains part of their "model of humanity," the oppressed will, as Paulo Freire says, simply become oppressors in their turn,[80] following the sad example of native populations, observed by Frantz Fanon, where nationalism has only meant "the transfer into native hands of those unfair advantages which are the legacy of the colonial period."[81]

At the very least, feminist reforms will be co-opted by the ruling male groups unless these reforms incorporate "alternative value systems that would include new concepts of power."[82] Patricia Collins is thinking along these lines when she discusses "power as energy [that] can be fostered by creative acts of resistance." Opposing such power to that of domination, she connects this creative power with "the power to self-definition and the necessity of a free mind."[83] Rejecting the kind of strength U.S. policy has too often presupposed and contrasting that "power-over" with something quite different—"power-with"— Sharon Welch warns that eschewing the power of domination is difficult, even for those fighting to make the world safer and less oppressive: "To ask for elimination of nuclear weapons is to desire total control, a humanly impossible degree of domination. It presumes an immoral control of the actions of others now and in the future and misses a different sort of power, the influence that our disarmament might have."[84]

Although bell hooks is quite right that feminists must work out alternatives to the power-over exemplified in domination, perhaps she is a bit hasty in dismissing the latter from feminist strategy. Feminist reforms will no doubt be co-opted by the ruling male groups, regardless of what strategies are used and what kind of power is utilized. Thus, the problem is not co-optation, since that is inevitable, but rather the use of means that undermine and render impossible the end sought. But what if the end sought can be achieved in no other way; or worse, what if not using the unacceptable kind of power would result in an even stronger system of domination and destruction? Carol Anne Douglas quotes with approval Charlotte Bunch's affirmation that patriarchal domination and destruction can be ended only through the power dynamics already at work in the domination and destruction.[85] However true that may be, we should fear, with bell hooks, that uncritical use of the same kind of power will make impossible any move to a different and better world. If feminists are to use the kind of power they reject, they must do so by maintaining a clear sense that, though necessary in situations where all options are violent because of the violence of others, such measures are immoral as means and are clearly banned by the ideal toward which they strive. Much more will be said in behalf of morally dubious and even immoral strategies in Chapter 5.

While it is important to recognize the active and vicious systems of power over others in which we live, bell hooks argues that women bonding out of shared victimization is dangerous. It is dangerous because it simply reinforces rather than challenges sexist ideology, which "teaches women that to be female is to be a victim." It is dangerous, moreover, because women cannot afford to see themselves as powerless since their very survival may depend upon their own action, hence on their "continued exercise of whatever personal powers they possess."[86]

For women to see themselves simply as powerless is distorting and dangerous in many ways. First, because it perpetuates the myth of women's helplessness, it continues to obscure and hide from view the history of women's resistance to oppression, a history that some, like Adrienne Rich,[87] have tried to make visible.

Second, as Sarah Hoagland recognizes, victimization "ignores a woman's choices," thereby denying women's moral agency.[88] To acknowledge choices does not mean that women choose or are to blame for their own oppression, nor does it free oppressors from responsibility for their actions. Rather, with Patricia Collins, it affirms "that there is always choice, and power to act, no matter how bleak the situation may appear to be."[89] Seeing themselves as victims obscures whatever control might be exerted by women over their own lives and saps the energy women have used to make significant accomplishments. Paula Giddings suggests that the Afro-American woman has been able to accomplish so much "because she had an unshakable conviction: The progress of neither *race nor womanhood* could proceed without her." Giddings adds what is no doubt at least equally important: "And she understood the relationship between the two."[90]

Third, victimization also encourages a fear and a hiding that is dangerous. As Audre Lorde says, whatever an individual hides out of fear can be used against her. Realizing that silence is no protection, Lorde says she has developed, as a protective mechanism for herself, the strategy of speaking first. For her, though, this is more than just "an imperfect but useful argument for honesty" since the moral agency one thus exercises reveals that "that visibility which makes us most vulnerable is that which also is the source of our greatest strength."[91]

Fourth, to see women merely as victims obscures the ways women themselves exercise oppressive power over others, whether, for example, as women over their children or as white women over nonwhite women and men or as middle- and upper-class women over poor women and men. In discussing the "oppressor's nightmare" of realizing that those he has oppressed are not in fact so very different from himself after all, Cherríe Moraga proposes that "women have a similar nightmare, for each of us in some way has been both oppressed and the oppressor. We are afraid to look at how we have failed each other. We are afraid to see how we have taken the values of our oppressor into our hearts and turned them against ourselves and one another. We are afraid to admit how deeply 'the man's' words have been ingrained in us."[92]

Fifth, concentrating attention on women as victims tends to divert attention away from the complex network of power relations to a simplistic "focus on particular agents or roles that have power, and on agents over whom these powerful agents or roles have power." This dyadic modeling of power, according to Iris Young, results from the atomistic bias of distributive paradigms of power and obscures the institutionalization of power, "the larger structure of agents and actions that mediates between two agents in a power relation." As she says, "One agent can have institutionalized power over another only if the actions of many third agents support and execute the will of the powerful."[93] Thus, in three poignant instances provided by Michèle Le Doeuff, this dyadic model fails to recognize (1) that the way the French Head of State deferentially receives the Pope can encourage a village pharmacist to attempt publicly to shame and thus intimidate an unmarried woman who comes to him for birth control pills, (2) that silent and unprotesting passersby can support the continued battery of a wife whose skull is fractured even though she fled to the street hoping for protection, and (3) that a newspaper's indulgence of admitted racists who beat a Tunisian worker to death in Nice in 1987 can "sign a blank cheque for the violence done by others."[94] The network of power relations is further complicated by the ways self-oppression plays into our victimization.[95]

Finally, seeing themselves as victims keeps women from examining, and creating alternatives to, the prevailing notion of power as power over others. It thereby accepts and helps to perpetuate a culture which, as Margaret Randall observes, makes a book like *Women Who Love Too Much* into an instant best-seller while leaving unwritten and for the most part unthought the much needed *Men Who Hit Too Much*.[96] Bell hooks merely alludes to possibilities of power over self when she quotes Nancy Hartsock's view that power can be "understood as energy, strength, and effective interaction."[97] This reflects the truth of Sandra Lee Bartky's acknowledgment that "[t]he consciousness of victimization is a divided consciousness," divided between the awareness of the injury and the sense of exposure and diminishment, on the one hand, and, on the other, the "joyous consciousness of one's own power, of the possibility of unprecedented personal growth and of the release of energy long suppressed."[98]

Even women's traditionally ascribed passivity can, as Virginia Woolf observes, provide possibilities for effective interaction. While working women may have more real power in the sense that their not working to make, for example, munitions could materially affect the course of a war, sometimes even those who seem totally powerless and passive— e.g., "daughters of educated men"—can make their absence felt and their presence desirable. This is possible, of course, only if those in power require in some way the attention or approval of the "outsiders," a condition that frequently limits who can in this way make their absence felt and their presence desirable to women connected with the dominant.[99]

Woolf refers to these individuals who supposedly remain outside as the "Society of Outsiders," a characterization to which Janice Raymond objects, preferring as she does the term "inside-outsider": "because it helps to make clear the dual tension of women who see the man-made world for what it is and exist in it with worldly integrity, while at the same time seeing beyond it to something different. The term also highlights the reality of women who know that they can never really be insiders yet who recognize the liabilities of the dissociated outsider."[100] Woolf ultimately makes the same point, however, when she observes that these "outsiders," by displaying indifference, can sometimes help to modify or even abolish institutions: "[T]his use of indifference by the daughters of educated men would help materially to prevent war. For psychology would seem to show that it is far harder for human beings to take action when other people are indifferent and allow them complete freedom of action, than when their actions are made the centre of excited emotion."[101] But Raymond has a different explanation for those occasions where women's turning away from men's spectacles is effective: "Men prove they are agents in this world only in contrast to the passivity of those who watch and are thus acted upon. Yet women who watch are never really passive. They are active in consolidating the spectacle of male bonding. Without women watching, male activity of any sort would be recognized for what it often is—passivity."[102]

Thus, if women define themselves as sufferers, they will not see, much less take advantage of, the possibilities open to them, and, as Raymond says, "will settle for the world as men have made it."[103] It is necessary to understand the intricacies and fluidity of the power relations that victimize women and many men, even while implicating many of these individuals in victimization of others and of themselves. This understanding is vital to the disclosing of actual and possible points and strategies of resistance and will encourage individuals to go beyond what is demanded by traditional ethics (namely, performing or avoiding certain deliberate actions) to assume responsibility for the "unconscious reactions, habits, and stereotypes [that] reproduce the oppression of some groups."[104] Finally, it is important so that we can be clear both about what we reject as well as alternatives for which to strive. This is especially true in a context of what Margo Adair calls "polished ignoring," in which, as in our society, "[i]t is taboo to name power."[105]

CONCLUSION

Feminists, then, armed with outrage at violence and oppression, an awareness of freedom, ambiguity, and difference, and an ideal of objectivity, will approach the development of an ethics carefully and critically and with an especially acute concern that this development not exacerbate the plight of victims of violence and oppression. At the same time, attuned to problems of co-optation by the status quo, feminists will anticipate and try to keep such problems from derailing the struggle against violence and oppression. The analysis of equality and power is especially important to this development.

In the next two chapters, I shall examine the major alternatives to an ethics of freedom. These alternatives are the positions developed within traditional Western ethical theory: Aristotelian ethics, utilitarianism, ethical egoism, and Kantian ethics. Later, in a chapter on love, I shall consider a more recent development, an ethics of caring. As these positions are examined, their strengths and weaknesses will be explored as well as how they fare when compared to an ethics of freedom.

NOTES

1. Hoagland, *Lesbian Ethics: Toward New Value*, p. 134.
2. Frye, *The Politics of Reality: Essays in Feminist Theory*, pp. 66-72.
3. MacKinnon, "Feminism, Marxism, Method, and the State: Toward Feminist Jurisprudence," p. 136.
4. MacKinnon, *Toward a Feminist Theory of the State*, pp. 121-22.
5. Young, *Justice and the Politics of Difference*, p. 100.
6. Frantz Fanon, *The Wretched of the Earth*, trans. Constance Farrington (New York: Grove Weidenfeld, 1968), p. 77.
7. John Rawls, *A Theory of Justice* (Cambridge, MA: Harvard University Press, 1971), pp. 12-13, 120.

8. This is a term coined by Charlotte Perkins Gilman, "From *The Man-Made World*," in *Visions of Women*, pp. 396-97, when she found no term to characterize male monopolization of human standards and all human activities although many terms existed for pointing to an excess of the female in human affairs.

9. Joan Kelly-Gadol, "Social Relation of the Sexes: Methodological Implications of Women's History," in *Feminism & Methodology*, pp. 16-17.

10. Davis, *Women, Culture, and Politics*, pp. 122, 131.

11. Jean Grimshaw, *Philosophy and Feminist Thinking* (Minneapolis: University of Minnesota Press, 1986), pp. 100-101.

12. MacKinnon, *Feminism Unmodified*, p. 86; *Toward a Feminist Theory of the State*, p. 120.

13. Marie-Aimée Helie-Lucas, "Women, Nationalism and Religion in the Algerian Liberation Struggle," *Opening the Gates: A Century of Arab Feminist Writing*, ed. Margot Badran and Miriam Cooke (Bloomington: Indiana University Press, 1990), pp. 107-8.

14. Nabawiya Musa, "The Difference between Men and Women and Their Capacities for Work," trans. Ali Badran and Margot Badran, *ibid.*, p. 266.

15. Spivak, p. 91.

16. MacKinnon, *Feminism Unmodified*, p. 71; *Toward a Feminist Theory of the State*, p. 98.

17. Sandra Harding, "Introduction," in *Feminism & Methodology*, ed. Sandra Harding (Bloomington: Indiana University Press, 1987), p. 6.

18. Patricia Hill Collins, p. 234.

19. Welch, p. 137.

20. Young, "Impartiality and the Civic Public: Some Implications of Feminist Critiques of Moral and Political Theory," in *Feminism as Critique: On the Politics of Gender*, ed. Seyla Benhabib and Drucilla Cornell (Minneapolis: University of Minnesota Press, 1987), p. 69.

21. Le Doeuff, pp. 41-42, 97.

22. Welch, p. 136.

23. Harding, p. 9.

24. Carol Anne Douglas, *Love and Politics: Radical Feminist and Lesbian Theories* (San Francisco: ism press, 1990), p. 37.

25. Frye, *The Politics of Reality: Essays in Feminist Theory*, pp. 66-72.

26. Patricia Hill Collins, pp. 236-37.

27. MacKinnon, *Toward a Feminist Theory of the State*, p. xv.

28. bell hooks, *Feminist Theory: from Margin to Center* (Boston: South End Press, 1984), p. 71.

29. Luce Irigaray, *This Sex Which Is Not One*, trans. Catherine Porter with Carolyn Burke (Ithaca, NY: Cornell University Press, 1985), p. 33.

30. Frye, *The Politics of Reality: Essays in Feminist Theory*, p. 38.

31. Hoagland, *Lesbian Ethics: Toward New Value*, pp. 214, 60.

32. bell hooks, *Feminist Theory: From Margin to Center,* p. 71.

33. MacKinnon, *Feminism Unmodified*, p. 99.

34. Dworkin, *Intercourse*, p. 147.

35. Raymond, pp. 153-54.

36. *Ibid.*, p. 140.

37. Hoagland, *Lesbian Ethics: Toward New Value*, p. 54n.

38. Nye, p. 232.

39. Audre Lorde, *Sister Outsider* (Trumansburg, NY: Crossing Press, 1984), pp. 121, 115, 122, 51.

40. Sartre, "The Republic of Silence," *The Atlantic Monthly* (December 1944), p. 39.

41. In *Mercy*, Andrea Dworkin raises some provocative questions concerning the limitations of Sartre's claim. In her Prologue, a woman's voice ("Not Andrea") praises Sartre's moral eloquence—"a beautiful truth, beautifully expressed"—and claims with great conviction that it "applies to the situation of women [*Mercy* (New York: Four Walls Eight Windows, 1991), p. 2]." Ensuing chapters, in the voices of "Andrea" at various ages, raise serious doubts as to how easily this famous quotation from Sartre applies to the situation of women.

At age nine, "Andrea" is fondled by a man, a stranger, in a movie theatre when she is first allowed by her mother to go alone. Caught in a network of rules that work against any autonomy on her part (be polite to adults, don't make noise in theatres, don't yell or cry), she is further confused and invalidated by the behavior of adults who love her, such as her mother, when her report of the event is constantly interrupted by the question, "But did anything happen?" Her efforts to explain that something very serious did happen finally are dismissed with "thank God nothing happened [pp. 5-6, 20]." She is even scolded for wearing black bermuda shorts, for probably having thereby given her attacker the impression he was dealing with someone older, a scolding that leaves the little girl with the impression that such an attack would have been proper had she been older—and with the desire not to grow up to such treatment (p. 10).

At age 18, "Andrea" is forced into sex against her will but is not certain she has been raped since, as she says, "I wasn't a virgin or anything; he forced me but it was my own fault [p. 46]." The "peace boys" with whom she works at the War Resisters League reinforce her view that it was her own fault by regarding her as a "bourgeois" female who was "spoiled and had everything and needed to be fucked more or to begin with [p. 47]." Since they opposed violence yet joked, with those who sought conscientious objector status, about the "rape" of women, she concludes that whatever rape is, it must not be violence (p. 49). In fact, even though they rush anxiously to secure quick release for imprisoned male protesters (since "[i]n jail men get raped... [p. 65]"), the peace boys are enormously amused about what is done by jail doctors to her and other female protesters after they are arrested. Once again, her own perceptions about being violated are invalidated and she concludes she was not really raped: after all, the brutal exams had been performed by doctors, without a penis being involved, and besides, "if I wasn't a virgin it didn't matter what they did to me because if something's been stuck up you once it makes you dirty and it doesn't matter if you tear someone apart inside [p. 68]."

As she experiences one debasing and brutal sexual attack after another, she learns that "it is always best to sleep with men before they force you [pp. 86, 177]" and becomes silent and "blank inside [p. 56]," "always tired and ... always afraid [p. 193]," convinced that "I am fucked, therefore I am not [p. 114]." *Contra* Sartre, she concludes, "There's a special freedom for girls; it doesn't get written down in constitutions; there's this freedom where they use you how they want and you say *I am, I choose, I decide, I want*—after or before, when you're young or when you're a hundred—it's the liturgy of the free woman [p. 178]."

Finally, a seemingly nice cabbie rips up the inside of her throat with the forceful and excruciatingly painful thrusts of his penis (inspired, she figures, by the pornographic film *Deep Throat*), leaves her unconscious, and takes her much-loved dog. With her pain and her loss, she begins to understand and to object to what men do to women and girls (e.g., her uncle's sexual abuse of his five daughters along with similar abuse by others of other infants). She begins to see how this abuse is responsible for all the "small suicides" later as the women, grown up, try to "numb the pain that comes from nowhere but somewhere [pp. 300, 285]." Imagining "a Massada for girls, a righteous mass suicide [of all women who had been similarly treated as little girls]," she concludes, "it makes Auschwitz look small [p. 286]."

She sees her own situation in clear contrast to that of Huey Newton, a black activist, oppressed yet defiant. She is haunted by a picture she saw after he had been shot by the police. Though in pain from the shot and from the twisted position in which his body had been secured, he remains defiant: "Even if he's been fucked in his life..., he ain't been fucked; it ain't what he is [p. 244]." In that picture, "Andrea" sees what she needs to learn—that one can manage "to stay alive and to reach for dignity at the same time. . . ." In contrast to what she imagines a photograph of herself would show, there is in Huey "no look of shame or coyness on his face, he ain't saying fuck me [pp. 241-43]." Somehow, he has not learned—or has unlearned—the lesson that "Andrea," as a woman, has learned too well: not just to acquiesce and to smile to speed up the torture and to keep from being hurt more but to identify as victim.

No longer a pacifist, she ends up studying karate, determined to give back the pain she has had inflicted on her (p. 314), unable to distinguish one man from another (p. 318).

The Epilogue gives the response of a sophisticated, liberal voice of a "Not Andrea," one who is theoretically committed to recognizing the positive value of pain, denies there are victims, and admits to enjoying inflicting pain on her own lover, defining feminism as a matter of "letting go" and doing what men do (p. 341). This voice, like the liberal feminists she presumably represents here, challenges Dworkin, referring to her as "the Grand Inquisitor Dworkin" and as "the simple-minded demagogue who promotes the proposition that *bad things are bad* [p. 334]."

Dworkin gives herself the final say by adding an Author's Note at the end, simply citing there statistics about rape and attempted rape, ending with acknowledgments of the abuse of Linda Marchiano, aka Linda Lovelace, as she "starred" in *Deep Throat* and of her later triumph (pp. 343-44). In this way, she validates the experience of the novel's "Andrea" and notes that this character is far from alone in her struggle for freedom.

42. Lorde, pp. 132, 123.

43. Pateman and Gross, p. 54.

44. Barbara Smith and Beverly Smith, "Across the Kitchen Table: A Sister-to-Sister Dialogue," in *This Bridge Called My Back: Writings by Radical Women of Color*, p. 121.

45. Lorde, p. 77.

46. Jaggar, *Feminist Politics*, p. 196.

47. Hoagland, *Lesbian Ethics: Toward New Value*, p. 55.

48. Richard A. Wasserstrom, "Racism and Sexism," in *Philosophy and Women*, ed. Sharon Bishop and Marjorie Weinzweig (Belmont, CA: Wadsworth Publishing, 1979), p. 8.

49. Sara Ann Ketchum and Christine Pierce, "Separatism and Sexual Relationships," *ibid.*, p. 171.

50. Jaggar, *Feminist Politics*, p. 295.

51. Virginia Held, "Marx, Sex, and the Transformation of Society," in *Philosophy and Women*, p. 162.

52. Janet Radcliffe Richards, *The Sceptical Feminist* (Boston: Routledge & Kegan Paul, 1980), p. 172.

53. MacKinnon, *Feminism Unmodified*, pp. 171-72.

54. Raymond, p. 13.

55. Frye, *The Politics of Reality: Essays in Feminist Theory*, pp. 125, 79.

56. MacKinnon, *Feminism Unmodified*, p. 4. David L. Kirp, Mark G. Yudof, and Marlene Strong Franks, *Gender Justice* (Chicago: University of Chicago Press, 1986), cite several such cases, including *Craig v. Boren,* which challenged the denial of beer sales to young men under age twenty-one while young women at age eighteen were permitted to buy beer (pp. 93-94), *Weinberger v. Wiesenfeld* challenging the Social Security Act's provision of financial assistance to a widow but not to a widower who remained home to care for children (p. 101), and *Mississippi University for Women v. Hogan* in which a man successfully sued for the right to enter a previously all-female nursing program (p. 107).

57. Patricia Hill Collins, pp. 193-94.

58. bell hooks, *Feminist Theory: From Margin to Center*, pp. 15, 18.

59. *Ibid.*, pp. 19, 24.

60. *Ibid.*, pp. 25, 73-74.

61. Frye, *The Politics of Reality: Essays in Feminist Theory*, p. 1.

62. bell hooks, *Feminist Theory: From Margin to Center*, p. 35.

63. As Kay Lindsey, "The Black Woman as Woman," *The Black Woman: An Anthology*, ed. Toni Cade (New York: New American Library, 1970), p. 87, says: "To be a Black woman, therefore, is not just to be a Black who happens to be a woman, for one discovers one's sex sometime before one discovers one's racial classification. For it is immediately within the bosom of one's family that one learns to be a female and all that the term implies."

64. Patricia Hill Collins, p. 227.

65. Nye, p. 116.

66. Phyllis Chesler, "The Men's Auxiliary: Protecting the Rule of the Fathers," in *Women Respond to the Men's Movement: A Feminist Collection*, ed. Kay Leigh Hagan (San Francisco: HarperSanFrancisco, 1992), p. 138, "found that when fathers fight they win custody 70 percent of the time, even when they have been absentee or violent fathers" and notes that "other studies have demonstrated that when men fight they win custody anywhere from 50 to 80 percent of the time—whether or not they have been involved in child care or the economic support of the family."

67. MacKinnon, *Feminism Unmodified*, p. 34.

68. Rosemarie Tong, "Sexual Harassment," in *Women and Values: Readings in Recent Feminist Philosophy*, ed. Marilyn Pearsall (Belmont, CA: Wadsworth Publishing, 1986), p. 157.

69. *Ibid.*

70. As Tong, *Women, Sex, and the Law* (Totowa, NJ: Rowman & Littlefield, 1984), p. 77, says, such supplementation "would require the law to confront squarely its male-biases—a major review for which it may not be ready."

71. *Rabidue v. Osceola Refining*, 584 F. Supp. 419, 435 (E. D. Mich. 1984).

72. MacKinnon, *Feminism Unmodified*, pp. 114, 115.

73. Alice Walker, "Coming Apart: By Way of Introduction to Lorde, Teish and Gardner," in *You Can't Keep a Good Woman Down* (New York: Harcourt Brace Jovanovich, 1979), pp. 41-53.

74. MacKinnon, *Feminism Unmodified*, pp. 63-65, 35, 105, 28.

75. Kathryn Pyne Addelson, "Moral Revolution," in *Women and Values*, p. 306.

76. Friedrich Engels, "The Origin of the Family, Private Property, and the State," in *Philosophy and Women*, p. 176.

77. MacKinnon, *Toward a Feminist Theory of the State*, p. 239.

78. Woolf, pp. 69-70.

79. *Ibid.*, 72.

80. Paulo Freire, *Pedagogy of the Oppressed*, trans. Myra Bergman Ramos (New York: Continuum, 1990), p. 30.

81. Fanon, p. 152.

82. bell hooks, *Feminist Theory: From Margin to Center,* p. 88.

83. Patricia Hill Collins, pp. 223-27.

84. Welch, p. 39.

85. Douglas, p. 224.

86. bell hooks, *Feminist Theory: From Margin to Center,* p. 45.

87. Adrienne Rich, *Compulsory Heterosexuality and Lesbian Existence* (Denver: Antelope Publications, 1982), pp. 23-24.

88. Hoagland, *Lesbian Ethics: Toward New Value*, p. 50.

89. Patricia Hill Collins, p. 237.

90. Giddings, p. 349.

91. Lorde, pp. 74-75, 98, 42.

92. Cherríe Moraga, "La Guera," in *This Bridge Called My Back: Writings of Radical Women of Color*, p. 32.

93. Young, *Justice and the Politics of Difference*, p. 31.

94. Le Doeuff, pp. 256-67, 282-83.

95. See Andrea Canaa, "Brownness," in *This Bridge Called My Back: Writings by Radical Women of Color*, p. 232.

96. Margaret Randall, "'And So She Walked Over and Kissed Him . . .': Robert Bly's Men's Movement," in *Women Respond to the Men's Movement,*, p. 145.

97. bell hooks, *Feminist Theory: From Margin to Center*, pp. 90-91, 89.

98. Sandra Lee Bartky, "Toward a Phenomenology of Feminist Consciousness," in *Philosophy and Women*, p. 254.

99. Woolf, pp. 119, 113.

100. Raymond, p. 232.

101. Woolf, p. 109.

102. Raymond, p. 241.

103. *Ibid.*, p. 184.

104. Young, *Justice and the Politics of Difference*, pp. 149-51.

105. Margo Adair, "Will the Real Men's Movement Please Stand Up?" *Women Respond to the Men's Movement*, pp. 59, 58.

Chapter Three

The Place in Ethics of Natures and Needs

To settle questions of ethics, many have turned to allegedly factual considerations. They ask such questions as "What kinds of creatures are involved?" and "What need, if any, is being satisfied by the action?" Plato and Aristotle have been followed by a host of thinkers who conclude, allegedly from observations of human behavior, that particular ways of acting are dictated and others prohibited by what it is to be human. Similarly, many have tried to show that human beings have specific needs, perhaps organized in a hierarchical fashion, enabling them to determine which behaviors are morally proper and which are not. Such appeals to biology and nature underlie many contemporary discussions, perhaps even, as Catharine MacKinnon suggests, the expressions of "anguish and embarrassment [over the fact] that women in positions of power behave just as badly as men." She objects to all such appeals, anguish, and embarrassment: "The question whether women would exercise power 'differently' always smells faintly of the body, as if women might be congenitally nicer or would mother the country as head of state or would clean up corruption because of a genetic affinity for cleaning."[1]

What role do factors such as alleged natures (or essences) and needs play in ethics? That is the main question addressed in this chapter. Once the role of supposedly biologically determined human nature and needs in ethics has been settled, the issue of socially determined natures and needs will be examined. This examination will reveal that natures and needs are not so easily discarded in ethics as a glib rejection of biological determinism might lead one to suppose.

87

HISTORICAL SURVEY

Many have argued that biology determines a woman's future at least to the extent of limiting or enhancing her desires, needs, capacity for rationality, and other capabilities. Those who disagree often point to the difficulty in distinguishing, in human beings at least, "natural" factors (caused, for example, by genes and hormones) from "artificial" ones (produced by education and other forms of social conditioning).

Others, such as Virginia Woolf, point out how frequently "Nature is called in" to support the societal "sex-taboos" and yet how infrequent and delayed are actual efforts to test claims about what "Nature" allegedly decrees. When permission is finally granted "to have the brains that the professors said that Nature had made incapable of passing examinations examined," the examinations are passed. Yet, even when the examinations are passed and the professors proved wrong, little is gained: "Still Nature held out. The brain that could pass examinations was not the creative brain; the brain that can bear responsibility and earn the higher salaries. It was a practical brain, a pettifogging brain, a brain fitted for routine work under the command of a superior."[2] One claim about nature is simply replaced by another, presumably until the latter is tested and proved wrong, at which point "nature" will no doubt be invoked in another way, in a process that, illogically but unfortunately, can continue without end.

Moreover, when tests or studies are done, too many are rigged or otherwise distorted. As Alison Jaggar observes, animal studies attempting to justify human gender roles are fundamentally flawed inasmuch as they fail to recognize that animal behavior differs from human behavior, namely, that animals generally behave in a more instinctive and less flexible manner, that animals are "much less dependent on postnatal learning, and . . . not subject to the same sort of self-conscious reappraisal."[3]

Sometimes animal behavior is used to support an extremely hasty generalization. Such is the case in the infamous 1965 Moynihan Report, which purported to trace the "deterioration" of black society to the "deterioration" of the black family, which was then traced to pressures of racism and discrimination. These pressures supposedly were harder on black males than on black females, with the result that the presumably proper dominant-submissive relation of husband and wife was reversed in the black community. Paula Giddings joins the ranks of critics, such as Robert Staples and Albert Murray, who argue that Afro-American women in fact have had little power over either families or society. This lack of power is reflected in salaries: black women's salaries on average are considerably lower than those of both black men and white women. Although even the evidence cited in the report itself clearly showed the black matriarchy hypothesis to be myth, nevertheless Daniel Patrick Moynihan still maintained that males had suffered more from racism and discrimination, supporting his claim with the amazing "scientific" claim that "The very essence of the male animal, from the bantam rooster to the four-star general, is to strut."[4]

In addition, many studies of "nature" simply describe animal behaviors in question-begging ways. E. O. Wilson in his controversial but widely cited work on what he calls "sociobiology" links various human behaviors and traits with supposedly similar animal behaviors and traits, thus appearing to demonstrate that the former are natural, the result of evolutionary design. In the process, however, he makes highly questionable moves. For example, Sarah Hoagland discusses the way Wilson simply equates "female *receptive* posture" with "female *submissive* posture" when discussing mating behavior in animals. As she observes, this equation makes domination by males definitionally a part of female/male mating behavior. Wilson's work and the work of others also proceed, according to Hoagland, under "a feminine stereotype [within which] no behavior *counts* as resistance to male domination." Thus, "'femininity' normalizes male domination" and consequently "is a concept used to characterize any group which men in power wish to portray as requiring domination."[5]

Jean-Jacques Rousseau's discussion of women may come closer than most to admitting the actual methodology of much research into their alleged nature. He forthrightly declares that the proper method for distinguishing differences owing to sex from other differences is the following: similarities between men and women indicate characteristics of the species, whereas *any* differences have to do with the characteristics of sex.[6] Interestingly enough, as Margaret Canovan notes, this simplistic approach violates Rousseau's own mandate to "lay aside all the accretions and corruptions of centuries of social life."[7]

Furthermore, his observation concerning the consequences of sex makes explicit what is probably the underlying assumption common to all those who regard biology as destiny for a woman, but not for a man. The consequences of sex, Rousseau claims, are entirely different for a woman than for a man since, "[whereas] the male is a male only now and again, the female is always a female," with everything reminding her of her sex and her whole life focused around it.[8] Here Rousseau seems to be guilty, first, of doing what Hoagland accuses church and state fathers of doing, namely, choosing "one of the many things women do and decid[ing] to call *that* women's function,"[9] and, then, viewing the particular activity as all-consuming. Were he to regard femaleness as narrowly as he views maleness, apart from occasional "intrusions" of this narrowly conceived sexuality into both women's and men's consciousness and activities, a fairly androgynous view of human life outside the bedroom would no doubt result.

Arthur Schopenhauer and Friedrich Nietzsche see the propagation of the species as the particular and unique natural destiny of women. For Schopenhauer this destiny is deterministic and inescapable. Nietzsche suggests that women are biologically determined and develop certain "masculine" tastes only when something goes awry. For example, he claims, "when a women has scholarly inclinations there is generally something wrong with her sexual nature." According to Nietzsche, the "first and last function" of women is to bear robust children.[10]

José Ortega y Gasset proposes that being "in reference to a man" is what distinguishes woman and constitutes her "destiny." Apparently recognizing that his discussion of women seems to commit him to the outrageous claim that his existentialist views about humanity fail to apply to half the human race, Ortega hastens to deny that this destiny is purely mechanical and argues that it merely "guides" or "directs," but does not "drag," her life.[11]

Frequently, rejections of determinism or at least of strong notions of destiny have come from would-be liberators of oppressed segments of humankind. For example, John Stuart Mill, Charlotte Perkins Gilman, and Simone de Beauvoir argue that biology is no more a destiny for a woman than for a man. Although, they agree, there may be certain things either that women are precluded from doing because of their sexual constitution or that they may not be able to do as well as men, all three question the extent of these disabilities and, in particular, raise doubts about how many result from education and conditioning rather than from some natural or inherent inferiority.[12]

Similarly, Mary Wollstonecraft, who challenges Rousseau on most issues concerning women, counters that a woman is and ought to be a woman with her lover; otherwise she is, like a man, a rational creature and needs to develop her understanding. A woman's excessive regard for her body has been cultivated in her by education, not by nature.[13]

When appeals to nature are examined, their weaknesses become apparent. First, the variety of these appeals to nature must make us suspicious. Too often, it seems, nature is examined in such a way that it simply reflects the opinions of the observer. Thus, for example, Diderot is convinced from what he has observed that the husband should generally have the determining voice in a marriage "since ordinarily men are more capable than women to decide matters of detail,"[14] while his contemporary and fellow countryman Rousseau is equally as certain that women should be subordinate to men even though, or partly because, women have *better* heads for detail.[15]

Similarly, this examination may simply reflect the race, class, or gender interests of the observer. For example, researchers have developed an imposing list of characteristics "naturally" accruing to blacks (particularly when their slavery was being supported), to colonized groups, to Asians and other ethnic groups when their cheap labor was desired, and to women. Those against slavery, colonization, disadvantaged labor groups, and male supremacy are generally unable to discover the natures allegedly justifying the subordination and frequently succeed in unmasking the interests promoting such "discoveries." For instance, Andrea Dworkin points to the irrationality of naturalistic claims about women and their alleged sexual availability to men when she notes that the "logical inference" from the fact that human females do not have estrus or go into heat like other female animals "is not that we are *always* available for mounting but rather that we are never, strictly speaking, 'available.'"[16] Furthermore, frequently the claims about "women's" nature are in conflict with the claims about the natures of slaves, colonized groups, and other ethnic groups, all of which presumably contain women.[17]

Second, such attempts to decipher nature raise a question about what is really being examined. Mill and others question how we know which of the actual mental and physical differences between men and women are natural and which are the result of education and circumstance (nurture).[18] Whatever the answer, it cannot be Rousseau's simplistic proclamation that "where man and woman are alike we have to do with the characteristics of the species; where they are unlike, we have to do with the characteristics of sex."[19] No matter what the factors claimed to distinguish male and female human beings in our society, recent cross-cultural studies have found other societies in which almost all are reversed.

Third, the adequacy of the sample on which these claims about men and women are based can be questioned, even in terms of the philosopher's own society. Mill observes: "the most favorable case which a man can generally have for studying the character of a woman is that of his own wife: for the opportunities are greater, and the cases of complete sympathy not so unspeakably rare." Since few men have had occasion to study closely more than one woman, Mill concludes, "one can, to an almost laughable degree, infer what a man's wife is like, from his opinions about women in general."[20] This may, in fact, help to explain the diversity found in these opinions.

NATURE'S ALLEGED
SUPPORT FOR HIERARCHY

One of the most frequent uses to which nature and natures have been put is to support hierarchy. For those who view hierarchy as natural, the main question concerning human relationships is who should rule whom; and this question is decided on the basis of physical or mental superiority, or both. Thus, Aristotle argues, the female is a "deformed" male and, therefore, "the male is fitter to command than the female."[21] His views of superiority and inferiority and of the right of the superior to control the inferior lead him also to approve the institution of slavery, but without applying to slaves themselves the principle that the male is fitter to command. As Elizabeth V. Spelman observes, he avoids this consistent application of his principle *within* the institution of slavery itself by claiming that the slave's function within the state is determined by his or her being a slave, not by the fact of being male or female. Spelman suggests that the very fact the male slave is not superior to the female is, for Aristotle, "one of the marks of [the male slave's] inferiority."[22]

The alleged physical inferiority of women to men often is the basis for the conclusion that men must rule in marriage although considerable disagreement exists over whether this inferiority goes beyond the purely physical and would therefore preclude women from ruling or participating in the rule of societies. Agreeing the superior should rule, for example, Montesquieu argues that women's "natural weakness does not permit them to have the pre-eminence" in families, although it may in fact make them good administrators of empires by giving them "more lenity and moderation."[23] For Rousseau, a woman's reproductive capacity—her physical weakness and consequent "intervals of inaction"— are enough to tip the scales, however otherwise evenly balanced, in favor of the man.[24] On the other hand, pointing to the "intrinsic weakness of her reason" ("unfit as she is, in comparison, for the requisite continuousness and intensity of mental labor"), Auguste Comte argues for the woman's subordination to the man.[25] But like Montesquieu who never explains why family rule requires physical strength whereas the rule of empires does not, Comte never shows that rule of either families or societies requires particularly continuous and intense mental labor, much less that women are incapable of the requisite labor.

The alleged weakness of women is sometimes said to be physical and sometimes mental. According to Aristotle and Schopenhauer, it is both. Schopenhauer sees women as weak in both body and mind and seems to regard this dual weakness as extremely obvious even to those with the most minimal powers of observation: "You need only look at the way in which she is formed to see that woman is not meant to undergo great labor, whether of the mind or of the body."[26]

All the problems previously seen in appeals to nature affect the various attempts to use these appeals to support hierarchy. First, these appeals are too diverse and contradictory to one another to withstand serious examination. The very diversity and conflict among the "observations" used to justify dominance reflect the fact that frequently such claims are little more than ruses to camouflage the interests of the dominant.

Second, a generally unacknowledged hazard in all such attempts is that individuals are products of nature *and* of society. It is arrogant or thoughtless to ignore the multifarious ways individuals are molded by training and expectations, as well as by the denial of options, to behave and be in certain ways.

Third, the observations on which these claims are based are likely to be inadequate to support sound conclusions. They are probably too few in number and too limited in scope. The few women who are observed usually will be unrepresentative, since most or all will be drawn from the observer's socioeconomic class, race, country, and period of history. An even more damning factor limiting the adequacy even of the observations of this sparse and unrepresentative group of women is the fact that the observers are members of a dominant group while their observations concern members of a subordinate group. As Marilyn Frye notes, members of a dominant group are subject to an arrogance permitting and even encouraging them to ignore their subordinates, often in the interest of continued or additional control. Therefore, observations by the dominant of the subordinate are likely to be unreliable as well as coercive.[27]

Finally, there is no way an examination of nature in all of its diversity could possibly justify the universal subordination of women to men, certainly not the unlimited subordination generally recognized by the laws of the societies in which these thinkers lived. If the argument for subordination proceeds from the principle that the superior are to dominate the inferior, then the universal domination of women by men could be justified only if *all* men could be shown to be superior to *all* women in certain relevant ways. This simply cannot be done inasmuch as any serious perusal of human beings will reveal virtually no capacity of which it can be said that, vis-à-vis the exercise of this capacity, all women are worse than all men. Some writers even comment on the remarkable *similarity* between women and men, agreeing with biopsychologist Jerre Levy that "the differences are 'rather minor compared to differences between people of the same sex: of all the variations we observe among people, eighty to ninety-five percent of them are *within* men and *within* women.'"[28]

According to the premises with which this support of hierarchy begins, what is needed to justify across-the-board domination of women by men is a marked, universal, and unfailing difference between women and men. Even a comparative weakness such as these thinkers "observe," whether of body or of mind, will not do, partly because it will not be sufficiently marked and partly because it will be a difference that *will hold* among men themselves and frequently *will not hold* between an individual woman and a particular man. As Nancy Holmstrom observes, "most concepts of so-called natural kinds are cluster concepts"; in other words, they are concepts that define with a list of disjunctive properties, each of which is sufficient to characterize a thing as a thing of a particular sort. Such concepts, she says, carry no evaluative implications.[29]

Examining men and women as they are, without raising questions about what is and is not natural, Condorcet finds "that with the exceptions of a limited number of exceptionally enlightened men, equality is absolute between women and the remainder of the men."[30] Mill, too, recognizes a rough equality between women and the majority of men of his time: "The utmost that can be said is that there are many things which none of them [women] have succeeded in doing as well as they have been done by some men—many in which they have not reached the very highest rank. But there are extremely few, dependent only on mental faculties, in which they have not attained the rank next to the highest."[31]

Even Thomas Hobbes[32] and Diderot,[33] although believing the husband will generally be the superior, nonetheless acknowledge exceptions and propose that in any case the fitter of the two should rule, be it the husband or the wife. The appeal to nature can go no further than this. If it is granted that the superior ought to rule and even if it were found that generally men are superior to women in ways relevant to the activities required within a marriage, any individual exceptions would require special treatment. Otherwise, there will be marriages in which the inferior rules the superior.

Challenges have also been made to the extent of the "rule" one human being should be allowed over another. Mill recognizes the inconsistency of maintaining the virtually absolute mastery of women by men in an age that has rejected the legitimacy of slavery (and presumably the presumption that some are sufficiently superior to others that the former have the right to absolute rule over the latter). He sees a "monstrous contradiction" in abolishing slavery yet continuing "the law of servitude in marriage . . . in which a human being in the plenitude of every faculty is delivered up to the tender mercies of another human being, in the hope forsooth that this other will use the power solely for the good of the person subjected to it." He concludes: "Marriage is the only actual bondage known to our law. There remain no legal slaves, except the mistress of every house."[34]

Some thinkers supplement appeals to nature with religious appeals. For example, Jerome, a medieval Roman Doctor of the Latin Church, cites Paul's admonition that a woman is not "to have dominion over a man" and points to the Old Testament account of the consequence of the first sin: "after displeasing God she [Eve] was immediately subjected to the man."[35] Similarly, Thomas Aquinas adds to the woman's subordination to the man as her alleged natural superior the "subjection" supposedly following Eve's sin. This subjection is her punishment and involves "her having now to obey her husband's will even against her own."[36]

Such an appeal has certain philosophical advantages over an appeal to nature. First, it relies neither on the highly dubious claim that women are by nature generally inferior to men nor on the obviously false claim that each and every woman is mentally or physically weaker than each and every man. Second, affirming women's subjection to men as a punishment inflicted by God, such thinkers need not concern themselves with cases where superior women are subjected to inferior men. Although not a testament to the thinker's humaneness, even brutal subjection could be accepted as the woman's proper punishment for Eve's sin. Thus, a contemporary follower of Aquinas would not be troubled by Mill's claim that the wife's servitude is a "monstrous contradiction to all the principles of the modern world."[37]

Although the religious appeal has some philosophical advantages over the appeal to nature, the former also has some serious liabilities. Like nature, religious scriptures often act as a mirror and merely reflect the opinions of those who look therein for indications of "divine will" on specific matters. Lucretia Mott, a nineteenth-century Quaker minister, makes this point when she maintains that were Judeo-Christian scriptures "read intelligently . . . the solemn covenant of marriage may be entered into without these lordly assumptions and humiliating concessions and promises." Not only do these scriptures not justify the "assumed superiority, on the part of the husband, and the admitted inferiority, with a promise of obedience, on the part of the wife," but also, according to Mott, there is no good reason to suspend the wife's legal existence and to surrender her property to her husband, actions with cruel consequences for many wives.[38] Like Mott, Charlotte Perkins Gilman rejects such readings of "God's will" and indignantly charges that "the guileless habit of blaming women for the sin and trouble of the world" just shows what a mess an overly masculine approach can make even of a religion of life and love such as Christianity.[39]

Second, the religious appeal presumes the authority of some scripture or other. Even if the scriptures cited were clear and unequivocal, which they are not, such religious appeals are singularly unconvincing to those who do not accept the particular scripture, or perhaps any scripture, as evidence of divine will.

Thus, whatever advantages a religious appeal may have over secular appeals to nature, these advantages evaporate when the appeals are challenged by those critical of overly masculine readings of scriptures or by those who simply do not accept particular scriptures (or any scriptures) as authoritative. Like appeals to nature, religious appeals will be persuasive only to those who accept the particular readings of "nature" or of scripture; and this means that such appeals all lapse into a problematic circularity.

POSITIVE USES OF ESSENCES
AND COSTS THEREOF

In the Enlightenment tradition, thinkers have urged the essential humanity of slaves, of women, of conquered or colonized people. If members of these various groups could be shown to be rational, for example, then certain conclusions could be drawn not only as to how they should act but also concerning how they should be treated. Some feminists have tried to wrest from male maligning the assertion of a female nature or essence and to affirm the value of previously undervalued female attributes, maintaining that this nature makes women more moral, more peaceful, or more mothering than men. Although the earlier domesticity movement is a precursor of this development within contemporary feminism, Linda Alcoff connects this move primarily with feminists like Mary Daly, Adrienne Rich, and numerous individuals within the peace movement.[40]

While these traditions have been important, leading to many significant developments in moral, political, and legal aspects of thought and society, and to a deeper and more adequate appreciation of women's historical contributions and attributes, there are serious dangers in such approaches to overcoming oppressions. First, the emphasis on "natural" characteristics of individuals or groups of individuals suggests to many that these characteristics are unchangeable. This presumption in fact underlies and guides much of the debate over "natures," but it is false. As Sarah Hoagland notes, our society tries to treat and change many problems that are "natural," such as various diseases and even genetic problems.[41]

Second, there is the danger recognized by Peter Singer in his argument for animal rights. Singer observes that if factual similarities are relevant to how individuals should be treated, then any factual dissimilarities are relevant, too. Thus, if further study documents average differences between or among racial groups or between genders, then different treatment of these groups may be warranted.[42] As much as Wollstonecraft and Mill try to justify the inclusion of women in politics and morality, their attempts may thus be undermined by their own methodology. Even radically unconventional nurture and expectations of girls may not produce women with a sense of justice like that which men tend to have (whether it would be desirable to do so is a different issue). Girls may continue to make moral judgments in ways more similar to those of the girls studied by Carol Gilligan than to those of the boys studied by Lawrence Kohlberg.[43] If girls and women stubbornly continue to be "different" from boys and men, arguments for equal treatment become weakened to whatever degree they are based on claims of similarity and to the extent they buy into (as they inevitably do) both the assumption of the male as the norm[44] and the arrogance of those who arrogate to themselves the prerogative of determining who is to be included in the human community and to be "granted" rights.[45]

Third, claims about essence or nature, while liberating in some instances, frequently move in the opposite direction and become moral straitjackets. They have taken such a turn in condemnations of behaviors said to be "unnatural," such as the physically expressed affection of homosexual lovers for one another. Similarly, suppositions about women's alleged maternal natures and their "natural" docility (suppositions never consistently applied to women of all races and classes) have led to cruel dismissals as "unnatural" of such diverse events as the middle-class rejection of motherhood by Charlotte Perkins Gilman and the killing of her own infant by a slave woman who refused to raise a child for the torments of slavery. As Sarah Hoagland points out, "the concept of 'woman' is not based on a bedrock of female behavior. Rather, the concept of 'woman' determines what counts as normal female behavior."[46]

On the other side, such appeals to nature have protectively held in place much violence against women of all races, against blacks, native Americans, and various other ethnic and racial groups, men as well as

women, and against children. Such violence has been justified and
rendered inevitable, even encouraged, with claims about men's inability to control their sexual urges[47] and about the naturalness of their
aggression. Belief in natural essences may, in addition, augment a
tendency of language noted by Hoagland, to turn, for example, what
is *done* to a woman by another (battering) into something that *happens*
to her (being battered) and finally into a part of her *nature* (a battered
woman), thus transforming something usually done by men to women
into a part of the nature of the women.[48]

Moreover, in various ways, such appeals have been used to buttress
theories of society mandating structures of domination and subordination and the violence preceding and consequent to such structures.
Assumptions of natural differences not only render plausible contract
theories with their presumptions of a natural conflict of interests and
of consequent competition among the potential members of society but
also obscure other and better theoretical options. Hoagland quotes
approvingly Alison Jaggar's counterclaim that if we begin with the
facts of reproductive biology then competition will appear puzzling
and problematic, not natural.[49]

Catharine MacKinnon cautions against the "special benefits" approach to legislation (and Carol Gilligan's "special attributes of wom-
en" approach to ethics, which MacKinnon sees as parallel). This approach affirms difference and thus, "when difference means dominance,
as it does with gender, means to affirm the qualities and characteristics
of powerlessness."[50] As Linda Alcoff recognizes, this danger is compounded by the fact that the "special attributes" under discussion were
developed "[u]nder conditions of oppression and restrictions on freedom of movement." Even if these attributes were developed—and
served—as survival skills in conditions of oppression, their affirmation is likely to promote those conditions and thereby solidify "an important bulwark for sexist oppression: the belief in an innate 'womanhood' to which we must all adhere lest we be deemed either inferior
or not 'true' women."[51]

Fourth, Judith Butler observes that claims about essences and theories based on them will always have difficulty accounting for individuals who do not exemplify those essences or fit into the theories. Such
individuals can be dismissed as simply deluded or as not "really" women.
On the other hand, and more properly, instead of dismissing these obvious
counterexamples, the claims and the theories about the "essential feminine," even the more general claim of natural necessity, should be
reexamined and rejected.[52]

Finally, claims about essences or natures have a damaging psychological effect on individuals who are led to see themselves through what is usually a distorting lens and through what is almost always a confining stereotype. Often individuals are placed in no-win positions by alleged essences—like femininity—that involve dual and conflicting roles, such as those of wife and mother.[53] Generally, as Toni Cade Bambara notes, stereotypic notions of masculine and feminine are an obstacle to individual development as well as to the development of political consciousness: "I always found the either/or implicit in those definitions antithetical to what I was all about—and what revolution for self is all about—the whole person. . . . It seems to me you find your Self in destroying illusions, smashing myths, laundering the head of whitewash, being responsible to some truth, to the struggle. That entails at the very least cracking through the veneer of this sick society's definition of 'masculine' and 'feminine.'"[54]

Even the most positive and liberating Enlightenment notions of human nature have had the negative effect of perpetuating the split between reason and passion or emotion, a split Sarah Hoagland quite rightly deplores.[55] Such a split has had unfortunate effects on theories about human development as well as on the actual development of both male and female individuals. Particularly devastating effects have resulted from the "somatophobia" (a term coined by Elizabeth Spelman, meaning "fear of and disdain for the body"[56]) generally connected in Western society with this split. These effects have been particularly pronounced on women, associated as they have been with body throughout Western tradition. This association has been used to justify the assignment of certain tasks to women and generally to support domination and exploitation.[57]

Less liberating notions have introduced similar splits within individuals or between the individual and what she or he is supposed to be but clearly is not. For example, the oppositional "natures" male and female are characterized so that many, perhaps most, individuals do not fit comfortably into either and can fit only by denying a great deal of what they feel, think, and do and of how their bodies look and are constituted. Some who physically do not fit neatly into either of these dichotomous "natures," as Marilyn Frye points out, are actually reconstructed either chemically or surgically. Thus, "persons (mainly men, of course) with the power to do so actually *construct* a world in which men are men and women are women and there is nothing in between and nothing ambiguous."[58]

Admittedly, society devises additional "natures" for those who do not fit emotionally or psychologically into the male/female dichotomy—such as "tomboys," "sissies," etc. In spite of their occasional grudging respect, these additions do not help since they continue to suggest some essential inadequacy or other. The message in all this, as Frye suggests, is that the sexes are clearly distinct and that this distinction is preeminently important.[59]

HIGH COSTS OF SIMPLY
DENYING ESSENCES

Since the liberating aspect of essences or natures seems to come at a rather high price, we do well to seek an ethics with at least as much liberatory potential but without the dangerous and likely-to-backfire affirmation of essences. After all, women, in the systems of oppression with which we are familiar, have been defined as lesser beings, natural, emotional as opposed to rational, the weaker sex, deformed males, and generally, as Simone de Beauvoir would say, "other" (where "human" and all accompanying attributes have been arrogated to males, and not even to all of them).

Confronted by such negative social and philosophical definitions, women may be tempted to deny they have a nature at all. But this, as Linda Alcoff argues, is dangerous. If we "reject the possibility of defining woman as such at all," then the very point of departure for feminist theory and feminist politics vanishes. We are left with "the neuter, universal 'generic human' thesis that covers the West's racism and androcentrism with a blindfold."[60]

Thus, to deny women a nature in any sense accomplishes many things we should find dubious and dangerous. It denies embodiment, situatedness in the material world and in a network of relations, in a way very much to the detriment of women. Basically, this is what some reform of law has accomplished. Recognizing all, at least in principle, as just human beings and equal before the law has resulted in gross injustices to women and children in workplace decisions, divorce decrees, custody disputes, and murder convictions of women who have been battered by men and who responded in their own defense with what is denounced as "inappropriate" and "unnecessary" violence.

If Alison Jaggar is correct, and I think she is, the ways women are perceived have important consequences for them, both legally and socially:

> The contemporary perception of women as sexual objects imposes social penalties on women who do not express their sexuality in a way pleasing to men. Women are expected to present themselves as subtly or blatantly titillating to men and to achieve sexual gratification through intercourse,

even though this sexual practice is far more conducive to male than to female orgasm. The perception of women as sexual objects restricts more than their sexuality: it also encourages sexual harassment, makes it difficult for women to be taken seriously in non-sexual contexts, and provides a covert legitimization of rape. In these ways, it limits women's freedom to travel safely alone and denies them equal opportunities in public life.[61]

This perception is reflected in various social pressures, as Janet Radcliffe Richards has pointed out, from the general expectation that women will take responsibility for domestic matters in their homes and be available when needed by husbands and children, to the approval of women's behavior when they do not put themselves forward and when they go along with what men suggest, to the advice magazines give women on not threatening men and on leading men while making them think they took the initiative, to the expectation that the married woman will take the husband's name. In other words, this perception is reflected in social pressures that "work to make individuals suited to the wishes of *other* people."[62]

This means, as Simone de Beauvoir says, that women are "made," not born: "[I]t must be repeated once more that in human society nothing is natural and that woman, like much else, is a product elaborated by civilization. . . . Woman is determined not by her hormones or by mysterious instincts, but by the manner in which her body and her relations to the world are modified through the action of others than herself."[63] Catharine MacKinnon agrees, claiming that gender is "a nonnatural characteristic of a division of power in society," a "congealed form" of "the organized expropriation of the sexuality of some for the use of others."[64]

Whatever the disadvantages to men in the present social system, Richards observes, men, on the whole, "seem to be in no hurry to end these sex distinctions," and, as she thinks, with good reason. After all, power is generally recognized as a good thing to have, and for the dominant "it is excellent that there should be a class of people on hand" among whom each member of the dominant group usually will be able to find at least one who is "acquiescent, available, and a general provider of personal comforts."[65]

Merely denying essences or natures will not necessarily resolve the problems giving rise to such notions in the first place. After all, "essences" or "natures" reflect something important about the social world in which an individual finds herself or himself. They are, as MacKinnon says, male power "incarnate," not just something in our heads (such as a false way of seeing). Although this power is illusory in the ways it justifies itself, "namely, as natural, universal, unchangeable, given, and morally correct," nevertheless, as constitutive of social relations this power is real and not illusory. Thus, "Male power is a myth that makes itself true."[66] Quite apart from how we may have internalized these "natures," they reflect something significant about us as particular individuals, regardless of how ill-fitting the particular essences applied to us may feel or actually be. Even if the disparity between ourselves and the notions of male or female seems enormous, we are forced to recognize that one or other of these categories is constantly being applied to each individual and to his or her behavior. Such categorization continues to create hurdles, to open and close doors to particular individuals, and to set parameters in which, for better or worse, all members of a society must move and have their being.

Simply to deny the existence of such essences is to deny both the ways individuals are seen by others and much in the ways they see themselves. Worse, though, it denies the quite objective, institutionalized structures with which each must contend, structures objectively delimiting and thereby limiting freedom in myriad ways. As MacKinnon says: "If a woman is defined hierarchically so that the male idea of a woman defines womanhood, and if men have power, this idea becomes reality. It is therefore real. It is not just an illusion or a fantasy or a mistake. It becomes *embodied* because it is enforced."[67] Consequently, MacKinnon rejects "liberal feminism," which " sees sexism primarily as an illusion or myth to be dispelled, an inaccuracy to be corrected." She rejects, as must we, such feminism in favor of a more adequate one that "sees the male point of view as fundamental to the male power to create the world in its own image, the image of its desires, not just as its delusory end product."[68] As Rita Manning argues, the recognition of a "situated self," replacing what Michael Sandel has called the "unencumbered self," is much less likely to distort and mask oppression.[69]

In general, simply to deny the existence of essence in any sense will perpetuate systems of oppression by mystifying them and keeping us from becoming sufficiently aware of the ways they curtail our choices and limit our vision. All women relating to white men ignore these systems at their own peril. They thereby, as Marilyn Frye points out, ignore the arrogance with which males, specifically some white males, arrogate to themselves the power to admit creatures to personhood. Racially mixed groups of individuals relating to each other ignore a similar prerogative on the part of any in the groups who are white, a choice of those who are white to hear or not hear, a privilege consequent to their membership in a group that is self-defining.[70]

Of course, from what has been said previously about nature, it should be clear that mere recognition of difference will not do. By itself, acknowledgement of the differences of those who are indeed "different" (from those who are taken as the standard or norm) adopts and will only reinforce "the point of view of male supremacy on the status of the sexes"[71] and the point of view of white supremacy on the status of the races. It also is likely to reinforce the class relations built into the status quo as well as the heterosexism of the society.

Instead of treating difference in a way that buttresses the status quo, feminists must heed MacKinnon's cautions and recognize difference as cutting both or all ways, inasmuch as women are as different from men as men are from women, blacks are as different from whites as whites are from blacks, etc. What is significant in a difference like gender, for example, is not difference but dominance. As MacKinnon says: "Explaining the subordination of women to men, a political condition, has nothing to do with difference in any fundamental sense. Consequentially, it has a *lot* to do with difference, because the ideology of difference has been so central in its enforcement." In this way, gender is recognized not as nature but "as the congealed form of the sexualization of inequality between men and women."[72]

This is to affirm something like what Alcoff calls "positionality." This is a way of saying that gender is indeed relevant, "an important point of departure," but that it is "not natural, biological, universal, ahistorical, or essential": "When the concept 'woman' is defined not by a particular set of attributes but by a particular position, the internal characteristics of the person thus identified are not denoted so much as the external context within which that person is situated."[73]

A RESOLUTION EMPHASIZING AMBIGUITY

What is needed, then, is recognition and critique of such congealed essences and the ways they circumscribe human freedom, along with an affirmation of freedom and liberation from oppression. With its emphasis on freedom and the moral imperative to recognize one's own and others' freedom, Sartre's ethics offers what we seek.

Of crucial importance to feminists is Sartre's recognition of freedom. But the freedom he acknowledges is not the absolute freedom often ascribed to him. It is a situated freedom, circumscribed and affected by the actions of others over whom the individual may have no control. While Sartre does remind victims of their responsibility for their own attitudes and actions to the extent they have a choice, he does not, as

Herbert Marcuse and others claim, blame the oppressed for their own oppression and thereby relieve oppressors of their responsibility. It is this analysis of the intricacies of freedom which enables Sartre to take both oppression and the oppressed seriously.

Of particular interest to feminists concerned with oppression are Sartre's examples of the homosexual man with the "champion of sincerity" and of the anti-Semite and Jew, illustrating as they do the limited options resulting from certain social structures and interactions. The homosexual in Sartre's analysis is confronted by one who demands he confess to "being what he is." The person who confronts him is a familiar type, not like the gays of today who believe in "outing" other gays still hidden in closets, but more the disapproving puritan who believes "confession is good for the soul" and "a sin confessed is a sin half pardoned." The other resists, quite rightly, the "crushing view" that his past actions "constitute for him a destiny." But, at the same time, he fails to acknowledge, *even to himself* that his past acts are the acts of a homosexual. Instead, affirming that his future decisions may make him something quite different, he denies *being* a homosexual. By heeding only his future, he refuses to accept the responsibility he has for his past actions and their significance as well as their consequences. It is this refusal, not his denial of homosexuality to one who solicits an unacceptable confession, that manifests the bad faith of the homosexual. Thus, he and his confronter make parallel but opposite errors: where the homosexual refuses to accept having a past, his challenger refuses to recognize a human being as anything more than his past. As Sartre recognizes, both this homosexual and the champion of sincerity are in bad faith; neither is able to acknowledge the ambiguous connection of past and future that is human existence.[74]

The Jew Sartre describes is in a situation somewhat like that of this homosexual. Like the champion of sincerity, the anti-Semite reproaches the Jew with *being* a Jew; and, like the homosexual of Sartre's example, the Jew is unwilling to identify with the essence held up by the other. Unlike the homosexual, however, the Jew is confronted with a nature almost totally, Sartre thinks, a product of anti-Semitic society, having little or nothing to do with the Jew's acts or physical being. Presumably, the homosexual at least has some history of homosexual activity or inclination, although his past may bear no further resemblance to the furtive and sordid image held up to him by the champion of sincerity. On the other hand, the Jew may see absolutely nothing of himself or his past activity in the image of greediness, graspingness, or other vileness held up by the anti-Semite. Thus, Jews may have an even more difficult time than homosexuals recognizing themselves in the image with which anti-Semitic and homophobic society demands they identify.

Because the Jew is confronted by anti-Semitic society with a na-ture—Jewishness—having little or nothing to do with the Jew's phys-ical being or past, Sartre concludes the Jew is "overdetermined"; the Jew, Sartre says, "has a personality like the rest of us, and on top of that he is Jewish."[75] This is apparently what leads Sartre to be less harsh when he discusses the bad faith of the Jew who follows the admonition of the democrat and "forgets" about being a Jew.[76] Since society is responsible for placing the Jew in such an untenable posi-tion, Sartre is uncomfortable affixing moral blame to the Jew's inau-thenticity. The Jew does nothing to place himself in this position and is even hard-pressed to recognize anything of himself in the "phantom personality, at once strange and familiar, that haunts him and which is nothing but himself as others see him." In times of calm, Sartre goes on to tell us, the Jew even has nothing to revolt against as she or he "dances" with others the "dance of respectability."[77]

Sartre's analysis of the situation of the Jew has considerable rele-vance for the situations of black men and women and of women of all races in a racist and sexist society like the United States. Like Jews, blacks and women have difficulty recognizing themselves in the dom-inant views of them as black and as women. Like Jews, they, too, confront all the ambiguity of the human condition, including the necessity of recognizing themselves in the usual ways human beings are seen by others—for example, to use another of Sartre's illustrations, as jealous if discovered while spying through a keyhole on a lover.[78] In addition, though, society imposes on individuals such as blacks and women a "phantom personality" that haunts them in everything they do, taints their successes, and renders them somehow responsible for the activ-ities of all other blacks or of all other women.

Moreover, black women and other women of color are doubly "haunt-ed" inasmuch as racism and sexism confront them with a twofold "phantom personality" (Alice Walker refers to this situation as "the condition of twin 'afflictions,'"[79] and Frances Beale calls it "double jeopardy"[80]). Elements of one aspect of this personality may conflict with elements of the other, as Sojourner Truth so eloquently observed, rhetorically inquiring "Ain't I a woman?" to each of the claims about women used by men against suffrage for women, and as Bonnie Thornton Dill more recently notes.[81] Still, the dominant society may use each in turn as suits its purpose, expecting, for example, the black woman in question to identify herself with each aspect and to assume full responsibility for the activities of all other blacks *and* of all other women.

Given the "overdeterminedness" of blacks and women, feminists should no doubt, with Sartre, hesitate not only to condemn the inauthentic Jew but also to judge harshly those who "forget" their "color" and/or their femaleness. Like Sartre, feminists must reject both the democrat's universalistic claim (we are all just human beings) and his disregard for the racist and sexist realities. Although Sartre himself fails sufficiently to note the parallel, something similar needs to be acknowledged with respect to homosexuality since much of society's image thereof also constitutes a phantom personality bearing no resemblance to the reality lived by a particular homosexual.

Sartre opens interesting paths into the nature/nurture debate. Though clearly and definitively on the side of nurture, his analysis broadens our understanding and helps us realize that the "natures" of Jews, blacks, women, and gays in a racist, sexist, and homophobic society are not merely subjective ways individuals of these groups have been raised to see themselves. The "natures" also reflect objective structures of the society (for example, features of language, institutions such as marriage, and laws) as well as the ways the individuals are seen by others. Sartre's analysis can help us to understand how, however much we may wish to reject any such thing as Jewish, black, female, or gay "natures," we must recognize these as quite real, not as natural but as socially constructed, not as inescapable destinies but certainly as real factors to be dealt with, frequently limiting the "bouquet of possibilities"[82] open to individuals.

Finally, Sartre's analysis of the Jew reminds us how little these extra "natures" of Jewishness, blackness, femaleness, and gayness may have to do with the actual choices and activities of any particular Jew, black, woman, or gay. With many people of color and most women, there may be more in the way of physical attributes warranting their identification as people of color and as women than in the case of Jews, but even those attributes will be as tenuous for many individuals as those that identify the Jew. Similarly with gays, there is at least something in their past (attraction or activity) warranting their identification as gays although that attraction or activity very likely was not experienced with the negative overlay with which society confronts them. Certainly, though, how people of color, gays, Jews, and women are regarded by society may have little or nothing to do with any of the activities and choices of the individuals so regarded.

NEEDS AND FREEDOM

Some ethicists have attempted to ground ethics in needs. Attractive and tempting theories have been proposed, such as Erich Fromm's *The*

Art of Loving, where human needs are alleged to form a hierarchy, with the deepest need being "the need to overcome . . . separateness, to leave the prison of . . . aloneness." Examining alternative ways to overcome this separateness (orgiastic states, conformity with the group, creative activity, and various forms of love) and finding each, except what he calls "mature love," to be a failure, Fromm's strategy presents a fairly involved argument to convince his readers to move their lives in certain directions.[83] The argument is hypothetical, to the effect that recognition of oneself in Fromm's account of the human predicament, acknowledging the need to overcome separateness as one's deepest need, and acceptance of Fromm's analyses of the failures of alternatives, should lead to the practical conclusion that one ought to seek a relationship of "mature love."

The notion of "needs" to which such ethics appeal generally presupposes a universal answer to the question, "What is it to be human?" Unfortunately, it often ignores the reality of quite different needs resulting from individual differences as well as from institutionalized differences of race, sex, and class.

Moreover, often these needs are characterized according to the interests of the dominant group or groups. For example, slaves once were thought to be the sort of creatures who "need" to be ruled and women (at least, white, middle- and upper-class women) have been viewed as "needing" the secure confines of home, the paternalistic care and protection of a father or husband, and "freedom" from economic responsibility and intellectual stimulation. Given the social and economic pressures on all oppressed groups, even the most well-meaning observer will be unable to distinguish between those "needs" into which these groups have been manipulated by the dominant and needs they would have on their own apart from such manipulation. Simone de Beauvoir notes that women are "made" and not born.[84] The same holds for other oppressed groups. Any ethics must beware of ascribing, as Charlotte Perkins Gilman would say, "[w]hat we see immediately around us, what we are born into and grow up with, be it mental furniture or physical, . . . to the order of nature."[85] This is particularly true where the conflation of the commonplace and nature becomes the basis of ethical conclusions that in turn reinforce and perpetuate the oppressions built into the status quo.

Thus, while "need" purports to be descriptive as well as normative, it, alas, is not separable from ideological considerations. Even the descriptions upon which claims about needs are based will reflect both the interests of the dominant who usually make the observations and the ways those interests have molded all individuals in societies, both those who are dominant and those who are not.

Is the notion of "freedom" equally susceptible to such social constructions and conscious and unconscious manipulations? I think not. First, anyone can understand goal-directed behavior of others even when the goals sought are not those he or she would seek. To understand goal-directed behavior requires no assessing of what is sought and no distinguishing between mere wants and desires and those things the individual "really needs."

Second, we can understand others' appeals for our assistance, and we can respond with help for no other reason than that this individual is seeking this goal. We do not need to adopt the goal ourselves or to recognize it as "legitimate." Morally speaking, we should be able to see it as not oppressive and as generally morally permissible, but this is an inescapable moral requirement of all our actions and is less subject to manipulation and distortion than is the determination of the legitimacy of needs. We can dream with Sartre of a society in which there will be no oppression and everyone can appeal to everyone.

The recognition of freedom will not, of course, totally escape distortion and manipulation since freedom is certainly affected by ideology and limited by social constructions. With Sartre, we can acknowledge constraints on our lives and agree that some of these are common to all human beings, which is to say they are part of what it is to be human. However, even what is regarded as the human condition, as Sartre calls it, is affected by ideology. Although such a universal condition as embodiment seems unproblematically a part of this condition, Western culture has ascribed this condition in a limiting way to females but not to males. Recognizing this, de Beauvoir finds it necessary to remind male thinkers[86] that a man's "anatomy also includes glands, such as the testicles, and that they secrete hormones."[87] Other aspects of the human condition may or may not be recognized, depending on the thinker's sensitivity and class position as well as race and gender. For instance, Sartre, along with many contemporary feminist thinkers, recognizes more interdependence among human beings than does Mill.

In addition, constraints on human existence are subject to considerable change (e.g., medical advancements) and may be subject to the actions of others (e.g., premature deaths caused by chemicals or radiation from waste or power plants). It thus seems preferable to allow a place for such considerations while not making them, or needs, central to ethics.

HUMANISM, ARROGANCE, AND
THE CHARGE OF "SPECIESISM"

Peter Singer is known for leveling the charge of "speciesism" at ethical theories based in some way or other on claims that only human beings have rights or only their pleasure and pain need be recognized.[88] Does an emphasis on freedom open an ethics to a similar charge?

The answer to this question necessarily seems somewhat ambiguous. From one point of view, the answer is quite clearly, No. That perspective recognizes the interconnectedness of human freedoms and sees such recognition of interconnectedness as quite readily and naturally expandable to include animals and even inanimate objects.

From a rather different point of view, though, something Singer might see as speciesism inevitably creeps in when we ask to what degree and in what way this recognition of interconnectedness would require us to respect animals and things. It is, after all, the interconnectedness of human freedoms that requires each to will and actively further the freedom of all. While our actions depend on animals, plants, and things, as well as on the actions of our fellow human beings, these dependencies are radically different. Where each of us needs the active assistance or at least the noninterference of other human beings, the support of animals, plants, and things is needed in a different way. We need the latter neither to assist nor to refrain from intervening (since we do not generally believe they are capable of such assisting or refraining), but rather just to be.

The humanism affirmed by an ethics of freedom thus is capable of avoiding not only the arrogance Marilyn Frye sees in traditional humanism but also some of the worst aspects of speciesism. The recognition of the dependence of one's life and action on animals, plants, and things, as well as on other human beings, should result in an enhanced respect for *all* of these and the roles they play in sustaining life and action.

This humanism is also able to avoid what Frye calls the arrogance of a more traditional humanism since it neither assumes the superiority of all human beings over every member of every other species nor justifies treating members of those other species "with contempt, condescension and patronage." Arrogant humanism has all too often been used even against other human beings, leading Sartre, like Frye, to condemn "our humanism" as "nothing but an ideology of lies, a perfect justification for pillage; its honeyed words, its affectation of sensibility were only alibis for our aggressions."[89] Sartre explicitly dismisses as "absurd" a humanism that takes man as an end in himself (as though he is not "still to be determined") and that allows individuals to plume themselves over the accomplishments of others.[90]

The humanism proper to an ethics of freedom would join Frye in rejecting the arrogant teleologism of the perceiver who believes "everything that is is resource of man's exploitation," believing "everything exists and happens for some purpose, . . . imagining attitudes toward himself as the animating motives [of the things he tends to animate]."[91]

CONCLUSION

Although natures and needs are problematic and even objectionable as bases for ethics, a feminist ethics must acknowledge both, at least as social constructions creating objective barriers for some and privilege for others. While freedom must be affirmed (and this includes the recognition that human beings create themselves through their choices and actions), it is necessary nevertheless to acknowledge the extent to which the choices and actions of some seriously restrict the choices and actions of others. One result of such curtailment is an "overdetermination" of the latter—a situation in which they find themselves with a nature through which all of their actions will be seen by others and, to the extent they have internalized it, even by themselves. Although such natures may be difficult for the overdetermined individuals to identify with, these determinations, along with their embeddedness in institutions, must be acknowledged. After all, they delimit and limit possibilities and consequences in a real way.

NOTES

1. MacKinnon, *Feminism Unmodified*, p. 219.
2. Woolf, pp. 139-40.
3. Jaggar, *Feminist Politics*, p. 108.
4. Giddings, pp. 324-27.
5. Hoagland, *Lesbian Ethics: Toward New Value*, pp. 39f, 40, 39, 41.
6. Jean-Jacques Rousseau, "From *Emile*," in *Visions of Women*, p. 197.
7. Margaret Canovan, "Rousseau's Two Concepts of Citizenship," in *Women in Western Political Philosophy*, ed. Ellen Kennedy and Susan Mendus (New York: St. Martin's Press, 1987), p. 88.
8. Rousseau, "From *Emile*," pp. 197-98.
9. Hoagland, *Lesbian Ethics: Toward New Value*, p. 94.
10. Arthur Schopenhauer, "From 'On Women'"; Friedrich Nietzsche, "From *Beyond Good and Evil*," in *Visions of Women*, pp. 270-76, 330-33.

11. José Ortega y Gasset, "From *Man and People*," *Ibid.*, p. 452.

12. John Stuart Mill, "From *The Subjection of Women*"; Charlotte Perkins Gilman, "From *Women and Economics*" and "From *The Man-Made World*"; Simone de Beauvoir, "From *The Second Sex*," *Ibid.*, pp. 288-98, 391-94, 396-404, 440-48.

13. Mary Wollstonecraft, "From *Vindication of the Rights of Woman*," *Ibid.*, p. 224.

14. Denis Diderot, "From the entry 'Woman' in the *Encyclopedia* of Diderot and d'Alembert," *Ibid.*, p. 182.

15. Rousseau, "From *Emile*," p. 206.

16. Dworkin, *Intercourse*, p. 139.

17. This is a point Elizabeth V. Spelman observes, primarily in connection with philosophy and feminist theory. See Spelman, *Inessential Woman: Problems of Exclusion in Feminist Thought*.

18. Mill, "From *The Subjection of Women*," pp. 293-94.

19. Rousseau, "From *Emile*," p. 197.

20. Mill, "From *The Subjection of Women*," p. 291.

21. Aristotle, "From *Politics*," in *Visions of Women*, p. 66.

22. Spelman, *The Inessential Woman*, pp. 42-43.

23. Montesquieu, Baron de, Charles-Louis de Secondat, "From *The Spirit of Laws*," in *Visions of Women*, p. 165.

24. Rousseau, "From *A Discourse on Political Economy*," *Ibid.*, p. 196.

25. Auguste Comte, "From *The Positive Philosophy*," *Ibid.*, p. 281.

26. Schopenhauer, p. 270.

27. Frye, *The Politics of Reality: Essays in Feminist Theory*, pp. 66-72.

28. Kirp *et. al.*, pp. 53-54.

29. Nancy Holmstrom, "Do Women Have a Distinct Nature?" in *Women and Values*, pp. 52-53.

30. Marie-Jean-Antoine-Nicolas Caritat, Marquis de Condorcet, *On the Admission of Women to the Rights of Citizenship*, in *Visions of Women*, p. 210.

31. Mill, "From *The Subjection of Women*," p. 293.

32. Thomas Hobbes, "From 'Philosophical Elements of a True Citizen,'" in *Visions of Women*, p. 147.

33. Diderot, p. 182.

34. Mill, "From *The Subjection of Women*," p. 295.

35. Jerome, "From *Against Jovinianus*," in *Visions of Women*, p. 85.

36. Thomas Aquinas, "From *Summa Theologica*," *Ibid.*, p. 112.

37. Mill, "From *The Subjection of Women*," p. 295.

38. Lucretia Mott, "From 'Discourse on Woman,'" in *Visions of Women*, p. 327.

39. Gilman, "From *His Religion and Hers*," in *Visions of Women*, p. 404.

40. Linda Alcoff, "Cultural Feminism versus Post-Structuralism: The Identity Crisis," *Signs: Journal of Women in Culture and Society*, Vol. 13, No. 3 (Spring 1988), pp. 408-13.

41. Hoagland, *Lesbian Ethics: Toward New Value*, p. 95.

42. Peter Singer, "All Animals Are Equal," in *Ethics and Public Policy*,

ed. Tom L. Beauchamp and Terry P. Pinkard (Englewood Cliffs, NJ: Prentice-Hall, 1983), pp. 390-91.

43. See Gilligan, *In a Different Voice: Psychological Theory and Women's Development*.

44. MacKinnon, *Feminism Unmodified*, pp. 34, 63.

45. Frye, *The Politics of Reality: Essays in Feminist Theory*, pp. 66, 69.

46. Hoagland, *Lesbian Ethics: Toward New Value*, p. 15.

47. Rich, *Compulsory Heterosexuality*, p. 17, refers to "the mystique of the overpowering, all-conquering male sex drive, the penis-with-a-life-of-its-own," a mystique in which "is rooted the law of male sex-right to women, which justifies prostitution as a universal cultural assumption on the one hand, while defending sexual slavery within the family on the basis of 'family privacy and cultural uniqueness' on the other."

48. Hoagland, *Lesbian Ethics: Toward New Value*, pp. 17-18.

49. *Ibid.*, p. 250.

50. MacKinnon, *Feminism Unmodified*, pp. 38-39.

51. Alcoff, p. 414.

52. Judith Butler, "Variations on Sex and Gender: Beauvoir, Wittig and Foucault," in *Feminism as Critique*, p. 142.

53. Caroline Whitbeck, "Theories of Sex Difference," in *Women and Values*, p. 39.

54. Toni Cade, "On the Issue of Roles," in *The Black Woman: An Anthology*, pp. 101, 108.

55. See Hoagland's chapter on "Integrating Reasoning and Emotions," *Lesbian Ethics: Toward New Value*, pp. 155-97.

56. Spelman, *The Inessential Woman*, p. 126.

57. Jaggar, *Feminist Politics*, pp. 186-87.

58. Frye, *The Politics of Reality: Essays in Feminist Theory*, p. 25.

59. *Ibid*, pp. 25, 27.

60. Alcoff, pp. 405-7, 436.

61. Jaggar, *Feminist Politics*, p. 179.

62. Richards, pp. 142-43, 131.

63. de Beauvoir, "From *The Second Sex*," p. 443.

64. MacKinnon, *Toward a Feminist Theory of the State*, p. 95, 4, 3.

65. Richards, p. 143

66. MacKinnon, *Toward a Feminist Theory of the State*, pp. 99-100, 104.

67. MacKinnon, *Feminism Unmodified*, p. 119.

68. MacKinnon, "Feminism, Marxism, Method, and the State: Toward Feminist Jurisprudence," p. 137.

69. Manning, pp. 2-3.

70. Frye, *The Politics of Reality: Essays in Feminist Theory*, pp. 49, 111, 115.

71. MacKinnon, *Feminism Unmodified*, pp. 34, 42-43.

72. *Ibid.*, pp. 51, 6.

73. Alcoff, p. 413.

74. Sartre, *Being and Nothingness*, trans. Hazel E. Barnes (New York: Philosophical Library, 1956), p. 58.

75. Sartre, *The Anti-Semite and Jew*, p. 79.

76. Frye, *The Politics of Reality: Essays in Feminist Theory*, pp. 116-17, notes that individuals who, like Sartre's democrat, "graciously" let other individuals "pass" as normal/white/non-Jewish/heterosexual/etc., are as arrogant as the bigot, though "often considered a nice person and not a bigot." All, she points out, "are arrogating definitional power to themselves and thereby asserting that defining is exclusively their prerogative."

77. Sartre, *The Anti-Semite and Jew*, pp. 78, 79.

78. Sartre, *Being and Nothingness*, pp. 259-60.

79. Alice Walker, "One Child of One's Own: Meaningful Digression Within the Work(s)—An Excerpt," in *But Some of Us Are Brave: Black Women's Studies*, p. 40.

80. Frances Beale, "Double Jeopardy: To Be Black and Female," in *The Black Woman: An Anthology*, pp. 90-100.

81. Bonnie Thornton Dill, "The Dialectics of Black Womanhood," *Feminism & Methodology*, p. 105.

82. Sartre, *Notebooks for an Ethics*, p. 432.

83. Erich Fromm, *The Art of Loving* (New York: Bantam Books, 1963), pp. 8-17.

84. de Beauvoir, "From *The Second Sex*," p. 443.

85. Gilman, "From *The Man-Made World*," p. 397.

86. Since existing systems of oppression force many men daily to recognize their embodiment, if not their hormones, many other men may not need this reminder.

87. de Beauvoir, "From *The Second Sex*," p. 441.

88. See Peter Singer, pp. 387-402.

89. Sartre, "Preface," *The Wretched of the Earth*, p. 25.

90. Sartre, "Existentialism is a Humanism,"in *Existentialism from Dostoevsky to Sartre*, ed. Walter Kaufmann (New York: World Publishing, 1956), pp. 309-10.

91. Frye, *The Politics of Reality: Essays in Feminist Theory*, pp. 43, 67.

Chapter Four

Freedom versus Pleasure and Universalizability

The other major Western traditions in ethics are ethical egoism, utilitarianism, and Kantian ethics. In these, not nature and needs, but pleasure or happiness (for ethical egoism and utilitarianism) and universalizability (for Kantian ethics) are the bases on which the rightness of action is to be judged. In this chapter, I shall raise what I believe are significant philosophical and feminist objections to these ethical theories and argue that an ethics of freedom more adequately resolves fundamental moral problems, especially those of concern to feminists.

Although I shall examine primarily the philosophical formulations of these positions in Jeremy Bentham, John Stuart Mill, and Immanuel Kant, it should be noted that all of these proposals for ethics are founded on or at least have their counterparts in ordinary moral experience. Bentham and Mill argue that, in fact, human beings generally do judge actions morally on the basis of their consequences (pleasure or happiness). Though utilitarians differ among themselves as to the meaning of pleasure or happiness, they are convinced nonetheless that their moral strategies have the support of common sense and ordinary experience.

Even more than utilitarianism, ethical egoism is thought to be empirically based. Many of its adherents believe that, when thinking clearly and not badgered or saddled with guilt trips by others, people make moral decisions according to how actions affect themselves. Convinced of the truth of psychological egoism—that people always or generally do act in their own self-interest—ethical egoists do little more than to encourage enlightenment in this pursuit and rebut those who make us feel guilty for doing what egoists are convinced we should and very likely will do anyway.

Kant derives his moral imperative from reason rather than from experience. Nevertheless, his imperative gains a certain plausibility for those who realize how often they have made a related move by asking, "What if everyone were to do what I am about to do?" We frequently seem to use universalizability as a test of moral rightness. After all, if we cannot affirm that others should do the same thing in similar circumstances, what could we possibly mean by saying *we* should do it? Are we not making exceptions of ourselves? Can this ever be morally justified? Are we not rather opting out of morality? Even ethical egoists seem determined to convince others that everyone should seek her or his own interest.

While the previous chapter argued the superiority of freedom over essences and needs as a basis for ethics, this chapter examines the initially quite plausible appeals to pleasure or happiness and to universalizability and how freedom fares as a foundation for ethics when compared with them. Though my analysis is far from comprehensive in terms of contemporary variations on these themes, I have tried to explore options within each of these ways of doing ethics and thus to expose fundamental problems which are likely to affect most if not all variations.

My overriding concern is that these ethical theories ultimately do little to challenge oppression and violence, particularly when systemic. I shall argue that an important part of the inadequacy of each is its separation of intention and consequences and its inadequate view of what it is to be a human being.

PLEASURE AND HAPPINESS

Many ethicists have proposed pleasure, one's own or others', as the central yardstick against which actions are to be evaluated morally. To determine whether an action is moral, they say, we must look to its consequences; if those consequences are, on the whole, more pleasurable (or less painful) than consequences of alternative actions, then the action is moral.

In oppressive societies, considering the consequences of proposed actions as they affect *everyone* may indeed be revolutionary. Surely, Bentham's labor reform proposals seemed so to many in his society. No doubt, though, many of his proposals were passed only because legislators saw them as necessary to dispel the threat posed by increasing worker dissatisfaction. Certainly, more extensive reform would have been enacted had the pains and pleasures of all in fact been weighed equally, as demanded by Bentham's careful calculus of consequences.

Ideally, following this utilitarian mandate would result, as Mill believed, in the abolition of many if not all of the most glaring and egregious abuses of power over others, such as slavery and the denial of legal and political rights because of class, gender, or race. I say "ideally" because even Mill has great difficulty escaping the limitations imposed on his own perspective by his privilege along the lines of class, gender, and race. For example, Andrea Nye observes the influence of class-privilege in Mill's claim that, rather than move into the workplace, married women should be educated companions for their husbands. Here, as she says, "the tone of deadening public opinion that Mill in other contexts so deplored is clearly audible," rendering the equality he extolled in marriage a possibility only for "the idle rich."[1] Moreover, as Sarah Hoagland points out, he evinces limited ability to understand harm and the response to it, particularly "the absolute devastation and rage of those who have been violated by white, imperialist, male social structures," and was unable to fathom "that establishing british [sic] culture through colonialism was either exploitation or a violation of individuals or social groupings."[2]

Even with greater sensitivity on the part of practitioners, utilitarianism does not offer enough in the way of corrective power. On the contrary, utilitarianism offers considerable support for the status quo, particularly when the abuse of power is subtle. After all, change never comes without some cost, and the fundamental and consequently disruptive change contemplated by feminists and others working against oppression is likely to come at considerable cost, if it comes at all.

In fact, contrary to the optimism of Bentham and Mill, utilitarianism is more likely to condemn than to offer solace or support to reformists and revolutionaries, particularly if they work for extensive and enormously disruptive change in the society. After all, the greater the disruption, the more unforeseen and even unforeseeable factors may intervene between the disruptive activity and the hoped-for outcome. This means the conscientious utilitarian probably will find the good consequences toward which radical reform or revolution is aimed too uncertain to warrant the far more certain disruption and suffering. To the extent utilitarianism demands action be justified by the greater amount of good to be achieved (actually anticipated consequences), effective challenges to fundamental, oppressive institutions and structures of a society are apt to be rejected. Only in those cases where the suffering caused by such institutions and structures is itself extreme will the gamble be justified and probably not even in all of those cases.

In addition, utilitarianism mutes the critique of society and restricts possibilities of action by beginning with the way things and people are and determining, on the basis of the present makeup of both individuals and societies, which actions can do the most good and the least harm. Utilitarianism, at least Bentham's egalitarian utilitarianism, simply observes that people do experience pleasures or pains and notes the circumstances under which these occur. Its next step is to determine the right action—whatever action maximizes pleasure over pain in any given circumstance. Utilitarians of this sort, however, as Alison Jaggar notes, will be limited by their agnosticism vis-à-vis values, precisely because "they have no critical standpoint from which to resist conventionally accepted criteria of achievement or success," in other words, conventional views of happiness.[3] They can point out hidden or unconsidered costs outweighing and hence morally invalidating ends conventionally proclaimed to be those all should seek. However, a utilitarian like Bentham is hard-pressed, on utilitarian grounds alone, to condemn those *who derive pleasure*, for example, *from imposing their wills on or oppressing others.*

Such indiscriminate and uncritical appeal to pleasure and pain is particularly problematic when we consider the ways oppressive systems construct and structure individual pleasure. After all, oppressing can become a very elaborate and complicated "acquired taste" for the dominant; and, perhaps even more problematic, some aspects of being oppressed may become an "acquired taste" as well for the oppressed. Thus, many sacrifices will not even be figured as sacrifices in a pleasure/pain calculus. On the contrary, if the oppressed have become sufficiently acclimated to oppression, these sacrifices may be reckoned by the utilitarian as benefits! Catharine MacKinnon notes this danger: "For the female, *subordination is sexualized*, in the way that dominance is for the male, as pleasure as well as gender identity, as femininity. Dominance, principally by men, and submission, principally by women, will be the ruling code through which sexual pleasure is experienced [italics added]." Just as subordination is eroticized, so is physical violence, with the result that "sexual desire in women, at least in this culture, is socially constructed as that by which we come to want our own self-annihilation."[4]

Less conventional about pleasure than Bentham, Mill comes close to recognizing the extent to which dominance and violence are sexualized. Arguing for women's rights, Mill considers and rejects an argument for "the rule of men" based on the claim that women accept this rule voluntarily. The argument appeals to the "fact" that women "make no complaint, and are consenting parties to it [the rule of men]." In response, Mill notes, first, "a great number of women do not accept it." Second, though acknowledging that large numbers of women *do* accept this rule, he observes that this acceptance is not exactly free and uncoerced. Women accept the rule because they have been taught it is necessary and good; they have even been cajoled and subtly threatened out of challenging it. Since men want willing rather than unwilling slaves, women are manipulated into positions where they accept and even want male dominance.[5] Recognizing this manipulability of human beings, Mill is aware that calculating the pleasures and pains of individuals is not as unproblematic as Bentham would have us believe.

Partly to deal with the fact that some human beings have been manipulated into what Lucretia Mott calls "hugging" their chains,[6] Mill proposes a complication for Bentham's calculus of pleasures and pains: pleasures and pains are to be evaluated not just in terms of quantity but also in terms of quality. Thus, the utilitarian must evaluate some pleasures as qualitatively better than others and maintain that right actions maximize "happiness," a goal incorporating this recognition of qualitative differences among pleasures.

This is seriously problematic, though. The interjection of qualitative considerations requires an appeal beyond pleasure and pain and thus renders utilitarianism incoherent. After all, initially pleasure and pain were presented as the ultimate appeal. Now it turns out, some pleasures and pains are more ultimate than others, and no criteria are available for determining these degrees. All Mill can do is propose one who has experienced both "higher" and "lower" pleasures as the arbiter of disputes. Presumably we could encase such a pleasure expert in glass and place him or her alongside other standard measures such as former Supreme Court Justice Potter Stewart, well known for his claim that although he could not define obscenity he knew it when he saw it![7] Of course, in neither case is opposition silenced since aficionados of "lower" pleasures and of obscenity will no doubt question how adequately these are experienced and appreciated by such alleged experts. This is further complicated by the fact that whole segments of society are prevented from acquiring the experiences necessary for arbitrating such disputes.

Mill remains in his own eyes a utilitarian by opting for freedom while professing his hope that the "higher" pleasures of freedom in the long run will offset even its most intense pains and make up for any resultant losses of "lower" pleasures. But this is an article of faith on Mill's part, connected more, it seems, with his high evaluation of freedom than with any empirical evidence warranting expectations of objectively greater pleasure on the part of the oppressed were they released from their submission and allowed to vote and to determine their own lives. To his credit, Mill seems convinced that freedom for everyone is to be sought, regardless of whether in fact this would lead to a net increase in pleasure. In *On Liberty*, he characterizes "utility" broadly and without direct reference to either pleasure or happiness as "in the largest sense, grounded on the permanent interests of man as a progressive being." There he claims as vital to those "permanent interests" the freedom to pursue "our own good in our own way, so long as we do not attempt to deprive others of theirs, or impede their efforts to obtain it."[8]

If they desire to remain utilitarians, ethicists can legitimately ask only in carefully circumscribed ways whether individuals *should* experience pleasure of whatever type and degree in the particular circumstances in which they experience it. If a utilitarian can envision alternatives involving sufficiently greater amounts of pleasure, then it is certainly appropriate to criticize present pleasure-seeking and to propose the pursuit of those alternatives. John Rawls defends utilitarianism along these lines when he says, "The utilitarian can always say that given social conditions and men's [and women's] interests as they are, and taking into account how they will develop under this or that alternative institutional arrangement, encouraging one pattern of wants rather than another is likely to lead to a greater net balance (or to a higher average) of satisfaction."[9]

However, as long as pleasures and pains are the ultimate appeal, Mill's efforts to the contrary notwithstanding, it is illegitimate for this ethics to critique the way things are on the basis of dreams of *fundamentally* different individuals and relations and of ways of actualizing both. After all, to reconstruct human existence along the lines of ideals that are difficult and painful to implement is quite clearly unacceptable on utilitarian grounds—unless, that is, we have sufficient grounds for believing that the restructured individuals and society are likely to experience significantly greater pleasure than present individuals and society, enough to more than counterbalance the almost certain pain of the transition. The grounds we would require are rendered difficult if not impossible to obtain by the fact that the painstakingly reconstituted pleasures of individuals in a radically restructured society cannot even be clearly imagined, given present realities. Most likely those experiences would be virtually unrecognizable as pleasures given our presently constituted ones. The requisite comparisons between the reconstituted and our present pleasures would be extraordinarily problematic. Thus, although reform of institutions, of societies, and of individual behavior is consistent with and often demanded by utilitarianism, any real reform of human "nature" (that is, of the way human beings are now constituted by whatever combination of nature and nurture is at work in their development) is beyond the scope of such moral vision.

As long as individuals are raised as they now are, utilitarian appeals to pleasure will easily justify much to which feminists must object. For example, justification of the sacrifice on the part of girls and women will be especially easy as long as boys are raised, as they presently are, to expect service from females and girls to believe that their "highest" or deepest and most intense pleasure and fulfillment are to be found in serving others, particularly males. In fact, individuals so raised are likely to experience pleasure when they are (and pain when they are not) playing their respective roles in the prescribed service. A woman in such a society is likely to tolerate considerable pain rather than risk the guilt she would experience were she not to serve.[10] In fact, precisely because of her expectations and acclimation to her condition, her pain may *be* less than the total pleasure to which her actions give rise. Thus, the acclimation of women to their socially appointed roles of service actually supports the continuation of this service by lessening the average or aggregate utility of change and even of protest.

Mill believes that this is one point at which he can critique the social conditioning and discount the pleasures many women take in their service to males, but this is harder to do than he seems to realize. True, he can note that many women are not happy with their current positions; and it is indeed legitimate, even necessary, for a utilitarian to take their dissatisfaction into account. But when he tries to discount the satisfactions of others by indicating all the training, threats, and cajoling that go into producing this result,[11] he is on much less stable ground. Whatever combination of social forces accounts for the contentment or satisfactions of these women, they are nevertheless content or at least experiencing pleasure that cannot be ignored. Even Mill's more qualified talk of quality of pleasure as opposed to mere quantity does not offset this difficulty. As long as the ultimate appeal is happiness, he is required to show that alternative arrangements would result not just in greater average or net happiness (quality balanced against quantity of pleasure) but also in sufficiently greater happiness to offset the misery of dislocation and change. Thus, utilitarianism's very appeal to pleasure or happiness tends to undercut and make quite difficult any feminist critique of and challenge to the positioning of women in roles of service to men.

In addition, affirming pleasure as the end of any action and the quantity of pleasure as the criterion of its rightness automatically places individuals of all sorts in a precarious moral position. Utilitarianism may too easily demand that the pleasure of some, even their lives, be sacrificed for the greater pleasure of others. Similarly, pain may be demanded of some if it will bring greater pleasure for others, provided this increases the average or net amount of utility.

To avoid placing particular individuals in such precarious situations, an ethicist might reject a moral standard that requires each to maximize the pleasure of all and affirm instead that moral agents seek to maximize only their own pleasure. No longer will an individual agent be included only as one among many whose experiences must be calculated to determine which actions maximize pleasure and are, therefore, right. By recognizing no greater good beyond each individual's own good, this move allows the agent steadfastly to maintain and pursue his or her own interest and to deny, at least on ethical grounds, demands that that interest be sacrificed to others. No matter how much a sacrifice on the part of a particular agent might actually be in the interest of others, individuals are morally entitled to pursue their own interests and not to sacrifice themselves or their interests for others. This ethics thus would not side with the larger number and demand the interests of one or a few be sacrificed in favor of the interests of many. Of course, neither would it side with the one (nor, for that matter, with feminist concerns for victims of oppression). Rather, it continues to proclaim that each should do whatever is in his or her own interest.

By placing all interests on the same level, both individually and collectively, ethical egoism appears to alleviate the precariousness of those whom utilitarians would sacrifice for the greater good; but it does so by increasing the level and extent of the precariousness. While it is true that the theory would not side with those who demand sacrifice of others, it is just as true that the theory gives those designated for sacrifice by others no moral leverage with which to confront and challenge these demands. Moreover, instead of proposing a single set of interests for the sake of which some may be justifiably sacrificed, ethical egoism establishes multiple individual and collective interests for the sake of which the sacrifice of others may be legitimately demanded and pursued. What the theory does is to place virtually all individuals in the precarious position in which utilitarians placed only some.

Moreover, many ethicists have challenged ethical egoism on other grounds. Admittedly, some of the challenges miss their mark. An example is Rawls's proposal that ethical egoism fails as an ethics by virtue of its not being able to rank competing claims.[12] This proposal begs an important question by assuming that competing claims can and should be ranked, presumably in some objective and commonly agreed-upon way, an assumption that ethical egoism rejects. It is also an assumption to which I object since it seems to beg the question in favor of certain ethical theories and to demand what some theories, Sartre's theory of value included, regard as unfeasible. While I recognize the desirability and even necessity of an ethics "ranking" some claims, e.g., the conflicting claims of oppressors and liberators concerning the acceptability of oppression, I do not believe it is possible to do this for more than a select few. To the extent that values (and even the criteria to which we appeal when justifying them) are the result of choice, to "rank" other competing claims consequent to those choices is impossible.

Others, like Kurt Baier, raise more serious challenges to ethical egoism. Baier argues that moral claims become impossible for the ethical egoist since the same action would then be right for K (assuming that it is in K's interest) and wrong for B (assuming that it is not in B's interest).[13] Another way to illuminate this incoherence Baier sees in ethical egoism is by questioning what the ethicist is doing in urging others to look after their own interests. Surely the one who urges this is not, or at least should not be, saying it is *morally right* for others to maximize their own interests. This will not do since, after all, the ethical egoist is not a detached and disinterested observer but, presumably, an interested individual and, speaking as such *and* as an egoist, should urge others to act in the *ethicist's* own interest.

To meet this objection, some have argued that each (or, at least, society) is likelier to be better off if everyone act egoistically. In doing so, they presume something like providence or an invisible hand adjusting interests to one another, a presumption that ignores—and is seriously challenged by—the reality of oppression. Like Adam Smith, they may thus endorse egoism as the best means to accomplish an end that is essentially utilitarian.[14]

It is not, of course, the case that *all* of our interests are in conflict; clearly they are not. Many of us would no doubt say the same of our experience that Sarah Hoagland says for hers: "Yet in considering what most contributes to the development of my work, I find that it is *not* those around me giving up their goals to pursue mine. What helps me is others vitally and intently pursuing *their* goals."[15] Such overlapping of interests, however, does not sufficiently help the ethical egoist. After all, the ethical egoist is indiscriminately addressing everyone in society as presently constituted, a society in which we clearly recognize serious and sometimes devastating conflicts of interest. While Hoagland rejects the presumption of inevitable conflict among interests (on which contract theorists like Thomas Hobbes proceed), her main dispute seems to be with bringing this presumption into the smaller group with which she is trying to establish a community (and perhaps into a better larger society of the future). Though she opposes self-sacrifice as a viable way to resolve problems resulting from disharmonious interests, she does not and could not conscientiously urge the pursuit of any and all self-interest, including the interests of oppressors and of those with considerable stake in the status quo of the larger heterosexist society.

This does not mean that urging others to be egoists might not occasionally pay off for an individual egoist like Ayn Rand, whose books made money and who was in demand as a lecturer. Her urging others to be egoists was consistent with her egoism: she profited from it in ways she apparently valued. However, her particular *activity* of urging others to practice egoism may very well be in her interest, and thereby consistent with *what* she urges, without the latter being *coherent* when applied universally, specifically to those whose active pursuit of their own interests would conflict with and undermine her own.

Baier's challenge to the coherence of ethical egoism as a moral theory becomes apparent if we imagine a rather dramatic shift of opinion and potential power throughout the world while Rand is writing and publishing. If enough individuals throughout the world were to become aware that it is in their interest to bring down the capitalism in which Rand's views were formerly so congenial and if she thought that continuing to urge others to pursue their own interests would encourage the overthrow of capitalism, surely she would cease this dissemination of her theory. Such cessation would indicate to me that she was indeed an egoist. The recognition that most egoists in such circumstances would no longer preach or think they should preach ethical egoism indicates to me a fundamental problem. If what she had been urging suddenly becomes impossible to urge in such a revised scenario and if, as I believe, most of us are in similar positions, ethical egoism becomes an ethical theory that no one would dare to articulate, not even in clandestine ways. Even the most powerful oppressors would be more likely to further their own interests by affirming publicly an ethics of rights or of altruism. There is every reason for them to follow the sage advice Machiavelli once offered in *The Prince* to rulers.

I can imagine an egoist like Rand rejecting my scenario as impossible, given that she is urging that everyone do what is actually, not just perceived to be, in her or his own interest, and that the overthrow of capitalism could not possibly be the result of an enlightened pursuit of anyone's self-interest. But a blanket rejection of this possibility would itself be difficult if not impossible to support, without appealing to that fanciful and highly dubious invisible hand (and doing so in a completely nonutilitarian way).

Although ethical egoism does not resolve the problem of precariousness discussed previously, it would, if tenable, resolve one serious difficulty confronting utilitarianism, a problem having to do with the value of pleasure or happiness. This value is theoretically unproblematic as long as we consider particular agents who are urged to maximize precisely the pleasure or happiness they are presumed to value, namely, their own. When utilitarians urge everyone to maximize the net or average amount of pleasure in the world, however, they are not thinking of particular subjects who will themselves experience the pleasure they bring about. Even though Bentham and Mill see society as just an aggregate of individuals and the common good as nothing more than an aggregation of all the individual goods, it is still the case that agents are to act in pursuit of pleasure most or at least much of which will not be experienced by themselves. This means that individuals frequently must act to realize pleasure for others but not for themselves. Even if we grant that each individual values pleasure, that does not mean that each values the experience of pleasure by others; and it is surely not unproblematic to move from the claim that each values his or her own pleasure to the very different and unrelated claim that each values the pleasures of all. It simply will not do, as Rawls recognizes, "to adopt for society as a whole the principle of rational choice for one man," whether by postulating an impartial spectator or by some other ruse.[16]

The assumption underlying utilitarianism must be not just that pleasure is inherently valuable, that is, valuable in and of itself, to any agent, but also that this value remains constant for each agent, no matter who is to experience the pleasure. While society is able, as Bentham proposes, to use pleasure and pain to manipulate individuals into caring about the pleasures and pains of others, the resulting psychological move seems insufficient to buttress the ultimate indifference, required by utilitarianism, to the question of who is to experience the pleasure and pain. One who applies Bentham's calculus or Mill's more complicated way of evaluating the utility of actions must value pleasure or happiness wherever it occurs and try to weigh consequences evenhandedly, regardless of who is affected. Bentham's proposed manipulation of individuals into caring about the pleasures and pains of others leaves individuals valuing primarily their own pleasure but, in a secondary way, valuing the pleasure of others (to the extent that the valuers are or will be affected by it). I cannot see how that would be sufficient to motivate or even enable them to engage in the calculations of utility demanded by Bentham and Mill. After all, these manipulated individuals remain psychological egoists, albeit egoists who care about the happiness of others; and as such they simply cannot, I think, be indifferent to the question of who is to experience the pleasure or happiness.

Moreover, utilitarianism seems on particularly weak ground in requiring the agent to value pleasure, even though it is the pleasure of someone else, instead of requiring the agent to value *the individual who is to experience this pleasure*. The perplexing requirement of utilitarianism then leads to many difficulties when utilitarians try accurately to assess, in their pleasure or happiness calculus, the killing of an individual. What they do not and cannot include in their calculation is *the individual* whose death is being considered. No doubt, they think this has been done since they seem to believe that an individual, like a society, is nothing more than the aggregate of its parts and, in the case of an individual, the parts are simply the experiences of pleasure and pain. Surely, though, no matter how plausible David Hume's rejection of a substantial self somehow hidden behind all the individual's experiences, a human life is more than a collection of pleasures and pains; and even a thoroughly unhappy individual cannot be simply written off. A central factor—the individual as a freedom, as one who chooses the value of both life and happiness—is omitted in this consideration; and that factor simply is not reducible to or commensurable with pleasures and pains (whether of that individual or of others), all the efforts of utilitarians notwithstanding. It is, after all, individuals who *experience* pleasures and pains and who *delimit the values of such experiences*; thus, the individuals themselves cannot be weighed in as nothing more than the totality of those experiences.

Others must matter in some fundamental way to the agent; otherwise, the only reason for valuing or disvaluing the pleasures and pains of others is the egoistic one—how do they affect the agent? Any other reason is lacking once we assume that each is a psychological egoist. Treating the moral value of the individual as nothing more than a collection of experiences of pleasure and pain together with his or her effects on others parallels Bentham's and Mill's treatment of society as nothing more than a collection of individuals, but it does nothing to give an individual any reason besides pure self-interest to value or disvalue others *or* their experiences. Surely an individual can *take an interest* in others and in society as a whole; but to do so is a choice and to make such choice central to an ethics requires at the very least a view of human beings that does not allow them to be reduced to the sum of their pleasures and pains. Thus, by its failure to regard the individual as anything more than the sum of her or his pleasures and pains, utilitarianism seems mired in an egoism that inevitably undermines its injunctions to maximize utility.

FREEDOM CONTRASTED WITH
PLEASURE / HAPPINESS

Instead of judging actions in terms of their consequences, an ethics of freedom asks whether actions respect human freedom, the agent's and others'. Such an ethics does not readily allow the sacrifice of an individual for the pleasure or happiness of others. After all, it recognizes that individuals who are centers of autonomy and choosers of values are incommensurable with both their own and others' pleasures and pains.

At the same time, an ethics of freedom does not preclude, to the same degree as utilitarianism, risk and sacrifice, even of life, for the sake of human freedom, that is, to challenge oppression. For utilitarianism, risk and sacrifice must be weighed against realistic expectations for improvement in overall or average utility. Where expectations are quite modest or uncertain, risk and sacrifice will probably not be in order, morally speaking, for utilitarians. This will tend to leave unchallenged all but the worst forms of oppression. Complicating this analysis is the fact that the oppressions themselves must be evaluated only in terms of pain and suffering, *not* in terms of their effects on freedom. Given the capacity of oppression to inure the oppressed to their conditions, the more psychologically effective the oppression, the less likely that utilitarians can point to suffering sufficiently great to warrant any considerable risk or sacrifice. Even if it seems clear that less oppression would increase utility, the cultivated acceptance, contentment, and even pleasures of the oppressed will serve to render unjustifiable any substantial risk for the sake of what will be at best fairly slight improvements in utility.

Whereas utilitarianism seems to require acceptance, respect for human freedom allows for critique of and opposition to the perverse transformation into pleasure, by a lifetime of acclimation, of subordination and degradation. Thus, when "[o]ppression tries to defend itself by its utility," a defender of freedom, like Simone de Beauvoir, can object that something is useful only relative to human beings and that "nothing is useful if it is not useful to man; nothing is useful to man if the latter is not in a position to define his own ends and values, if he is not free."[17]

With a criterion of freedom, we are able to distinguish between good and bad pleasure and good and bad pain. Clearly, some pleasures and many pains interfere with human freedom while some pains and some pleasures lead to the growth, understanding, and critical awareness without which freedom atrophies. We can see that freedom is not absolute, not an all-or-nothing affair. On the contrary, it can be re-stricted and enhanced. As a result, some individuals operate out of a severely curtailed freedom, many out of almost none at all. We be-come aware of the fact that freedom can be used both oppressively (that is, to circumscribe the freedom of some for the sake of others) and to counter oppression. In countering violence, freedom sometimes must engage in violence,[18] since otherwise it affirms the oppression.

An ethics of freedom shares a problem with an ethics based on pleasure: like pleasure, freedom must be recognizable if it is to offer any guide to action. Mill confronts an objection along this line from those who claim pleasure is too subjective, too difficult for anyone not experi-encing it to validate and measure. His response, and an appropriate one, is to remind such objectors that no ethics can withstand the supposi-tion of "universal idiocy."[19] In other words, given our awareness of ourselves and a considerable fund of common human wisdom, we often have enough information to determine what sorts of pleasurable and painful responses a particular action is likely to evoke in others. In other cases, we have an obligation to secure, if possible, the informa-tion we need. Mill's optimism concerning our ability to ascertain like-ly consequences is certainly greater than that of Sharon Welch; the latter claims: "the fatal flaw of the human species is the lack of com-mensuration between our ability to act and our ability to imagine the consequences of our actions."[20] Whether Mill's optimism is warranted or not, the point remains that if feminists appeal to freedom as the basis for morality and as somehow providing a guide for action, then freedom and oppression must not be too difficult to recognize and to assess.

An ethics of freedom will not be as quick as Mill to make a snappy retort to this challenge, since feminist theory and other critical enter-prises have made us painfully aware of how invasive the prevailing systems have been with respect to our inherited "common wisdom," even what we think we know of ourselves. We have found that systems of oppression mystify both freedom and oppression. To break through the denials and distortions requires enormous and ongoing critical effort.

This difficulty is compounded by the fact that many will turn the very recognition of mystification into the relativistic challenge that opposing claims about "reality" simply reflect different (and, presum-ably, equally valid) ways of seeing things. From such relativism emerges the frequently voiced argument that challenges to oppression are fun-damentally incoherent since, if denied opportunity to continue oppressing, former oppressors will in turn feel—and presumably be—oppressed. The issue, though, is: *are* they oppressed? Does denying would-be oppressors the opportunity to do what they want mean that they are thereby oppressed? Is preventing them from oppressing the same as systematically circumscribing their freedom in the interests of others? This is a question that can and must be answered in the negative and without the relativistic presumption that all ways of seeing are equally valid.

In spite of the difficulty in attaining an adequate understanding of freedom, given the ways it is mystified in our culture, there is no cause for despair. Most of us begin with some understanding of freedom and of how interconnected individual freedoms are with one another. This understanding, so basic and difficult to obliterate, frequently surfaces in spite of the strongest indoctrinations to the contrary and no doubt causes oppressors many uneasy moments. It leads to discomfort, even for the relatively uncritical, when commonly accepted explanations are offered in support of exploitative situations and relations. Moreover, we have an ever-growing mass of critical studies of which it behooves us to become aware; and numerous opportunities exist for consciousness raising.

This is not to deny that there are some who need but truly have neither the time nor the energy, nor possibly the ability, to read and to take advantage of such opportunities, those whose options are limited by oppression to, as Sartre says, choosing the sauce with which they are to be eaten.[21] A few, as Simone de Beauvoir recognizes, may be kept by others in such a perpetual twilight of awareness they become aware neither of their own freedom nor that of others.[22] To acknowledge such cases poses a challenge to the rest of us to confront and overthrow existing oppressions; it in no way undermines *our* recognition of oppression and its unacceptability.

Our understanding of freedom and the subtle ways it is curtailed may of necessity always be in process; Jean Grimshaw, for example, points to our slowly changing understanding of the realities recently reconceptualized as sexual harassment and women's domestic labor (with the latter finally viewed as *work*).[23] Similarly, the complex realities of classism, heterosexism, and racism are gradually being acknowledged and examined; analyses have found their way into even fairly traditional college and university courses and texts. Although it is hard not to be discouraged with the slowness of change and the continuing inadequacy in our understanding, the fact that moral sensitivity is in constant flux (and that consequently the moral adequacy of our choices varies accordingly) does not invalidate our ethics. It just means we act with less certainty than our society generally finds comfortable. We affirm ambiguity in a culture particularly resistant to any ambiguity in morality.

ARE UNIVERSALIZABLE ALTERNATIVES
ALWAYS POSSIBLE?

For some, universalizability, not pleasure, is the ultimate criterion for evaluating actions morally. Foremost among them is Immanuel Kant with his "moral law"—the famous "Categorical Imperative"—which he thinks reason capable of giving to itself. He develops several versions of this imperative. Two versions mention "maxims" (the subjective principles of actions): "Act only on that maxim through which you can at the same time will that it should become a universal law" and "Act as if the maxim of your action were to become through your will a universal law of nature." The third mentions "persons" (by which he means rational individuals) instead of maxims: "Act in such a way that you always treat humanity, whether in your own person or in the person of any other, never simply as a means, but always at the same time as an end."[24]

Marcus George Singer gives a plausible account of Kantian universalizability. The maxim of an action includes not just "the context of the act" but also the end sought by this agent and is to be formulated from the agent's perspective. Singer argues that, although maxims are sometimes the objects of moral judgments, maxims may not be necessary and may even be misleading, given that not every action is based on a maxim. Though the agent's perspective is central in the formulation of maxims, that perspective is left behind by the attempt to universalize maxims (or actions, if Singer is correct). Now one asks: what if everyone followed this maxim or acted in this way? As Singer argues, Kant wants the criterion of universalizability to reveal those cases where "if everyone were to act in this way, no one would be able to." This is not a generalization argument which would take us back to utilitarianism by pointing to undesirable consequences of everyone's acting in this way. Rather, it simply makes the point "that if, as a consequence of everyone's acting or trying to act in a certain way, no one would be able to, then no one has the right to act in that way— without a reason."[25]

Two of Singer's examples of universalization focus on rape. In the first, admittedly not intended "as a serious possibility," he argues that one could not will to be raped since "being raped involves being subjected to violence involuntarily—that is, *against one's own will*—and if the individual we are imagining were willing to have this happen to everyone, including himself [*sic*], then, by hypothesis, it would not be against his own will, and would not be *rape*." Universalizing is redundant in this case, as Singer notes, since the contradiction arises in the individual's hypothetical wish to be raped. The second example involves trying to will that everyone act as the would-be rapist wishes to act. This would require willing that everyone rape and, consequently, that potentially everyone be raped, including himself; and the latter, as we just saw, is impossible.[26]

Although he indicates that special circumstances may make force permissible, Singer concludes, "One who wishes to force another to do something against his own will could not be willing to have everyone do the same, for he could not be willing to be forced to do something against *his* own will, and this is what this would almost certainly involve." Interestingly, Singer omits such qualification when he says, "This is sufficient to show the immorality of such things as sadism and human exploitation, and such institutions as slavery." In other cases, for example, lying, he does qualify his conclusions: "this is sufficient to establish the rule against lying, which requires that any lie must be justified, and not that every lie must be wrong. What more is needed?"[27]

To see how even Singer's admirable interpretation of the universalizability criterion begs an important question, consider a man beating a woman in an attempt to enslave her.[28] Following Sarah Hoagland's example of a Kantian argument against slavery, this action is clearly wrong: "[I]f I willed it [slavery] universally, then I would be included among those to be enslaved; and as a slave I would not be a being who could will laws. In other words, I would be willing myself to be a being who could not will anything—a contradiction. Thus, it is not possible for me to will such a law morally."[29] Such a batterer is, then, acting immorally, according to Kantian ethics. He cannot will, as Singer would say, that everyone engage in the kind of force he is using since this would ultimately force him to do something against his own will. To do so would require that he will himself forced to act against his own will, which, as we have seen, is impossible.

The problem is that, as a result of exactly the same reasoning, neither can the woman who is being battered universalize the force that she or others might use to stop the battering. By affirming force to stop the battering, she would be ascribing to force to prevent someone from doing what he wills. Now she would be willing that force be used against her to prevent her from battering should she ever will to do so. Surely, she can no more will to be forced to do or not to do something against her will than can the batterer. Thus, Singer's rule against force would seem to count against much that she might do in her own self-defense, including asking law-enforcement agencies to prevent further beating. This is surely a case where Singer would appeal to his claim that such rules only require that exceptions "must be justified."

Perhaps the woman could justify her use of force as an exception to the rule against force, since, after all, she is using force in order to free herself from the force of another. Perhaps she could will that force be used to prevent her from raping or battering, should she ever will to do so. Certainly, she can avoid placing herself in that position; thus, by willing never to rape or batter, she can avoid an actual conflict with her will and thereby avoid willing that she be forced to act against her will. The batterer cannot so easily invoke similar reasoning to justify himself as an exception if he is forced to cease his battery. He and the rapist can, however, invoke similar reasoning earlier when the Kantian is challenging their actions. Conceivably, batterers and rapists may consistently adhere to the principle that might makes right. With such adherence, why can they not will themselves to be sexually attacked and battered by any who are sufficiently powerful? Granted, this means that the sexual attack is no longer, strictly speaking, rape and that the battery is also no longer strictly speaking against their will. Unlike Singer, though, they will not be chagrined to see that in some sense their activity makes, for example, rape no longer possible. Rather, they are far more likely to wonder why others make such a big deal of activities like rape. Eerily enough, what began as a purely hypothetical possibility begins to sound quite plausible as a description of the way the brutal and brutalizing often see the world and moral reasoning.

Like the woman using force against her batterer, such rapists and batterers simply resolve not to will in a particular way; and this may allow them to universalize what they are doing. Surely this is not what Singer has in mind, given that he seems unwilling to entertain any legitimate exceptions to sadism, human exploitation, and slavery; but it is difficult to see how this can be argued.

If the woman is not to use force, just what is she morally permitted to do? What if she considers making a false promise in order to flee from her batterer? On the surface, at least, such a promise may differ little from Kant's example of making a false promise when in need of money. A maxim to make false promises when in danger or in need could never as such become a law of nature, inasmuch as such a maxim "must necessarily contradict itself," as Kant says: "For the universality of a law that every one believing himself to be in need [or in danger] can make any promise he pleases with the intention not to keep it would make promising, and the very purpose of promising, itself impossible, since no one would believe he was being promised anything, but would laugh at utterances of this kind as empty shams."[30] Once again, Singer would say that all this shows is that, as with lying, false promises are generally morally impermissible. Thus, the woman must justify herself as an exception, a difficult if not impossible task.

Kant quite rightly recognizes that a maxim allowing the making of any false promises one might wish or believe helpful to meet any kind of need or degree of danger opens the door to too much. It thereby contradicts the very function of promising on which it relies. Perhaps, though, such contradiction could be avoided by restricting such false promises to cases *where one really is in need or in danger, and desperately so* (possibly where this need or danger is *the result of immoral behavior on the part of others, possibly even the ones to whom the false promises are made*). In this way, exceptions might be built into the initial formulation of the maxim or action. Kant rejects such exceptions, claiming that, by making consequences the point of the behavior, the exceptions would make the promiser legally and morally responsible for all ensuing consequences, no matter how horrendous or unanticipated.[31] In fact, though, building in such exceptions is consistent with the recognition by our legal system that contracts made under certain forms of duress and deceit are not enforceable.

Even such careful and limited formulation of exceptions has problems, though. If these false promises are believed to be not morally binding, would anyone accept them? If not, then we find ourselves once again in the position of willing promises (under certain conditions) that render promises (under those conditions) impossible. Here, though, things are a bit more complex since certain false promises may not appear to be a problem for everyone. As long as the recipients of the false promises are unaware of the need and danger in which the immoral behavior of others has placed the promisers, accepting the promises might seem simple enough. However, knowing that factors like need, danger, and immoral coercion could render the promises null and void, these recipients would be wise not to rely on the promises alone but to demand evidence and reassurance that those factors played no important role in eliciting the promises. Any indication to the contrary would surely render such promises unacceptable as promises.

On the other hand, if need, danger, and immoral coercion are *known* to exist, then no one would accept the promises thus elicited. Surely Kant is right that, under these circumstances, "no one would believe he was being promised anything, but would laugh at utterances of this kind as empty shams."[32] Though many batterers deny to themselves as well as to others the danger in which they place their victims and the immorality of the battering, any who do clearly acknowledge both the dangers and the immorality would see such promises for what they are—ways to escape—and not as promises. Thus, false promises under any conditions seem to raise the same question.

This reasoning undermines Singer's way of defending Kantian ethics from Kant's own allegedly mistaken use of it. Singer tries to show that Kant improperly applies his own universalization principle in the infamous example of an individual forced to answer a would-be murderer's inquiry concerning the whereabouts of the intended victim. Singer points out that "it would not be self-contradictory or self-defeating for everyone to lie . . . *in the specified circumstances.* . . . [T]he lie would be self-defeating—the murderer would fail to believe it—only if the murderer knew what the circumstances were, that is to say, only if he knew that his victim was in the house. But if he knew this the whole question would not arise in the first place." According to Singer, "The question, 'Could it be willed to be a universal law that everyone should lie in order to save an innocent man from harm?' practically answers itself. There is more ground for saying that it is impossible to will the opposite."[33]

Singer's suggestion that the "murderer" would fail to believe the lie "only if he knew that his victim was in the house" is not persuasive. True, the question asked by the murderer has to do with whether the intended victim is in this house (in which, in Kant's example, he has been allowed to hide). Presumably, though, according to Singer's formulation of a supposedly unproblematic and universalizable imperative, every moral individual who knows the intention of the murderer and the innocence of the intended victim would have just as good reason to lie. If so, a smart murderer would be able to anticipate a lie from anyone thought to be morally conscientious and not just from the individual actually hiding the intended victim. If clever enough, the murderer might be able to figure out the truth from one or more responses to carefully formulated questions; but this determination would not result from believing the lies. Ignorance of the facts in a particular case is not sufficient to lead a smart murderer to believe the response.

It looks as though adherence to Singer's reasoning is not sufficient to separate those cases in which it is morally permissible to lie and to promise falsely from those in which it is not. This is because he is relying on universalizability to accomplish what it cannot. Universalizing can, indeed, reveal conceptual difficulties in claims that one may lie or make false promises whenever one pleases. Surely Kant is correct that willing everyone to act in these ways would render both communication and promises impossible. Similarly, delineating circumstances in which it is morally permissible to lie and make false promises will no doubt make it difficult if not impossible to lie and make false promises in those circumstances. But is the latter difficulty, even assuming it is an impossibility, as serious as the former? It seems to me that while we cannot will a world in which communication and promises are impossible, we can will one in which lies and false promises are impossible precisely in those cases where truth should not be told and binding promises should not be made. To this extent, I believe, I am in agreement with Singer; where I cannot agree is with his presumption that universalization will enable us to determine when lies and false promises are morally permissible.

A world in which lies and false promises are impossible in some circumstances is, I think, close to the one in which we already live. It seems unlikely to me that promises and claims made, for example, at knife point are really taken by the wielder of the knife as promises or as truth solely or even mainly because of the immorality of making false promises or of telling lies. Rather, the one who threatens death very likely threatens it just in case the individual does not keep the promise or should the information turn out to be false. My hunch is that those who force promises or information know full well that promises and answers made in response to force are not normal promises and answers and must be insured, not by moral considerations, but by threats of force. Moreover, given that many or most who use force in this way do not themselves feel particularly bound by moral considerations, they would probably be no more inclined to accept the claims and the promises at face value even if morality unequivocally decrees all lies and false promises impermissible.

Whatever conceptual problems may result from recognizing that some promises are not legally or morally binding, those problems do not prevent a legal system such as ours from disallowing, as a matter of practice, some promises made under duress from counting as promises. Whereas Kantians seem to worry that exclusion of such promises from those that are legally binding would result in individuals in duress not being able to make promises, since those to whom the promises are made would see them as the empty shams they are, a legal scholar might point out that this is exactly what the exclusion is designed to accomplish.

Furthermore, a legal system can avoid undermining the ability of those in dire circumstances to make promises—and, of course, the enforceability of those promises even by those responsible for the circumstances—simply by failing or refusing to recognize the seriousness of most coerciveness and by discounting most danger. By making it very difficult to convince a court that a particular false promise should not be legally binding, a legal system will protect contracts in such a way that parties with the advantage generally will not fear unenforceability.

An example of the extent to which the legal system is able to ignore coerciveness occurred recently. Even the coerciveness of a knife-wielding man breaking into a woman's home and the life-threatening nature of AIDS did not prevent a grand jury in Austin, Texas, from concluding, on September 30, 1992, that she was consenting to sexual activity by begging her would-be rapist to wear one of her condoms, coaxing him into doing so by saying that she might have AIDS even if he did not. Fortunately, a different grand jury indicted the man on October 27, 1992, although it remains to be seen whether the man's defense will ultimately succeed: "If she didn't want to, why would she give me the condoms?"[34]

Kant's own analyses certainly offer little if any moral guidance to the battered woman previously discussed. The woman trying to escape the batterer might try to reformulate her options in accordance with other alternatives discussed by Kant. She might, for example, formulate her choices in terms of self-preservation or developing her talents. She could then examine Kant's examples of suicide and neglecting one's natural talents[35] to see what moral insight into her own situation she might glean. Since Kant claims it is impossible to universalize the maxim of suicide to avoid suffering and also impossible to will everyone's neglect of natural talents to indulge the moment's fancy, she could try to set up her alternatives in terms of suicide and neglecting natural talents.

It may be quite obvious to the woman that staying with the batterer will eventually lead to her death at his hands. Admittedly, this is not the same as Kant's example of suicide to avoid suffering: if she stays to be beaten and killed by the batterer, she clearly does not do so to avoid additional suffering. She may stay simply because he has convinced her that she deserves to suffer or that she has no other options. Perhaps her options are severely limited by virtue of being involved in a relationship consuming so much time and energy that she has not been able to develop any of her talents, abilities, and even awareness beyond those absolutely necessary for day-to-day survival with the batterer.[36] This suggests that Kant's ethics simply presumes a basic level of self-respect and awareness of options that systematic oppression prevents some individuals from attaining or maintaining.

On the other hand, mindful of the statistics on women who are killed when they try to leave situations like hers, she may realize that she has a better chance of survival if she stays with her batterer. Even if she retains enough self-respect and awareness of options so that she can make a clear choice of survival, it is far from clear that she should leave.

If she chooses to stay, however, she may be an example of the servility discussed by Thomas E. Hill, Jr.[37] By treating herself merely as a means to someone else's ends, she supposedly violates the third formulation of the Categorical Imperative;[38] she lacks, Hill says, respect for her own rights. Recognizing the difficulty in explicating exactly what, if anything, Kant intends to add to the universalizability criterion by this formulation of the Categorical Imperative, we might rephrase her plight in terms more like those of Singer: even if allowing herself to be beaten and perhaps killed is not obviously self-contradictory, willing that she be thus controlled (even against her will) would be. This rephrasing brings to light a problem: if she is truly servile, she has so conformed her will to her abuser's that there can be no conflict between his control and her will. Surely Kant is right that such servility is morally unacceptable even if its unacceptability does not become readily apparent when she attempts to universalize her choice of conformity.

If she is not to be servile, she must conclude that she should escape the batterer's control. At that point, Kantian ethics seems to put her in a bind. What if she cannot escape without lying to the batterer or making false promises or violating him in some other way? Without lies and false promises, and sometimes more serious measures, many women have been unable to escape battering and even death at the hands of the batterers. What if she cannot escape the batterer without killing him? If she recognizes servility as morally unacceptable, what is she to do? Though Kant grants that it is permissible to defend ourselves against violence, he nevertheless forbids even lying except, in self-defense, when a declaration, later to be used against the individual, is "extorted by force." But this exception, like that for false promises, is problematic to Kant[39] and quickly revoked: "A liar is a coward; he is a man who has recourse to lying because he is unable to help himself and gain his ends by any other means. But a stout-hearted man will love truth and will not recognize a *casus necessitatis*." A man who fails to recognize duties "far greater than life and which can often be fulfilled only by sacrificing life" is "a worthless man [who] values his life more than his person."[40]

If women are to be held to the same moral standards as men (something by no means obvious for Kant[41]), then a woman should avoid worthlessness and love truth to the same degree as the "stout-hearted man." This apparently means not lying even when lying is necessary for self-defense.

Indeed, the right to defend oneself seems severely limited, particularly for women and others without power. Not only is there "always something mean" about a lying promise, but "[i]nsidious, underhand conduct" is "far viler than violence." Even if the other is at fault in some important way (if, for example, he is a swindler demanding information from me to which he has no right and which he will use against me), Kant concludes that though my lie is not unjust to him, nevertheless "my conduct is an infringement of the rights of humanity." Although death may be the alternative to not telling lies, Kant denies that "necessity" can cancel "morality": "If, then, I cannot preserve my life except by disgraceful conduct, virtue relieves me of this duty because a higher duty here comes into play and commands me to sacrifice my life." Thus, condemning Lucretia for killing herself rather than allowing herself to be sexually "dishonored," he observes how much better it would have been to defend "her honour unto death." Such defense of honor, he says, "would have been right; for it is no suicide to risk one's life against one's enemies, and even to sacrifice it, in order to observe one's duties towards oneself."[42] For many battered women, Kant's concern to avoid disgraceful conduct and infringing the "rights of humanity" effectively bars all the doors through which they might escape their persistent batterers and leaves them to stoutheartedly defend themselves "unto death."

The woman being battered is likely to find herself either in the untenable position of this "stout-hearted" individual or, at best, at a moral impasse: if she treats the batterer in accordance with universalizable maxims, she will not lie, make false promises to him, or use force against him. Given the realities of the situation, this very likely means that she will do nothing—or at least nothing effective—to protect herself. Thus, she continues to be battered. This in turn means that, to the extent she is aware of options and able to choose, she allows him to treat her, and thereby in some sense treats herself, in a way that cannot be universalized. She cannot will to be controlled against her will. On the other hand, if she were to do what is necessary to escape the battering, she would use force against him to end the battering, thereby immorally controlling him against his will. Nor is it permissible for her to lie or make false promises, or to do anything "underhanded," in order to escape. Whatever she does, she seems to be caught, as a result of the manipulations and abuse of another, in a situation where she is unable to act morally.

Like many ethics, Kant's is an ethics for a world in which others act morally most of the time. By presuming such a world, Kantian ethics and Kant himself are unable to take the realities of violence seriously and thereby place themselves in a position where convention, not moral considerations, determines what is disgraceful conduct, e.g., that women are "dishonored" by rape. While Kant's solicitude for women's sexual "honor" reflects a distorted sense of what constitutes integrity in women, nevertheless it clearly indicates how easily Kantian morality can side with convention, barring not only social critique and challenge but also the doors through which women might escape the violence against them.

One remaining possibility looks promising as a way to resolve the dilemma confronting those who seem to face, at best, only immoral options as the result of the violence of others.[43] This alternative is suggested by Kant's recognition, in *Perpetual Peace*, of war as "only the sad recourse in the state of nature (where there is no tribunal which could judge with the force of law) by which each state asserts its right by violence and in which neither party can be adjudged unjust (for that would presuppose a juridical decision); in lieu of such a decision, the issue of the conflict (as if given by a so-called 'judgment of God') decides on which side justice lies."[44] Given the separation of the private from the public spheres, a Kantian could argue that, to the extent the private is cordoned off by society and placed beyond the purview of law, the private realm is itself a state of nature. To the extent a woman in a relationship with a man—or, for that matter, a woman—cannot seek or get help from properly constituted authorities, she is in the same position as a state violated by another; and her response, like that of the state, cannot be judged legally unjust because it is beyond the reach of juridical decision.

Perhaps Kantians could agree that responses to violence in such situations are beyond the reach of moral as well as legal judgment. Legally, this seems eminently preferable to our present system which ignores the often deadly consequences for women of the privacy it upholds. By recognizing the impropriety of applying laws to those placed in a state of nature by society's constructions of the private, the legal system at least would allow the abused and the battered to take effective steps to protect themselves.

With this move, an ethics can condemn the original acts that created the state of nature, if these are known; but, once a state of nature has been created, the ethics is unable sufficiently to judge and to guide actions. While it will not condemn it also will not encourage the use of violence to escape violence. Where oppression and violence are systemic, this failure to move beyond condemnation of the original acts supports the status quo. Kantian ethics thus renders even its own condemnation of violence and oppression ineffectual by placing some of the most important attempts to respond and to resist totally outside the purview of morality. Such an ethics is unacceptable.

Moreover, by leaving unchallenged the respect for a privacy that places so many in desperate straits, Kantian ethics fumbles the opportunity to guide an oppressive world or society toward a less oppressive future. Leaving resistance and oppression to fight it out, so to speak, while ethics officially remains morally neutral between them serves only to reinforce the oppressive violence of the status quo.

THE PROBLEM OF INACTION

A second concern is that Kant's emphasis on intention tends to privilege acting and thereby to ignore the harm often done through inaction, whether the result of unchosen, inadvertent inattention or deliberate choice. A focus on intention precludes the former's having any moral relevance and thus allows no condemnation even of great harm caused by carelessness, negligence, or unself-conscious arrogance. Only deliberate or studied inattention, clearly a matter of intention, would fall within the realm of morally scrutizable action since it involves deliberate choice of inaction.

Is even such deliberate choice of inaction, though, sufficiently subject to moral objection in Kant's ethics? For example, if I am an acquaintance of the woman and the batterer previously discussed, I may try to resolve my moral obligations by not getting involved, perhaps absolving any sense of guilt on my part by looking soulfully at her, when next she turns up bruised and aching, to let her know I sympathize with her suffering and to acknowledge the immorality of the way she is being treated. By keeping my distance, I explicitly try to avoid treating either her or the batterer in nonuniversalizable ways. I busily engage myself in acting on clearly universalizable maxims having nothing to do with either of them. In this way, I try to live morally, reminding myself of Kant's affirmation that one is not responsible for the use other's make of one's right actions. Yet surely such distancing of myself is morally problematic. This is what society has been doing with battering, a fact recognized by feminists today as a moral outrage. Unfortunately, however, it is what Kantian ethics seems to encourage with its stress on intention.

Perhaps, though, this suggests what is false: that explicitly formulated intentions are readily available to avoid complicity in violence and oppression. Onora O'Neill raises a related question when she asks whether Kantian ethics requires any actions, e.g., famine relief, to prevent human suffering. Acknowledging Kant's duty of beneficence (requiring "that we act on *some* maxims that foster others' ends"), she challenges the claim that "[a] conscientious Kantian . . . has only to avoid being unjust to those who suffer famine and can then be beneficent to those nearer home." She proposes that the complicated economies of the contemporary world make keeping our moral hands clean considerably more difficult than many would like to admit. She argues:

> Only if we knew that we were not part of any system of activities causing unjustifiable deaths could we have no duties to support policies which seek to avoid such deaths. Modern economic causal chains are so complex that it is likely that only those who are economically isolated and self-sufficient could know that they are part of no such systems of activities. Persons who believe that they are involved in some death-producing activities will have some of the same duties as those who think they have a duty to enforce others' right not to be killed.[45]

Although it follows that in cases where one is involved in, e.g., "death-producing activities" one has an obligation, within Kantian ethics, to stop those activities or at least to cease one's involvement, it may not be obvious which should be done or how. While Kantian ethics seems to give no guidance, O'Neill's analysis at least shows that intentional and even unintentional participation in such activities is forbidden by Kantian ethics. What her arguments do not suggest and what Kant's analyses give us little reason to hope for is any way to support an obligation to act against oppression and violence by non-participants. This ethics, then, is more demanding than many realize, though considerably less demanding than utilitarianism.

When Kant dismisses generosity as a "superfluity," he suggests that, given the extent to which poverty results from unjust actions, generosity is superfluous in reality and not just in ethics: "A man who is never generous but never trespasses on the rights of his fellows is still an honest man, and if everyone were like him there would be no poor in the world."[46] What he does not acknowledge is how important it might be for others to address and to try to relieve or to abolish poverty in a world where many are quite unlike this honest man.

O'Neill's analysis goes a long way toward unraveling objections that Kantian ethics neglects or disallows all moral condemnation of inaction. For example, given the complex system fostering violence against women, her analysis suggests that Kantian ethics might be able to condemn the actions of many who watched for so long, not wanting to "get involved," while Kitty Genovese was stabbed time and again by an attacker outside a New York apartment building. Similarly, given the same analysis, a negative moral judgment may be forthcoming in the case of many or most who do nothing about battering. The problem will be only that of determining to what degree, if any, individuals are "involved" in the complex system fostering violence against women. Probably most of those in these two cases are not involved as directly in the killing or battering in the sense O'Neill's investors are involved in companies whose policies contribute to famine. However, some may be implicated in the sense of profiting in some way or other from the system, much as do those who buy the less expensive products generated by companies' management and investment decisions. Others may have actually contributed to the maintenance of the system through preaching, teaching, and example.

While those who formulate and implement policies creating or perpetuating conditions fostering violence against women should have the most strenuous obligation to change the conditions and to alleviate the suffering caused by them, nevertheless, it is problematic to suggest that those who do not create, implement, maintain, or profit have no obligation to change the system (unless they fulfill their general obligation to be beneficent in no other way). This allocation of responsibility serves to perpetuate the status quo by placing the greatest amount of responsibility for social change on those least likely to do anything about it and possibly none on the rest, many of whom would be likely to do something. Indeed, those who are held responsible for social change on this view are those most likely, as Catharine MacKinnon might say, to continue eroticizing women's subordination and promoting the view of women and even female children as wanting, asking for, and indeed being made for violent treatment such as rape, battery, sexual harassment, child sexual abuse, and forced prostitution, "all presented in pornography as sex, sex, sex, sex, and more sex, respectively."[47]

Moreover, it is disconcerting to think that whether individuals have any obligation, other than a general obligation to be beneficent, could be determined only after a lengthy and very difficult analysis of the situation and of their involvements in it. The feminist analyses required if we are accurately to gauge levels of involvement in systems of oppression are sufficiently complex and demanding of sensitivity that most people will remain not only oblivious to obligations of this sort but also impervious to all efforts to get them to see such obligations. To further complicate matters, traditional oppressive social structures create, as Sarah Hoagland observes, additional resistance to recognizing certain choices as choices because, as she says, the tradition "cannot afford to acknowledge that participation is a choice."[48] The more fundamental and pervasive the social structure in question, the more this resistance comes into play and must be overcome before individuals can see *any* involvement much less correctly assess their *levels* of involvement in systems of oppression.

That some obligations will be obscure and not readily apparent to an unsensitized agent is no doubt inevitable at some level in any ethical theory. The problem with obscurity in this theory is that a general obligation to prevent individuals from suffering the violence of others needs to be among the theory's most fundamental and obvious obligations. Beginning with this obligation, we progress to complicated analyses and to carefully honed distinctions between the systematic violence of oppression and the sometimes necessary violence of those who work against oppression. As our understanding of the complexity of situations grows, our obligations gradually become more refined and more finely tuned; but the point is that they are motivated both individually and theoretically by the initial recognition of the general obligation to prevent violence. If this obligation is forthcoming only in particular cases and often only *after* complicated analysis, there seems to be nothing to motivate the analysis.

A Kantian might respond that the obligation not to trample on the rights of others is sufficient to require individuals to be sure they are not implicated whenever they see rights being trampled, but I am not sure this is enough. What, after all, is to impel individuals to study a situation to make sure they are not implicated in any way unless they initially recognize that the situation should not be allowed to be? In a society that encourages its members to think in terms of individual rather than collective responsibility, an ethics that absolves the non-involved from responsibility encourages those who observe someone trampling the rights of others to assign responsibility to the trampler. Widespread and complex systems of oppression with no key perpetrators on whom to focus moral condemnation are likely to escape entirely any deep moral probing.

This danger is compounded by the fact that systems of oppressions spin out complex ideologies, in addition to that of individualism, to distort and render invisible the intricacies of the oppression and thereby to obscure involvement in it. Thus, any awareness of an obligation to work against oppression is likely not to emerge at all. Given the Kantian presumption that moral action is always possible and given what I believe to be a necessary entailment of this presumption—that generally everyone does as she or he ought—Kantian ethics buttresses rather than critiques such ideologies.

For feminists, it is especially problematic that an ethics gives us little motivation to break with the individualism of the society and to undertake the study necessary to determine responsibility in a complex network of relations. If we cannot begin with agreement not just about the wrongness of oppression but also about our responsibility to do something to stop it and to prevent further occurrences, we are not likely to make much progress in feminist social analysis itself. After all, just such acts of violence and the responses of others to them usually are at the roots of such analysis: it is generally the recognition of the unacceptability of this sort of violence which ignites critical consciousness and continues to fuel feminist thought.

Thus, although O'Neill's analysis of Kant's ethics is probing and sensitive, it does not take Kant far enough, for reasons endemic to his position and over which O'Neill has no control. It is Kant, after all, who focuses on universalizable intentions and who fails to acknowledge the prevalence of violence and oppression, instead envisioning a world in which generosity is superfluous. It is Kant who allows those who do not violate any rights and who are generally beneficent to have no responsibility to prevent such violation by others. And it is Kant who fails to consider that what he says about the state of nature in *Perpetual Peace* may apply not just to nations but also to women and others involved in relationships regarded as beyond the purview of law and morality.

PROBLEMS OF RATIONALITY, UNIVERSALISM, AND THE KINGDOM OF ENDS

Kantian ethics faces problems besides those of insufficient recognition of inaction and of prohibiting effective response in situations of violence. Feminists have objected to the fact that Kant's view of autonomy privileges the rational will and opposes it to anything emotionally or physically based. As Sarah Hoagland says: "[Kant] argued that the moral individual is one who uses pure reason (logic) to determine what to do and then, by exercising his will, acts from duty alone to rise above his emotions or inclinations and hence his nature." To preserve this reason/emotion split, Kant regards "autonomy and morality [as] achievable only if we fragment our selves," distancing our moral selves from all passion, desires, and wishes.[49]

By privileging rationality, he makes human wills appear disembodied and outside all relationships, at least to the extent the wills are rational and autonomous. Since this is the position in which society has typically envisioned some but not all males and no females, this understanding of the will is invidious. It becomes especially invidious and likely to strengthen rather to critique ongoing violence and oppression when, as Hoagland observes, the notion of "autonomy" "begins to imply the idea of self-control," which, in turn, fits a bit too nicely into the dominant ideology of control of others.[50]

The primarily male reference of autonomy and rationality becomes quite apparent when Kant turns his attention to women. Not surprisingly, he characterizes women's virtue in terms antithetical to everything he has said about morality. In particular, he joins the conventional praise of women's sensitivity, even while claiming that women tend to shun evil, not because it is evil, but because it is ugly.[51] What Kant calls the "beautiful virtue" of women, contrasted with the "noble virtue" of men, is, according to what he says elsewhere, not a virtue at all. If women act out of attraction to the beautiful and aversion to the ugly, they shun evil only because it is ugly, avoiding it out of inclination and not, as they should, simply because it is wrong.[52] Failing to do their duty simply because it is duty, they should be blamed, not praised, were Kant true to his principles.

When, in other contexts, he discusses women, Kant gives himself license to sneer at, ridicule, and basically treat as deformities any who step outside the roles conventionally assigned to women. He says: "A woman who has a head full of Greek . . . or carries on fundamental controversies about mechanics . . . might as well even have a beard; for perhaps that would express more obviously the mien of profundity for which she strives."[53] Kant's own practice raises serious doubts about whether his proclamations about rationality, autonomy, and duty apply to women and even about whether and how one recognizes other creatures, quite different from oneself, as rational.

Kantian ethics assumes that human beings, indeed all rational beings, simply by virtue of being rational, are sufficiently like one another to make the Categorical Imperative work as the ultimate (and sole) principle of ethics. In the context of oppressive societies, the historical constructions of race, class, and gender may result in individuals who are quite different from one another and from socially established norms of rationality. Racism, classism, and sexism tend to hide from the dominant the very humanity, and surely the rationality, of the dominated. We see this in Kant's own treatment of women.

Although I am not sure how, Kantian ethics, as opposed to Kant's own application of his own principles, may be able to condemn such nonacknowledgment of any who are indeed rational beings. Still, though, serious problems remain. Race, class, and gender are parts of individual embodiment, not just institutionalized relationships. It is not clear that such aspects of embodiment can be represented adequately either in maxims or in descriptions of actions, particularly since Kant's ethics is premised on regarding and treating all individual human beings merely as rational beings. More important, though, since those outside a system of oppression may have no prima facie duty to abolish the oppression, there seems to be little in Kantian ethics to motivate, either theoretically or practically, such careful honing of maxims. Kant's own inadequate analyses and answers when other factors besides rationality come into play offer some indication of how easily this ethics sides with convention and existing power arrangements.

Lest Kant's failure to take women seriously as rational beings be seen as no more than a failure to take his own principles seriously, we need to observe that he has similar problems with men when recognition of their embodiment is forced by circumstances. Just as he does not deal adequately in his ethics with women, so he fares poorly even when discussing a man whose embodiment is rendered inescapable as a result of his being threatened with murder. To one who hides the intended victim, Kant advocates not lying about the friend's whereabouts if asked by the attacker (and compelled to answer—it is morally permissible, he thinks, not to answer). If he lies to protect the innocent friend, he "must answer for the consequences, however unforeseeable they were, and pay the penalty for them even in a civil tribunal." This means that if telling what is believed to be a protective lie inadvertently leads the murderer to the intended victim,[54] the liar is legally and morally responsible for the victim's death, whereas one who tells the truth simply follows duty and thereby bears no responsibility for consequences, apparently no matter how horrendous.[55]

This example simply cannot be said to be an anomaly in Kant's theory. Like the stout-hearted man, the individual forced to answer the would-be murderer's request for information concerning another's whereabouts apparently will love truth, will value "his person" (and presumably that of the intended victim, whatever that would mean) more than the life of either, will avoid "[i]nsidious, underhand conduct," and thus will not "violate the right of mankind" by lying. If moral, the individual who is questioned will not lie and will hope for the best, namely, that the villain is unsuccessful or that the intended victim comports himself well and, unlike Lucretia, dies, if he must, fighting (by whatever means are allowed morally) for his honor, not at his own hands to escape suffering.[56]

While there may be comfort in knowing that individuals thus victimized are regarded as "wronged," there is something seriously amiss in an ethics that leaves victims so much at the mercy of the immoral. It is difficult to agree that somehow it is more important not to lie to one who does not deserve it than to protect one who, because innocent and about to be killed, is deserving. Kant's satisfaction over having done the morally right thing by not lying, even though another uses his answer to do what is morally wrong, places too much emphasis on the purely cognitive aspect of the intention on which the agent acted, ignoring its connection with action embedded in a world of other agents, institutions, and even yielding or recalcitrant objects. While the agent intended only not to lie and did not intend to harm to his threatened friend, the agent's participation in the ensuing harm is inescapable since he *knew*, even if he did not consciously will, the likelihood of the harm, given the violent intent of the questioner. A more adequate ethics would describe *what* was done in terms of its context.

While this example is used by Kant as a reductio ad absurdum of the utilitarian concern for consequences, it is remarkably consistent with his analysis elsewhere of self-defense. In my earlier examination of the latter,[57] I objected that Kant's concern with disgraceful or dishonorable conduct failed to take seriously the complexity of the positions in which individuals are placed by the immoral activities of others. Now I am suggesting that this failure is at least partially the result of his concern to treat the subjects of moral duties as rational and not embodied beings.

Kant's emphasis on rationality obscures, even enables him to deny, the moral relevance of an important aspect of intention: that the intention of the friend is manifested by his actions and that his actions are events in the world, creating features of the world that others can then use to their own ends. Although Kant denies it, the willingness to risk the life of the friend rather than tell a lie makes the answerer morally as well as causally complicit in the murderer's scheme precisely because it is clear that the information will be used to carry out the murderer's intent. This is not a case of ignorance stemming from inattention; rather, Kant allows the friend to fulfill his duty to humanity by avoiding lies even though well aware how his answer will be used. To claim, as Kant must and does, that the friend has no moral responsibility concerning the use the other will make of his answer reflects Kant's separation of intention from action, a separation grounded in his connection of autonomy with rationality. With his emphasis on rationality, he finds himself, consistently enough, more worried about lying and being underhanded than about preventing rape and murder. Treating and valuing individuals solely in terms of their rationality, Kant is hard pressed to take sufficiently into account the embodiment that renders them subject to torture, rape, and murder, to coercion, and to classism, racism, and sexism, and that frequently makes even apparently nonparticipant onlookers causally and morally complicit in all of these.

Finally, Kant's ethics makes the serious mistake of treating as relatively unproblematic the ideal of the kingdom of ends ("a systematic union of rational beings under common objective laws" where each member has "a dignity—that is, an unconditioned worth" by virtue of the fact each "obeys no law other than that which he at the same time enacts himself"[58]). Although recognizing this as an ideal—even a regulative one—and not as reality, Kant fails to realize that, given societies with systematic oppression, this ideal in fact can be and is counterproductive when used to determine the right action. If my previous analysis is correct, trying to act, in situations of violence, in accordance with Kantian ethics is problematic since these efforts are apt to reinforce existing oppressions and to render even less possible similar action on the part of the oppressed.

Failing to recognize how even the best intentioned effort will be co-opted and used to reinforce the status quo, this ethics advocates the sort of wishful thinking that works only in fairy tales. This is the sort of moralistic theorizing that urges, for example, "color-blindness" in business, educational, and legal decisions without any awareness of or concern for the ways racism informs not just deliberate actions but also institutions and numerous aspects of life in a racist society. It is almost as if those who endorse this thinking believe human beings can do away with racism by clicking their heels together and repeating, "There is no racism here." This treatment of the ideal is like the "dreamy idealism" of audiences who respond to Catharine MacKinnon by asking her to create a "design of life after male supremacy":

> [This] requests a construction of a future in which the present does not exist, under existing conditions. It dreams that the mind were free and could, like Milton, make a heaven of hell or a hell of heaven. The procedure is: imagine the future you want, construct actions or legal rules or social practices *as if* we were already there, and that will get us from here to there. This magical approach to social change, which is methodologically liberal, lives entirely in the head, a head that is more determined by present reality than it is taking seriously, yet it is not sufficiently grounded in that reality to do anything about it.[59]

While Kant turns attention in the right direction, with his focus on will and the kingdom of ends, his emphasis on intention and on the rational will as law-giver leads ultimately to an ethics of disembodied wills, defenseless victims, and an unfortunate encouragement of an idealistic or magical approach to ethics. His ethics tends to ignore concrete individuals and their suffering except where some are specifically involved in violating the rights of others. Even then, the violators are only condemned; either the victims are not morally permitted adequate means to stop the violations or their responses are placed outside the purview of ethics. Moreover, the uninvolved are recognized as possibly having no duty to stop the violations or to aid the victims. Given its seeming inability to motivate, theoretically or individually, an adequate understanding of levels of involvement in systems of oppression, Kantian ethics moves too easily into a legalism in which it is permissible to ignore not just great suffering but also great oppression, socially or individually based.

While utilitarians must justify the suffering and oppression of some as necessary for the greater good, Kantians need not concern themselves with any such rationalizations as long as they act with good intentions and are not implicated in the suffering and oppression. When acting morally, Kantians are not responsible even for foreseen consequences of their own right actions, much less for those of others' actions. Thus, Kantians' consciences will not be troubled by suffering and oppression of which they are not intentionally a part. Even with O'Neill's analysis broadening the scope of that of which one is intentionally a part, a Kantian ethics still offers a protective cover for the inaction of those not directly implicated in situations of violence and oppression.

Thus, Kantian ethics, along with ethical egoism and utilitarianism, fails as an acceptable feminist ethics. All of these ethics fail to place proper emphasis on the individual, either by treating individuals as disembodied wills unaffected by oppressive social institutions and structures or by assuming that individuals are nothing more than aggregates of their pleasurable and painful experiences. In addition, all ultimately fail sufficiently to address much morally outrageous violence. In their different ways, they all support the status quo and undermine the reformist and revolutionary activities of feminists and others concerned with oppression.

WILLING ONE'S OWN FREEDOM AND THAT OF OTHERS

If an ethics of freedom is to succeed where others fail, it must emphasize individual will but take great care to recognize the material and social embeddedness of this will. Moreover, this ethics must condemn systems of oppression as well as individual acts violating the freedom of others. Even more, it must support active resistance to such oppression and violence.

In the preceding chapter, we saw that Sartre's ethics acknowledges the will and the freedom of the individual but also is sensitive to ways the body and society situate the will and structure the range of options through which this freedom is to be played out. Especially important

for feminists is the recognition of societal oppression as "overdeter-
mining" the oppressed by creating for them "natures" that objectively
delineate and limit their options and dictate the ways individuals and
their actions are seen by others and even by themselves.

Sartre places willing and working for one's own and others' freedom at the center of ethics. Although values have no objective existence independent of human choice, nevertheless oppression is immoral and must be resisted. Violence, too, is morally unacceptable, yet
sometimes unavoidable and necessary in a context of oppression and
violence. He thus provides an ethics supportive of feminist reform and
revolution. Yet because Sartre has been so frequently misunderstood,
much more must be said about his treatment of freedom, moral judgment, and violence.

Keenly aware of human freedom, of the temptation to deny it in
ourselves, and of the extent and frequency of oppression, Sartre argues
that we ought to will our own and others' freedom. He argues this
while denying any objective values and with, I think, a maximal openness to whatever individuals may choose as values. His moral judgment is limited to condemning those who try to deny freedom, either
their own or that of others.

While there are no grounds justifying certain values over others or
warranting the imposition on others of the values any particular individuals happen to choose, Sartre nonetheless proposes limits for morally acceptable choices. Any choice denying freedom is morally unacceptable. Whatever values we individually choose, we must will our
own freedom, since our freedom is a necessary precondition for any
choosing and consequent action.[60] This is very like the hypothetical
imperative disparaged but recognized as analytic by Kant: whoever
wills the end wills the means.[61] In Sartre's analysis, though, freedom
is recognized as a precondition to whatever ends individuals may choose
rather than as a means to any end. As a precondition of all value, freedom
underlies all choice and thus acquires a positive value through any
choice of value. Kant himself recognizes something like this when, in
arguing against suicide, he maintains that "it annuls the condition of
all other duties; it goes beyond the limits of the use of free will, for
this use is possible only through the existence of the Subject."[62]

A similar recognition holds, for Sartre, with respect to the freedom
of others. Inasmuch as human existence is an ambiguous, embodied
existence, human beings are always vulnerable to others; and to the
extent their activities take place in a world of others, the success of
their projects depends at least on the noninterference of others and
often on active assistance. To recognize being-for-others is to acknowledge

the extent to which one's acts are not totally within one's own power. As Simone de Beauvoir says: "[B]y taking the world away from me, others also give it to me, since a thing is given to me only by the movement which snatches it from me. To will that there be being is also to will that there be men by and for whom the world is endowed with human significations. One can reveal the world only on a basis revealed by other men. No project can be defined except by its interference with other projects."[63] Thus, in willing one's own ends, one must will not just the noninterference of others but also their active aid, hence their freedom as precondition of that aid.

Here, Sartre and de Beauvoir are not judging means by the ends they accomplish but rather, once again in the analytic spirit of "whoever wills the end wills the means," affirming something about what it means to will any end. Whatever one wills, one implicates all others and thereby wills for everyone. Though the authentic individual does not, as Hazel Barnes observes, "insist that everyone must go where he goes," authenticity does require that the individual hold as absolute "the possibility of choice."[64]

Thus, Sartre maintains in his writings, not that others should always choose in the same way, but that others should be free, and that, wherever possible, everyone should act to eliminate oppression. His actions supported and exemplified these claims. He and de Beauvoir frequently manifested their "willingness to put their lives and honor on the line in support of human dignity," behavior some have erroneously seen as evincing the spirit of "seriousness"—an attitude of bad faith toward values—as given, ready-made, not created by free choice.[65]

The move from willing to acting, however, is not the unwarranted move many take it to be. Rather, choosing and acting are not separable: to choose a value is, at least in appropriate circumstances,[66] to act on it, and, similarly, to act is to make value choices, however much we may try to avoid such choosing. Separating choice from action leads to an "abstract ethics . . . that of the good conscience"—"the idea that one can be good without changing the situation"—a morality Sartre clearly rejects in *Notebooks for an Ethics*.[67] Sharon Welch presents a similar view of action as the basis for her "ethic of risk": "To act means to determine what will happen through that single action, to ensure that a given course of events comes to pass."[68]

Sartre quite properly objects to those who, like his character Garcin in the play *No Exit*, think they can divorce choice from action: "A man," Garcin declares, "is what he wills to be."[69] Sartre himself agrees rather with Inez's response to Garcin: a man is what he does. For Sartre, an individual's intentions and even potentiality are manifest in, though not simply reducible to, actions. Even Garcin is unable to distinguish his intention from his act. He tries to convince himself he fled his country to further the revolution; yet his death left his action standing alone and uninterpreted. Since no actions followed it, this lone action is ambiguous. He cannot be sure whether his choice was the pragmatic choice of a dedicated revolutionary or the skin-saving choice of a coward.

If, then, choosing and willing are inextricably connected, moral beings must will and act to further the freedom of all. To be moral, one must will the freedom of others; and this requires, in appropriate circumstances, working against their oppression. It is not enough simply for an individual not to oppress others. For Sartre, inaction is often action: if one could do something to prevent oppression but chooses not to do so, then to that extent one is actively involved in and supportive of the oppression.

Although acting against oppression may jeopardize the actor's life, the action may simply follow from an awareness of freedom as the foundation of all values, not from the spirit of seriousness that refuses to question the givenness of all values. This is just to recognize freedom as embodied and not merely as a contextless will. It involves the acknowledgment that an embodied will is very much dependent on other freedoms and is affected by their nonrecognition as well as vulnerable to their imposition of physical and psychological restraints.

Moreover, to act against oppression is not, in turn, to oppress those who wish to practice oppression, although, if successful, the action will curtail their freedom to act in oppressive ways. To the extent that oppressive action denies the freedom of others, it is unacceptable and should be stopped. Doing nothing to end the oppression is often tantamount to allowing it to continue and, therefore, is to that extent an endorsement of and a participation in the oppression. By rejecting the acceptability of oppression, action against it affirms rather than denies freedom, even that of would-be oppressors: it says, in effect, that no one, not even former oppressors, should be oppressed. Admittedly, action against oppression will violate the freedom of the oppressors by limiting it, constraining it, perhaps even doing them bodily harm. To use constraint and bodily harm in order to object to constraint and bodily harm is indeed most problematic for those who will and try to further the freedom of all. Yet the only other option in such cases—to allow and thereby endorse violence and oppression—is clearly unacceptable. Violence is unavoidable. In such cases, those who recognize the immorality of violence must violate the freedom of some in order to deny that the violation of freedom is acceptable. To reject violence in such instances, violence is necessary.

Does this mean that violence against oppressors creates new oppression? Paulo Freire correctly recognizes that former oppressors will not feel liberated and will see themselves as oppressed by virtue of being denied the opportunity to oppress others. Every claim that one is oppressed, however, need not be accepted at face value, particularly claims based on the assumption that only the would-be oppressors are human beings while other people are merely "things."[70] If oppression is, as Marilyn Frye suggests, "a system of interrelated barriers and forces which reduce, immobilize and mold people who belong to a certain group, and effect their subordination to another group,"[71] then stopping oppression does not itself involve creating new oppressions. Would-be oppressors are simply not allowed to oppress; however they may feel, they are not, by the mere fact of being prevented from oppressing, thereby subordinated to anyone else. Simply to be denied opportunity to subordinate others is not to be subordinated. Although they are prevented from doing what they wish, they are not thereby oppressed.

Sartre's recognition of embodiment is an acceptance of multiple ambiguities, one of the most important of which is the ambiguity of agents who act in oppressive situations not of their own making. While freedom can be curtailed in any number of ways, those whose freedom is curtailed are not responsible for limitations imposed upon them and which they cannot change. At the same time, if there are *any* options available to them, they are responsible for whatever choices they make among these. This understanding of freedom thus encourages heightened awareness of the range of choices available to those whose freedom has been curtailed. This understanding of freedom supports revolutionary thinking in the oppressed and encourages victims to avoid defeatism and the sense of powerlessness that comes from seeing themselves merely in terms of their victimization.

Without blaming the oppressed for the limitations others impose, as Sarah Hoagland[72] and others accuse him of doing, Sartre nevertheless relentlessly focuses on whatever freedom remains *within* those limitations. In so doing, he stresses a notion of freedom quite similar to Hoagland's own conception of moral agency (though she fails to realize how similar), namely, "the ability to choose in limited situations, to pursue one possibility rather than another, to thereby create value through what we choose, and to conceive of ourselves as ones who are able to and do make choices—and thus as ones who are able to make a difference for ourselves and each other in this living."[73] While oppressors are responsible for the limitations they impose on the range of options available to the oppressed, the latter are responsible for what they do and thereby make of themselves within those limited opportunities.

CONSEQUENCES AND
INTENTIONS REVISITED

Feminist ethics must recognize the obvious, that both intentions and consequences are important. It very often does make a difference to us to learn the intention of the agent. However, the consequences of an action also matter in our evaluation of the actions, particularly if those consequences were or could have been anticipated. As Hoagland says: "[W]hen someone does us an injury, it generally matters to us whether or not she intended to harm us. . . . Nevertheless, it is not another person's intentions which hurt me. . . . If I am harmed, it is another person's (or group's) actions which harm me; and that is so whether they act intentionally, from ignorance, or are coerced in certain ways."[74] Part of the inadequacy of utilitarianism is its ignoring the intentions and indeed the agent, except to the extent the agent's pleasures and pains are taken into account like everyone else's. On the other hand, part of the problem faced by Kantian ethics is its heedlessness of the consequences of actions, particularly whether they leave oppressions unchallenged and suffering untreated.

An ethics of freedom can and does maintain intentions and consequences in tension, refusing to negate the significance of either or to try to reduce without remainder one to the other. Sartre maintains this tension in large part by undercutting the foundation on which the distinction between utilitarianism and Kantian ethics rests—the clear separation of act and intention.

For Sartre, on the contrary, though not simply reducible to one another, act and intention are inseparable just as are being-for-others and being-for-oneself. Action requires embodiment and embeddedness in the world. Since an action is an effort to do something, it can be blocked or impeded, either by one's own temporary or permanent disabilities or by the resistance of things or others. To act requires, if not the assistance of others, at least their noninterference. While the agent cannot control all the factors necessary for accomplishing the intention expressed in the action, nonetheless the agent's intention to achieve a certain result demands the exercise of whatever control is possible over all of these factors. So the agent has some responsibility for at least some consequences. Whatever they are, they evince to some degree the agent's intention.

Thus, for Sartre, actions are always seen in a rather intricate context. The will is embodied and acting. Both embodiment and acting develop in social situations. This freedom has little to do with Kant's autonomous self and is more properly interpreted along the lines of Hoagland's "self in community"—a self that "emerges through our interactions with others."[75]

Sartre's emphasis on a contextualized freedom enables him to avoid the dreamy but harmful idealism of those who invoke the kingdom of ends with inadequate recognition of the oppression and violence involved in the status quo, with insufficient allowance for acts that would resist and overthrow this oppression and violence, and with little or no awareness of the extent to which the ethics they build around this notion of a kingdom of ends perpetuates the oppression and violence. His understanding of freedom allows him a standard beyond the pleasures, needs, and values constructed by oppressions, a standard by which societies, institutions, and individual actions can be critiqued and in terms of which strategies for overthrowing systems of oppression can be evaluated and supported.

NOTES

1. Nye, p. 20.
2. Hoagland, *Lesbian Ethics: Toward New Value*, p. 259.
3. Jaggar, *Feminist Politics*, pp. 174-75.
4. MacKinnon, *Feminism Unmodified*, pp. 7, 54.
5. Mill, "From *The Subjection of Women*," p. 289.
6. Mott, p. 326.
7. According to Albert C. Skaggs, journalists facetiously made this suggestion for Justice Stewart years ago.
8. Mill, *On Liberty* (New York: Appleton-Century-Crofts, 1947), pp. 10-11.
9. Rawls, p. 262.
10. See Jaggar's observation, p. 45, that the assumption of a natural egotism is much more appropriate when discussing the behavior of contemporary males than when considering that of females.
11. Mill, "From *The Subjection of Women*," pp. 288-89.
12. Rawls, p. 136.
13. Kurt Baier, *The Moral Point of View: A Rational Basis of Ethics* (Ithaca, NY: Cornell University Press, 1958), pp. 189-90.
14. I owe this observation to Claudia Card.
15. Hoagland, *Lesbian Ethics: Toward New Value*, p. 90.
16. Rawls, pp. 26-27.
17. de Beauvoir, *The Ethics of Ambiguity*, trans. Bernard Frechtman (New York: Citadel Press, 1964), p. 95.

18. Although Sartre, *Notebooks for an Ethics*, p. 207, distinguishes "defensive violence" ("a recourse to violence directed against nonviolent processes") from "counterviolence" ("a riposte to some aggression or effort to secure a hold maintained by force (State)"), he goes on to undermine this distinction to some extent. He explicitly acknowledges, for example, the violence of much apparently nonviolent activity, such as "a unilateral break in a tacit contract that I made with the other" when refusing to discuss an issue any further and using *ad hominem* attacks to silence the other in a discussion (pp. 207-12).

19. Mill, *Utilitarianism, Readings in Moral Philosophy*, ed. Andrew Oldenquist (Boston: Houghton Mifflin, 1965), p. 272.

20. Welch, p. 108.

21. Sartre, *Notebooks for an Ethics*, p. 331.

22. de Beauvoir, *The Ethics of Ambiguity*, p. 37.

23. Grimshaw, pp. 87-88.

24. Kant, *The Moral Law*, trans. H.J. Paton (New York: Barnes & Noble, 1963), pp. 88-89, 96.

25. Marcus George Singer, *Generalization in Ethics: An Essay in the Logic of Ethics, with the Rudiments of a System of Moral Philosophy* (New York: Alfred A. Knopf, 1961), pp. 245-49, 253, 275.

26. *Ibid.*, pp. 265-67.

27. *Ibid.*, pp. 267, 259.

28. See Kathleen Barry, *Female Sexual Slavery* (Englewood Cliffs, NJ: Prentice-Hall, 1979).

29. Hoagland, *Lesbian Ethics: Toward New Value*, p. 257.

30. Kant, *The Moral Law*, p. 90.

31. Kant, "On a Supposed Right to Lie From Altruistic Motives," in *Critique of Practical Reason and Other Writings in Moral Philosophy*, trans. and ed. Lewis White Beck (Chicago: University of Chicago Press, 1949), pp. 347-48.

32. Kant, *The Moral Law*, p. 90.

33. Marcus George Singer, pp. 232-33.

34. *The Atlanta Journal/The Atlanta Constitution*, October, 25, 1992, p. A14; October 28, 1992, p. A10.

35. Kant, *The Moral Law*, pp. 89-91.

36. For more discussion of Kant's "imperfect duty" to develop one's natural talents and the duty to abstain from suicide, see Kant, *ibid.*, pp. 89-92.

37. Thomas E. Hill, Jr., "Servility and Self-Respect," in *Moral Philosophy: Classic Texts and Contemporary Problems*, ed. Joel Feinberg and Henry West (Belmont, CA: Dickenson Publishing, 1977), pp. 484-93.

38. Kant, *The Moral Law*, pp. 96-98.

39. This is true whether we examine his critical or his precritical work.

40. Kant, *Lectures on Ethics*, trans. Louis Infield (Indianapolis: Hackett Publishing, 1963), pp. 232, 228-29, 154.

41. See Kant, "From *Observations on the Feeling of the Beautiful and Sublime*," in *Visions of Women*, pp. 241-47.

42. Kant, *Lectures on Ethics*, pp. 232, 227, 157, 151.

43. This was suggested to me by C. Grant Luckhardt.

44. Kant, *Perpetual Peace*, trans. Lewis White Beck (New York: Bobbs-Merrill, 1957), pp. 7-8.

45. Onora O'Neill, "Kantian Approaches to Some Famine Problems," in *Ethics and Public Policy*, pp. 208-9, 218.

46. Kant, *Lectures on Ethics*, p. 211.

47. MacKinnon, *Feminism Unmodified*, p. 203.

48. Hoagland, *Lesbian Ethics: Toward New Value*, p. 54.

49. *Ibid.*, pp. 159, 258. For further discussion of Kant's notion of autonomy and feminist objections to it, pp. 159, 251, 257-58.

50. *Ibid.*, p. 144.

51. Kant develops these claims in *Observations on the Feeling of the Beautiful and Sublime*, trans. John T. Goldthwait (Berkeley: University of California Press, 1960). Relevant selections from this work are included in *Visions of Women*, pp. 241-47.

52. Kant, *The Moral Law*, p. 108.

53. Kant, "From *Observations on the Feeling of the Beautiful and Sublime*," in *Visions of Women*, p. 242.

54. That telling a protective lie certainly may lead to the death of the intended victim is part of Sartre's point in his short story "The Wall." Sartre's larger point, though, is quite unlike Kant's: to unmask the bad faith of the prisoner who tells the lie, confident that he has control over what is actually beyond his control.

55. Kant, "On a Supposed Right to Lie From Altruistic Motives," pp. 347-48.

56. Kant, *Lectures on Ethics*, pp. 229, 154, 232, 228, 149-50.

57. See my discussion of Kant on self-defense under "Are Universalizable Alternatives Always Possible?" earlier in this chapter.

58. Kant, *The Moral Law*, pp. 100, 103, 102.

59. MacKinnon, *Feminism Unmodified*, p. 219.

60. Sartre, "Existentialism is a Humanism," in *Existentialism from Dostoevsky to Sartres*, p. 307.

61. Kant, *The Moral Law*, p. 86.

62. Kant, *Lectures on Ethics*, p. 149.

63. de Beauvoir, *The Ethics of Ambiguity*, p. 71.

64. Barnes, *An Existentialist Ethics* (New York: Vintage Books, 1967), p. 109.

65. Thomas C. Anderson, *The Foundation and Structure of Sartrean Ethics* (Lawrence: Regents Press of Kansas, 1979), p. 149.

66. This qualification is important given Sartre's recognition in his war diaries, *The War Diaries of Jean-Paul Sartre*, trans. Quintin Hoare (New York: Pantheon Books, 1984), p. 36, "that there exist in me a certain number of full, effective willings which are nonetheless not conjoined with realization." For some of these, there simply is, at the moment, nothing to do given the "far-away" nature of the decision, such as his intention to answer a letter "tomor-

row" or his decisions concerning his more distant return to civilian life. Even in the war diaries, though, Sartre (*ibid.*, p. 35) rejected what he called "empty volitions" and regarded as "an excellent precaution" the "severe, moralistic decision" that judges the intention by the result. Thus in 1939, Sartre (*ibid.*, p. 37) clearly says, "[w]ill needs the world and the resistance of things." The dreamer, "victim of ... [his] omnipotence, ... [is] bound hand and foot by his absolute power [*ibid.*]."

67. Sartre, *Notebooks for an Ethics*, p. 17.

68. Welch, p. 3.

69. Sartre, *No Exit*, trans. Stuart Gilbert, *No Exit and Three Other Plays* (New York: Vintage Books, 1955), p. 44.

70. Freire, p. 43.

71. Frye, *The Politics of Reality: Essays in Feminist Theory*, p. 33.

72. Hoagland, *Lesbian Ethics: Toward New Value*, p. 200.

73. *Ibid.*, p. 231.

74. *Ibid.*, p. 216.

75. *Ibid.*, p. 145.

Chapter Five

The Role of
Violence In Ethics

Feminist ethics should begin by recognizing the facts that violence pervades the societies with which we are most familiar—particularly our own—and that much of this violence is directed toward women. Given this recognition, there is a legitimate place for anger, not just subjective rage, but something more like what Aristotle might call righteous indignation, an anger that fuels both reformist action and revolutionary consciousness.

Marilyn Frye has discussed the difficulties women face in having their anger recognized by men even as anger, much less as legitimate.[1] Here I am not so much concerned with the legitimation of such anger, though legitimation is psychologically vital in an individual's development of a sense of self and movement toward feminism. I am more concerned with the ways feminist ethics can support and encourage such anger and help develop a critical consciousness and a determination to work diligently and effectively to overcome systems of oppression wherever they are found.

In this chapter, I examine violence and the way "the feminine" is related to it. From a recognition of violence as endemic to the social systems with which we are familiar, I conclude that fundamental change is required and that the reformist as well as the revolutionary must sometimes engage in violence—when acts of violence are seen as the only ways to resist the violence of others and to move beyond oppressive situations. At the same time, I share Sartre's concern that such active violence be kept limited and seen as unjustifiable, lest violence be endorsed as an acceptable means and thus corrupt and undermine our goal of a society in which individuals would not be violated and

used merely as a way to achieve the ends of others. This means that
we must walk a fine line between refusing to engage in any violence—
even in certain situations where there is no way to avoid at least complicity
in the violence of others—and endorsing violence as a morally justifiable means when it would be efficacious. To make that point, Sartre
speaks enigmatically and, for many, no doubt, in a seemingly self-
contradictory manner by affirming that though violence is sometimes
"necessary" it is never "justifiable." What he means, however, can be
unpacked and related to similar pronouncements and underlying concerns in others.

VIOLENCE—WHAT AND WHY

Feminists long have realized how central violence is to traditional
theories of society. There may, however, be less clarity and certainly
less agreement concerning exactly what is encompassed by the term.

Generally, violence seems to be conceived in terms of a continuum
of power relations involving some sort of coercion. Violence is placed
at one end of the spectrum, the end depicting an extraordinary degree
of coercion. The remainder of the continuum—the nonextraordinary
degrees of coercion—is then thought to refer to acceptable behavior.
This is particularly true in a society that too easily interprets "the ordinary"
as "the normal," and the latter as the way things should be.

Understanding violence as part of a continuum of coercive and for
the most part acceptable behavior has a disastrous effect on any effort
to challenge violence. On the one hand, it places challengers in the
uncomfortable casuistic position of drawing lines to determine at precisely what point coercion becomes too much and therefore wrong. On
the other hand, it allows upholders of the status quo to profess bemusement about so much fuss being made over what will be in many cases
only a slight increase in the degree of coercion. Challengers of the
status quo are hard pressed to criticize and to find anything amiss with
the remainder of the actions on the continuum, or at least with all but
the most brutal; and defenders, seeing these other actions passed over
as permissible, feel justified in not being morally outraged over actions differing only in degree from the permissible.

As a result, Catharine MacKinnon's and Adrienne Rich's questioning whether any important qualitative differences exist between sexual
harassment, rape, and ordinary heterosexual intercourse can either be
dismissed as "radical" or incorporated as a rationalization of actions,

much in the manner of the rapist quoted by MacKinnon as claiming "he hadn't used 'any more force than is usual for males during the preliminaries.'"[2] Similarly, Frye's analysis of and objection to the control men exert over women through arrogance is likely to be rejected as unfairly castigating most male/female relationships or used to buttress the pity or contempt, often felt, she proposes, for men who, not sufficiently adept at gaining control through arrogance, resort to beating women.[3]

Though it will include a great many actions not normally so characterized, a more adequate understanding of violence focuses on the coercion at the heart of all the actions in the continuum of coercive behavior. Violence must be seen as the coercion itself, the control exerted by someone over the will, intellect, or limbs of another. Such control is itself a violation of the other's freedom, whether the control is physical force or a more subtle limiting of the possibilities confronting the other. As Paulo Freire says, "Any situation in which some men prevent others from engaging in the process of inquiry is one of violence." Such prevention treats the latter as objects by alienating them "from their own decision-making."[4]

One of the greatest difficulties facing such an understanding of violence is the way social and political theorists, through the centuries, have incorporated the view that conflict is normal, natural, and indeed fundamental to human existence and, therefore, that control and domination are inevitable and necessary for the functioning of any society. As Sarah Hoagland observes, social contract theories typically have perceived men as "violent and aggressive as well as egoistic and solitary" but able to rise above this natural state by exercising a rational capacity, realizing "they could maximize their self-interest if they were to give up some of their natural rights, such as the right to pillage and plunder their neighbors, to a central authority which could regulate pillaging and plundering, thus creating order and 'cooperation.'" These theories have perpetuated what Hoagland calls the "masculine myth" that making choices requires having control over situations. Such theories also have disparaged caring for others as undermining an individual's moral agency.[5]

G. W. F. Hegel is an example of a thinker who presents conflict as inevitable for civilization. He sees the care and nurture required to bring an individual to the point of consciousness as operating purely at the level of nature. To reach self-consciousness, the level of awareness necessary for society and for "higher" developments of thought, individuals require recognition from others outside their families. This recognition is achieved only through struggle, one so serious that Hegel sees it as a "life-and-death struggle," even though ideally it does not end in death but in the subjugation of one to the other—the famous slave-and-master relationship.[6]

Hegel's master/slave dialectic is illuminating in a number of ways. First, it is important to note that what was desired by each of the parties in conflict was reciprocity, *mutual* recognition of one another. This is not, of course, what they achieve; consequently, what they achieve through conflict does not accomplish their purpose. Neither receives the recognition for which each fought so vigorously. The master *appears* closer to such recognition than the slave, but this appearance is deceptive. Even though the master is recognized by the slave, the slave's recognition of the master as master hardly counts, inasmuch as the master deigns to recognize the slave as little more than a thing, an almost inhuman consciousness. By definition, what the master wants cannot come from a slave,[7] so what results is a futility, similar to the futility Sartre later recognizes: what the master wants is simply impossible once the other is rendered a slave.

A second critical feature of this relationship based on conflict is that it is the slave who, according to Hegel, is able to secure the recognition originally sought, not by fighting with yet another consciousness, but by working on nature. The slave plants, cooks, makes things to meet the master's needs, and through this work comes to self-consciousness as the result of seeing himself[8] externalized, seeing the forms he imposes on things. Conflict must be surpassed since it is unsuccessful; and labor is what ultimately accomplishes for the slave the result for which both slave and master were striving. The conflict may represent a stage, even a necessary one, in human development, but it certainly is not consistent with Hegel's portrayal of this stage to see it as any more than a temporary step in the development. The most it achieves positively seems to be the slave's confrontation with his own death, an awareness of his own mortality, thought by Hegel to be necessary if the slave is to move beyond unfulfilling servitude to the recognition of himself in his work.

The necessity of such conflict, even as a transitional stage, has been challenged by Sartre. In *Notebooks for an Ethics*, Sartre objects that the inessentiality of the slave does not constitute for the master quite the dialectical problem Hegel thought it did. Hegel's analysis presumes the master is alone with the slave, whereas in fact they are not alone. In the company of other masters, the master is recognized, Sartre suggests, in a way that compensates for the failure of recognition by the slave.[9]

While Hegel's master and slave presumably preexist societies and their institutionalization of slavery, Sartre's objection bears important resemblances to a feminist response to Hegel based on acknowledging the love, nurture, and conflict previously experienced by his hypothetical individuals. Although Hegel is postulating individuals in a time before societies, both Sartre and feminists challenge the assumption of such a presocial time or family out of which individuals can arise and begin their "ascent" toward self-consciousness. To question this assumption is to question whether conflict and domination are, after all, essential to the development of consciousness. Clearly, if the master achieves the recognition he sought from other masters or from a doting family member, then he achieves this recognition without domination and even without conflict of the sort singled out by Hegel.

A different way in which theorists and the rest of us are apt to think of conflict, violence, and dominance as necessary features of society is in terms of a criminal justice system. Hoagland indirectly questions this necessity by arguing that the community she and other lesbians are trying to create can do without punishment. In actually existing criminal justice systems, she observes, punishment is "not uniformly meted out"; as a recent case demonstrated, "being a rich, white, christian preppy male who murders a female he has sex with" greatly reduces the risk of punishment. In addition, she argues, even in an ideal criminal justice system, deterrence punishment is exploitative by virtue of selecting a person to be punished according to the anticipated effects on others. Finally, any punishment will be part of a system that preserves the social order and consequently leaves many crimes unnamed, "especially the crimes of those in power." In fact, she says: "a state can do exactly the same things as mean and nasty individuals; only when the state does them, they're called 'legal.' And the state has far greater capacity to do them."[10]

The main problem running through and underlying her objections is that "'Justice' is a concept that exists to sort out competing claims within a system that has as its axis dominance and subordination." Consequently, "if in our communities we continue to choose to flirt with ritual violence—in the form of punishment, in the form of controlling and humiliating another with or without her consent—then dominance and subordination will become part of lesbian meaning."[11] In her refusal to endorse a system officially preserving coercion and dominance, she rejects violence and agrees with Audre Lorde's observation that *"the master's tools will never dismantle the master's house."*[12]

WOMEN'S RELATIONS TO VIOLENCE

Apart from the role the feminine plays in masculinist ideology, women's relations to violence are likely to be important factors in maintaining the status quo. These relations include women's relations to war, their general lack of preparation for engaging in violence (either aggressively or self-protectively), their frequent exclusion from competitions and trainings for competitions, and their treatment by legal and moral systems both when violence is used against them and when they in turn use violence against their attackers.

In *Three Guineas*, Virginia Woolf describes what she sees as men's and women's different relationships to and views of war. Noting that "to fight has always been the man's habit, not the woman's," she lists the reasons males have fought: "war is a profession; a source of happiness and excitement; and it is also an outlet for manly qualities, without which men would deteriorate." Whether this difference between men and women is "innate or accidental," she says, "[l]aw and practice have developed that difference." Consequently, "[s]carcely a human being in the course of history has fallen to a woman's rifle; the vast majority of birds and beasts have been killed by you [men], not by us; it is difficult to judge what we do not share."[13]

Like Woolf, Nel Noddings notes how differently men and women relate to violence. Though courts often fail to acknowledge this difference, she finds it helpful in explaining why many women who kill their batterers receive prison sentences instead of being treated like others who kill in self-defense. For Noddings, the notion of a "fair fight," which underlies much of the legal system, represents a "distinctively masculine" attitude. Speaking for herself but no doubt also voicing an attitude shared by many women, Noddings writes: "I would not fight unless I absolutely had to. . . . But if I had to, the stakes would be so high that I could not possibly consider a 'fair fight.'"[14] While Noddings assumes that the response of women who kill their batterers is outside the parameters of "fairness," Rosemarie Tong questions this. She suggests, on the contrary, that judges and jurors do not take sufficiently seriously the actual deadliness of the force that many of these women confront; otherwise, their actions *would* fit within the legal recognition that "deadly force may be used to combat deadly force."[15] Perhaps Tong and Noddings both are right.

Noddings objects to the "wildly fantastic notion," reflected in the law and promulgated by simulation in competitive games, "that life can [and should] be conducted as a 'fair fight.'" Such games are not mere "harmless sublimation of aggressive instinct and even admirable training for competent performances of various kinds"; they may be shunned by women, not because of women's socialization, but because they tend to "see clearly the loss of playfulness in such games."[16]

Women who are neither raised on competitive games nor taught as children how to defend themselves from physical attack are thereby positioned in an important respect outside the law. In fact, for the most part, their nurture is radically opposed to a preparation for self-defense. First and foremost, many are simply not taught and are actively discouraged from learning on their own the necessary physical techniques. Furthermore, the games girls are taught and actively encouraged to play do not develop their muscles in ways even minimally conducive to self-protection; and "feminine" clothing and shoes often would not permit the requisite movements. As a result, women as a rule are no match for their male attackers. Even males who face odds as formidable as those confronting many battered women probably have difficulty remembering and following rules of "fair play" learned in their competitive childhood games.

Even if there are reasons many or most women would respond very differently from many or even most men in situations of violence, why would men, who have set up and for the most part enforced the law, have treated women and those crimes affecting only women (or defined so as to affect only women) so differently? In fact, some of the differences are rather peculiar and cry out for explanation. A disbanded comedy/singing group in Atlanta, Georgia, calling itself Sisters of No Mercy, a number of years ago did a routine in which the male "alleged" victim of a mugging was asked at the trial of the accused mugger questions similar to those a rape victim is asked at a trial of the accused rapist: "Why, knowing the dangers, were you out walking at night in such an area?" "Weren't you just flaunting your wealth by wearing an expensive suit?" and "Since you have given money away, how do we know you were not doing so again, but changed your mind?" While we find such questions ludicrous when asked of mugging victims, particularly males, we need to be much clearer why many in our society believe questions like these *should* be asked of rape victims.

Marilyn Frye observes that even the meaning of coercion changes drastically when it is applied to rape victims. In armed robbery, coercion is applied at some distance and the will of the victim is engaged: "Under her own steam, moving her own limbs, she removes her money from her pocket and hands it to you." She is coerced, not because anyone else controls her limbs, but rather because circumstances are manipulated so that, of the options available to her, giving the robber her money seems the most attractive or the least unattractive. In rape, coercion often is denied unless the victim is physically overcome and not in control of her limbs or of the positioning of her body. Thus, signs of struggle are sought in the rape case but not in the mugging. As Frye observes, "The curious thing about this interpretation of coercion is that it has the consequence that there is no such thing as a person being coerced into *doing* something."[17]

Actually, this is only *one* curious thing about the notion of coercion frequently applied to cases of rape. Another curious thing is its long history, going back, as Hoagland notes, to Aristotle's explanation of an action "done under constraint" ("to which the initiative or source of motion comes from without, and to which the person compelled contributes nothing"), and yet applied so selectively today.[18] Apart from its application in cases of rape, this very limited notion of coercion seems not to play much of a role, at least officially, in our legal system; even contracts signed under duress or fraud are considered null and void. Yet unofficially it plays an important and unacknowledged role as a fallback position for what counts as coercion and duress in various situations beyond the experience of those who make and administer laws. Thus, for example, this limited concept of coercion operates as a way to discount claims that individuals are exploited and oppressed: ignoring the coercive aspects of the situations in which these individuals are operating (the way real alternatives are limited or nonexistent), the discounters stress the fact that no one was forced to take the particular jobs, to accept the low pay, to live in the substandard housing, or to pay the higher costs for necessities.

By not clearly distinguishing itself from the widely used and more acceptable understanding of coercion, this limited notion, selectively used, effectively obscures certain ways the freedom of some can be curtailed and circumscribed by others, particularly in situations where power differences exist and have been institutionalized. In other words, the use of this limited notion of coercion obscures the fact that the oppressed are already victims of coercion in the broader sense, as the result of the way others have manipulated circumstances and thereby the options of the oppressed. As Hoagland correctly observes, such a limited understanding of coercion is simply not appropriate in conditions of oppression.[19]

Frye takes Sartre as well as the judicial system to task for presuming that if the raped woman moved at all as the result of her own choice then she is not innocent but complicit. While it is true that Sartre calls attention to the freedom exercised even by one who is coerced, he does not thereby make the victim responsible for her own rape. For Sartre, to the extent a coerced individual has and makes choices, those choices are hers and ones for which she bears responsibility. Thus, she is responsible for making a particular choice if there were *other* choices she could have made but did not. She is responsible, however, *only* for that over which she has control. She is not responsible for the range of choices available to her precisely because this has been chosen for her by someone else. Just because she is not responsible for those ways she is forced and otherwise coerced, her exercise of her own freedom within parameters established by others by no means frees rapists or other coercers from responsibility for their manipulative and violent actions; nor does this mean their actions are not to be seen as rape or whatever other kind of coercion they may be.

One way to explain how differently crimes like rape and mugging are treated is by pointing to our legal heritage. Maimonides, codifying Jewish law in the twelfth century, discusses rape as a crime of one man against another. Consequently, the penalty for rape will depend upon the status of both the rapist and the "girl's" father, her beauty, whether she has had "intercourse" before, and the age and bodily "structure" of both the violated and the violator. The penalties for rape and seduction are discussed in a section of Maimonides' *Book of Women* entitled "Virgin Maiden." Even the location of this discussion is revealing inasmuch as the compensation for the "blemish" inflicted on the "girl" is not required if she is not a virgin, there apparently being no additional "blemish" in such cases. Moreover, Maimonides indicates there will be no penalties if no man is injured by her treatment: if she "wants to be divorced, or is widowed, she has no claim to anything whatsoever."[20]

A view of daughters and married women as property had roots not only in Jewish law but also in Christian thought and no doubt informed early formulations of rape laws in the United States. If rape was considered primarily a crime of property, this would explain why rape laws were formulated so only girls and women could be raped. After all, rape would be a crime against a man's property; and another law would be needed to deal with the superficially similar but obviously radically different sexual crime against his person.

The view of rape as a crime of property may help to explain some aspects of the ways rape is conceived socially and treated legally. Even fairly recent discussions of rape in the women's movement have had great difficulty confronting and undermining the stereotype of rape as a crime committed by a male of a lower socioeconomic class against a female of a higher. Though not at all related to the actual realities of rape in the United States, the paradigm of rape has all too frequently involved a black male and a white female, with class aspects as well as racial ones entering the picture in subtle but important ways. By implicitly appealing to class, the paradigm suggests and no doubt furthers the continued assimilation of rape to property crimes in general, obscures the fact that most rapes are committed by males of the victims' own race and class, and even undermines the claim that the latter should be conceived as rapes. Thus, one would expect the laws on rape and the standard of evidence required by them to reflect aspects of this paradigm.

While this legacy helps to explain rape legislation in the United States, it does not go far enough in enabling us to understand why rape laws look and function as they do even at the end of the twentieth century. After all, legal theory and practice have undergone numerous reforms. Women (even wives[21]) have been clearly recognized as having rights, and sexist or gender-specific laws and legal procedures have been reworked in most states to give at least the appearance of gender-neutrality. Yet rape laws and court procedures seem to have been significantly resistant to change. Rape laws remain gender-specific in many states; marital exclusion is still included in many of those laws; and victims' sexual histories continue to make their way into rape trials. Moreover, evidence of struggle is still sought in these trials in spite of advice not to resist constantly being given to girls and women by police and others in authority.

What makes rape laws and procedures particularly resistant to a more enlightened point of view? Some of this recalcitrance might be explained by examining the way Western thinkers question women's inherent truthfulness. For example, according to Friedrich Nietzsche, because of women's constitution, "all truth (in relation to men, love, children, society, aim of life) disgusts them."[22] José Ortega traces this alleged untruthfulness (as well as women's "confusion") to their desire to keep their inner lives secret.[23] Arthur Schopenhauer believes that "dissimulation is innate in woman" and even argues that since they tell so many lies their evidence in court should carry proportionately less weight. He traces this untruthfulness not just to the weakness of their powers of reasoning and deliberation, but also to the general weakness of their position in society vis-à-vis men.[24] Maimonides, too, raises doubt about the veracity of women by not regarding them as "qualified" witnesses. One qualified witness, he concludes, is sufficient to counterbalance the opposing testimony of several women.[25]

If women were inherently untruthful, it at least would make some sense, in rape allegations, to take the man's word over the woman's as long as there are no other witnesses and as long as there are no visible signs of struggle. Such a presumption might explain the frequency with which rape is defined so it can happen only to females and thus can be treated legally quite differently from similar violations of men, such as aggravated sodomy.[26]

Although Maimonides may help us understand some of the reluctance to accept the word of a woman who claims to have been raped, more is at stake here. After all, the reluctance to fault the man is present even when there is considerable evidence of struggle. In fact, the reluctance persists even when there is no question of believing the woman's account of what transpired in preference to the man's story. For example, when the woman or girl is dead, her mute testimony that she was violated is still frequently ignored and preference given to the male's or males' account of how violent (but, of course, "consensual") sex "got out of hand" or how they believed she was consenting even though she had passed out and was choking on her own vomit while the various acts of "intercourse" were going on.

Alison Jaggar's account of the situation explains this tendency to side with the accused male by pointing to the normalization and consequent legitimation of rape by patriarchal ideology's definition of women as sexual objects. She says: "Because patriarchal culture defines women as sexually passive or receptive, it is thought reasonable to interpret a woman's uninterested behavior as expressive of sexual interest. Sometimes even outright refusal is interpreted as assent."[27]. Another factor explaining this problem and its legal treatment is the way this ideology presents, as fact, the myth that men have an almost overwhelming drive toward heterosexual intercourse.

When the culture normalizes rape, it is women and girls rather than men and boys who are seen to be at fault in cases of alleged rape. This means, given the "known" sexual propensities of the male, females who do not desire "intercourse" simply should not place themselves in situations where it can happen to them. Of course, this ignores the fact that situations allegedly inviting rape cover virtually all situations in which individuals find themselves. With definitions of women and myths about men, society relocates responsibility from the violator to the victim.

But why would a culture normalize rape? Marilyn Frye connects the coercion involved in rape with the coercive influence of the arrogant eye. The arrogant male eye expects women to conform to its expectations and either disregards any incongruities or regards the woman who does not meet the expectations as somehow having something "wrong" with her. This arrogant eye places women, particularly younger women, in binds where neither sexual activity nor sexual inactivity is acceptable: in the one case she is loose and in the other she is frigid;

in the one case, if she is raped, she wanted it and in the other she needed it, and in neither case therefore could she have been *raped*.[28] If the arrogant male eye is typically manipulative of the woman's options and thereby coercive, those who make laws *and* participate in this arrogance would themselves clearly be in a bind if they tried to make male coercion of women illegal. Probably it would not occur to them to do so, so great and so hidden is the arrogant eye's power to create "reality."

Frye suggests, too, that even though relatively little is done concerning crimes against women, such as rape and battering, other men may have contempt for those who rape and batter. Although such men, particularly batterers, are generally said to suffer from "low self-esteem," Frye sees the real "problem" of such men as "a lack of arrogance." Thus, "as men they 'know' they are supposed to be centers of universes, so they are reduced to trying to create by force what more successful men, men who can carry off masculinity better, create by arrogant perception."[29]

Like Frye, Catharine MacKinnon analyzes the coerciveness of rape, sees the arrogant manipulation generally involved in sexual intercourse in a heterosexist society, and concludes that heterosexual intercourse in such a society is akin to rape. She objects to Susan Brownmiller's unexamined distinction between rape as violence and intercourse as sexuality, noting, "Never is it asked whether, under conditions of male supremacy, the notion of 'consent' has any meaning."[30] Similarly, bell hooks sees men as operating too much under notions of masculinity "that equate manhood with ability to exert power over others, especially through the use of coercive force" and observes that both women and men are socialized to equate violence with love.[31]

In fact, the presumption that heterosexual intercourse is domination is so pervasive the equation operates, probably without awareness, even in allegedly scientific discourse. Remember Sarah Hoagland's observation of how easily E. O. Wilson's supposedly descriptive account of male/female sex among selected nonhuman animals slips from calling the female's posture "receptive" to calling it "submissive" and thus definitionally equates heterosexual intercourse with domination of the female. Finding this presumptive linkage between the female and subordination in the dominant culture's stereotype of femininity, Hoagland notes how the stereotype rules out anything that could *count* as resistance to male domination and, moreover, how it serves to characterize all groups "requiring" domination. Thus, what might otherwise be seen as sabotage by slaves will be perceived as "clumsy," "childlike," or "foolish," and acts of resistance by Jews to Nazis will be either simply not "seen" or else characterized as examples of compliance (e.g., hurling themselves against electrified fences). Similarly, she claims, in our society, women who kill their batterers after years of constant abuse are advised by lawyers to plead insanity and are more often convicted when they plead self-defense: "As a result, the judicial system promotes the idea that a woman who effectively resists aggressive acts of male domination is insane. Insanity, thus, becomes part of women's nature, and resistance to domination becomes institutionally nonexistent."[32]

PROTECTION/DOMINATION

Frequently, unequal judicial and moral treatment of individuals (and groups) has been justified by the claim that they must be treated differently "for their own good." This justification presumably means either the treatment they then receive is better than they would otherwise merit or be able to secure on their own, or such treatment protects them from harms they would bring on themselves or elicit from others. The claim that the unequal treatment protects and is in the best interests of the protected deserves examination, particularly when the parties involved are adults and all as nearly sane as a society permits.

A good place to begin this examination is with gallantry, a special treatment of women, at least some women, long encouraged by our society. Gallantry often is cited as a benefit to women and as a civilizing influence on the whole society, thus something we should certainly hesitate to destroy or even seriously to threaten. Any costs of this "benefit" are never mentioned. Inasmuch as most benefits loudly touted by society come at some or even considerable cost to the recipients, we would do well to begin our examination here.

Gallantry is an unmerited tribute paid, as David Hume recognizes, by a superior to an inferior. According to Hume, the male finds himself in a position analogous to that of the host among his guests: the male is physically and mentally superior to the female and, in a civilized society, he, like the host, generously "alleviates" that superiority and consequent authority "by a studied deference and complaisance for all her inclinations and opinions." In barbarous nations, Hume adds, this authority is displayed by making women abject slaves or by beating, selling, and killing them.[33]

There is in gallantry, then, something tantamount to irony since the inferiority is feigned; however, not just any feigned inferiority will do. The gallant feigns inferiority in order to bring himself down to or below the level of the person toward whom his behavior is directed. It must be presumed he is in fact superior to her.

While some, like Mary Wollstonecraft and Soren Kierkegaard, see the insult in gallantry, given a presumption of superiority fairly likely to be false in any particular case,[34] others, like Hume, extol gallantry as vital to civilized society. Gallantry represents a generosity that softens the sting of the natural inferiority of women and their subjection to the authority of men. Kant, too, views gallantry as a tactful half-truth whereby, for example, a married man makes more palatable his rightful authority over his wife by manipulating appearances so she seems to have a voice in their affairs.[35] Similarly, George Santayana presents "gallantry of the mind" as a civilized sort of behavior in conversations with ladies, a behavior akin to the "natural courtesy toward children and mystics"—"a habit of respectful concession, marking as it does an intellectual alienation as profound as that which separates us from the dumb animals . . . , radically incompatible with friendship."[36]

But is gallantry a civilizing factor in human affairs? I think not. For it to be, certain conditions must—but, in fact, do not—hold. First, men must be inherently superior to women. If women's inferiority to men is the result of education and of institutions and mores depriving women of experiences and recognition vital to their development, then, rather than a civilizing factor, gallantry is part of a unjust system depriving half the human race of those things necessary for meaningful freedom.

This raises the whole nature/nurture controversy and the question Mill and Condorcet, among many others, ask: How do we know what women's capacities are when all we can observe is their behavior as shaped by education, rules, and regulations created by men? In addition, claims about women's inferiority arrogantly fail to acknowledge individual differences among men as well as among women. As Mill so aptly notes, there is hardly any human pursuit in which women have not achieved a ranking of second or third place, thereby showing themselves superior in the pursuit to many men.[37] Thus, this aspect of the claim that gallantry civilizes leaves the insult standing.

Second, the recognition of gallantry as a civilizing factor requires an acknowledgment of the right of the physically stronger and mentally superior to rule those who are physically and mentally weaker. The assumption that the allegedly superior have the right to rule the allegedly inferior has been challenged throughout the ages in terms of men ruling other men. As Wollstonecraft says, "The *divine right* of husbands, like the divine right of kings, may, it is hoped, in this enlightened age, be contested without danger."[38] Her analogy is not overstated, given its historical use in support of legal recognition of lesser rights for women. Rosemarie Tong cites Blackstone's discussion of English common law "which not only permitted husbands to beat their wayward wives, but instructed wives to 'kiss the rod that beat them.'" She notes the "sharp contrast" in the way this law dealt with husband killing, likening it to murdering the king and, consequently, striking "at the root of all government."[39]

In his review of Horace Bushnell's *Women's Suffrage* and Mill's *The Subjection of Women*, William James challenges one understanding of gallantry's civilizing effect on society. Quoting Bushnell's effusive praise of a commonplace act of gallantry, James characterizes Bushnell's underlying assumption: "that our yielding to women in small matters demands as *quid pro quo* on their part that they refrain from crossing our path in larger affairs; and that if they become our rivals in these latter, we shall no longer scruple to push them to the wall wherever we find them."[40] James thus calls attention to Bushnell's own recognition of *the lack of generosity* in the gallantry he praises so profusely *for its generosity*.

While recognizing the lack of generosity in Bushnell's *quid pro quo* analysis of gallantry, James goes on to object that men are not likely to push women "to the wall wherever we find them." What will prevent such treatment, he thinks, is "the mere animal potency of sex": "An individual man, however his interests may clash with those of an individual woman, will always shrink from appearing personally like a brute in her presence."[41]

This response is false, given what we know of the violence women suffer at the hands of men—most frequently of men who profess to love the women they abuse. What makes his response interesting, though, is the readiness to grant Bushnell's assumption that men respond to each other (their equals and therefore their rivals) by pushing them "to the wall wherever we find them." Among men there seems to be only competition, with no place for manners, generosity, or ethics. If so, Bushnell's concern for gallantry as introducing some civility into human affairs certainly can be appreciated, although the civility of gallantry simply removes women from this harsh treatment by removing them from any competition with men. Here James's only response is to express hope based on "the mere animal potency of sex" for women's survival in this bleak, competitive world where might prevails. Other civilizing factors—like education—that might affect even men's relations with each other are not mentioned, an interesting omission for one who spent such a large portion of his life connected with educational institutions.

Although gallantry is arrogant and insulting in its assumption of men's superiority to women, what about those cases where the individual woman is not equal or superior in rank or ability to the gallant man? Should not such a woman acknowledge gratefully the generosity of the man's behavior? Since nothing seems particularly insulting in the behavior of Hume's hypothetical host toward his guests, why should what Hume considers parallel behavior of a man toward a woman be insulting or problematic?

First, a caveat about such cases is in order. Gallantry has always been selective in terms of its recipients. Anna Garlin Spencer, a late nineteenth- and early twentieth-century thinker, says, "The much vaunted 'chivalry of men,' the proudly assumed 'reverence for womanhood' paraded in public addresses on the glory and moral excellence of our present civilization, do not work far down in the social scale."[42] As she and many others[43] acknowledge, slave and working women have been subjected to some of the hardest and most health-destroying conditions and have received the least compensation for their work, even though, as Sojourner Truth eloquently proclaims, they, too, are women. Recognizing the black women's treatment both by white men and women and by black men, one of Zora Neale Hurston's characters describes the black woman as the "mule" of the world.[44] A bit of respect and deference could have improved the lot of such women considerably.

Gallantry's double standard belies the gallant's claim that women, solely by virtue of their gender, are frail and in need of respect and special treatment. The gallant's position is thus inconsistent and self-serving, tailored as it is to his own male interests when, for example, he pursues a woman, and easily retailored to his profit interests when he wishes to take advantage of female labor. Even the law's much-vaunted "protections" of women have been, as Catharine MacKinnon says, "condescending *and* unreal, in effect strengthening the protector's choice to violate the protected at will, whether the protector is the individual perpetrator or the state."[45]

Though many of the women most in need of respect and deference never receive any, still there are cases where the gallant is objectively superior to the individual he favors with his behavior. Even in such cases the insult of gallantry persists. To the extent the gallant praises qualities he would find despicable (or at best worthy of indifference) in himself or in men who are his equals, he is engaging in a duplicity that degrades rather than flatters.

Moreover, to the extent the gallant treats the woman with respect just because she is a woman, the act implicitly generalizes. To be regarded as exemplifying "woman" may be momentarily uplifting for her, until, that is, she realizes that her inferiority to the man is thereby attached to "woman," thus enabling him to assert his superiority to all women.

This easy sense of superiority on his part should enrage her. Gallantry is a game he can play to gain a sense of superiority, but not one she can play with the same result should she encounter a man inferior to herself.

The man who becomes angry when a woman rebuffs his gallant behavior or otherwise refuses to play his game probably sees his behavior as containing, if not an insult, at least the presumption of his superiority to the recipient of his "generosity." He wants her to accept gratefully because he wants her affirmation of his superiority. By refusing to play the game, she not only refuses to affirm his superiority but also makes him look foolish: as though it was important to him to open the door or as though he actually values the characteristics he was praising. By refusing to play his game—a game in which she is set up from the outset as the loser—she asserts equality, thereby becoming, in his eyes, his rival. Just as Bushnell fears, he is ready to push her "to the wall."

Sarah Hoagland sees in the special protection exemplified in behavior like gallantry the promotion of an image of women as helpless. In fact, to be protected, a women must dress and act in ways that not only fit this image but also render her less able to protect herself. Moreover, she must act as men say she should. Finally, for women to be protected, they must be depicted as prey—which requires that there be predators. Consequently, Hoagland sees it as a "mere matter of logic that men will depict women as evil and step up overt physical violence against them in order to reaffirm women's victim status." Thus, she says: "Heterosexualism is a way of living . . . that normalizes the dominance of one person in a relationship and the subordination of another. As a result, it undermines female agency."[46] Her analysis is essentially the same as MacKinnon's: "male supremacy is a protection racket."[47]

Some feminists have questioned whether similar arguments hold against the protections and privileges accorded to children in contemporary Western society. For example, Alison Jaggar suggests that the limitations imposed on and the alleged compensations offered to young people should be carefully examined to see if "those privileges are as illusory as the false respect accorded to women in sexist society." She proposes: "[This examination] needs to consider how far the helplessness of children, like that of women, is socially imposed. Just as oppression creates females who are 'feminine' (whining, irresponsible and competitive with other women), so it may be that oppression creates young people who are 'childish' (whining, irresponsible and competitive with their siblings)."[48]

VIOLENCE PROTECTED BY "PRIVACY"

Inasmuch as battering, rape, and child abuse, both sexual and non-sexual, are perpetrated by men in the vast majority of known cases, their treatment by the judicial system might be the result simply of unacceptable sexism, patriarchal attitudes, and male arrogance. Other explanations have been offered, though, including a rather Kantian concern for the intention of the perpetrator and the possibility that maintaining such a double standard in the law was deemed necessary to protect the "sanctity" of family and home.

In the name of fairness, judges and jurors might look at a perpetrator's intention, worrying about the injustice of punishing one who thought he was doing the right thing or, in the case of rape, really believed his victim was consenting. For the same reason, the abuser's love of his victims may be taken more seriously than the actual harm he inflicted. MacKinnon notes the way similar emphases on intention in rape laws and their enforcement jeopardize women, given that "men are systematically conditioned not even to notice what women want." She asks, "From whose standpoint, and in whose interest, is a law that allows one person's conditioned unconsciousness to contraindicate another's experienced violation?"[49]

A utilitarian, on the other hand, might try to argue that the double standard is necessary to protect the intimacy and privacy of family and home. Utilitarians are likely to agree with Mill that the greatest good will be achieved only if human beings are allowed as much self-determination as possible. Thus, they will argue for minimal governmental interference in the so-called private affairs of citizens. Instead of prohibiting interference in cases where individuals' behavior affects only themselves or other consenting adults, though, too often they draw a curtain over family and home, a curtain to be lifted only in cases of particularly egregious abuse and perhaps not even then. Too often this curtain protects virtually all that goes on beyond closed doors: *assent is presumed given because the activity occurred or normally occurs behind closed doors*. This means that individuals who are harmed by strangers and who are harmed in the so-called public sphere will be treated quite differently than those (mainly women and children) who are harmed in the home and by individuals with whom they are related or familiar. It even means that those who are harmed in ways deemed appropriate only to intimate relationships will be treated quite differently than individuals harmed in other ways.

Other utilitarian reasons have been offered for protecting the privacy and intimacy of family and home and thus distinguishing and treating so differently "public" and "private" harms. One line of reasoning has to do with the concern that efforts to prevent harm may only create additional harm. The argument goes something like this. If an individual (male) is not coping well with the competitive and demanding environment of the workplace, surely society adds one more layer of stress for him if it gives members of his own family rights against him, such as the right not to be abused. Moreover, if the law becomes involved in "protecting" those members from him, those very individuals are likely to suffer additional serious harm if the family is broken up and loses its chief means of financial support. Instead of examining ways protection could avoid such harm, this argument leaves the abused to fend for themselves and extends its primary solicitude to the abusers, who, we are told, frequently were abused when they were young.

A rather different but still utilitarian argument justifies denying men and women the same rights, particularly in the family, arguing that this denial helps to secure a stable social order. As David L. Kirp, Mark G. Yudof, and Marlene Strong Franks more recently propose: "By denying an independent legal status to the married woman, this paternalism was meant to minimize family strife; in that sense, the law helped to secure a stable social order."[50]

William James affirms something like this when he challenges the equality of men and women for which Mill argues. James objects that the "representative American" dreams of home as a haven, a place of refuge from the struggle, the failure and humiliation, of the "outer world": a "tranquil spot where he shall be valid absolutely and once for all; where, having been accepted, he is secure from further criticism, and where his good aspirations may be respected no less than if they were accomplished realities." But, James cautions, the security and repose essential to his ideal are not easily attainable "without some feeling of dependence on the woman's side—without her relying on him to be her mediator with the external world—without his activity overlapping hers and surrounding it on almost every side, so that he makes as it were the atmosphere in which she lives."[51] The requisite dependence would seem to entail minimal or no recognition of rights she could exercise against him.

While this argument supports legal respect for the privacy and sanctity of the home and family, it is deeply flawed. After all, what is James's argument but an expression of the arrogance of which Marilyn Frye speaks? How else are we to understand his confusing of the "representative American," whose desires James voices, with the male? How else can we understand the way James so unabashedly either ignores the desires of women or subsumes them under the desires of men? What else can we make of his inability to recognize that what he says cannot even apply to many men who not only cannot afford such dependent wives but also have neither the time, energy, nor money to mediate between the world and wives whom they shelter in artificial cocoons? How else could he be so smugly satisfied with the status quo that he, unlike Virginia Woolf, would not even raise a question about whether "the public and the private worlds are inseparably connected; that the tyrannies and servilities of the one are the tyrannies and servilities of the other"?[52]

We are left to conclude that men's, not women's, privacy is protected by the legal system and by the public/private distinction itself. MacKinnon observes, in fact, that women are not allowed privacy under male domination: "The very place (home, body), relations (sexual), activities (intercourse and reproduction), and feelings (intimacy, selfhood) that feminism finds central to women's subjection form the core of privacy doctrine. But when women are segregated in private, one at a time, a law of privacy will tend to protect the right of men 'to be let alone,' to oppress us one at a time."[53] This is in part, she believes, because the private is conceived as the realm of choice where "consent tends to be presumed." Although such a presumption is voided by coercion, it is nevertheless quite difficult for anything supposedly private to count as coercion. This conception of the private thus gives their urgency to questions like "Why would one allow force in private[?]—the 'why doesn't she leave[?]' question asked of battered women."[54]

This understanding of the private may lead theorists to misrepresent and misunderstand what happens both "in public" and "in private." For example, in their book *Gender Justice*, Kirp et. al., present the private as a sphere of "sexual intimacy, procreation, and childrearing, informed by affection, trust, privacy, and responsibility." Not surprisingly, they then are unable to find anything "inherently oppressive" in the condition of the "American" housewife, certainly "nothing akin to such unambiguously imposed forms of association as slavery and apartheid."[55] They seem unaware of the fact that they are accepting at face value the *social meaning* of the one while looking critically at the *reality* of the other. If they were to consider only the social meanings of slavery and apartheid (as constructed by the societies institutionalizing these), they probably would not find much "inherently oppressive" about these institutions either. We know, *contra* the social rationale of what was going on, that slaves were indeed human beings and that they were held against their wills, raped, beaten, tortured, and killed under slavery, just as we know that women today are human beings, often held against their wills, raped, beaten, tortured, and killed by their husbands, lovers, fathers, brothers, and male "friends."

When Kirp et al. turn to the public "realm," they carry with them the optimistic social meaning of the private. Thus, they quickly rule out the hypothesis that men are "homosocial," "interested in working with other men, not women," and "have created segregated working conditions in order to associate with one another." Proclaiming this to be a "couple-oriented" society and citing the fact that hiring women would be in the self-interest of employers given the prevailing wage differential between men and women, they conclude: "Arguments based on employer's prejudices against women strain credulity." Though they acknowledge early in their book that a household with a sexist or racist bent may give a similar bent to the society,[56] they later seem unable to comprehend that the sexist hierarchy perpetuated in the home might explain the couples orientation of our society, the prevailing wage differential, *and* the homosocial nature of the distribution of power in the workplace and in politics. The resulting, somewhat confusing social order may indeed "strain credulity" for individuals who reject ambiguity and who expect rationality and particularly consistency in the realm of human affairs; but feminists must acknowledge the ambiguous and seemingly inconsistent situation so succinctly described by Letty Cottin Pogrebin: "That although we are a relentlessly *heterosexual* society, our nonromantic interactions are overwhelmingly '*homosocial*.'"[57]

Agreeing that the very way "woman" is conceived precludes privacy, Andrea Dworkin interprets the "privacy" of intimate relations a bit differently. For her, women are understood in terms of their sexuality, a sexuality perceived as a hole, a hole making a woman accessible to men: "a hole between her legs that men can, must, do enter"; this entry opens her up, splits her down the center, and occupies her "physically, internally, in her privacy." Unlike the hole men also have—the anus, which also can be entered—"[t]his hole, her hole, is synonymous with entry." This, in turn, supports the ideology that "men fuck women because the women attract, are sensual, are pretty, have some dimension of beauty or grace, however lowdown or elegant, that brings on desire," thus ignoring, as Dworkin observes, all the "ravaged junkie-prostitutes on our contemporary streets" and "toothless bawds of history who got fucked more than the elegant ladies by all accounts." It also protects men's boundaries and dominance by limiting male penetration to the hole only a woman has, it being regarded as an abomination, according to sodomy laws, to "fuck men as if they were women."[58]

For Dworkin, this conceptualizing of woman means a woman "is, in fact, human by a standard that precludes physical privacy, since to keep a man out altogether and for a lifetime is deviant in the extreme, a psychopathology, a repudiation of the way in which she is expected to manifest her humanity." This preclusion of privacy helps Dworkin understand why "*[v]iolation* is a synonym for intercourse," explaining the "deep recognition in culture and in experience that intercourse is both the normal use of a woman, her human potentiality affirmed by it, and a violative abuse, her privacy irredeemably compromised, her selfhood changed in a way that is irrevocable, unrecoverable."[59]

In addition, Dworkin agrees with Catharine MacKinnon that sexual privacy functions as a shield for men. It means, Dworkin says, "a man has a right to shield himself when sexually using civil inferiors." Since laws have actually required sexual compliance from women (for example, the marital exemption in the rape laws of many states), she concludes, "Any act so controlled by the state, proscribed and prescribed in detail, cannot be private in the ordinary sense."[60]

While the private is thus not in actuality outside the purview of or even very different from—and certainly not opposed to—the public, the distinction itself is likely to obscure the similarities and exaggerate the differences, as Nancy Fraser suggests.[61] Of course, such obfuscation may be an essential rather than accidental feature of the distinction and may serve theoretical as well as practical interests. For example, Andrea Nye argues, the public/private distinction is vital if democratic theory is to sustain the illusion that society is made up of competing individuals: noncompeting individuals whose existence would otherwise challenge the theory can be in effect hidden in the privacy of the family and represented in society by the male head of the household. Moreover, since the family is necessary for the functioning of democratic society, the latter cannot recognize any rights the exercise of which would deflect women from marriage and motherhood.[62]

As Iris Young indicates, such ideological use of the public/private distinction may be consequent upon "defining privacy as what the public excludes." She urges feminists to preserve the public/private distinction but with a new understanding of privacy as "that aspect of his or her life and activity that any individual has a right to exclude others from." No longer would any social institutions or practices be excluded a priori from public discussion and expression. Moreover, such a revised notion of privacy places the onus for any such exclusion on individuals and thereby acknowledges the following principle: "no persons, actions or aspects of a person's life should be forced into privacy."[63] Patricia Collins suggests that African-Americans communally constructed a recognition of privacy much along the lines advocated by Young: during slavery, for example, "[t]he line separating the Black community from whites served as a more accurate boundary delineating public and private spheres for African-Americans than that separating Black households from the surrounding Black community."[64]

THE NECESSITY OF REVOLUTION

As we saw in Chapter 1, individuals' attempts to transform themselves and their relationships are problematic. As bell hooks points out, "[t]he ethics of Western society informed by imperialism and capitalism are personal rather than social." She warns: "This particular form of cultural imperialism has been reproduced in feminist movement in the form of individual women equating the fact that their lives have been changed in a meaningful way by feminism 'as is' with a policy of no change need occur in the theory and praxis even if it has little or no impact on society as a whole, or on masses of women."[65] Sartre, too, rejects individual solutions. Though individuals may try to love one another and to treat each other with respect, as ends, they can never escape the reach of the oppressive structures of the society surrounding them.

Sartre illustrates the impossibility of individual solutions in his play *The Chips Are Down*. In the realm of the dead, a purely theatrical device for Sartre, two individuals discover their love for each other and feel such love should have had a chance to flourish while they were alive. When Eve Charlier and Pierre Dumaine are given the opportunity to return to the world of the living in order to try to love each other "with perfect coincidence and with all their . . . might," they find themselves divided by class and torn by other loves and loyalties. Although they love each other, their love is contaminated by gender and class oppressions they cannot escape.[66] They recognize the limiting features of class just after Pierre murmurs, "If I had only met you before." When Eve asks what he would have done, Pierre starts to answer, but "the words die on his lips." They watch an elegant, pretty young woman with a poodle on a leash step out of a chauffeured limousine. She passes a young workman who carries an iron pipe on his shoulder. As the two pass without even looking at each other, Pierre recognizes class differences separating and making them invisible to each other. To Eve he observes: "She is your kind, only not as good as you. And he is my kind . . . not as good as me, either."[67]

According to Sartre, oppressions and scarcity result in a "depth of darkness" in the individual, "things which refuse to be said . . . which resist being said to another."[68] This sounds like Kant when he says: "If all men were good there would be no need for any of us to be reserved; but since they are not, we have to keep the shutters closed."[69] Nevertheless, unlike Kant, Sartre affirms transparency as necessary "before true social harmony can be established": "A man's existence must be entirely visible to his neighbor, whose own existence must be entirely visible in turn."[70]

Some opacity, like some alienation, however, may be inevitable. Sartre suggests this when he says in *Search for a Method* that human beings "are always conditioned by others."[71] Moreover, Iris Young is no doubt correct that part of the difficulty with transparency to others is that if we do not understand ourselves with this kind of clarity, it is impossible to be clear to others. Even if opacity is inevitable, though, what is ultimately significant in our moral relationships with one another, for Sartre as well as for Hoagland, is visibility or intelligibility to one another, not justification (since there are no objective values to justify our choices and actions). While Sartre would no doubt agree with Young that the goal of transparency along with the goal of community can be sought in a way that denies freedom and obscures difference,[72] he proposes that these can be sought in another way—as regulative[73]—and is convinced individuals cannot be sufficiently intelligible to each other as long as they live in societies that engender starvation and that alienate human freedom through various types of oppression.

Revolution is necessary. Reform will not and cannot suffice. Reform, by definition, simply perpetuates the existing value structures. At best, it improves and thereby strengthens them by, as Fatima Mernissi says, offering "palliatives," and superficially "replastering" the system. This, she observes, requires resources that many countries cannot afford; thus, she concludes, "Muslim societies *cannot* afford to be reformist."[74] Neither, though, can other societies afford mere reform. If existing value structures are what we ultimately hope to change, our efforts at reform are singularly futile and even counterproductive. The very process of arguing for change is often self-defeating. For example, as Sarah Hoagland says: "[I]n addressing and defending women's rights, she [the arguer] is implicitly acknowledging that women's rights are debatable. She is, by that very act, affirming that there is a legitimate question concerning women's rights, even if she is quite clear about the answer she espouses. And she is agreeing that society has a 'right' to determine women's place."[75]

Acknowledging "society's" right to make such determinations is especially damning inasmuch as what needs to be challenged is precisely, as Marilyn Frye recognizes, the arrogance of those who see themselves as constituting the conceptual community and thus arrogate to themselves the prerogative of determining who is and who is not a person and who does and who does not have rights.[76] Since Hoagland's arguer cannot question men's rights or their competence to make such decisions "without appearing radical beyond reason," she is, by her own argument, "solidifying status quo values which make women's but not men's rights debatable in a democracy."[77]

As bell hooks and others have recognized, if we do not understand the ideology and structures of dominance, we are likely not to see how our behavior, however well intentioned, is prescribed by those structures and thereby perpetuates them.[78] Sartre's analyses of oppression and resistance are important contributions to the political analysis needed by those who seek to change society in fundamental ways.

WHY THE MAXIM OF VIOLENCE
SHOULD BE REJECTED

Oppression is a complex network of individual and institutional relations. It places resisters in an ambiguous position. Sartre's analysis of this ambiguity deserves an important place in a feminist ethics.

The situation of the oppressed varies greatly from one type of oppression to the next. As Simone de Beauvoir indicates, oppression may be so severe that those oppressed never become aware even minimally of themselves and their options and, as a result, can quite properly be said to have no freedom.[79] As Sartre himself became increasingly aware of oppressions, he, too, recognized the way the freedom of many is so seriously curtailed as to be little more than the freedom "to choose the sauce with which it will be eaten."[80] Sounding very like Sartre but writing considerably later, Frye describes this predicament as one in which "[o]ne can only choose to risk one's preferred form and rate of annihilation."[81]

As Sartre considers resistance to oppression, he wrestles with issues that continue to plague feminists, in particular, what means are permissible in pursuit of a goal and whether violence can ever be condoned. He notes that some means undermine the ends to be realized by them. His examples of this include lying and violence.

In analyzing lying as a revolutionary strategy, Sartre recognizes a serious danger of which too few practitioners of utilitarianism have been sufficiently cognizant: that some means "perpetuate oppression with the pretext of putting an end to it." The interconnectedness of means and end is clearly acknowledged when Sartre discusses the permissibility of lying in order to overthrow oppression: lying is not permissible in cases where "it helps to create a *lied-to* and *lying* mankind; for [those] who take power are no longer those who deserve to get hold of it; and the reasons one had for abolishing oppression are undermined by the way he [or she] goes about abolishing it."[82] It follows that some means must be rejected because they perpetuate, rather than help to end, oppression.

Adrienne Rich's discussion of the consequences of lying is similar;
however, unlike Sartre, she makes no claims about the general permissibility or impermissibility of lying. Rather, she questions, first, the
likely effect on the liar: is, for example, "a life 'in the closet'" likely
to "spread into private life, so that lying (described as *discretion*) becomes
an easy way to avoid conflict or complication. . . , a strategy so ingrained that it is used even with close friends and lovers?" Then she
turns to the effects on the one to whom the lie is directed, asking "Why
do we feel slightly crazy when we realize we have been lied to in a
relationship?" She answers:

> Because I love you, because there is not even a question of lying between
> us, I take [your] . . . accounts of the universe on trust. . . . I fling uncon-
> scious tendrils of belief. . . , across statements such as these, statements
> made so unequivocally, which have no tone or shadow of tentativeness.
> I build them into the mosaic of my world. I allow my universe to change
> in minute, significant ways, on the basis of things you have said to me,
> of my trust in you.[83]

Like lying, many instances of rebellion have undesired and undesirable consequences. Hoagland discusses some on these. For example,
rebellion against society, even when aimed at changing structures
recognizably in need of change, may simply reinforce those structures.
This is certainly true where the form of rebellion chosen "fits the
parameters of what counts as rebellion from the dominant perspective." Her caution leads to an important extension of Sartre's point.
Various activities, e.g., pregnancy and drug addiction, are delineated
within an oppressive system as acceptable forms of rebellion and are
tolerated inasmuch as they can be used as a "safety valve." They are
used to channel challenges to the system in ways fundamentally harmless to the system itself.[84] Certainly, much violence in our society is
of this sort.

More generally, though, since it contradicts that end, violence is to
be rejected as a means of establishing a society where each respects
and treats every other as an end and not merely as a means. "A means
contradicts an end," Sartre says, "when it allows one to attain this end
in appearance while it secretly ruins it in reality." Sartre illustrates
this with a case of rape, which, he says, "allows one to obtain the body
of a woman *once*, but if I want to be the real possessor of this body
for life or a long relationship, it ruins this possibility."[85]

This may seem to many an unfortunate example for Sartre to use in
what I think is his only real discussion of rape. For him, in this rare
treatment of such violence, to characterize a rape as possibly a mis-

guided attempt to capture the body of the woman "for life or a long relationship" may suggest that typically all rapes issue from such misguided—and, some would claim, misnamed—love. Sartre himself suggests no such thing, depicting this kind of rape as quite differently motivated than others; and he, too, criticizes the appropriative love motivating it.

Nevertheless, the example is illuminating. Surely there are instances of violence such as Sartre depicts, where, for example, the perpetrator acts at least partly out of a desire to "get" or "hold" a woman otherwise deemed unattainable or whom he is afraid of "losing." Sartre has shown in *Being and Nothingness* how problematic this kind of appropriative or possessive love is (and more will be said concerning this in the next chapter). Here, though, he argues that, whatever tenuous "holds" an individual can achieve over another's consciousness, the violence of rape is apt to undermine and destroy their continued possibility. While such violence may be the ultimate in control, it, like torture, either alienates the consciousness controlled or else, by forcing it to completely embody or objectify itself, turns it into something other than the consciousness over which control is sought.

A similar means/end problem renders problematic any utilitarian ethics. To will whatever means is necessary to achieve an end is *the maxim of violence*, where violence seems to be understood quite literally as violation, as treating the other merely as means. "A lie," for example, "places the other's freedom in parentheses."[86] Sartre challenges precisely this openness to any means necessary as insidious to the utopian goal of treating all human beings as ends in themselves. To put his point in a slightly different way, a way suggested by Hoagland, the maxim of violence fits very neatly into "patriarchal justification for exercising power in the sense of 'control' or 'power-over' or imposing one's will on others," a justification that "ranges all the way from the blatant 'might makes right' to the subtle ideology of 'protection' of the 'weak' and 'defenseless.'"[87] Exercising such power perpetuates and reinforces rather than undermines the structures of dominance.

The use of violence as a means is thus problematic in several ways. Ideologically, it supports the prevalent understanding and use of power. Moreover, by treating others in the way forces of oppression urge as necessary and warranted, those who fight for a better society make it more rather than less remote. Both they and the recipients of their violence are affected in negative ways by the violence and rendered less able to be the sorts of people who would and could live in a better world, a consequence noted by Bat-Ami Bar On in her discussion of terrorism. Agreeing with Conor Cruise O'Brien that "terrorism" is usually used, purely rhetorically, to designate "politically motivated violence *of which we disapprove*," Bar On proposes that terrorism is problematic because it is a coercive practice, using terror as "a means to an end other than itself," in which "a self is intentionally eroded and a will is intentionally broken." It is thus, she argues, not only a cruel practice but one that makes its practitioners cruel ("people who feel no compassion or kindness and are inhospitable") and its victims "fearful with diminished selves organized around the experience of the fear of the loss of their strength of will." She questions whether such people could enjoy the promised benefits.[88]

In fact, Sartre tells us in *Notebooks for an Ethics*, to use violence as a means involves self-deception, bad faith, since this is "Manichean," involving a belief "in an order of the world that is given yet concealed by bad wills," and since it pushes destructions while counting "on the richness of the world to support them and perpetually to provide new things to be destroyed." The connection between bad faith and violence goes even deeper, inasmuch as the lie, so central to the understanding of bad faith, always is made in the name of freedom, and "occurs as though one were saying: 'If you freely want to reach this end, you ought freely to choose the means to attain it, therefore you ought to be willing to be lied to if necessary [the maxim of violence].'"[89]

Consequently, Sartre proposes a different way of treating means and ends, a way, incidentally, that avoids defeatism in the event that the goal to be attained may be unachievable: the goal must be viewed, not as exterior and indifferent to the means, but rather as "the organic unity of the means." In other words, such a goal "is not the last link in the causal series A, B, C, D, E, F (which, in effect, would allow us to assert that the end is indifferent to the means), instead it is the organic totality of the operation." If the end is seen in the means and not as totally separate from them, each means will be a "prefiguration of the city of ends."[90] Instead of working to achieve some distant or even unactualizable utopia with whatever means are necessary, each and every means will be chosen because it partially embodies the ideal. Each means is thus in some sense an *achievement* of the ideal; the dangerous and destructive conflict of means with end is thereby avoided.

THE NECESSITY OF VIOLENCE

Despite his cautions and his rejection of the maxim of violence, Sartre is quite aware that absolutely nonviolent resistance to oppression may do little to bring into existence a kingdom of ends and in fact often reinforces systems of oppression in which some are treated merely as means for the pleasure or profit of others. Thus, in his Preface to Frantz Fanon's *The Wretched of the Earth*, Sartre condemns believers in nonviolence, disputing their claim to be neither executioners nor victims: "Very well then; if you're not victims when the government which you've voted for, when the army in which your younger brothers are serving without hesitation or remorse have undertaken race murder, you are, without a shadow of doubt, executioners." Only in a situation without previously existing violence would claims in support of such passivity be at all plausible.[91] Since violence is morally unacceptable, Sartre concludes, "ethics is not possible unless everyone is ethical."[92]

In saying this, Sartre does not intend to sanction an "anything goes" attitude. Rather, he is attempting to deal with a problem of dirty hands. His point is that in situations of violence there are no unambiguously good alternatives. Whatever one does will be violent: one must either sanction the previous violence or exercise a different violence against it. The latter will probably be preferable to the former, but it will and should be troubling. Thus, as Fanon observes, "everybody will have to be compromised in the fight for the common good. No one has clean hands; there are no innocents and no onlookers. We all have dirty hands; we are all soiling them in the swamps of our country and in the terrifying emptiness of our brains. Every onlooker is either a coward or a traitor."[93]

If Sartre is correct, oppression stands in the way of acting morally, creating the city of ends and treating others as ends, and also in the way of developing an ethics, since the latter can and will be used by the oppressive system against those who seek change. Consequently, oppression and the violence that challenges it are of central importance. I suspect that he never felt sufficiently confident that his analyses would not be used to support the status quo and that that is the main reason he never completed and published the *Notebooks for an Ethics*.[94]

Sartre comes close to affirming the violence of revolt as moral when he presents as a "moral law" the following: "in the case of *impossibility*, the choice of the Good leads to reinforcing the impossible, what we have to choose is Evil in order to discover the Good." His point, I believe, is that in what he calls impossible situations respecting the freedom of all is impossible and trying to act so as to respect freedom simply places us in a hopeless bind. This may result in our trying to choose not to choose or at least in our choosing action which at least does not add to the already existing violence. Either way, we act in such a way that we reinforce the existing violence; and this, Sartre is saying, is unacceptable. Thus, we must choose violence in order to affirm that violence is unacceptable.

To suggest that this violence is moral or that violence is an acceptable means when used toward a good end would not be a proper way to characterize what this "moral law" means. Such a characterization omits or denies too much that is vital to Sartre's analyses. After all, he has emphatically recognized that violence (as part of the organic unity of the means) "is an alteration of the whole series of means and therefore of the end." Violence simply cannot be seen as moral; to see it as moral (or justified) is to slip into a complacency vis-à-vis violence that changes the end we seek. No longer will our goal be the eradication of violence but only the eradication of violence that does not lead to a good end. Yet, in spite of the immorality of violence, it is sometimes necessary. Ultimately, this apparent dilemma concerning violence is resolved, in a very Sartrean way, with the affirmation of ambiguity: although violence cannot always be avoided, neither can it be justified. Rather, it must be condemned, not just by the morality of right (a morality that supports the status quo), against which it revolts, but also, and more importantly, by the morality of the city of ends, toward which the revolt may indeed be progress. He says: "[I]f the goal is concrete and finite, if it is part of a future available to man, it has to exclude violence (at least in that it should not itself be violence or evil), and if one is obliged to make use of violence to attain this goal, at least it [the violence] will appear as unjustified and *limited*. This will be the failure at the heart of the success."[95] Surely this dilemma is what Sartre has in mind when he later says, in *Saint Genet*, "*any* ethic is both impossible and necessary."[96]

It should be clear by now that this resolution does not mean that the revolutionary in an oppressive society is totally beyond good and evil and that anything goes. Nor does it follow that ethics can give absolutely no guidance in such situations. The revolutionary confronts a society in which violence is woven through the status quo. Sartre is clear that this violence is unacceptable and that it should not be allowed to continue. He is equally clear that avoiding all violence is likely to strengthen the status quo and thus condone the violence that permeates it. Yet to accept violence as a legitimate means to a good end is also unacceptable since that acceptance and use will undermine movement toward the city of ends. If violence is avoided, there is no movement whatsoever toward a better society; if violence is condoned, then the goal of a better society is compromised. Thus, while the goal may require revolutionary violence, in order not to compromise the goal itself, we must be very clear that violence is not thereby rendered an acceptable means and that the maxim of violence is not endorsed.

Sartre's affirmation of dirty hands is thus more than acknowledgment of conflicting values and moral obligations. It is rather a very conscious way to keep the end in view in a series of actions where there is no way that the goal can be seen as the organic unity of the means. Sartre's struggle with violence resembles, though his resolution of the dilemma greatly differs from, that of Camus's "just assassins." In the play (*The Just Assassins*), one of the assassins argues that he must give his life to demonstrate that all murder, including the assassination of which he is guilty, is unacceptable, even when the victim is pivotal in maintaining a society where children starve.[97] Sartre would, I think, dismiss the assassin's proposal as itself manifesting an unacceptable desire for moral purity, agreeing instead with the assassin's fellow terrorist Dora that "It's easy, ever so much easier, to die of one's inner conflicts than to live with them." Sartre would, though, certainly appreciate the dominant concern, voiced by the assassin, Kaliayev: "I refuse to add to the living injustice all around me for the sake of a dead justice." In the play, the Chief of Police, Skuratov, cynically acknowledges how difficult that is to do: "One begins by wanting justice—and one ends by setting up a police force";[98] and he clearly knows from experience how far one has then strayed from the goal. Sartre and Camus's assassin are trying to allow violence under certain circumstances without condoning the maxim of violence.

However impossible *and* necessary an ethics, Sartre's ethics included, his analyses of violence and oppression offer a much-needed antidote to traditional moral theory. By proposing as end the utopian kingdom of ends rather than pleasure or happiness and by demanding the end be visible in the means chosen to actualize it, Sartre parts company with utilitarians who find it both too easy to justify violence and too difficult to justify a serious challenge to the status quo. In addition, he parts company with all utilitarians by rejecting their "seriousness" vis-à-vis the alleged value of pleasure or happiness.

More important, though, is the recognition of the untenable position in which traditional ethical theories place the revolutionary. Like Sarah Hoagland, Sartre sees the ways traditional ethical theories condemn revolutionary action. Not only do traditional ethics allow next to no resistance on the part of women whom men beat, but, according to Hoagland, the ethical considerations forced on most of them "involve how to maintain the family unit, how to work with their husband's problems, how to restore his 'dignity,' how to help the children adjust—in short, how to go on as a (heterosexual) woman." Thus, she says: "[T]he function of such judgments is not to encourage the integrity of the individual in her choices. It is rather to maintain the social order and specific relationships and avenues of hierarchy within it."[99] Part of the problem is that, as Sartre recognizes, in an oppressive society any ethics is co-opted to reinforce the status quo. Worse, though, even an ethics focused on abolishing oppression turns against its followers and either renders them ineffectual or decrees them evil unless they are able to walk a fine line, such as Sartre proposes, affirming both impossibility and necessity.

While Sartre is quite different from more traditional ethicists in the support he offers those who work against oppression, his analysis of the impossibility of some situations is far from new.[100] In her analysis of *The Agamemnon*, Martha C. Nussbaum reflects on the "necessity" under which Agamemnon has been placed. This "necessity" is having to choose between two undesirable options: sacrificing his daughter Iphigenia to appease Artemis's anger, on the one hand, or, on the other, not sacrificing Iphigenia in which case, according to prophecy (which he accepts), all will die, including Iphigenia. His downfall, as Nussbaum presents it, lies not in his sacrifice of Iphigenia, but rather in the moral smugness that sets in once he makes his decision to sacrifice her. As she says, "Once the decision is reached, the case appears soluble, the competing claim 'counts as nothing'." Sounding very like Sartre, Nussbaum goes on to say, "A proper response, by contrast, would begin with the acknowledgement that this is not simply a hard case of discovering truth; it is a case where the agent will have to do wrong."[101]

She sees Agamemnon condemned by the Furies, but also by morality, for not responding to this "necessity" as a "good person" would:

> [T]he good agent will also feel and exhibit the feelings appropriate to a person of good character caught in such a situation. He will not regard the fact of decision as licensing feelings of self-congratulation, much less feelings of unqualified enthusiasm for the act chosen. He will show in his emotive behavior, and also genuinely feel, that this is an act deeply repellent to him and to his character. Though he must, to some extent, *act* like a person "who is called by the worst names," he will show himself to be utterly dissimilar to such a person in "passion," in the emotional dispositions that form a part of his character. And after the action he will remember, regret, and, where possible, make reparations.[102]

Thus, Agamemnon is condemned for ignoring the moral complexities of the situation. He adopts the maxim of violence—the end justifies the means—in which the complexity is abolished and, according to which, one of these clearly unacceptable alternatives triumphs as unambiguously the right thing to do.

Nel Noddings's analysis of some acts of violence resembles the analyses offered by Sartre and Aeschylus in acknowledging the "impossibility" of the situations in which many find themselves. However, Sartre's analysis goes beyond hers in at least two ways. First, he supplies the political analysis so lacking in her view. By recognizing the violence in which the agent is immersed—both the prior and the ongoing violence embedded in the status quo and perpetuated by it—Sartre makes us cognizant of a problem of dirty hands: that failure to act against oppression and violence will often make us complicit in them. This recognition of dirty hands acknowledges the impossibility of avoiding involvement in the violence and in the structures of oppression all around us.

Second, Sartre recognizes the problematic position in which this oppression places those who are concerned with the development of ethical theory. Thus, as we shall see in the next chapter, although Noddings's ethics is very close to Sartre's vision of an ethics in a kingdom of ends (the ideal society toward which we must strive), his is quite different from hers in recognizing the dangers, even the impossibility, of acting as though the ideal society has been realized or even can be unproblematically sought. Unlike both Noddings and Rita Manning, he is aware that an ethics appropriate to utopia cannot serve as a direct guide to action in an oppressive society.

Sara Ruddick, in her book *Maternal Thinking: Toward a Politics of Peace*, develops an analysis of war and violence remarkably similar to Sartre's: "[P]eace is not sharply distinguished from war," she observes; what is called peace "includes many violences and is often secured by violence." Peacemakers, she says, must constantly seek out and identify those violences and their costs, thus developing the political critique so lacking in Noddings. Moreover, Ruddick denies that a peacemaker's pacifism requires an absolute renunciation of violence. She suggests, "[p]eacemakers can remain sturdily suspicious of violence and able to count its costs in the best of causes yet refuse to judge from a distance that violent response of others to violent assault on them." In this, she, like Noddings, maintains a suspicion of violence yet acknowledges that even "the sturdiest suspicion of violence is of no avail to threatened peoples who do not have alternative nonviolent ways of protecting what they love and getting what they need."[103] Yet unlike Noddings and more like Sartre, Ruddick seems cognizant of the fact that the violence she pledges herself to ferret out may place her in a position where she cannot avoid violence herself.

I found myself confronted with this recognition of violence as both unacceptable and necessary at a recent retreat for the board of Men Stopping Violence. In discussing her role in the organization, Kathleen Carlin, the executive director, expressed her profound discomfort with the exercise of power over others, even while acknowledging its necessity in cases where she is unable to persuade individuals to discontinue behavior that, as she sees it, is or encourages battery. What she finds comfortable, she said, is leading with the consent of those led. This admirably feminist understanding of the kind of power we should exercise seems to me quite appropriate. At the same time, her awareness that she cannot permit battery or its encouragement seems equally appropriate. She is, after all, hired to lead a group of men who acknowledge their own conditioning both to be abusive and to accept abuse of women and who recognized early in the life of the organization that they needed her help if they were to change themselves and other men. Interestingly enough, the same problem with power will arise as those men work with groups of batterers, particularly with those mandated to the program by the courts. While these men, too, are working for a society in which exerting such power over others is inappropriate and unacceptable, they daily face situations in which they must intervene—even with the sort of power they abhor—in both individual and systemic violence against women.[104]

CONCLUSION

We are left, then, with the uncomfortable conclusion that violence must be condemned by our ethics while it is nevertheless sometimes necessary. To condone the violence of the status quo, whether actively or by doing nothing to challenge it, is unacceptable. Such violence is definitely in conflict with the affirmation of freedom envisioned in the ideal of the city of ends. At the same time, condoning whatever violence is needed to unsettle the status quo is also unacceptable: justifying such violence as a means endorses the maxim of violence, which in turn serves as a cornerstone for the status quo. Worse, though, endorsing violence compromises the end to which the violence was to serve as means. Thus, condoning violence both supports and undermines the actions of revolutionaries who fight against oppression. It supports their actions insofar as the actions are violent but momentarily at least serve the revolutionaries' ends; however, it undermines revolutionary action by distorting and undermining the end of human freedom in the name of which the oppression is fought.

Yet simply to condemn violence in a situation of oppression also supports the status quo and makes the goal of human freedom nothing but an idealistic and ineffectual dream. Those who work to end oppression must therefore adhere to an ethics in which acts of violence are clearly condemned; at the same time, these reformers and revolutionaries must recognize that oppressive societies and the violence of others sometimes place individuals in impossible situations where violence cannot be avoided. Acting against the oppression may of necessity involve violence; but not acting against the oppression affirms, collaborates with, and even reinforces the oppression and its violence.

While violence is inevitable in such situations, the individual who confronts this "impossible" dilemma must be careful to choose violence on the side of human freedom and against oppression, as difficult and morally wrenching as such decisions may be. In opposition to Audre Lorde, we must conclude that the "master's tools" may be necessary in dismantling the "master's house,"[105] even though they are morally unacceptable as tools for building a better society.

NOTES

1. See Frye, *The Politics of Reality: Essays in Feminist Theory*, pp. 84-94.

2. Rich, *Compulsory Homosexuality*, p. 14, quotes MacKinnon.

3. Frye, *The Politics of Reality: Essays in Feminist Theory*, p. 72.

4. Freire, p. 73.

5. Hoagland, *Lesbian Ethics: Toward New Value*, pp. 250, 13, 120.

6. G.W.F. Hegel, *The Phenomenology of Mind*, trans. J. B. Baillie (New York: Macmillan, 1949), pp. 232-33.

7. See the commentary on Hegel's "Lordship and Bondage" by Alexandre Kojève, *Introduction to the Reading of Hegel*, trans. James H. Nichols, Jr. (New York: Basic Books, 1969), pp. 21-22.

8. Because this encounter seems to be presented as a male/male scenario, I am leaving the pronoun masculine and bequeathing to other scholars questions about the assumed universality of antagonism between consciousnesses and whether Hegel's master/slave dialectic sheds any light on the subordination of women to men. Linda Alcoff and I have written a paper, "Lordship, Bondage, and the Dialectic of Work in Traditional Male/Female Relationships," *Cogito* 2, no. 3 (September 1984): 79-93, which explores limited aspects of the latter question.

9. Sartre, *Notebooks for an Ethics*, pp. 452, 454.

10. Hoagland, *Lesbian Ethics: Toward New Value*, pp. 263, 267, 264.

11. *Ibid.*, pp. 264, 271.

12. Lorde, p. 112.

13. Woolf, pp. 6, 8.

14. Noddings, *Caring: A Feminine Approach to Ethics & Moral Education*, p. 118.

15. Tong, *Women, Sex, and the Law*, p. 146.

16. Noddings, *Caring: A Feminine Approach to Ethics & Moral Education*, p. 118.

17. Frye, *The Politics of Reality: Essays in Feminist Theory*, pp. 56, 54.

18. Hoagland, *Lesbian Ethics: Toward New Value*, p. 209.

19. *Ibid.*

20. Maimonides, "From *The Book of Women*," in *Visions of Women*, pp. 99-101.

21. Kirp *et al.*, p. 31, observe that in terms of legal rights, married women were much worse off than their unmarried sisters through much of the nineteenth century. They quote Blackstone's "classic eighteenth century account of the common law," in which he observes that "'the very being or legal existence of the women is suspended during the marriage.'"

22. Nietzsche, "From *Human, All-too-Human*," in *Visions of Women*, p. 337.

23. Ortega, "From *Man and People*" and "From *On Love*," in *Visions of Women*, pp. 450-53, 456.

24. Schopenhauer, p. 272.

25. Maimonides, p. 99.

26. In Georgia, for example, rape is defined in such a way that only women can be raped. A sexual violation of one man by another thus must be considered under a different law, that specifying aggravated sodomy, even though men who are thus attacked sometimes seek counseling and assistance from rape crisis centers and evince psychological trauma and response similar to those of women.

27. Jaggar, *Feminist Politics*, p. 261.

28. Frye, *The Politics of Reality: Essays in Feminist Theory*, p. 3.

29. *Ibid.*, p. 72.

30. MacKinnon, "Feminism, Marxism, Method, and the State: Toward Feminist Jurisprudence," p. 144.

31. bell hooks, *Feminist Theory: From Margin to Center*, pp. 122-25.

32. Hoagland, *Lesbian Ethics: Toward New Value*, pp. 40-45.

33. David Hume, "From 'Of the Rise and Progress of the Arts and Sciences,'" in *Visions of Women*, p. 155.

34. Wollstonecraft, pp. 224-25; Kierkegaard, "From *Stages on Life's Way*," *ibid.*, pp. 303-4.

35. Kant, "From *Anthropology from a Pragmatic Point of View*," *ibid.*, p. 252.

36. George Santayana, "From *The Life of Reason*," *ibid.*, p. 406.

37. Mill, "From *The Subjection of Women*," *ibid.*, p. 293.

38. Wollstonecraft, p, 223.

39. Tong, *Women, Sex, and the Law*, p. 127.

40. William James, "A Review [of] 1. Women's Suffrage, the Reform Against Nature, by Horace Bushnell, New York, Scribner, 1869, [and] 2. The Subjec-

tion of Women, by John Stuart Mill, New York, Appleton, 1869," in *Visions of Women*, p. 363.

41. *Ibid.*

42. Anna Garlin Spencer, "From *Woman's Share in Social Culture*," *ibid.*, p. 387.

43. Kirp *et al.*, p. 37, note how poor were the working conditions of many women—as well as of many men—even at the beginning of this century.

44. Zora Neale Hurston, *Their Eyes Were Watching God* (Chicago: University of Illinois Press, 1978), p. 29.

45. MacKinnon, *Feminism Unmodified*, pp. 104-5.

46. Hoagland, *Lesbian Ethics: Toward New Value*, pp. 30-31, 29.

47. MacKinnon, *Feminism Unmodified*, p. 31, acknowledges that the notion of a male protection racket is one she owes to others. She cites Susan Rae Peterson's use of the term in a paper, originally read in 1976, "Coercion and Rape: The State as a Male Protection Racket," *Feminism and Philosophy*, ed. Mary Vetterling-Bragin, Frederick A. Elliston, and Jane English (Totowa, NJ: Littlefield, Adams & Co., 1977), pp. 360-71. Earlier (1971), though, Susan Griffin discussed chivalry as a "protection racket" in "Rape: The All-American Crime," included in the same volume, p. 320; and she acknowledges (p. 318) even earlier recognition of the reality if not the actual terminology by quoting Mae West: "Every man I meet wants to protect me. Can't figure out what from."

48. Jaggar, *Feminist Politics*, p. 154.

49. MacKinnon, "Feminism, Marxism, Method, and the State," p. 146.

50. Kirp *et al.*, p. 32.

51. James, p. 362.

52. Woolf, p. 142.

53. MacKinnon, "Feminism, Marxism, Method, and the State," p. 148.

54. MacKinnon, *Feminism Unmodified*, p. 100.

55. Kirp *et al.*, pp. 17, 62, 72.

56. *Ibid.*, pp. 149, 19.

57. Letty Cottin Pogrebin, *Among Friends: Who We Like, Why We Like Them, and What We Do With Them* (New York: McGraw-Hill, 1987), p. 251.

58. Dworkin, *Intercourse*, pp. 97, 122, 155-59.

59. *Ibid.*, p. 122.

60. *Ibid.*, pp. 147-48.

61. Nancy Fraser, "What's Critical about Critical Theory? The Case of Habermas and Gender," in *Feminism as Critique: On the Politics of Gender*, p. 36.

62. Nye, p. 24.

63. Young, "Impartiality and the Civic Public: Some Implications of Feminist Critiques of Moral and Political Theory," p. 74.

64. Patricia Hill Collins, p. 49.

65. bell hooks, *Feminist Theory: From Margin to Center*, pp. 28-29.

66. These examples will receive further treatment in Chapter 6.

67. Sartre, *The Chips Are Down*, trans. Louise Varése (New York: Lear, 1948), pp. 92, 80.

68. Sartre, "Self-Portrait at Seventy," in *Life/Situations*, trans. Paul Auster and Lydia Davis (New York: Pantheon, 1977), p. 12.

69. Kant, *Lectures on Ethics*, pp. 224-25.

70. Sartre, "Self-Portrait at Seventy, p. 13.

71. Sartre, *Search for a Method*, trans. Hazel E. Barnes (New York: Alfred A. Knopf, 1967), p. 80.

72. Young, *Justice and the Politics of Difference*, pp. 230-32.

73. For more discussion of this, see Chapter 6.

74. Fatima Mernissi, *Beyond the Veil: Male-Female Dynamics in Modern Muslim Society* (Bloomington: Indiana University Press, 1987), p. 175.

75. Hoagland, *Lesbian Ethics: Toward New Value*, pp. 57, 26.

76. Frye, *The Politics of Reality: Essays in Feminist Theory*, pp. 48-51.

77. Hoagland, *Lesbian Ethics: Toward New Value*, p, 26.

78. bell hooks, *Feminist Theory: From Margin to Center*, p. 76.

79. de Beauvoir, *The Ethics of Ambiguity*, pp. 37-38.

80. Sartre, *Notebooks for an Ethics*, p. 341.

81. Frye, *The Politics of Reality: Essays in Feminist Theory*, p. 3.

82. Sartre, *What Is Literature?*, p. 282.

83. Rich, "Women and Honor: Some Notes on Lying," in *Women and Values: Readings in Recent Feminist Philosophy*, pp. 355-56.

84. Hoagland, *Lesbian Ethics: Toward New Value*, pp. 58-59.

85. Sartre, *Notebooks for an Ethics*, p. 180.

86. *Ibid.*, pp. 199, 202.

87. Hoagland, *Lesbian Ethics: Toward New Value*, p. 119.

88. Bat-Ami Bar On, "Why Terrorism Is Morally Problematic," in *Feminist Ethics*, pp. 108, 109, 116, 122.

89. Sartre, *Notebooks for an Ethics*, pp. 174-75, 202.

90. *Ibid.*, pp. 172, 435, 167.

91. Sartre, "Preface," *The Wretched of the Earth*, p. 25.

92. Sartre, *Notebooks for an Ethics*, p. 9.

93. Fanon, p. 199.

94. Others, such as William L. McBride, find problematic elements and difficulties in that work and claim rather that Sartre's inability to resolve those problems led to his cessation of work on that volume. McBride, *Sartre's Political Theory* (Bloomington: Indiana University Press, 1991), dismisses the *Notebooks for an Ethics* as a "confused text [p. 84]," abandoned by Sartre because it contains "much that is utopian and idealistic, in the most negative senses of those words [p. 40]."
    I find these criticisms rather confusing and, if I understand them correctly, mistaken. I take it that utopian goals are seen as realizable albeit in some remote future (and hence cannot be regulative) and that ideals are idealistic (and hence not properly regulative) when they cannot be approached asymptotically. Sartre recognized the improbability of achieving the goals cited by McBride as utopian and objected to any limiting of ourselves to such goals: "As soon as a goal is assigned to the human species and this goal is finite, as soon as one pictures it as reality, everything falls into darkness, the

human species become ants." At the same time, if it is beyond attaining for each generation, "this is discouraging." Sartre's conclusion is: "This signifies that each person has to realize it and yet it is still to be realized [Sartre, *Notebooks for an Ethics*, p. 448]." To the extent that the goals offered in the *Notebooks* by Sartre are utopian, they apparently can be pictured as reality and thus cannot suffice, if we take Sartre's argument seriously. Otherwise, "the human species become ants." What is required to prevent this is that there be, *in addition,* regulative goals that are not utopian in this sense.

I assume, then, that McBride's problem is that to the extent that Sartre offers goals that are utopian they, too, cannot be regulative. His challenge, if I am correct, is that other goals developed in the *Notebooks* are idealistic and, as such, they, too, cannot be regulative ideals. What is "idealistic" for McBride about the *Notebooks* can be understood best in contrast to what he would find acceptable as a regulative ideal, e.g., the ideal of overcoming scarcity: "the idea of a potential overcoming of scarcity might prove useful as a sort of limiting-concept, an asymptotically approachable goal against which genuinely possible historical change for the better could be measured [p. 110]." Instead, McBride says that in the *Notebooks*, "Sartre, the philosopher of action, the sworn opponent of idealism, has committed himself to a regulative ideal that seems not only to be never completely realizable, as is the case with all regulative ideals, but to be thoroughly unapproachable: no asymptotes here! [p. 82]."

But must ideals be asymptotically approachable in order to avoid the charge of idealism and in order to serve as regulative ideals? Interestingly, McBride early in the book rejects the critics he disparagingly calls "harmony theorists," who propose as serious alternatives to Sartre's "concrete relations with others" that "there can be such privileged, sheltered relationships [of love, friendship, and social solidarity, 'permanent and entirely without the potentiality of violent conflict'] of both a dyadic and perhaps even a communal sort, and moreover that it is on such ideal relationships that we ought to concentrate our attention [p. 20]." McBride seems clear enough here that such relationships are impossible, certainly in society as presently constituted and, I think, in any society, and that "such an approach to social theory is at best self-deceptive, and is sometimes even a deliberate effort to encourage others not to reflect on the conflict-filled reality of the world around them, in the interest of preserving existing social hierarchies that have no rational basis [p. 20]." It seems to me that believing in asymptotic approaches to an ideal of harmonious relationship is similarly self-deceptive and supportive of social hierarchies, but does that mean that harmony cannot serve as a regulative idea? Pursuing such a goal as harmony, taken as a regulative ideal, will result in perpetual dissatisfaction with all of our actual relationships. It will inspire us to try harder to achieve whatever harmony is possible and to value any momentary intimations of unity, no matter how fleeting. Finally, it will challenge us to work more diligently to overthrow oppression of every sort.

Also, McBride seems to have little difficulty with Sartre's example of childrearing, referring to it as a "fascinating analysis [p. 72]." Yet it, too, involves a problem of impossible goals. As McBride himself presents it, Sartre's "nonoppressive childrearing entails treating children as free here and now rather than suppressing their present freedom in the name of such a future time ["at which he or she will be 'allowed' to make free choices"]." At the same time, Sartre recognizes that this is simply not the way things are or can be: "the mere fact that nonoppressive parents are 'allowing' their children to act freely and must always be prepared to intervene in order, for example, to prevent an inexperienced young child from harming him- or herself shows that there is always some element of lying and ruse involved in such relationships even at their best [pp. 72-73]."

    Though an important ideal, respectful, noncoercive treatment of a child is nonetheless an impossibility. It is quite unlike "the idea of a potential overcoming of scarcity." It simply cannot be a "limiting-concept" as McBride understands such. Without denying the very condition of children, childrearing cannot asymptotically approach this goal. While I believe that the ideal of nonoppressive childrearing allows us to distinguish, at least to some extent, better from worse childrearing (and most assuredly allows us to condemn manipulative control of the child for the benefit of others and even for a distant future desired for the child by others), I am very uncomfortable with the idea of asymptotic approach to this ideal. My discomfort reflects Sartre's own discomfort, expressed in the *Notebooks*, with "the maxim of violence." Like Sartre, I am convinced that parents should remain uneasy with the coerciveness in even their best efforts at nonoppressive childrearing. To see one's effort as asymptotically approaching the ideal is either to mask the coercion or to justify it in terms of some future realization of the child's freedom; and the latter takes us right back to the oppressive childrearing to which Sartre was offering an alternative.

    95. Sartre, *Notebooks for an Ethics*, pp. 406, 172, 207.
    96. Sartre, *Saint Genet*, trans. Bernard Frechtman (New York: New American Library, 1964), p. 247.
    97. Albert Camus, *The Just Assassins*, in *Caligula & Three Other Plays*, trans. Stuart Gilbert (New York: Vintage Books, 1958), pp. 233-302.
    98. *Ibid.*, pp. 297, 260, 281.
    99. Hoagland, *Lesbian Ethics: Toward New Value*, p. 25.
    100. Similarities between what Sartre says about these and the treatment of certain choices in ancient Greek tragedies was brought to my attention by C. Grant Luckhardt, who also suggested the analyses of Martha C. Nussbaum, *The Fragility of Goodness* (New York: Cambridge University Press, 1986), for their clarity in illuminating the ancient dilemmas.
    101. *Ibid.*, pp. 34, 42.
    102. *Ibid.*, p. 43.
    103. Ruddick, *Maternal Thinking: Toward a Politics of Peace*, pp. 138-39.
    104. For further discussion of the work of Men Stopping Violence and Carlin's role in it, see her essay "The Men's Movement of Choice," *Women Respond to the Men's Movement: A Feminist Collection*, pp. 119-25.
    105. See Lorde, "The Master's Tools Will Never Dismantle the Master's House," in *Sister Outsider*, pp. 110-13.

Chapter Six

Recognition of Love as an Ideal

While we seek an ethics that clearly sees and condemns oppression and that does not discourage all revolutionaries and reformists fighting for change, at the same time we need a vision of what can be. We require as much clarity as possible concerning the positive ideals under which individuals are to act. Thus, some characterization of love and of the vision informing our ethics is in order.

Various analyses of love and friendship can serve to illuminate our way in this characterization. Of particular importance are Sartre's views of love and the city of ends as well as Nel Noddings's ethics of caring.

MOTHERING/PATERNALISM

Emphasizing reciprocity, Sartre's and Noddings's ideals of human relationships seem less vulnerable to distortion within oppressive societies than the ideal of "mothering" as it has been developed by others. As Sarah Hoagland notes, "mothering" often appeals to "unconditional love," "an ideal of unconditional opening or giving." Quoting bell hooks's claim that such an ideal is involved in the stereotype of the mammy, she questions how well such an ideal can serve today's society. Unconditional love fosters society's judgment of our fundamental "rottenness" by its affirmation "that we can be loved no matter how rotten we are." Moreover, such love is "amorphous and indiscriminate," and "ultimately, makes no sense and . . . works only to distort a relationship." Most significantly, it affects women's relationships with one another by the way it "undermines reciprocal interaction between mothers and daughters and so encourages incompetency and ageism among us."[1]

In addition, seeing such unconditional love as a good thing, particularly for women to do, and calling it "mothering," reinforces the attachment of love to roles women but not men are expected to play. This is especially dangerous since the traditional role of self-sacrifice is still generally expected of women. Feminists must be careful in any endorsement of love, lest they inadvertently strengthen the ways men's dominance of women is embedded in the status quo. In her 1970 analysis of abortion, Judith Jarvis Thomson makes quite clear the way previous laws against abortion had uncritically assumed expectations of female self-sacrifice. As she notes there, society demanded through such laws an extremely high level of Good Samaritanism from the pregnant woman vis-à-vis the fetus while requiring not even the most "Minimally Decent Samaritanism" of others. To emphasize her point, she cites as examples the thirty-eight people who witnessed from their apartments the long and drawn-out murder of Kitty Genovese in the late 1960s in New York, but failed (and were not required by society) to do anything, including to call the police, claiming they did not want to become "involved."[2]

Even a careful attempt, such as Sara Ruddick's, to define "mothering" so it neither sentimentalizes the work "mothers" actually do nor limits this work to women is too easily co-optable by a society in which women have been and continue to be viewed as the caretakers of children as well of men and of the infirm. While both those who care for children and those who work for peace have much to learn from Ruddick's work, it is, nevertheless, important to recognize, as she herself does, the "reactionary sound" of her discussion of "mothering" and the need for feminist transformation of maternal pacifism if such pacifism is to become a "public good."[3] Ruddick's analyses are particularly insightful when she discusses issues of violence, power-imbalances, and coercion in "mothering" itself. Such love proceeds with great caution, always with awareness of the independence of the child and concern for her or his preservation, growth, and social acceptability.[4]

Although respectful of the other's freedom and independence, Ruddick's "mothering" is premised on the particular vulnerability of the child and the power imbalance between the "mother" and the child. What we need to recognize is how this vulnerability of the child and the power imbalance between the child and adult(s) render this relationship inherently violent and thus a poor model for caring and moral adult relationships. Sartre's analysis of childrearing demonstrates the violence endemic to childrearing. The most liberating childrearing is that which enables "the child to be able to choose his own good when he grows up." Since "many of his childish projects will go against this end," an enlightened parent must intervene in some of those projects. To keep the child from consequences she or he does not intend, the adult limits the child's freedom. Though done with the best of intentions for the child's welfare and though perhaps truly necessary to keep the child from harm or to provide for her or his future freedom, the limitation is nonetheless violence: "In violence one treats a freedom like a thing, all the while recognizing its nature as freedom."[5]

Even attempting to reason with an older child often will "minimize his freedom" since the reasoning will inevitably leave much out that is necessary for the child to truly understand and will only create in the child "the habit of believing in the principle of authority." By virtue of being a child, the child's knowledge and comprehension are such that "[t]he child chooses himself in error and this choice runs the risk of being definitive; and we know that this choice orients him toward consequences he did not *intend* and does not intend." Sartre sums up the situation in terms of impossibility:

> [T]he essence of the adult/child situation is that *I cannot* treat the child as freedom; and neither can I treat him as a thing. He himself wants to be treated as a freedom and at the same time for me to impose a rational universe upon him that he can take confidence in. In the father/child hierarchy, there is a failure, as in every human hierarchy—which presupposes a qualitative impermeability. As for the position of the father over against the child, it necessarily constitutes him on the level of immorality. For ethics, he is immoral.[6]

I take this not as an argument in favor of hierarchy but rather as acknowledgment that some violence is inevitable. This seems very much in line with Sartre's recognition that some alienation is unavoidable.

Given the power imbalance in even the most enlightened parent/child relationship, however, this hierarchical relationship simply cannot be taken as a model for relationships between individuals who are both responsible adults, whatever their existing differences in wisdom, strength, foresight, or other abilities. We cannot continue such paternalism into adulthood, since, as Sartre says, we limit the violence in the education of the child by "clearly consider[ing] the age of adulthood as a regulative principle and concrete, everyday emancipation as the real end." This means:

The child has to be taught to judge and choose for himself in every case,
since, as freedom, he ought to be recognized for himself. And this emancipation as an immediate end must serve the future. In other words, we
have to renounce seeing the future man in the child as an absolute end that
justifies every means, instead considering that this end can be attained
only if, in each case, the situation of the child is the means of his concrete
and real emancipation. The future has to be seen through the perspectives
of the present, we have to comprehend that it is *the future of this present*,
giving each present along with the future it foreshadows an absolute value.[7]

Mothering, therefore, is problematic as a model for adult relationships since it primarily characterizes a necessarily hierarchical situation and thus suggests that hierarchy is acceptable even in relationships among adults. Moreover, echoing the cultural view of women as
mothering not just children but husbands and male lovers as well, it is
particularly dangerous as a model for heterosexual relationships. Those
who develop mothering as a model for adult relationships too often
uncritically presume power on the part of wives/female lovers, thereby
masking the real lack of physical, legal, and economic power on the
part of most women in such relationships. And, of course, even with
Ruddick's constant reminders to her readers not to take "mothering"
as gender-based, nevertheless, given the culture, the term will inevitably reinforce the cultural stereotype of women as the ones who are
to do the caring and nurturing.

As a model for adult relationships, paternalism in any form seems
unacceptable. Ultimately, in the words of Sarah Hoagland, paternalism
requires and affirms power-over another, a power-over that abrogates
the other's moral agency: "paternalism (1) justifies interrupting or even
abrogating a person's integrity 'for her own good'; (2) validates the
idea that someone has a right, indeed an obligation, to dominate (protect, coerce, and so on) someone else under certain conditions and so
force her into a certain dependency; and (3) gives credence to the idea
that such dependence benefits an individual." This sort of acting *for*
as opposed to *with* another arrogantly regards another as better able to
determine what is good for a person (an arrogance that often masquer-
ades as objectivity), encourages atomistic individualism, and is thus
counter to the appropriate assistance to others that Hoagland calls
"attending."[8] As Ruddick observes, attentive love, an idea developed
by Simone Weil and later by Iris Murdoch, demands a knowledge of
and respect for the independence and desires of the other and opposes
"fantasy"—"intellectual and imaginative activity that has blindly put
itself in the service of consolation, domination, and aggrandizement."[9]

Quite apart from whether women were "victimized by policies designed
to protect them" and from whether the rules governing their conduct

were "honestly seen as women's best interest," paternalism requires "the assumption that the beneficiaries are in fact helpless, or at least less competent than the deciders to make their own life choices." Acknowledging this, David Kirp et al. go on to say: "Should that prove untrue, the argument for paternalism collapses, and the intervention is unmasked as an assault on the personal dignity of those whose lives have been unfairly constrained."[10] Feminists, of course, recognize the falseness, in all but a tiny percentage of cases, of the presumption of women's helplessness or incompetence. Even in those cases where it is true, the moral situation is problematic if the more competent has played a role—even a passive one—in producing the helplessness and incompetence of the other. If, for example, women must "pay" for their protection by some men from other men with a studied helplessness, with a delicacy that requires underdeveloped muscle structure and no training in self-defense, and with clothes that prevent defensive movement or even much movement at all, then their "protectors" are indeed in a morally unacceptable position by requiring that women cater to an unchallenged social view of themselves as prey in order to deserve protection from those who would be predators.

Paternalists step in and take over where those who help simply offer assistance. Where Sartre's helper respects the other's choice, one who acts paternalistically decides for the other. Paternalism affirms dominance, not reciprocity.

As long as dominance structures human society and the individual relationships within it, even the allegedly self-sacrificing love of the dominated for the dominating is likely to be tinged with manipulativeness and deviousness. They are, after all, the only means available to the powerless to influence the direction of events. Admittedly, such measures may be used for good, much as Nora acted manipulatively and deviously in the best medical interests of her husband in Ibsen's play *The Doll's House*. However, as Judith Andre has argued, manipulation and deviousness are always morally problematic behaviors.[11] In addition, as Larry Blum, Marcia Homiak, Judy Housman, and Naomi Scheman point out, such behavior, even when used as Nora used it, is still likely to prove harmful by giving or reinforcing in the dominant a distorted idea of themselves.[12]

HIERARCHY'S ALLEGED
ROOTEDNESS IN HUMAN DESIRES

Some thinkers see dominance as desirable at least in some intimate relationships, specifically in those between men and women, since, it is claimed, only in marital arrangements involving dominance can men—and possibly women—achieve what they *want*. Paternalism is not what leads these thinkers to conclude the husband must rule the wife. It is rather demands issuing from the perceived wishes, sexuality, or moral requirements of at least one and possibly both the parties.

Some of the wants and wishes to which these thinkers appeal are not particularly praiseworthy or even healthy. For example, Nietzsche sees subordination as something women have used "to get themselves supported, like drones in a beehive.[13] Kierkegaard proposes submission as the form always taken by woman's devotion to man, "perhaps because woman has a bad conscience about [the egotism of her devotion]."[14] Similarly, Simone de Beauvoir observes, many women prefer to "take shelter in the shadow of man" to avoid the demands and responsibilities of adult freedom.[15] These all seem good reasons to *change* the traditional approach to marriage although, of the three cited, only de Beauvoir draws this conclusion.

Making a more convincing case for hierarchy, Nietzsche proposes that subordination and domination are precisely what the two sexes want from each other in love: "woman" sees love as "complete surrender (not merely devotion) of body and soul" and a man who loves a woman "wants precisely this love from her."[16] More recently and with more flourishes, Ortega extols the wonderful "pre-established harmony" in the desires women and men have for each other: "[T]he essence of femininity exists in the fact that an individual feels her destiny totally fulfilled when she surrenders herself to another individual. Everything else that the woman does or is has an adjectival and derivative character. In opposition to this marvelous phenomenon, masculinity presents the deep-rooted instinct which impels it to take possession of another person."[17]

Many of the same responses can be made to this claim about the way women and men love as were made to the appeals to nature. Does observing the loves of men and women really indicate anything very clearly about their differences? Can observation tell us anything about the essentials of feminine and masculine loves; or does it only reveal the way these have been formed by social expectations, training, and manipulation? Are not men's reports concerning such loves more likely to reflect primarily their own preferences, interests, and limited relationships with their wives and, at best, a few other women? Such discussions of the ways men and women love not only omit any mention of intimate, loving relations between women and between men, but also implicitly disparage or deny a priori the very possibility of such. Finally, even if general differences are found, what, if anything, follows concerning the mutual love of a particular man and a particular woman or of two specific individuals of the same sex?

This last question is by far the most important. As Bertrand Russell notes, there are many women who do not desire to subject themselves to their husbands[18]—or, we might add, to acquire a husband in the first place. Even Ortega, contemporary that he was to de Beauvoir, cautions us not to assume that particular women and men will conform perfectly to the essences of femininity and masculinity since "the classification of human beings into men and women is, obviously, inexact."[19]

Such inexactness, however, only complicates the issue. It will not do simply to dismiss individuals who do not fit the alleged patterns as "slaves" or "not really women" or to instruct them to accept, even though it does not meet their needs, the institution of marriage established for those who better fit the patterns. On the other hand, if those who do not fit the patterns are entitled to set up differently organized marriages and relationships to meet their needs, then the arguments purporting to establish the subordination of women to men in marriage fail. Far from showing that men and women should establish marriages in which wives are subordinate to husbands, these arguments show, at most, only that some people prefer such relationships. Whether these people are in the majority is dubious, given the armchair speculation often offered in support, but also irrelevant in terms of dictating patterns for others. Furthermore, we must question, as do Adrienne Rich and others, whether those who do "want" such marriages would continue to do so in a less coercive society.[20]

William James, as we have seen, presents a variation of this argument when he maintains that the "representative American" really wants a wife who is dependent. He wants a "tranquil spot" where he does not constantly have to fight to secure his position but "where he shall be valid absolutely and once for all." The security and repose essential to James's ideal require, as he acknowledges in what surely is a classic understatement, "some feeling of dependence on the woman's side."[21]

We might ask how easily attainable these goals are even with the woman's dependence, but it is more crucial to note the ease with which James justifies women's dependence for men's comfort and happiness. There is certainly no recognition of the cruelty that wives' legal and physical dependence has brought in its wake and no concern that such treatment of women might be morally problematic or unjust. The home of which James writes may offer a man some protection from and solace against his enemies; but, as Alison Jaggar argues, it all too frequently does not offer any protection and solace to the woman:

[T]he woman's enemy is within the door as well as outside it. He is present in the incestuous father and in the abusive husband—perhaps even in the political activist who requires her to support his work through domestic and sexual service. From the perspective of a woman, the nuclear family is not a haven in a heartless world; it is one of her workplaces, perhaps her only one, and the one in which she suffers some of her most direct oppression.[22]

To any who think of marriage as "an equal bargain" in which sexual availability is traded for support, Catharine MacKinnon responds: "[I]n any place where one cannot prosecute for marital rape, the woman's obligation to sexually deliver is effectively enforced by the state. The support obligation that men supposedly provide overwhelmingly is not."[23]

Moreover, others express chagrin over the consequences on men and boys—and, more broadly, the consequences on democracy itself—of this dependence of their wives and mothers. Certainly, even if men's goals of security and repose were easily attainable with women's dependence, the consequences of such dependence on women themselves as well as on men and society must be evaluated as an unwarranted expense for men's comfort.

It is also important to ask whether women, if their wishes were considered, would want exactly the same thing, namely, their own security and repose, even if their security and repose require the dependence of men. Why should women's wishes not be granted the same consideration James accords to those of men? Audre Lorde addresses the inherent unfairness of respecting men's but not women's desires as well as the incompatibility of those respective desires when she says: "It has been said that Black men cannot be denied their personal choice of the woman who meets their need to dominate. In that case, Black women also cannot be denied our personal choices, and those choices are becoming increasingly self-assertive and female-oriented."[24]

Of course, if women and men want incompatible things and either group's getting what it wants means the other cannot get what it wants, then both sets of wishes cannot be granted the same consideration James accords to men's. Thus, compromise might be in order. Perhaps, though, some of these desires *should* be accorded *no* consideration—if, that is, one or both groups desire what is morally unacceptable. This would apply even if men and women happen to have compatible desires, for example, as the result of growing up in a society like ours where both women and men are raised to want the dominance of men over women and where such dominance is eroticized. Given the conditioning and careful coercion exerted to this end, as Mill points out, it is hardly amazing to find many women accepting their subservience and even desiring it.[25] Even if many women do want their own subservience, this is not sufficient to warrant their subservience, any more than the desire of a slave to remain in servitude is sufficient to warrant his or her continued servitude.

Finally, we need to ask whether men—or women, for that matter—should try to secure such absolute justification in the eyes of another human being. Admittedly, few would choose to go from one battle-field—their work—to another—their homes. James, however, only replaces one dilemma with another just as faulty. He would have done better to examine whether it is healthy for human beings to set up work as a battlefield and whether it is any more advisable to try to set up home as a haven of perfect acceptance. Acceptance secured at the cost of the freedom of the one who accepts is bought at a high—and morally unacceptable—price. Furthermore, inasmuch as the acceptance involves the dependence of the accepting party, it is problematic as acceptance. Surely what is desired is free and uncoerced acceptance by an equal; acceptance by one who is dependent can never be quite adequate since the dependent are placed by their very dependence in a position in which refusal to accept and approve their masters jeopardizes their security and even their existence. With good reason, those who are free seldom respect to any great degree the opinions, or the acceptances, of those who are dependent upon them.

HIERARCHY ROOTED IN SEXUAL ACTIVITY

A final argument for "the most unlimited subjection of the woman to the will of her husband" comes from J. G. Fichte, who claims a moral ground for the surrender of the woman's very personality to her lover. His argument is a difficult one; but since it touches on several important issues, I shall develop it at length.

The argument proceeds like this. Even though the sexual impulse is natural, men and women must experience it differently. This impulse appears "in its true form," he says, in men who seek its satisfaction "as an end in itself, since it can be satisfied through activity." If women were similarly to seek satisfaction of the sexual impulse as an end, they would, according to Fichte, make a "pure passivity" their end. This, he believes, is irrational: "The character of reason is absolute self-activity; pure passivity for the sake of passivity contradicts reason, and utterly cancels it." Thus, a woman, inasmuch as she is rational, can give herself up to her sexual impulse only if it assumes a different character—"the character of an impulse to satisfy the man."

She thus maintains the dignity of reason by "voluntarily mak[ing] . . . herself [a] means in virtue of a noble natural impulse—love!" In this "moral" form of love, "[h]er own dignity requires that she should give herself up entirely as she is, . . . and should utterly lose herself in him." Fichte concludes, "[t]he least consequence is, that she should renounce to him all her property and all her rights."[26]

Fichte's argument goes far beyond any except perhaps the religious one in attempting to support the subordination of one human being to another. For him, such subordination is not merely a means to satisfy men's or women's wishes. Nor is it a means to meet an alleged "need," such as the man's "need" to be assured of the "legitimacy" of the children he is obliged to acknowledge and raise as his own—a "need" he can satisfy only if he is able to "superintend" his wife's conduct, according to Rousseau.[27] On the contrary, for Fichte, a wife must voluntarily surrender *all* her property and *all* her rights to her husband; otherwise, she is acting immorally and contrary to her very existence as a rational being.

Fichte's argument, however, is not compelling. First, he does not demonstrate that women cannot pursue the satisfaction of the sexual impulse without making "pure passivity" their end. He seems simply to believe this result follows from the nature of sexual activity itself. This suggests he is assuming the traditional view of this activity (active male and passive female); thus, his claim is based on arbitrary and unwarranted—and antiquated—views of the roles of the participants. At most, a woman seeking to maintain her dignity as a rational creature while securing her sexual satisfaction should conclude from Fichte's analysis that she, too, must be an active participant. In this way, sexual activity would come closer to being what Ruddick approvingly calls "complete sex." This is "reciprocal sex" where "[t]he partners, whatever the circumstances of their coming together, are equal in activity and responsiveness of desire."[28]

If Fichte's claim is not based on this active-male/passive-female view of the sex act, then I can think of only one other possible interpretation, an interpretation suggested by de Beauvoir's analysis of the way woman has been systematically rendered "the Other."[29] He might believe that if men actively pursue sexual satisfaction as a goal, then women, insofar as they are *not* men, cannot pursue this goal in the same way. Consequently, their pursuit must make them passive; and, since rational beings cannot rationally make passivity their end, women must not pursue sexual satisfaction as their goal.

If this is Fichte's argument, then it is a weak one. Difference between women and men simply cannot be used to require women and men to pursue goals differently: ludicrous results follow when we imagine this claim applied to basic life-sustaining activities like eating and drinking.[30] In addition, if this were Fichte's argument, it would be arbitrary whether he begins with the male or the female pursuit of sexual satisfaction; and the conclusion concerning who is to give up rights, property, and personality to the other would differ according to which gender stakes out for itself the active pursuit of this satisfaction, hardly an inspiring basis for moral claims.

Finally, even if, as Fichte claims, women and men were to experience the sexual impulse differently, with women experiencing it as love, his conclusion about the unlimited surrender of the woman's property, rights, and personality (symbolized by her surrender of her name) does not follow. At best, the sexual impulse is only one of many impulses seeking satisfaction in an individual's life. For an individual to surrender herself body and soul in the pursuit of any one of these seems an extreme over-reaction. She could, for example, meet Fichte's requirements (assuming their correctness for the sake of argument even though such correctness seems implausible) by experiencing the sexual impulse as love—the desire to satisfy the man—during the sexual activity itself without allowing this desire to rule each and every aspect of her life and possibly impede her satisfaction of other impulses. On the other hand, she could simply risk willing momentary passivity during the sexual activity itself. For a person to go to the lengths Fichte proposes just to avoid the contradiction of willing momentary passivity seems irrational indeed.

Fichte's argument, then, does not support the traditional dominance of the husband any more than did appeals to wants and needs. That men want an absolute acceptance of themselves or need to know what children are truly their own does not justify their keeping their wives dependent. As John Stuart Mill argues, even if women, too, were to want their own dependence, which universally they do not, this would not justify the traditional dominance of the husband, particularly as long as education, laws, and mores work together to limit women's opportunities and expectations and thereby to ensure as far as possible acceptance of subordination.[31] Justification of subordination by appeal to the good of the subordinated has been challenged too vigorously, too frequently, and too compellingly to retain any plausibility today. Moreover, the desire for one's own or another's dependence cannot justify, as de Beauvoir argues, morally problematic or otherwise objectionable dependence.

A NONHIERARCHICAL HOME

What else can be said to support hierarchy in marriage?

Few modern thinkers seriously maintain that a difference in capability alone justifies the rule of the superior over the inferior. This aristocratic presumption has been subjected to a great deal of philosophical attack and relatively little defense since the time of Plato and Aristotle. Instead, the modern support for a "head" of the family is more likely to resemble Thomas Hobbes's practical argument: if this society is to be durable, then one must "govern and dispose of all that is common to them both."[32] Opting on the side of male dominance, John Locke spells out the problem arising from disagreements in more detail: "But the husband and wife, though they have but one common concern, yet having different understandings, will unavoidably sometimes have different wills too; it therefore being necessary that the last determination, i.e., the rule, should be placed somewhere; it naturally falls to the man's share, as the abler and stronger."[33] Where there is no head, a serious disagreement between husband and wife will lead, according to Kant, to "nothing but wrangling"[34] or, according to C. S. Lewis, to the dissolution of the marriage.[35] Thus, in the interests of harmony and permanence, such thinkers conclude, marriage must have a head.

Those who challenge this argument often cite other human relationships that clearly do not need a head. For example, Charlotte Perkins Gilman points to friendship and love: "If it [marriage] needs 'a head' it will elect a chairman pro tem. Friendship does not need 'a head.' Love does not need 'a head.' Why should a family?"[36] Unfortunately, as long as marriage is proposed as an enduring relation with a common life and common property, this analogy will not do. At most, the analogy challenges the presumption that human relationships are impossible without a ruler.

Mill, too, points to other voluntary forms of association between two individuals where it simply is not the case "one of them must be absolute master [and] . . . still less that the law must determine which of them it shall be." In business partnership, he observes, "[though t]he most frequent case of voluntary association, next to marriage, . . . it is not found or thought necessary to enact that . . . one partner shall have entire control over the concern, and the others shall be bound to obey his orders."[37]

Mill's analogy is far better than Gilman's, since business partnerships usually involve at least some common property, are granted legal recognition, and frequently are long-lasting. C. S. Lewis, however, would probably object to the analogy since business partnerships would not be quite enduring enough to satisfy him. If business partners come to a serious disagreement, they can dissolve their partnership and go their separate ways. This is precisely what Lewis does not want to see happen in a marriage.

If the concern to make marriage as harmonious and enduring as possible is legitimate, then some way to resolve differences seems to be in order. But why should it be the rule of one over the other? Though agreeing with the need for a determining voice in cases of disagreement—in "situations that do not permit the interaction of separate wills"— Condorcet sees such situations as in fact few in number and rejects the rather extreme measure of decreeing that one should always be subordinate to the other. He urges instead the prerogative be shared, in each case the "deciding vote" being given to "that one of the two [who] will conform his [or her] will more closely to reason."[38]

Such a division of responsibility seems more consistent with the expressed concern for "the superior" to have the final say in conflicts requiring a joint decision. A particular man and woman are likely to be such that one is superior in some ways while the other is superior in terms of other skills and abilities. Surely a union is more likely to be harmonious and enduring if the more expert on the particular matter at hand has the determining voice each time a serious conflict of wills otherwise prevents a unanimous decision from being reached.

Moreover, this responds to other problems facing the purported need of marriage for a head. First, the discord arising from the abuse of authority no doubt would be greatly reduced, even without going so far as to grant David Hume's wish that "there were no pretensions to authority on either side; but that everything was carried on with perfect equality, as between two equal members of the same body."[39] Certainly it would diminish the extreme cruelty recognized by Lucretia Mott of allowing the wife to be "robbed" by her husband of her earnings with no redress by law.[40] And it seems likely to lessen the incidence of wife and child abuse.

By rejecting domination of one partner by the other, such marital distribution of authority in decision-making would allow also for a friendship between the two not possible in relationships with a hierarchical structure. Admittedly this is not a problem to some, like George Santayana, who find friendship between men and women simply precluded by their intellectual disparity, "an intellectual alienation as profound as that which separates us from the dumb animals."[41] Thinkers like Gilman, though, deplore the subservient wife and dominant h*sband of the traditional home and look toward "a nobler type of family," one combining the tenderness and permanence of love with "the broad deep-rooted friendliness and comradeship of equals."[42] Even Nietzsche recognizes slaves cannot be friends and tyrants cannot have friends.[43]

Condorcet's division of responsibility answers an objection raised by several thinkers concerning the social effects of the traditional hierarchical family. Mill blames this "present constitution of the relation between men and women" for "[all] the selfish propensities, the self-worship, the unjust self-preference, which exist among mankind."[44] Gilman, too, believes the traditional home develops unnecessary selfishness, but, even worse, is counter-productive in a democratic form of government: "For each man to have one whole woman to cook for and wait upon him is a poor education for democracy. The boy with a servile mother, the man with a servile wife, cannot reach the sense of equal rights we need today."[45] Thus, Condorcet's suggestion of a division of responsibility meets the concerns of those who see a dominant voice as essential if couples are to resolve differences; moreover, a division of responsibility resolves many of the difficulties and problematic or harmful consequences of the hierarchical traditional marriage.

The appeals to wants, wishes, and needs not only offer no support for a hierarchy in individual relationships, but also raise serious questions about whether the demands of morality would permit the traditional dominance/submission relation of husband and wife. Similarly, the arguments that marriage needs a head do not prove there should be a single head; even less do they prove the husband should be head and certainly not that the husband/father should be granted special rights by law over other members of the household. The only compelling argument examined thus far is not an argument for hierarchy but rather for providing within marriage, and, by extension, within whatever intimate relationships are meant to be relatively stable and permanent, some way of resolving disagreements when common action is needed. However, this argument does not establish the necessity of a recognized ruler in such relationships. At most, it indicates a need in stable unions for some division of responsibility, recognized at least by themselves, so disagreements can be resolved with joint action following the lead of the party who is likely to make the cooler and wiser judgment on the matter under dispute.

This suggests the liberal feminist proposal of individualized marriage contracts to allow for choice concerning the rights and responsibilities of the partners. As Alison Jaggar observes, by proposing alternative ways the state might control the most intimate and presumably most private of relationships, this proposal makes clear how uniformly controlled by the state this relationship has been and thus offers further challenge to the public/private distinction itself. From the perspective of allowing the individuals to determine their own relationships without the state intervening and dictating contours, she says, marriage would become more of a private matter by allowing the participating individuals to determine their own relationships. At the same time, but from a different perspective (that of making the intervention of the state explicit), she recognizes that marriage would thereby become, in a sense, less private: "As marriage contracts became more detailed, explicit and enforceable under the law, they would become indistinguishable from business contracts and it would become generally accepted that the details of family life should be regulated by the state."[46] For those concerned that privacy has for too long served as a cover for abuse, this acknowledged regulation of family would by no means be a bad thing.

REJECTION OF APPROPRIATIVE RELATIONSHIPS

Traditional views of human relationships are problematic, not just because of their emphasis on competition and hierarchy. They also err in the ways they depict love and friendship. Sartre's characterizations of kinds of love can help to make these errors apparent.

Most of Sartre's critics take the human relationships described in *Being and Nothingness* as exhaustive of what he sees as the possibilities. In so doing, they ignore not only his relationship with de Beauvoir, however limited in fact it may have been and however distorting and idealizing the descriptions given by both Sartre and de Beauvoir themselves. More important, concentration on *Being and Nothingness* neglects the interesting examples of loving relationships developed in his novels, plays, and short stories. Such critics also disregard his quite explicit later description of *Being and Nothingness* as an analysis of consciousness in bad faith.[47] With Iris Murdoch, they conclude that all human relationships are appropriative, attempts to capture the other's freedom, and that love is a "battle between two hypnotists in a closed room."[48]

For Sartre, individuals in bad faith attempt in various ways to flee from their freedom. To be human is to be free and responsible, even vis-à-vis one's own birth and bodily infirmities—factors over which, in a sense, one has no control, yet over which one has the important power of interpreting, of giving a significance to, of accepting or rejecting. Responsibility extends to the way in which one is seen by others and to one's being as an inert presence in the world. One is one's body, one's past, the way one is seen by others; at the same time, one is always free. This is the ambiguity of human existence.

For those in bad faith, the look of the other may be a threat inasmuch as it denies their freedom by seeing them as nothing more than objects. At the same time, the look may tempt them by virtue of the fact that they are thereby seen as things, as solid, as finished, rather than as free. The look destroys the very ambiguity bad faith seeks to escape.

Because the other sees this individual as what she or he is (a body, acting in certain ways in a certain context, with a particular history) and thereby bestows on her or him something like an essence, individuals in bad faith may try to incorporate the other's perspective into themselves, but without destroying it as freedom. Such individuals may identify with the object seen by the other (Sartre calls this the way of love, language, and masochism) and, when that fails to achieve their goal, confront the other's freedom on the ground of their own (the attitude of indifference, desire, hate, sadism). Both attitudes view relations in terms of appropriation; in the latter, the attempt is to possess and, in the former, it is to be possessed.[49]

The upshot of these discussions of the relations of love and desire, both essentially possessive and both requiring the dominance of one and the submission of the other, is that these relations are doomed to fail. Since they are attempts to capture the freedom of another or to abolish one's own, they cannot succeed. The one attempt is foiled by the fact that the freedom of the other remains out of reach; and, in the other, the harder one tries to be merely an object, the more one becomes "submerged" by the consciousness of subjectivity.[50]

Other depictions of relationships in Sartre's writings challenge the view of relationships as always appropriative and suggest nonappropriative possibilities for human relationships. These examples include the relationships of Eve and Pierre (*The Chips Are Down*), of Hoederer and Hugo (*Dirty Hands*), of Hilda and Goetz (*The Devil and the Good Lord*), of Lucie and Henri (*Men Without Shadows*), and of Anna and Kean (*Kean*).

Analysis of these relationships along with what is said about love in Sartre's more familiar writings reveals three quite different views of love. There is first the game-of-mirrors view of love—the view presented in *Being and Nothingness*. A second might be called the "common-enemy" view. And a third, the most important and least recognized, is a depiction of a kind of love capable of affirming human freedom, a lucid yet nonetheless joyful love, seeking perfect confidence and coincidence only as a regulative ideal.

The first view of love is the view with which readers of *Being and Nothingness* are quite familiar. At this level, "[s]adism and masochism are the revelation of the Other," as Sartre says in *Notebooks for an Ethics*. But, he adds, this sadism and masochism "only make sense . . . before conversion."[51] In this type of relationship, the lovers are in bad faith and seek to make use of each other in trying to hide their freedom and responsibility from themselves. Such lovers seek solitude because the look of a third party effectively destroys the game they play with each other. Their love requires sequestration because their appropriative projects cannot succeed and the look of another makes this apparent.

Second, there is a love between or among those who are, as it were, comrades in arms. Terror can produce this sort of love, as Sartre recognizes in the *Critique of Dialectical Reason* ("a practical bond of *love* between the lynchers [of traitors]").[52] This is the love Goetz (*The Devil and the Good Lord*) has in mind when he affirms, "To love anyone is to hate the same enemy."[53] Similarly, when Mathieu, in *The Age of Reason*, imitates Ivich's gesture and stabs his own hand, their common defiance of others' opinions brings them momentarily to a sense of intimacy they had not previously experienced and do not experience again.[54]

It is in terms of this sort of love Henri and Lucie (*Men Without Shadows*) are drawn closer through their tortured shame and suffering even as they are separated from Lucie's former lover Jean. Jean and Lucie are imprisoned with several of their comrades. Jean, the leader of the insurrectionary group, was captured separately, and the captors do not suspect his connection with the others. In fact, the others are being tortured for information concerning him. A triangle of sorts develops as Henri, one of the comrades, confesses his love for Lucie "because it doesn't matter any more." Lucie allows Henri to kill her young brother François who, they fear, under torture will reveal Jean's identity. Their shame and suffering bring Lucie and Henri together and separate them from Jean.[55]

A quite different kind of love emerges in other writings and other characters. This does not require a common enemy nor is it appropriative. Consider, for example, two relationships depicted in Sartre's fiction, one connected with sexual attraction and expression, the other not. Pierre and Eve (*The Chips are Down*) love each other but they neither have nor hate the same enemy. In fact, they are members of different classes and have different enemies and different loyalties pulling them apart and preventing them from loving each other "with perfect coincidence and with all their . . . might,"[56] a love they must achieve or, failing to do so, return to the netherworld of the dead. Similarly, Hoederer's apparently nonsexual love for Hugo (*Dirty Hands*) seems not to be connected with hatred of enemies. Even though both Hoederer and Hugo are Communists and active in the party, it is not at all clear they hate the same enemy. In fact, it seems to me obvious that they do not.

What can be seen in the love of Pierre and Eve is the recognition of a third kind of love, in which those who love strive in a positive and authentic way for a perfect coincidence, a perfect confidence. Given the ambiguity of human existence—the fact that human beings are a tension of opposites—coincidence with another cannot be achieved any more than can a coincidence of an individual with herself or himself. Although they do love each other, when they rejoin the living they are torn by conflicting loves and loyalties. Pierre tries to save his comrades from staging an insurrection that will be in fact only a trap for them. Eve is concerned about her sister Lucette whom Andre, Eve's husband, is trying to win over so that, after Eve's death, he can marry Lucette for her dowry just as he earlier married Eve for hers.

Unable to love each other with perfect confidence and not even the slightest of misgivings, Eve and Pierre return to the realm of the dead. There they meet two young people who, like Eve and Pierre earlier, have discovered they were "made for each other" and who also seek the opportunity to live their lives over. The new lovers eagerly ask if they really can try to do so. Pierre and Eve, we are told, respond with funny looks and gentle smiles, "'Try,' Pierre advises. 'Try it anyway,' murmurs Eve."[57]

Although Sartre admits that in this play he was having fun with a nonexistentialist determinism (in which the chips are down and lovers are meant for one another),[58] the play nevertheless suggests some important aspects of love. First, a love of perfect coincidence, of perfect confidence and no misgivings, is presented as an impossibility, given not just the ambiguous creatures human beings are but also oppressive social structures. This recognition should surprise neither Sartre's critics nor his admirers. What may surprise is the affirmation, in spite of this, of the attempt to love with perfect coincidence, an affirmation apparent in Eve's and Pierre's responses to the aspiring lovers. There is a wistfulness in their responses, but there is more: in their urging is a recognition of the importance of the attempt even though it cannot succeed. Ambiguity, a tension of opposites, and separateness are an ineradicable part of the human condition, yet the effort to harmonize and unify the inharmonious and disparate is vital to human striving, particularly to authentic striving.

Hoederer's relationship with Hugo is revealing as well. At his own peril, Hoederer recognizes Hugo's difficulty in growing out of his middle-class childhood and into a revolutionary. Hoederer respects Hugo's freedom and risks his own life in order to help Hugo grow up. Realizing Hugo has been sent as an assassin, Hoederer nevertheless presents Hugo with numerous opportunities to complete his mission, trusting him even though it may—and eventually does—mean Hoederer's own death. At each point, Hoederer's efforts backfire, and Hugo feels insulted, humiliated, made fun of, rather than loved and respected. For example, when Hoederer intervenes and tries to resolve the early antagonism between his bodyguards and Hugo, Hugo is outraged to find himself defended by Hoederer. Similarly Hoederer's trust of Hugo, even to the point of giving Hugo the opportunity to fulfill his assassination assignment, evokes from Hugo the response, "I hate you."[59]

In the play *The Devil and the Good Lord*, Sartre develops another character who, like Hoederer, loves without being loved in return and who also loves clear-sightedly, nonpossessively, and without bad faith. Hilda recognizes Goetz's misery, stays with him, and later confesses to Heinrich her love for Goetz, acknowledging only that Goetz has loved her "as much as he has loved himself."[60]

Against Goetz's fear of "coupling in public" ("under the eyes of God"), Hilda counters that love is a "deep night" hiding lovers from God's regard: "when people love each other, they become invisible to God." Goetz can be accurately characterized as loving "in opposition to God," an opposition he finds especially tormenting during "coupling." Hilda's love seems more indifferent to God; it appears not to matter to her whether God views her lovemaking or even whether God exists.

Hilda's love thus complicates Sartre's meaning when he discusses *The Devil and the Good Lord* and describes love as always "in opposition to God."[61] I believe he was speaking of an opposition with many manifestations. On one level is an opposition manifested by the sort of love exemplified by Goetz, a love premised on having the same enemy. In Goetz's love, a love that requires enemies, God can be seen as the enemy of last resort, an absolute necessity for lovers who love in opposition but who at any given moment may lack the "glue" of a present (and finite) enemy to hold them together. On the other hand, Hilda's love can be seen as opposing God only by virtue of itself being an absolute from within which she is totally indifferent to another, and opposing, alleged absolute, namely, God.

In response to Goetz's horror of sexual love ("how can I desire to hold in my arms this bag of excrement?"), she assures him, "[i]f you die, I will lie down beside you and stay there to the very end, without eating or drinking; you will rot away in my embrace, and I will love your carrion flesh; for *you do not love at all, if you do not love every-thing* [italics added]."[62] Hilda, unlike Goetz, accepts embodiment. She is not repulsed by the body or its functions and recognizes that to love Goetz is to love an individual who is embodied and not merely a disembodied mind, soul, or consciousness.

Finally, she loves without idealizing. She knows Goetz "will never be like other men. Neither better nor worse: different."[63]

Anna in *Kean* is similar to Hilda.[64] In the play, Anna has fallen in love with the actor Kean whom she has observed through many performances. When Kean, assuming he has dazzled her with his performances, seeks to shock and disillusion her by confessing he was "drunk as an Irish lord" during those performances, she indicates her thoroughgoing awareness of his drunkenness and acknowledges his various errors: calling other actors by the wrong names, inserting moving soliloquies from other plays. Mystified that she knew he was drunk and yet she "applauded all the same," Kean is told she applauded to encourage him and because she knew he must be unhappy.[65]

Anna sees Kean quite clearly and responds to what she perceives as his need somewhat as Hilda does to the suffering of the peasants and later to Goetz's misery: "So I made enquiries, and I found you were a drunkard, a libertine, crippled with debts, melancholy and mad by turns, and I said to myself: 'That man needs a wife.'" When she recognizes the prompter's love for Kean, she resolves "nothing will be changed"—Solomon (Kean's prompter) will live with her and Kean after they are married. Like Hilda, Anna seems unafraid of the eyes of the other. Finally, as she prepares to leave for America, she seems ready to accept defeat with good grace if Kean does not love her. Although she later admits to lying about leaving, as she says, to "make" Kean marry her, she nonetheless seems to be as clear-sightedly aware of Kean's freedom as she is of his character.[66]

In Hoederer's love for Hugo, Hilda's for Goetz, Anna's for Kean, and in the love of Eve and Pierre, Sartre exemplifies what he recognizes in *What Is Literature?*, namely, "that it is quite impossible to treat concrete men as ends in contemporary society." As in the cases of Hoederer and Hugo and of Eve and Pierre, the injustices of the age, classism, racism, sexism, etc., inevitably will intervene and vitiate "at the roots" the good one strives to accomplish.[67] Thus, Goetz remains the unlovable bastard, unable to accept himself and desiring only "to be a man among men." He moves from feeling more alone the more he is loved to acknowledging Hilda's love by incorporating her into himself and admitting her to his loneliness: "You are myself. We shall be alone together."[68]

Kean may appear more optimistic inasmuch as it ends with Kean linking arms with Anna and Solomon and saying, "My true, my only friends." However, it is difficult not to imagine the future Kean as he tries to make a living in America, whether by acting or not, once again wondering if his movement was truly an action or merely a gesture[69] and once again struggling with his existence as a bastard in the eyes of others.

Although it may be impossible today to treat men as ends, nevertheless, according to Sartre in *What Is Literature?*, the writer strives, as does Hoederer, to hold in tension the affirmations of revolution and the kingdom of ends. In the loves exemplified by Hoederer, Hilda, Anna, Pierre, and Eve, ambiguity prevails. Failure is inevitable; nevertheless they reach beyond such failure.

THE POSSIBILITIES OF AUTHENTIC LOVE

What these analyses indicate about the possibilities of love is to have been expected, given Sartre's view of humanity, freedom, and authenticity. There is a kind of love that recognizes and affirms the freedom of the beloved as well as one's own. However much social structures render problematic or impossible the expression or realization of such love, the authentic individual must affirm and actively support the freedom of others. To love authentically is to move beyond the sadomasochistic dialectic of enslaving freedoms to a "deeper recognition and reciprocal comprehension of freedoms" (a dimension lacking in *Being and Nothingness*, according to Sartre in *Notebooks for an Ethics*). For this love "*tension* is necessary: to maintain the two faces of ambiguity, to hold them within the unity of one and the same project." It is "something wholly other than the desire to appropriate."[70]

Authentic relationships, like other authentic activity, must maintain a tension between what is sought and what is achieved, between coincidence and inevitable alienation and separateness, between treating the other as an end and treating him or her as a means. An authentic individual can approach another with a confidence concerning human freedom, both the individual's own and the other's. Such love, as Sarah Hoagland says, borrowing a term from Julia Penelope, is a bonding, rather than a binding, since there is mutual respect and awareness of freedom rather than dependency, knowledge rather than ignorance. Each can feel power-from-within; neither will desire or feel power-over.[71]

The authentic individual has lost any illusions of being justified and made essential by another. This individual recognizes her or his own freedom and thereby, if Sartre's analysis in *What Is Literature?* is correct, already experiences a kind of joy. Like the writer, one who loves authentically can approach the other with confidence in freedom and with a trust and generosity.[72] Aesthetic joy and the joy of love may be momentary, but nonetheless they are intimations of the harmony sought in each case. As momentary, they may bring sorrow and negate the aspirations of those who sought therein to be justified and essential and to escape their freedom and responsibility. But for the authentic, such intimations may be taken in stride as temporal albeit fleeting and ambiguous embodiments of the ultimate but impossible goals toward which they strive. Once again, what is sought does not change when one becomes authentic, but the way it is sought does change.

Such love is not part of a morality attempting to fuse individuals into a single consciousness. The attempt to fuse two individuals into one was explicitly recognized, in *Being and Nothingness*, as the goal of bad faith and thereby rejected as the basis of authentic relationships. In *Notebooks for an Ethics*, Sartre warns against a morality of fusion as well as against a kingdom of ends that recognizes each consciousness only in its Kantian universality. Rather, the morality he approves would take each individual in his or her "concrete singularity."[73]

Although Sartre presents possibilities for human relations that are not appropriative and that go beyond Goetz's view of love as having the same enemy, nevertheless Sartre recognizes the ways the injustices of the age will inevitably intervene and vitiate "at the roots" the good one strives to accomplish. This means "it is quite impossible to treat concrete men as ends in contemporary society."[74] Eve and Pierre in *The Chips Are Down* have different enemies and are divided by class as well as other loyalties. Yet they affirm the attempt to love one another with perfect coincidence and confidence even while recognizing the impossibility of their goal.

FRIENDSHIP AND SEXUAL LOVE

While Western culture's traditional views of love emphasize what Sartre refers to as appropriation, they also treat differences in extremely dubious ways. A delightful exception is found in one of Plato's dialogues, although, as a spoof of another point of view, it is not his own view of the role of difference in sexual love. An examination of this role illuminates important but very negative assumptions in those traditional views.

In the *Symposium*, Plato recounts the course of events at a drinking party attended by Socrates. Those in attendance decide to give speeches in praise of love. One speech in particular is, I think, worthy of some attention. Delivered by Aristophanes, it purports to explain sexual love by returning to its supposed origins. The speech takes us back to fanciful earlier times when human creatures were quite unlike human beings today. These creatures were shaped like balls and consequently moved rapidly. Their bodies were basically doubles of ours, including two sets of sexual parts. They not only were fast, but generally remarkably self-contained, self-satisfied, and powerful.

In an effort to control these enviable creatures, the gods split them and rearranged their parts. Properly weakened, the halves began their search for each other. Since the former wholes, we are told, were diverse, some being male-male in terms of their sexual parts, some being female-female, and others being female-male, this accounts not only for the relentless search inherent in sexual love but also for those who seek lovers of the same sex.[75]

Plato's imagery highlights features of sexual love I have long thought important, even though Plato himself may not have taken it so seriously. First, from the outset, it quite clearly denies the heterosexist view of sexual love as "natural," healthy, or good only when it is heterosexual, anything else being a perverse and unhealthy mimicry of the "real thing." Second, it undermines the heterosexist view of women as somehow made for love and specifically to be dominated by men. On the contrary, the reconstructed creatures described in this myth are remarkably equal in their need for each other. Their desire is quite aptly described in Hoagland's terms as a desire for "connection."[76] Third, this explanation of love recognizes the generally unacknowledged sense of belonging, of fit, of wholeness, when one is so fortunate as to find one's "other half." Fourth, love presented in this way accommodates the similarities or sameness of lovers in a way not fashionable in Western thought,[77] while at the same time making room for the much more popular view of lovers as seeking in each other a completion, something they lack in themselves, an unproblematic claim if not developed in the direction of dependence.

There are indeed problems in this imagery. First, there is the difficulty just mentioned, that the incompleteness promulgated in the popular claim may suggest and even foster excessive dependency and thereby undermine moral agency. The initial integrity or wholeness of lovers must be affirmed as well as a view of loving relationships respecting and sustaining such integrity. Thus, the incompleteness presented in the myth must not be understood as lack of wholeness or integrity but rather as representing the fact that human beings are social beings and not totally independent and self-contained individuals. In other words, the view represented in the myth challenges our society's and many philosophers' view of autonomy in which individuals (generally only male individuals) are regarded as atomistic units.

Second, the imagery presents a view of lovers as somehow "made" for each other. While this may capture the experience of the initial attraction as, to a considerable extent, given and beyond choice, it falsely suggests that the "smitten" individuals are caught in a force stronger than both of them and cannot help but pursue the affair as far as it goes. It also falsely suggests that the ensuing relationship will be effortless. The natural determinism underlying such claims must be denied since it unduly restricts our view of the alternatives and denies the roles we play in choosing lovers, usually from those to whom we are attracted, and in actively working on relationships in order to maintain them.

Third, the imagery needs to be expanded to allow similar accounts of a multitude of relationships, not just sexual ones. Thus, it must accommodate the individual's need for connectedness to numerous individuals and the fact that most of the needed connectedness is not sexual.

With these qualifications, how can this view of sexual love increase our understanding of other forms of love? First, in its treatment of similarity and difference, Plato's story points to aspects of friendship and sexual love discussed by many feminists. Surely both friendships and sexual love require enormous amounts of similarity between those involved. When asked by her husband, whom she acknowledges as one of her "best friends," what she gets from her women friends and cannot get from him, Letty Pogrebin responds, "the other *me*" and seconds Ecclesiastes' claim that "The best mirror is an old friend."[78] Such emphasis on similarities among friends can be accommodated by the view that love can occur only between opposites. To do so, though, requires a radical separation between friendship (between equals or similars) and sexual love (between opposites), emphatically rejecting the possibility of any melding of friendship and sexual love in the same relationship. Moreover, if the differences separating men and women from each other are incompatible with friendship, they seem equally to rule out respect and even genuine communication, both of which require identification of one with the other. Such identification with one another is impossible where individuals are so different. All that is left is sexual attraction and, as Santayana claims, "an intellectual alienation as profound as that which separates us from the dumb animals."[79]

At the same time, Plato's myth reminds us of the impossibility of ignoring difference or of treating it simplistically. But here, too, the myth is at odds with the view that difference is paramount in love. Since only sexual love between men and women is affirmed in the latter, one difference thus seems to be regarded as essential. However, this is deceptive since, as we have seen, sexual difference is not a simple one. Though presumed purely biological or anatomical, sexual difference has all too frequently been assumed to connect with a whole battery of physical, emotional, psychological, class/economic, and even moral differences. In fact, sexism and heterosexism have led to the construction of gendered personalities in which these are connected— or at least appear so since otherwise the nonconforming individuals would be censured. The resulting assumption of difference—gender difference—presumes men are all the same and women are all the same and seems bemused when women sexually love other women and when men are lovers of other men. After all, since, according to this common view of sexual love, difference is essential, what could such lovers possibly offer one another except, perhaps, an unhealthy narcissism?

While I suspect they would be happy with the consequent that women are all alike, upholders of this view probably would demure from my claim that it results in the affirmation that men are all alike. They might try to claim that men are alike only in being "individuals," but that this means that men differ greatly from one another. In one sense, they are right; in another sense, their claim squares with neither their theory nor their practice. They are correct if they mean only that men take up different spaces, do different things appropriate to those of their gender, and say different things also appropriate to their gender. If that is all that is meant (and if I am right that differences like these are the only ones recognized by this theory), then women are just as much individuals; and any bemusement over women being attracted to women or being friends with women and even men is, on the basis of the theory, itself incomprehensible.

In another sense, though, the claim about individuality is inconsistent with both the theory and the practice of those who espouse it. After all, this theory disparages differences other than gender that might lead to a truly interesting concept of individuality. Moreover, its practitioners have been notorious for mocking, threatening, and even trying to reconstruct in numerous ways those males as well as females who do not manifest appropriate gender appearances, attractions, behaviors, qualities, and thoughts.

Those who uphold this framework frequently claim that friendship is possible without this vital difference of gender; some even see friendship as possible only between or among individuals who are alike, certainly *not* between men and women, and perhaps only among men.[80] Seldom, though, do they observe the way their disparagement of other differences makes friendship between men or between women just as unintelligible as it makes homosexual love. After all, propounders of this view can be asked the same question they ask of others, namely, assuming such likeness, what could such alleged friends possibly offer one another?

Why, too, if men are all alike and women are all alike, does one strike up a friendship with one individual and not another, convinced they are not interchangeable? Although an old friend may indeed become a good mirror and an other "me," presumably this friend's difference, certainly from other women and quite possibly even from "me," is what attracted in the first place. For many of us, at least, women—and men—are not simply replaceable ciphers; a woman seeking a friend like that described by Pogrebin often does not latch on to any woman who comes along, not even to the first one willing to be her friend. Nor does she necessarily restrict her search only to women; she may find that faithful mirror in a male who is more similar than different and who is willing and able to see and to hear her and to understand. Rather, in seeking a friend, one frequently seeks a level of sensitivity and emotional receptivity, along, perhaps, with intelligence, particular political commitments, a certain sense of humor, and many other qualities not found in others. Moreover, the fact that the friend is not "me" is what makes the perspective on "me" both of greater value than a real mirror and something quite different from that of a therapist who may reflect "me" while remaining somewhat detached.

This assumption of difference between the sexes and therefore of likeness within is the work of what Marilyn Frye calls the "arrogant eye." As she says, "The arrogant perceiver's expectation creates in the space about him a sort of vacuum mold into which the other is sucked and held." This is a mind unable to tolerate ambiguity and willing to go to great lengths, as Frye notes, to insure that each and every person is clearly male or clearly female, that men are men and women are women, and that same-sex lovers are regarded as deviates and, if possible, punished. This arrogant mind carefully molds individuals to its own expectations, sometimes through surgery and chemicals (when individuals are born with genitalia not fitting under society's dimorphism or later develop "inappropriate" secondary sex characteristics), sometimes through education (see Rousseau's *Emile*). If such molding fails, the arrogant eye may simply not see or credit differences or, where they cannot be ignored, will experience the incongruity as indicating "something wrong" with the individual or individuals themselves.[81]

For all the emphasis on difference in this view, its arrogance ends up postulating sameness (of all women, on the one hand, and of all men, on the other) and, even worse, creating difference that can be subsumed into the interests of the arrogant observer. Thus, though in one sense differences are maximized (those between men and women), in another they are minimized (those between men and those between women), and all so one set of interests can dominate and others can be manipulated and coerced to support and further the dominant interests.

This arrogance does not limit itself to sexual love. Friendship, too, is affected by the arrogance fostered by power relations in situations of oppression. As Frye points out, if women try to relate to one another in any way, these power relations will inevitably come into play. Thus, white women will always have the inescapable prerogative of hearing or not hearing those who are not white and of defining who is part of the group.[82] A similar prerogative exists and should be recognized in terms of class.

Sexual love, as seen by the arrogant eye, will involve, then, as Frye suggests, some variation of "[t]he attachment of the well-broken slave to the master." As opposed to this, there are voluntary friendships and loves, where one "can survive displeasing the other, defying the other, dissociating from the other." The "loving eye," contrary to the arrogant eye, "knows the independence of the other" and does not try to assimilate. It is, as Frye says, "generous to its object."[83]

The sexual love mandated by arrogance is a love in which there is no possibility of friendship since there is no equality, an essential ingredient of friendship, as Letty Pogrebin recognizes. It is a love in which the two participants have quite different views of intimacy: *"The average man's idea of an intimate exchange is the average woman's idea of casual conversation."* Moreover, in such love, women are unable to get from men the intimacy they need and, as long as men are allowed by society to feel superior to women, men, though able to get their intimacy needs satisfied by women, are unable to secure from women the requisite reassurance about their manhood. In addition, since men are indoctrinated with notions of manhood teaching them that *"affection is sexual and emotional,"* neither are most men able to meet their intimacy needs with other men. Thus, Pogrebin concludes, male/

female friendships are comparatively rare and a bit one-sided. Men need women as friends more than women need men as friends. Pogrebin argues the necessity of such relationships, not because women stand to gain a great deal from them, but rather because men need them so desperately, because "men who go their ways without women frequently make a mess of things" and because they learn from friendship what it is to be human.[84]

The loving eye, on the other hand, can appreciate difference since it recognizes separateness, boundaries, and different interests. Such an "eye" is also better able to discern similarities. Where genuine differences are appreciated, similarities will not be forced and artificial.[85] Only this approach to love and friendship can take seriously the second aspect of Plato's myth—the recognition that those who become friends and who love more than just sexually do so out of some deep-seated likenesses, such as seeing the world the same way, enjoying the same things, laughing at the same jokes, and having similar political and other commitments and convictions.

Neither differences nor similarities have been adequately appreciated in the Western tradition since generally only one difference—gender—has been seen as legitimate and even then narrowly interpreted in terms of heterosexual relations. According to Judith Butler, Monique Wittig sees the naming of sexual difference as the creation of such difference, a creation restricting "our understanding of relevant sexual parts to those that aid in the process of reproduction, and thereby render[ing] heterosexuality an ontological process."[86] This recognition of only one difference relevant to sexual love is heterosexist and has led, as we have seen, to the disparagement of sameness. At the same time, strangely enough, it has resulted in an enormous and uncritical assumption of the similarity of all women with each other and of all men with each other while reserving, as Frye so clearly sees, "[a]ll or almost all of that which pertains to love . . . exclusively for other men."[87]

Thus, two quite opposed views of love are at work in such heterosexism, one the common view of sexual love explicitly endorsed by heterosexism and in which only gender difference is relevant, the other a view more like that of Plato's Aristophanes in which similarities and perhaps other differences are thought enormously important.[88] Seldom, however, is this opposition explicitly brought to the fore. Recognition of the opposition should help us understand and perhaps appreciate more deeply Charlotte Perkins Gilman's amazement at as well as frustration with the long-standing theory and practice of raising male and female children to be almost as different as possible and then expecting them as adults to be able to love and work and play together in intimate relations.[89]

Loving in a way that comes to terms with and accepts both difference and similarity is difficult, theoretically as well as in practice. María Lugones reports developing her analysis of "'world'-travelling" in response to just such difficulties. Her analysis grew out of her recognition of the failures of women in the United States to love across racial and cultural boundaries and of her own failure to love her mother. In such failures she sees "the failure to identify with another woman, the failure to see oneself in other women who are quite different from oneself." Rejecting the arrogant love she was taught to feel for her mother, Lugones professes to be glad she did not learn her lessons well since such love would have been an identification with a victim of enslavement and thereby part of a process of learning to be a slave herself. What she proposes instead is a shift from arrogant perception to seeing her mother "with her eyes," going into her "world" and witnessing her own sense of her self and the way both she and her daughter are "constructed in her world." Similar "world"-travel is necessary if we are to love across other boundaries.[90]

What is needed is a caring that, as Sarah Hoagland says, involves "respect—for ourselves and each other—not establishing authority and chain of command (even benevolent): enabling, not controlling, playing with, not dominating, and so on." This caring "is a caring among those whom we would give the respect of peers whose abilities are quite varied."[91] Such relationship involves, as Audre Lorde says, "a totaling of differences without merging."[92]

Letty Pogrebin calls this sort of caring "feminist friendship" and claims that such friendships "unite the self and the other in pride, vitality, and strength." She elaborates:

> You feel it when you notice yourself assuming the best of a woman, not anticipating hostility or suppressing envy. You feel it when you are interested in what a friend thinks—not just about you and your activities but about *everything.* You feel it when your friends alter your perspective on life, help you sort out your problems, enlarge your goals and help you move toward achieving them, help you see yourself not as one isolated woman treated this way or that but as a vital member of half the human race.[93]

CONCLUSION

A feminist ethics must affirm as an ideal a love incorporating the reciprocity desired by Nel Noddings and the respect of each for the freedom of the other demanded by Sartre. It cannot be unidirectional caring in which the needs and wishes of one are central and those of the other are continually or for the most part ignored and considered less important. Nor can it be patronizing or paternalistic, imposing ends foreign to the other and presumably for the other's own good. Moreover, the ideal of love must incorporate the gratuity Sartre sees as vital in the relation of appeal/help. Love is a gift, an expression of generosity, an appreciation of and desire to be with and to help another, not necessarily because the one who loves profits therefrom or shares the other's goal. One helps another to achieve her or his goal just because it is the other's goal. Thus, such loving relationships require the freedom of all the parties and are incompatible with structures of domination and submission.

This is what makes an ethics of care inadequate and even dangerous if accepted uncritically in a situation of violence. An ethics of care will offer little guidance to those who work against that violence and will, in fact, do much to buttress a status quo that should be challenged rather than supported. At the same time, though, such an ethics is absolutely indispensable if it is taken as working out the parameters of the ethics that would guide the nonoppressive society we strive to create. In separating our ethical analyses into those applicable to the present society with all its violence and those appropriate to a society without oppression, we do little more than hone our double focus, as it were, endeavoring to become acutely aware of both the present with all its problems and ambiguities and of the future with all its potential and promise, trying to prevent present action from destroying future promise. All the while, we remind ourselves how poorly struggles against oppression would be served by an ethics proper to a nonoppressive future—if, that is, the ethics is taken as unproblematically applicable to the action of ourselves and our contemporaries.

Our views of friendship and sexual love must break with the view of sexual/gender difference as essential for sexual love and similarity as essential for friendship. Surely, numerous similarities are important, some may even be necessary, for sexual love and probably for all but the most perfunctory sexual relations. Surely, too, even the most narcissistic would be unable to sustain for long a friendship in which no significant differences emerge.

Finally, relationships of friendship and authentic love can flourish only where social structures of oppression do not exist to intervene in and to vitiate the caring activities of the parties involved. As ethicists, we must seek a social order in which reciprocity is always possible, in which individuals need not choose between dominance and submission, and in which each recognizes and respects all the others as ends.

NOTES

1. Hoagland, *Lesbian Ethics: Toward New Value*, pp. 98-99.
2. Judith Jarvis Thomson, "A Defense of Abortion," in *Women and Values: Readings in Recent Feminist Philosophy*, p. 276.
3. Ruddick, "Preservative Love and Military Destruction: Some Reflections on Mothering and Peace," in *Mothering: Essays in Feminist Theory*, p. 233.
4. See her careful development of these issues in her book *Maternal Thinking: Toward a Politics of Peace* (New York: Ballantine Books, 1989).
5. Sartre, *Notebooks for an Ethics*, pp. 191-92.
6. *Ibid.*, pp. 193-94.
7. *Ibid.*, p. 194.
8. Hoagland, *Lesbian Ethics: Toward New Value*, pp. 120, 139.
9. Ruddick, *Maternal Thinking: Toward a Politics of Peace*, p. 120.
10. Kirp *et. al.*, pp. 29, 30, 33.
11. See Judith Andre, "Power, Oppression and Gender," *Social Theory and Practice*, Vol. II, No. 1 (Spring 1985), pp. 107-22.
12. Larry Blum, Marcia Homiak, Judy Housman, and Naomi Scheman, "Altruism and Women's Oppression," in *Philosophy and Women*, p. 194.
13. Nietzsche, "From *Human, All-too-Human*," p. 334.
14. Kierkegaard, "From *Journals and Papers*," in *Visions of Women*, p. 315.
15. de Beauvoir, "From *The Ethics of Ambiguity*," p. 439.
16. Nietzsche, "From *The Joyful Wisdom*," in *Visions of Women*, p. 340.
17. Ortega, "From *On Love*," p. 457.
18. Bertrand Russell, "From *Marriage and Morals*," in *Visions of Women*, p. 421.
19. Ortega, "From *On Love*," p. 458.
20. See Rich, *Compulsory Heterosexuality*.
21. James, p. 362.
22. Jaggar, *Feminist Politics*, p. 241.
23. MacKinnon, *Feminism Unmodified*, p. 76.
24. Lorde, p. 63.
25. Mill, "From *The Subjection of Women*," p. 289.
26. J.G. Fichte, "From *The Science of Rights*," in *Visions of Women*, pp. 258, 254, 253, 255.
27. Rousseau, "From *A Discourse on Political Economy*," p. 196.
28. Ruddick, "Better Sex," in *Philosophy and Women*, p. 113.
29. de Beauvoir, "From *The Second Sex*," p. 442.
30. In fact, Janice Moulton, "Sex and Reference," in *Philosophy and Women*, pp. 107-8, develops a delightful and insightful analogy with a hypothetical "feeding behavior" as she critiques the notion of intercourse, an activity defined as beginning with the insertion of the erect penis into the orifice of choice and ending usually with the male's ejaculation or at least with his withdrawal. Despite the fact that

"[s]exual intercourse is an activity in which male arousal is a necessary condition, and male satisfaction, if not also a necessary condition, is the primary aim ..., sexual intercourse is thought by many to be an activity that involves (or ought to) both male and female equally [*ibid.*, p. 104]." While her analogy is designed to expose the ludicrousness of this assumption that intercourse involves the two "partners" equally, Moulton does not deny that women do sometimes experience orgasm during intercourse; after all, as she observes, "Sometimes the telephone rings, too [*ibid.*, p. 106]."

31. Mill, "From *The Subjection of Women*," p. 289.

32. Thomas Hobbes, "From 'Philosophical Elements of a True Citizen,'" in *Visions of Women*, p. 147.

33. John Locke, "From 'Essay Concerning the True Original, Extent, and End of Civil Government,'" in *Visions of Women*, p. 152.

34. Kant, "From *Anthropology from a Pragmatic Point of View*," p. 247.

35. C. S. Lewis, "From *Mere Christianity*," in *Visions of Women*, p. 438.

36. Gilman, "From *The Man-Made World*," p. 398.

37. Mill, "From *The Subjection of Women*," p. 293.

38. Condorcet, "From *Letters from a Dweller in New Heaven to a Citizen of Virginia*," in *Visions of Women*, p. 215.

39. David Hume,"From 'Of Love and Marriage,'" *Ibid.*, p. 157.

40. Mott, p. 327.

41. George Santayana, "From *The Life of Reason*," in *Visions of Women*, p. 406.

42. Gilman, "From *The Man-Made World*," pp. 397-98.

43. Nietzsche, "From *Thus Spake Zarathustra*," in *Visions of Women*, p. 341.

44. Mill, "From *The Subjection of Women*," p. 296.

45. Gilman, "From *The Man-Made World*," p. 397.

46. Jaggar, *Feminist Politics*, p. 198.

47. Sartre, *Notebooks for an Ethics*, p. 20, says: "Sadism and masochism are the revelation of the Other. They only make sense—as, by the way, does the struggle of consciousnesses—before conversion."

48. Iris Murdoch, *Sartre, Romantic Rationalist* (New Haven, CT: Yale University Press, 1953), p. 65.

49. See Sartre, *Being and Nothingness*, pp. 361-412.

50. *Ibid.*, pp. 378-79.

51. Sartre, *Notebooks for an Ethics*, p. 20.

52. Sartre, *Critique of Dialectical Reason*, p. 439.

53. Sartre, *The Devil and the Good Lord*, trans. Kitty Black (New York: Vintage Books, 1960), p. 145.

54. Joseph H. McMahon, *Humans Being: The World of Jean-Paul Sartre* (Chicago: University of Chicago Press, 1971), p. 117, observes that this gesture makes Ivich and Mathieu a "couple" for the rest of the evening, a solidarity that is experienced as "not far from joy."

55. Sartre, *Men Without Shadows*, trans. Kitty Black (London: Hamish Hamilton, 1949), p. 119.

56. Sartre, *The Chips Are Down*, p. 92.

57. *Ibid.*, p. 186.

58. Michel Contat and Michel Rybalka, *The Writings of Jean-Paul Sartre*, Vol. I, trans. Richard C. McCleary (Evanston, IL: Northwestern University Press, 1974), pp. 163-64.

59. Sartre, *Dirty Hands*, trans. Lionel Abel, *No Exit and Three Other Plays by Jean-Paul Sartre*, p. 233.

60. Sartre, *The Devil and the Good Lord*, pp. 97, 99, 111, 128.

61. Contat and Rybalka, p. 254.

62. Sartre, *The Devil and the Good Lord*, p. 133.

63. *Ibid.*, p. 147.

64. Many have not recognized that Sartre's writing includes such female characters as these. For example, Margery Collins and Christine Pierce, "Holes and Slime: Sexism in Sartre's Psychoanalysis," p. 121, disparage the female characters in Sartre's literary works, a disparagement seriously challenged by characters like Hilda and Anna.

65. Sartre, *Kean*, trans. Kitty Black, *The Devil and the Good Lord and Two Other Plays* (New York: Vintage Books, 1960), pp. 194, 195.

66. *Ibid.*, pp. 213, 220, 276.

67. Sartre, *What Is Literature?*, p. 269.

68. Sartre, *The Devil and the Good Lord*, pp. 145, 111, 146.

69. Sartre, *Kean*, pp. 279, 256.

70. Sartre, *Notebooks for an Ethics*, pp. 415, 507.

71. Hoagland, *Lesbian Ethics: Toward New Value*, pp. 147, 117-18.

72. Sartre, *What Is Literature?*, p. 49.

73. Sartre, *Notebooks for an Ethics*, p. 89.

74. Sartre, *What Is Literature?*, p. 269.

75. Plato, *Symposium*, trans. W.H.D. Rouse (New York: New American Library, 1956), pp. 86-89.

76. Hoagland, *Lesbian Ethics: Toward New Value*, p. 169.

77. Carol Anne Douglas, p. 203, credits lesbian feminism with the development of awareness "that opposition or being opposite is not a requirement of erotic love, and, in fact, works against one's possibilities of really knowing the other." However, it is important to note that this awareness has roots in Plato and was developed quite vigorously by Charlotte Perkins Gilman, "From *Women and Economics*," "From *The Man-Made World*," pp. 394, 400-401, when she bemoans the fact that women and men are reared with nothing in common, even their play as children being structured to prepare them for completely different sorts of work and activities. She notes that when a woman and a man marry, they do not work together either in the home or in society. Their totally different backgrounds as well as their being on different economic levels ill fits them even to play together. Perhaps that is why men's stories of love—their other main interest in addition to war, according to Gilman—always end with the conquest and why, as Letty Pogrebin observes,

p. 262, sex and sports are discussed by men "in much the same way." Maybe there is little more to say about the couple's relationship.

78. Pogrebin, pp. 309, 366-67.

79. Santayana, p. 406.

80. Raymond, p. 180, proposes that this claim may contain some truth even though it seems sexist as well as contrary to many women's experience. Inasmuch as the traditional view of men and women presumes men to be like one another and women to be all alike and then links timidity with women and risk-taking with men, many women are likely to accept these evaluations uncritically. Thus, many women will regard other women as boring and fail to see "the ways men turn risk into reckless behavior, a behavior that frequently masks necrophilic obsession."

81. Frye, *The Politics of Reality: Essays in Feminist Theory*, p. 69.

82. *Ibid.*, pp. 111, 115.

83. *Ibid.*, pp. 72, 75-76.

84. Pogrebin, pp. 18, 264, 332, 335-36, 254-55, 369.

85. Frye, *The Politics of Reality: Essays in Feminist Theory*, pp. 74-75.

86. Butler, p. 135.

87. Frye, *The Politics of Reality: Essays in Feminist Theory*, pp. 134-35.

88. We are thus led in the direction of Andrea Nye's conclusion that patriarchy is supported rather eclectically, even by theories and claims that are contradictory with one another. See her *Feminist Theory and the Philosophies of Man.*

89. Gilman, "From *Women and Economics*" and "From *The Man-Made World*," pp. 393-94, 401.

90. María Lugones, "Playfulness, 'World'-Travelling, and Loving Perception," *Hypatia*, Vol. 2, No. 2 (Summer 1987), pp. 6-8.

91. Hoagland, *Lesbian Ethics: Toward New Value*, p. 283.

92. Lorde, p. 163.

93. Pogrebin, p. 305.

Chapter Seven

The Role of Play
vis-à-vis Relativism,
Futility, and Revolution

How do we live with ambiguity? How do we act, sometimes in life and death situations, on values we have chosen? How can we render aid to individuals whose ends are not ours? These are questions an ethics of freedom must confront. Such questions seldom appear in Western philosophical ethics except as rhetorical, the intended effect of which is to dismiss without further argument any ethics where values are chosen or are otherwise "relative."

Since a feminist ethics of freedom thus confronts different questions from those facing many other philosophical ethics, an attempt to answer those questions requires explorations of some different topics. Play is one of those topics inviting our exploration and holding out hope for creative and satisfactory answers.

My belief that play may help to provide some needed answers had its inspiration in Sartre's ethics. There, play is presented as a way of resolving problems resulting from the choice of values in situations where ambiguity and failure are inevitable.

An impetus to push the possibilities of play a bit further came from references to play and playfulness in writings by feminist activists and theorists. While some of these references suggest something similar to Sartre's use of play, others refer to play or playfulness as a joyful celebration of freedom and love, however circumscribed these may be by oppressive structures and by threats of violence.

A few writers suggest that play can be a revolutionary strategy, a suggestion, incidentally, also found in Sartre. Like Sartre, Sarah Hoagland recognizes the ability to embrace ambiguity as essential to morality; and, like Sartre, she proposes that playfulness makes such embrace

possible. She cites Lugones's idea of "playful world travel" as a way
to "learn to love cross-culturally and cross-racially," describing this
activity as follows: "the ability to suspend not belief, but *disbelief.* It
is not our belief so much as our disbelief that leads us to discount
others and keeps us loyal to patriarchal perception."[1] Here play seems
both a revolutionary strategy and a way to live with relativism. This
dual role also is ascribed to play in Annette Kolodny's "playful plu-
ralism,"—"responsive to the possibilities of multiple critical schools
and methods, but captive of none, recognizing that the many tools needed
for our analysis will necessarily be largely inherited and only partly of
our own making."[2] Similarly, objecting to Robert Bly's *Iron John,* to
which they refer as "the bible of the men's movement," Jane Caputi
and Gordene O. MacKenzie propose that "mockery and reversal of
expectation" offer "one way out of the bonds of gender" by developing
"a grounding, not in iron, but in irony."[3]

In this chapter, then, I examine first the role play can serve in resolving
problems of both relativism and futility. In these resolutions, I draw
heavily from Sartre's work and from my own earlier analysis of his
ethics. Finally, with help from many disparate sources, I explore the
revolutionary possibilities of play.

PROBLEMS WITH RELATIVISM

A feminist ethics of freedom, such as I am proposing, will agree
with both Sartre's moral condemnation of freedom-denying activities
and his affirmation of the inescapability of value-choices. But the latter
affirmation is not unproblematic. Inherent in it is a value relativism
frequently challenged as untenable, with allegations either that such
relativism renders action impossible or that it leads to logical absur-
dity.

Soren Kierkegaard suggests one problem with the recognition of
relativism in ethics when he cautions that individuals become "hypothetical" if they attempt to create their own values *ex nihilo* apart from
any foundation in what they are.[4] If values depend on choice, then they
depend on choice both for their initial existence and for their continuation or endurance. Just as one was free not to choose a value in the
first place, so one remains free to alter or to tear down a value once
it is chosen. Thus, according to Kierkegaard, one becomes hypothetical because values depend not just on the original choice but also on
a constantly reiterated choice. This means, he believes, a choice must
continually be repeated before anyone can act on it—as a result, the

chooser of values will be like Zeno's runner, dividing the stadium to infinity but never completing the course. Unable to extricate himself from an infinite regress of choice, Kierkegaard's "hypothetical man," like Dostoevsky's "underground man," is plagued by the inertia of indecision. Like Buridan's ass or John Barth's Jacob Horner,[5] such individuals simply are unable to act.

In *The Concept of Morals*, W. T. Stace develops a different problem, one that, he thinks, confronts the ethical relativist on the psychological rather than on the logical level. If the ethical relativist is correct, Stace objects, moral judgments concerning other cultures and even other individuals in the same culture are at best expressions of the "vanity and egotism of those who pass them."[6] He fails to realize, however, that they are "vanity and egotism" only if they can be contrasted to moral judgments not subject to such failings, i.e., objectively based moral judgments, the possibility of which is denied by the ethical relativist. Thus, his objection may not trouble an ethical relativist inasmuch as it assumes what the ethical relativist denies, namely, an objective basis for moral judgments. It thereby begs the question.

In addition, Stace's worry about making moral judgments about other cultures and individuals treats moral judgments from a purely external point of view. This worry fails to recognize the externality of its own stance vis-à-vis moral judgments and that, from the perspective of those making these judgments, this challenge is simply nonsense. The perspective of the individual who makes the moral judgment in question in fact is quite different. From that perspective, there can be no serious question of whether moral values and principles apply to any others since to accept values and principles as moral is to affirm them in some sense as holding for everyone in similar circumstances. Moral judgments and commitments concerning both oneself and others are unavoidable since even inaction endorses the situation in which one finds oneself. An individual thus forced constantly to make moral judgments does not have the luxury presumed by Stace to make judgments only on her or his own action and then to ponder whether they could ever apply to others.

Stace also worries about whether individuals are capable of adhering to moral standards recognized as being no better than any others.[7] This criticism poses a more serious problem for an ethics based on freedom. Can individuals become aware of their freedom as the source of values without at the same time recognizing at each and every moment the freedom to maintain in existence or to abolish previously chosen values? Is Stace correct to fear this recognition of the arbitrariness and unjustifiability of values? Must it render difficult and highly unlikely

any individual's continued adherence to particularly demanding moralities? How can individuals not be demoralized? How can they continue in enterprises where the stakes seem so high but where there can
be no justification of their choices of values? After all, even sympathetic critics have feared that Sartre's and Simone de Beauvoir's
"willingness to put their lives and honor on the line in support of human
dignity seems to bear witness to the very spirit of seriousness they so
scornfully reject."[8]

THE PROBLEM OF FUTILITY

Another hurdle confronting those who attempt to develop a feminist ethics is posed by the feminist recognition that their most concerted efforts are likely to change very little and may even be co-opted to
reinforce and strengthen the very conditions that most need to be changed.
A feminist ethics must offer some resolution to the problems resulting
from an attempt to live with futility, particularly when, in an ethics of
freedom, futility is acknowledged from the outset as an inevitable aspect
of moral behavior.

Alison Jaggar suggests a need for something like play when she
points to "the problem of discovering viable ways of living in the long
haul toward a socialist feminist revolution, ways of living with contradictions that are presently ineradicable." As she says:

> The socialist feminist insistence that the personal is political has raised
> the possibility of liberating women through a total transformation of social
> relations. While this is an exciting prospect, the insight that the personal
> is political can, in the meantime, be a heavy burden to socialist feminist
> women. When racism, capitalism and male dominance are seen to pene-
> trate political organizations, the home and even the bedroom, socialist
> feminist women are left with no place of refuge from the struggle. They
> are always on the front lines.

Contradictions between feminist commitment and the often racist and
sexist elements in relationships that sustain even the most committed
are at least for now unresolvable. Fundamental changes in the structure of society would be required to abolish the institutional racism
and sexism which permeate the lives of all who are raised within the
institutions. Thus, Jaggar concludes, feminists "must discover how to
live with these contradictions in such a way as to find not despair and
defeat, but joy and strength in the struggle against them."[9]

In *Being and Nothingness*, Sartre laments the failure of all human projects. Man is a "useless passion"—haunted by an unachievable ideal of perfect coincidence with self. Sartre refers to this ideal as God and then argues that God is impossible. Insofar as actions pursue this impossible goal and all are doomed to fail, they are, he says, equivalent. Thus, in terms of their failure, "it amounts to the same thing whether one gets drunk alone or is a leader of nations."[10]

Although Sartre concludes that we always will be haunted by the desire to be God, he nonetheless affirms the possibility of a radical conversion from bad faith with its relentless pursuit of unity, a "faith" that deceives itself and believes that unity is possible. At the same time, he develops examples like that of Jean Genet who embody an alternative to bad faith and whose actions are not merely futile.

Individuals like Genet do not simply "neglect" their impossible goals and turn to possible ones, futility being thereby abolished; rather, according to Sartre, Genet pursued his impossible goal in a determined, clear-headed, earnest way until he managed to succeed in some very important ways even though he failed to achieve what he set out to do. Through his writing, Genet tried to get others to accept him as a thief. He "won" insofar as he secured his release from prison, had "honorable friends," was "received," recognized, and admired. He failed, however, inasmuch as his writing transformed both himself and "the Just" to whom it was addressed—"the Just" being those smugly self-righteous people who position themselves on the side of Justice and who so readily condemn individuals like Genet. Where "the Just" were disturbed by his writing, they recognized themselves and their possibilities in Genet's characters and thus showed themselves less than just. Through his writing, Genet, too, was changed by his discovery of himself as a man among men, "like everybody and nobody" but no longer the thief he had tried to get "the Just" to accept.[11]

Neither are impossible goals neglected and futility overcome by societies. In the *Critique of Dialectical Reason*, Sartre details attempts—by aggregations ranging from groups to institutions—to surpass the separated, unreciprocal existence of individuals (which he calls "seriality"). For Sartre, each attempt to create the group as a unity involves contradictions; this results eventually in a lapse back into seriality. The group's activity has limits: although it is formed in opposition to alienation, its activity always embodies itself and thereby alienates itself in matter; and this activity is the source of the group's undoing.[12] Although notable achievements may be made during this development from group to institution, for Sartre there is nonetheless an ultimate futility with respect to the attempt to achieve a community. Groups as well as individuals are thus haunted by an impossible ideal. For the group as for the individual, the unity sought cannot be attained.

Futility also plays a significant role in Sartre's novels, plays, and short stories. Often, however, as in his discussion of Genet, it is juxtaposed to the theme of "loser wins."[13] Individuals in Sartre's fiction are involved, like the mythical Sisyphus, in enterprises in which they cannot succeed in an unqualified way, though they may make quite noteworthy accomplishments.

Finally, futility is not overcome by conversion. Individuals who undergo Sartre's radical conversion thereby cease their self-deceptive denial of who they are and how values come into being through human choices. When they thus affirm their own freedom and that of others, that is, when they become authentic, they thereafter pursue ideals in a very different way; but this does not mean that they give up impossible goals, such as unity (the self-coincidence to which Sartre refers as "Being"). In *Notebooks for an Ethics*, he observes: "[t]he authentic man cannot suppress the pursuit of Being through conversion because there would be nothing else." For this reason, Sartre concludes, the authentic individual will always "be in some way poetic." Sartre suggests that the authentic must love the impossible but without loving failure and thereby becoming a poet.[14] Once again, authenticity is seen to involve maintaining uneasy tensions.

If all actions are recognized as futile, failing to achieve what is sought, how can we continue to pursue goals we realize cannot be accomplished? Like Stace's problem with relativism, the problem with futility is a psychological one. It looks as though the authentic individual depicted by Sartre would be demoralized. As attempts to realize impossible goals, all actions are equivalent in the sense that all are and must be failures; no actions come close to actualizing such goals. By recognizing the ultimate futility of human action, Sartre places all human beings in the frustrating position of Sisyphus. We are haunted by *value*, by the desire to be God (to coincide with ourselves), by the need to achieve community; yet inevitably our efforts fail as we try to coincide with our values, with ourselves, and with others. Because of the kind of beings we are, that is, an unresolvable tension between opposites (such as freedom and facticity), an unbridgeable gap remains: we cannot coincide with ourselves or others and, as long as we are, we remain free to alter our values. The problem of futility is how to live with this realization.

Thus, a Sartrean ethics must resolve more than the psychological problem of inevitable failure to achieve perfection. It must present a viable way of living with the realization that ultimately actions are futile precisely because the achievement of our goals requires the impossible, namely, that those opposing aspects of ourselves—e.g., freedom and facticity, being-for-ourselves and being-for-others—be unified rather than just held in an uncomfortable tension. Moreover, such an ethics must provide an answer to Kierkegaard's logical problem with chosen values and to Stace's more psychologically oriented challenge to an ethics based on such values. What Sartre says about "play" provides the resolution to all three problems.

PLAY AND THE SPIRIT OF SERIOUSNESS

Sartre contrasts play with the "spirit of seriousness" in which the "serious man" tries, in bad faith, to give himself "the type of existence of the rock, the consistency, the inertia, the opacity of being-in-the-midst-of-the-world." One who is serious, Sartre says, is concerned with consequences: "[A]t bottom [he] is hiding from himself the consciousness of his freedom; he is in *bad faith* and his bad faith aims at presenting himself to his own eyes as a consequence; everything is a consequence for him, and there is never any beginning. That is why he is so concerned with the consequences of his acts."[15]

Play is concerned with consequences, too, but in a different way. The serious person sees consequences as beyond her or his control; indeed, such an individual sees herself or himself as a consequence of other causes. In play, on the other hand, consequences are viewed as the result of free activity. Play is "an activity of which man[16] is the first origin, for which man himself sets the rules, and which has no consequences except according to the rules posited?" Play begins "[a]s soon as a man apprehends himself as free and wishes to use his freedom, a freedom, by the way, which could just as well be his anguish, then his activity is play. The first principle of play is man himself; through it he escapes his natural nature; he himself sets the value and rules which he has established and defined."[17]

In *Notebooks for an Ethics*, Sartre presents play as a break from the spirit of seriousness and as vitally connected with authenticity. In discussing risk, he says:

> I do not demonstrate my freedom just by the pure subordination of the external world; I also demonstrate it by accepting the contest [the challenge of another]. . . . At the same time, the *challenge* is a game. It is a break with the spirit of seriousness, [it is] expenditure, nihilation, passage to the festival. Indeed, the festival is liberation from the spirit of seriousness, the end of economics, the overthrowing of hierarchy, and the absorption of the Other by the Same, of the objective by intersubjectivity, of order by disorder. This will turn out to be the *apocalypse* as one of the extreme types of interhuman relations.[18]

Such play is not just a leisure time activity, as it is characterized by Johan Huizinga in his famous study of play.[19] Neither is it something to be grudgingly accepted, with Kant, as at least a way of staying occupied and sustaining one's energies and in that sense more like work than indolence-producing idleness.[20] Herbert Marcuse presents a Sartrean understanding of play when he describes it as "the play of life itself, beyond want and external compulsion," not because wealth and leisure have freed those who play from constraint, but rather because the "constraint [which] *is* the reality . . . 'loses its seriousness' and . . . its necessity 'becomes light.'" This play changes human activity into "*display*—the free manifestation of potentialities."[21]

Sartre's play is also quite different from the contest-play on which Huizinga focuses. While "the primary thing" of Huizinga's contest-play is to excel over others, Sartre's play can be noncompetitive. However, the two thinkers would agree that whenever playful activity involves competitiveness, this competitiveness is not, as Huizinga says, "in the first place a desire for power or a will to dominate."[22]

PLAY AS PARTIAL RESOLUTION
TO PROBLEMS OF RELATIVISM

On the basis of these statements about play, along with a little help from observations about ordinary play, we can construct resolutions to the problems of relativism and futility. These resolutions must deal, first, with both Sartre's denial of any preexisting justifications for our action and his affirmation of the necessity of creating and sustaining in existence our own values. Second, the resolutions must support continued activity even in the light of full recognition that, given human freedom and reality, an unbridgeable gap exists between our goals and our accomplishments.

In play, we create without being bound by any preexisting values, prescriptions, and proscriptions. Children at play create characters, dialogues, situations, and actions. While many of these merely mirror the scenes they have witnessed, some are quite different and even reflect different values than those taught by and evinced in the lives of their parents and teachers. Adults invent games and sustain them in existence, for example, by freely following the rules they have created, thus "*playing* the game."

Sartre's authentic individuals create their own values through their actions; but they recognize that their choices of these values are not necessary and ultimately are neither *supported* nor *justified* by any-

thing whatsoever. This is not to deny that some values may be supported and justified by other values within the rather complex network of
values held by any particular individual; it is rather to deny that there
are any ultimate values that serve as bedrock for all the others and are
themselves necessary and justified. Although considerations can be
invoked to *rule out* choices such as those of oppressors and those who
deny their own freedom, other choices are not thereby justified. Among
morally permissible choices, ultimately none are any more necessitat-
ed or justified than others. Like one who invents a game, those who
are authentic know they could have chosen differently; but, like the
creator of the game, they did not in fact do so. To say they chose is
to say they brought certain values and not others into being. This does
not mean, however, that the decisions are irrevocable. Rather, these
individuals remain free to revoke the chosen values as values. What
they cannot do is to abolish the fact of their having chosen these values.

Whereas both the creator of the game and the authentic individual
are thereafter free to alter or reject their game and chosen value respectively, both individuals may choose not to alter or reject and instead continue to act in accordance with their choices. There is no gap,
much less an unbridgeable one, between the choice of a value and action
in accordance with the choice. To act on a chosen value does not require
an infinite series of decisions in each of which one's previous value
decision is affirmed, any more than a runner is required to complete
an infinite number of movements before she or he can reach the end
of the stadium, Zeno's famous analysis to the contrary notwithstanding.

It is simply the case that choosing and acting are not separable. To
assume one can choose without acting or act without choosing, or avoid
both choosing and acting, certainly is to accept a position foreign to
Sartre's. Each of these alternatives is unacceptable. To assume that
one can choose without undertaking any of the actions available to
implement that choice endorses the sort of idealism that Sartre quite
rightly rejects. The idealistic freedom he rejects is the freedom of simple
formulas often erroneously thought to be Sartrean, aptly characterized
by William McBride as unreal and idealistic: "the heroic but ultimately unreal, idealist perception of freedom that is found in the Stoic slave
Epictetus or in the English poet's assertion that 'Stone walls do not a
prison make.'"[23] This idealistic view of freedom pretends that intention is disembodied and that responsibility does not extend to one's
own behavior and to what one may do to curtail and circumscribe the
behavior of others. Such pretense is a type of bad faith, is presupposed

by "abstract ethics" ("ethics of the good conscience . . . [that] assumes
that one can be good without changing the without situation"), and is
clearly rejected by Sartre.[24] To assume, on the other hand, that one can
act without choosing fails to recognize that acting involves value choices
and commitments. To choose a value is to act, in appropriate circumstances, on the choice; similarly, to act is to make value choices.

Furthermore, if Sartre is correct, as I believe he is, generally one
can avoid neither choice nor action. Not to choose is itself a choice;
and, generally, not to act is itself an action. Individuals' choices may
be seriously circumscribed by the actions of others; but to the extent
that any actions are available to them, they choose and act *within* the
restricting parameters set by others. Consequently, those who are thus
coerced are not responsible for the parameters themselves unless they
explicitly endorse them or choose not to resist when they can do so.

Since one can avoid neither acting nor choosing, it follows that the
hypothetical person's supposed problem of ever *beginning* to act cannot arise. Moreover, practice supports theory inasmuch as such a "problem" does not arise in the experience of those who both recognize values
as created and nevertheless act, sometimes even quite decisively.

If the problem is sustaining commitment, in the face of the realization
that chosen values have no external, objective justification, play offers
a resolution. Although this may be a more empirical and less properly
philosophical problem, at least an analogy with other forms of play
suggests a far less serious problem than Stace envisions. After all,
countless individuals have developed and played games demanding
extraordinary preparation, skill, and exertion. Surely some of these
individuals were aware of the existence of other, less demanding
possibilities, no more (and, of course, no less) objectively warranted
or justified. This suggests that Stace and those who agree with him are
merely begging the question in favor of absolutism. Otherwise, surely
the question "Why would an individual continue to adhere to demanding
standards?" would not appear so impossible to answer. Were they not
begging the question, they would at least be willing to entertain as a
perfectly acceptable, sufficient answer: "Because he or she chooses to
do so." Authentic individuals acknowledge what those who beg this
question will not, namely, freedom not only with respect to the world
and the values of others but even with respect to their own past choices.
They know that they and they alone create and sustain in existence the
values on which they act and that there are no other values than those
and like values created and sustained by other human beings.

The very question "Why would an individual continue to affirm previously chosen values?" either ignores the status of all other values (or, at least, ensembles of values) as equally unjustifiable or it assumes a freedom, short of killing ourselves, to cease choosing and acting. We may choose to end a game or discontinue a project. We may even do so for what we consider good and compelling reasons, reasons reflecting other—and perhaps conflicting—value choices. If, however, we can find no such reasons for continuing the game or the project on which we have been working, surely this, in itself, is insufficient reason to drop it. To play this objectivist game of demanding good and compelling reason, and to do so evenhandedly, requires sufficient reasons for *whatever* we do—even if we discontinue the project. Too many fail to recognize that for every "Why?" there is a "Why not?" just as difficult to answer. Many a project may be completed for no better reason than that it was begun.

Does this invalidate commitment, as critics have affirmed? Maurice Merleau-Ponty's challenge seems especially serious: "From the single fact that it is a question of committing *oneself*, that the prisoner is also his own jailer, it is clear that one will never have other bonds than those one currently gives oneself and that one never *will* be committed."[25] This challenge is partially correct: one is never completely bound by values one has chosen or by projects begun. One can always free oneself from the direction specified by one's own past choices and actions. However, to the extent Merleau-Ponty is correct, what he says indicates an advantage more than a disadvantage in the view of freedom to which he is objecting; surely what is meant by anyone who affirms freedom is that individuals are free to the extent that they are not bound either by their past or by the actions of others. In a 1970 interview, Sartre himself eloquently affirms just such a claim: "For I believe that a man can always make something out of what is made of him. This is the limit I would today accord to freedom: the small movement which makes of a totally conditioned social being some one who does not render back completely what his conditioning has given him. Which makes of Genet a poet when he had been rigorously conditioned to be a thief."[26]

Merleau-Ponty's challenge becomes a significant objection to the possibility of commitment only when it is conjoined with his seriously distorted view of Sartrean freedom as the "pure power of doing or not doing, a power that fragments freedom into so many instants, . . . the freedom to judge, which even slaves in chains have."[27] Yet this is a view of freedom Sartre, in his 1946 essay "Materialism and Revolution," quite rightly rejects as a "pure idealistic hoax."[28]

While Sartre gives examples of individuals who choose to fight the

privileges or dispossessions of class, to ignore hunger or other bodily
appetites, to take stands against injustices previously ignored, to quit
playing the buffoon for others, he recognizes that some aspects of existence
endure throughout such choosing and cannot be abolished. To some
degree, these aspects set the parameters of each choice. Moreover, in
situations of oppression, individuals may find their choices restricted
further by the actions of others.

Additionally, the individual's own past choices may have set up
circumstances in which her or his present choices are limited still more.
Inadvertently I may have developed habits that tend to keep me on a
course previously chosen. Even my own freedom vis-à-vis my past
commitments may not be so easy to exercise. I may have deliberately
acted so as to make a future change of direction quite difficult.

Moreover, although I may choose no longer to acknowledge a particular motivation as relevant to my present choice, as long as I remain
within the "ensemble of projects that I am, . . . my fundamental choice
of myself," I at most only modify secondary projects.[29] Given the
ambiguous relation of my transcendence and my freedom, being-for-
myself and being-for-others, being my past and not being my past, I
never can become an absolute subject; I cannot simply examine, at
each and every moment, a past commitment afresh and, as it were,
with no strings attached. Although particular choices may be justified
by appealing to more fundamental values or principles and those perhaps by appealing to yet others within this "ensemble of projects" that
the individual is, such justification cannot be made for the most fundamental values and/or principles, if there are any, or for the ensemble
as a whole. Sartre is concerned both to recognize the ultimate unjustifiability of one's choices at this level and to hold out for the possibility
of radical conversion, fundamental change of this ensemble. Since freedom
is not just inextricably connected with facticity, the past, and appearance for others, but already in some sense committed to an ensemble
of values, to act on this freedom requires more than Merleau-Ponty's
"magical fiat."

Even the spontaneous upsurge of unreflective freedom, the source
of fundamental choice of self, always is related ambiguously to facticity, the past, and being-for-others. Although this unreflective level
of freedom keeps one from being bound within one's previous fundamental choice of oneself, at the same time it will not be easy to dis-
engage from this fundamental choice, for, after all, to the extent that
it is a fundamental choice, it delimits all those things that can count,
for the one who operates within it (*not* for those who do not), as good
reasons for any choice.[30] A radical conversion, involving as it does an

alteration of such fundamental choice, seems hard won, not accomplished by "magical fiat."

From Sartre's analysis of freedom and reflection, I conclude that commitment is meaningful at each of two levels. First, in choosing, one may attempt to engage the future, to bind future decisions by making conflicting decisions as difficult as possible. This level of commitment is paralleled in Sartre's later writing by what the group does in its attempt to restrict or bind in advance, by promises and by terror, the freedom of its members. This level of commitment seems to be a vital aspect of many if not all choices inasmuch as willing generally involves at least some reference to a prolongation, into the future, of what is chosen. As Simone de Beauvoir says: "I can not genuinely desire an end today without desiring it through my whole existence, insofar as it is the future of this present moment and insofar as it is the surpassed past of days to come. *To will is to engage myself to persevere in my will* [italics added]."[31]

The practical import of this feature of will is that in acting one always finds oneself bound to some extent by past actions and, moreover, that one deliberately acts to bind, as far as possible, one's own future actions. While remaining free to "break" these bonds and to undermine past projects by launching a new one, individuals cannot change direction easily, given the momentum and all the "reasons" established by past choices.

Second, in a significant but different way, one's fundamental choice of self to a considerable extent binds one's future choices. If this choice values freedom, it requires an ensemble of projects and motivations that will call for actions in support of freedom. Thus, one is committed to such actions and to the rejection of oppression. Although fundamental choices can be called into question and this questioning may lead to a "conversion," such change is not likely to be easy nor does recognition of this possibility precipitate one into a limbo of paralysis. The possibility of conversion simply means there is a level of freedom underlying whatever an individual can or does count as a reason for choice.

Play can help those who understand and affirm the extent of our freedom and responsibility live with this fundamental choice of freedom, whether it is the original making of the choice, if there be such, or the continuing adherence to the particular choice, or a conversion from it. To some extent, one's fundamental choice is like one's decision to play a game: once made, the choice, like the decision to play the game, gives the chooser good and compelling reasons to act in a particular way or to execute one move rather than another. Yet the playful spirit is not itself provided thereby with similarly good and compelling reasons for its original decision to play the game. In fact, the decision itself may have no adequate motivation at all; but such a consideration will not dampen the spirits of the player. After all, precisely by choosing to play, the player has suspended not only the pretense of the serious that her or his actions are justified but also the rules of the serious, rules requiring justification of each and every choice others may make as well.

While play is important to those who affirm their own freedom and responsibility as well as the freedom of others, the analogy with games may suggest the possibility of a playful torturer. However, I think this suggestion is mistaken. The torturer, even one who constructs torture as a game, chooses not to recognize and affirm the connection between his or her freedom and that of the victim(s).[32] Yet the recognition is at some level unavoidable and one that the torturer must constantly mystify or disguise or otherwise hide from too conscious an awareness. This is tantamount to lulling oneself to sleep and is incompatible with the exhilaration with which an individual confronts freedom in play. Individuals in bad faith simply cannot allow even their own freedom to become too clear to themselves.

PLAY AS RESOLUTION TO
THE PROBLEM OF FUTILITY

The problem of futility is more difficult to resolve, and its resolution more centrally involves play. After all, particularly in a culture where winning is virtually everything, the recognition of futility will seem particularly demoralizing. Why, if we cannot or even just are not likely to win, should we keep trying? Surely not just my students have reacted quizzically to Albert Camus's presentation of Sisyphus as an "absurd hero," somehow happy and surely admirable in his moment of wisdom as he climbs back down the hill to pick up his stone for one more effort in what he clearly realizes is a futile task.[33] Why, many have asked me, does not Sisyphus just sit on his stone? Why does he keep trying when he knows the stone will not stay at the top of the hill? It will not do, of course, to emphasize the determinism in the older myth that Camus is retelling since we can see Sisyphus as a hero only if we posit a modicum of freedom on his part. If he returns to the stone only because he *must*, then he is simply performing his task in a robot-like manner; and that is that. Only if he somehow voluntarily returns for yet another try to accomplish what he knows to be impossible is he even interesting to us. Only then does Sisyphus rise above his fate and assert human values—or *his* values—in the face of insurmountable odds. Only then does Sisyphus's return indicate that there is something unacceptable, humanly speaking or perhaps just Sisyphusly speaking, about the way things are.

Friedrich Nietzsche describes an endeavor like that of Sisyphus as "remain[ing] faithful to the earth, . . . giv[ing] . . . the earth a meaning, a human meaning." Unfortunately, unlike Camus, Nietzsche ends up affirming the natural as the source of all legitimate values, thus returning to a seriousness about values and giving human choice too little recognition for its role in creating values. His characterization of the creator of new values as a child, innocent and forgetful, is a part of this naturalism and not at all useful to those who wish to build an ethics on freedom. However, he does emphasize the lightness and playfulness required in one who remains faithful to the earth while acknowledging eternal recurrence, Nietzsche's poignant symbol (and doctrine) of ultimate futility. Zarathustra demonstrates how difficult accepting and living with futility can be, as he "chokes" on the knowledge that "All is the same, nothing is worth while" and particularly on his "great disgust with man," on the painful recognition that "Alas, man recurs eternally! The small man recurs eternally!" Thinking of the "smallness," the pettiness of human beings, and the "fact" that all of this pettiness recurs eternally leads Zarathustra to despair and inertia: "Man's earth turned into a cave for me, its chest sunken; all that is living became human mold and bones and musty past to me. My sighing sat on all human tombs and could no longer get up." Only when he can look into this "abyss" and accept eternal recurrence, is he able, having killed the "spirit of gravity" (with laughter), to return with lightness to the world to dance, sail "uncharted seas," and generally "live dangerously."[34]

To understand how playfulness enables an individual to live with futility, we do well to turn once again to games. A consideration of the ways human beings operate when they are playing games helped us see how such playfulness resolves problems allegedly confronting the kind of relativism espoused by one who proposes that values come into being as the result of human choices. A player participates in a game *as if* the rules or values of the game have some sort of necessary and objective reality and validity. At the same time, as long as players are playing and not so caught up in winning that they mistake the game for something else, they recognize these rules and values as having no such necessity or objectivity. In other words, one who plays avoids the seriousness of those who no longer play.

In avoiding this seriousness, such an individual also avoids the serious person's reaction to futility. Even inescapable futility is not an insurmountable problem for those who play. In play, not only may we spend time and energy to unbalance balanced objects without much likelihood of success, but also we may exert great effort to balance unbalanceable objects and to fill sieves with water without *any* likelihood of success. A playful spirit of engagement makes possible full and frequently joyful concentration on the activity itself without the dispiriting often consequent upon recognition of the futility of the endeavor.

Does it make sense, however, to place life and honor on the line, as did Sartre and de Beauvoir? Did they, as has been claimed, thereby slip into seriousness? Although people frequently risk their lives in games, we tend to view play as a frivolous activity, suspecting those who risk their lives in play of doing so not for the game but for some reward external to the game itself. With such reasoning, *we* move into seriousness and thus beg a fundamental question by assuming there *are* ready-made values, some of which may warrant the risking of life and many of which clearly do not. More fundamentally, we beg the question Sartre deals with by presuming that an individual's own life *is* objectively valuable and that only something objectively higher in value could possibly warrant his or her risk of this life.

If Sartre is correct, *we* determine the extent to which our lives are valuable, as well as their value vis-à-vis other values. Even the value of freedom emerges in the context of willing other values, and those values in turn set the parameters for the valuing of freedom; for example, the freedom willed by the lucid daredevil may be part of a short life, but one lived intensely. The values created and sustained in play are not frivolous in comparison with those of the players' lives; no values exist apart from individuals' choices. Certainly there is no hierarchy of values independent of such choices. Serious human beings try to convince themselves (and others) otherwise, but their consternation over the irrationality of those who play "for keeps" cannot count as a legitimate objection to the nonserious play of those who are authentic.

The interesting thing about play as a resolution to the problem of futility is the way it changes both the nature and the outcome of the project. Authentic individuals and groups turn to some extent from impossible goals as such to what is within their control. This does not mean, however, that impossible goals will be abandoned. Rather, for the authentic individual, such ideals will become regulative.[35] To take goals as regulative is to take them as guiding behavior but not as depicting goals actually to be realized. To do so avoids the danger of what Sharon Welch calls "utopian thinking," namely, "the construction of the aim of moral action as the attainment of final, complete victory."[36]

Although individuals and groups may be unable ever to achieve the
harmony and unity represented by such ideals as God and organism,
the ideals nonetheless may guide behavior. Concretely, this would mean
that, instead of trying to be, for example, an identity of being-for-
others and being-for-self, individuals would strive to be (for themselves)
what they appear (to others) and to appear to be (to others) what they
are (to themselves). The authentic individual assumes responsibility
for and attempts to harmonize as far as possible those disparate aspects
of herself or himself while the individual in bad faith tries to unify, to
reduce them without remainder to one another, and, failing to unify,
then uses the impossibility of such unity as a justification for any and
all behavior.

As long as the city of ends is taken as a nonregulative ideal, that
is, as a goal actually to be realized, ethics confronts a dilemma. Either
this utopian goal is unrealizable, or it is only realizable in some distant
future. On the one hand, if the goal is not in fact realizable, if the goal
is merely ideal, then, as Sartre says, "hope disappears." On the other
hand, if the city of ends is regarded as realizable but only by projecting
this possible actualization into some far-distant future, then the end
remains beyond and outside the means and potentially able to justify
any and all means. It would then lead to "the maxim of violence": "the
end justifies the means."

To avoid defeatism and violence, Sartre proposes the goal be viewed
not "as being in relation to the means in terms of the exteriority of
indifference . . . [but rather] in terms of the organic unity of the means."
In other words, such a goal "is not the last link in the causal series A,
B, C, D, E, F . . . [but] is the organic totality of the operation."[37]

Because Sartre's resolution of his dilemma requires us to see the
end *in* the means, and not as totally separate from them, the means will
truly be a "prefiguration of the city of ends": "The solution of this
antinomy is not to distinguish the end from the means, but to treat man
as end to the same measure that I consider him a means, that is, to help
him think of himself and freely want to be a means in the moment
when and to the extent that I treat him as an end, as well as to make
manifest to him that he is the absolute end in that very decision by
which he treats himself as a means." Later in the same work, Sartre
states this antinomy and its resolution somewhat differently:

As soon as a goal is assigned to the human species and this goal is finite,
as soon as one pictures it as reality, . . . the human species become ants.
The given closes in on itself. The goal has to be infinite. But if it is beyond
attaining for each generation, this is discouraging, Therefore, it has to be

finite. This signifies that each person has to realize it and yet it is still to be realized. A *finite* enterprise for each person within humanity's infinite enterprise.[38]

Far from being a cause of despair, the human failure to coincide with self is the very basis of Sartre's ethics. As de Beauvoir recognizes: "[T]he most optimistic ethics have all begun by emphasizing the element of failure involved in the condition of man; without failure, no ethics; for a being who, from the very start, would be an exact coincidence with himself, in a perfect plenitude, the notion of having-to-be would have no meaning. One does not offer an ethics to a God."[39] Realizing the nonidentity of facticity and transcendence, and the inescapability of both, authentic individuals would affirm themselves as both, thereby seeing their facticity as subject to their freedom and their freedom as inevitably situated in their facticity. Thus, they harmonize and coordinate these aspects of themselves to the extent such aspects can be harmonized and coordinated.

Harmony and coordination are not sought in this manner by those in bad faith. In bad faith, individuals may try to achieve their ultimate goal through magic and incantations like one who faints in fear, thereby, according to Sartre, magically causing the "disappearance" of the threat.[40] By fainting, the fearful person relinquishes or denies responsibility for his or her body and its actions and retreats into pure subjectivity. Futility enters into the fainting behavior but entirely differently than it did in the foregoing discussion of the problem of futility. Fainting obliterates only the awareness of the threat. Although it might deceive, and thereby possibly thwart, an attacking animal by making the object of its attack appear dead, in other cases it does nothing to remove the threat. Rather, it may leave the one who faints totally vulnerable, unable to resist in any way or to escape from the threat. The consequences here are likely to be the opposite of the safety and security sought.

The waiter in Sartre's famous example seems to be in a similar position, inasmuch as his robotlike behavior is and will remain antithetical to what he sought: the *more* he becomes objectlike, the *less* he is the subjectivity-as-object he sought to become. The opposition between the goals and the actual consequences of actions makes apparent the moral problem with bad faith, namely, that those in bad faith try to will the end without willing the means. In this sense, consequences can count *against* an individual's actions and choices although, given the ultimate futility of human actions, consequences can never *justify* the value of any other actions and choices.

Sartre can say, then, as he does in his interview with Benny Lévy, that, contrary to an earlier characterization of despair, "human reality entailed essential failure" vis-à-vis one's fundamental goals and that nevertheless despair can acknowledge this essential failure without being the opposite of hope.[41] Hope, rather, is an "essential element of an action" inasmuch as "I cannot undertake an action without expecting that I am going to complete it."[42] This apparent reinstatement of hope makes sense only if fundamental goals are taken as regulative. For the authentic individual, the ideal of unity or coincidence will act only as a lure, as a perpetual challenge and constant source of dissatisfaction, without, however, being taken either as realized or as realizable—without, that is, being sought as a concrete aim. Thus, although impossible goals continue to guide the authentic, such goals must be understood and pursued as regulative, with concrete aims formed under their direction taking into account circumstances and probabilities.

This analysis allows Sartre to affirm a particular way of playing as appropriate to the authentic individual. Such individuals accept and affirm the futility of their efforts to actualize their ultimate goal; yet they continue to do what they can to accomplish it. In *Iron in the Soul*, for example, Mathieu recognizes the futility of his action and impending death—that ambushing those particular Nazi soldiers will "merely put their time-table out by ten minutes!" Although he recognizes its futility, he continues to shoot at the soldiers.[43]

Individuals like Hoederer (*Dirty Hands*) and Genet (*Saint Genet*) acknowledge and accept their freedom and the ultimate futility of their actions, yet enter the fray, resolved to control and change what they can. Although they may neither control nor change the course of history, nevertheless they act. They realize their finitude and essential ambiguity and work within these even while striving toward an impossible goal. Mathieu sums up this attitude as he indicts himself and a cohort for their previous political noninvolvement. Implicitly recognizing that their participation in politics might not have prevented the present confrontation, he still affirms: "At least you would have done all you could."[44] As Sartre says in *Notebooks for an Ethics*: "The historical agent has to accept that his action will be prolonged only as a proposal and that the spirit that animated him will continue to act only in the manner of a residue. But at the same time, *take every precaution to delay as much as possible the moment of alienation*."[45]

Feminists, too, must try to change the course of history. Oppressions should not be allowed to continue. A society in which the freedom on all is valued and respected is an ideal that dictates and guides feminist resistance. Yet our most concerted behavior is not apt to overthrow oppression and is certainly not going to realize a society in which the freedom of all is valued and respected. Our best efforts may only be co-opted and used to buttress and strengthen the status quo against which we strive. This is not to say that our efforts are for naught. After all, we may cause a little inconvenience. We may even make a difference in the lives of a few. Most important, though, our struggles will demonstrate the unacceptability of oppression and, if we engage in them well, may offer joyful albeit momentary intimations of the kind of world we seek: in the words of Mathieu, at least we would have done all we could. This simply cannot be accomplished otherwise than by a playful openness both to others and to the possibilities of failure.

PLAY AS REVOLUTIONARY ACTIVITY

Finally, what about the revolutionary possibilities of play?

Mikhail Bakhtin points to both the revolutionary potential and the reactionary uses of play in his discussion of carnival. Although he is interested in the "carnival sense of the world" embodied in some literature, he recognizes that carnivals are a primary locus in real life of this spirit with its characteristic "atmosphere of *joyful relativity.*" In the carnival, as he says, "life is drawn out of its *usual* rut, it is to some extent 'life turned inside out,' 'the reverse side of the world.'" During carnivals, "laws, prohibitions, and restrictions that determine the structure and order of ordinary, that is noncarnival, life are suspended." This means that "what is suspended first of all is hierarchical structure and all the forms of terror, reverence, piety, and etiquette connected with it—that is, everything resulting from socio-hierarchical inequality or any other form of inequality among people (including age)." In other words, "[a]ll *distance* between people is suspended, and a special carnival category goes into effect: *free and familiar contact among people.*"[46] During such festivals, "all participants entered, as it were, the utopian kingdom of absolute equality and freedom," albeit only for a "strictly limited" time.[47]

Carnival life sounds very like a temporary embodiment of the kingdom of ends where each may, as Sartre says, appeal to everyone else for help and where oppressive hierarchies are abolished. In fact, Sartre himself suggests something like this in his description of festival as "liberation from the spirit of seriousness, the end of economics, the overthrowing of hierarchy, and the absorption of the Other by the Same, of the objective by intersubjectivity, of order by disorder."[48]

Although carnival or festival may unsettle hierarchy and the spirit of seriousness, for the revolutionary, at least, something important is missing. What is missing is lasting effect on society and on its oppressive hierarchies. As Bakhtin observes, carnival is a form of *ritual* laughter, and such laughter is always linked with death *and rebirth*. Earthly authorities are ridiculed and put to the test in order "to force them to *renew themselves*."[49] Unless the authorities are totally unbending and unwilling to make even the most minor of concessions, such renewal favors and strengthens the status quo rather than challenging it in any really fundamental way. When the carnival ends, oppressive hierarchies are not substantially weakened but rather are purified and even strengthened by having endured the challenge. Thus, it would seem, they are more firmly entrenched than ever.

One problem with carnival is its very existence as ritual. As ritual, the carnival is removed from real life. Simone de Beauvoir notes this problem when she says, "The moment of detachment, the pure affirmation of the subjective present are only abstractions; the joy becomes exhausted, drunkenness subsides into fatigue, and one finds himself with his hands empty because one can never possess the present: that is what gives festivals their pathetic and deceptive character."[50]

In addition, the carnival is not only separate from real life but also, as a ritual, it has a clearly demarcated beginning and end. Everyone knows the carnival will end and something very like business as usual will take its place. This is part of what allows the sense of playfulness such license, even for those in power. Some features of the former ways of conducting business and other affairs may change as a result of the carnival, but everyone can be assured that fundamental aspects will not change and that all will be generally in the same hierarchical power arrangements once again. Commoners may be treated momentarily as kings and vice versa, but there is little chance of the hilarity of the moment permanently resulting in any such displacement.

Finally, real carnival frequently does not achieve the liberation of which its laughter is capable, according to Bakhtin, because it may lack the awareness necessary for it to express "a critical and clearly defined opposition." Without sufficient awareness, individuals and periods, like the Middle Ages, may allow to exist in their consciousness "side by side but never merg[ing]" both "the serious and the laughing aspect[s]" of the world, both the official and the carnival, both the pious and the grotesque. With awareness, Bakhtin believes, laughter can liberate "not only from external censorship but first of all from the great interior censor; it liberates from the fear that developed in man during thousands of years: fear of the sacred, of prohibitions, of the past, of power." Thus, he says: "[I]t unveils the material bodily principle in its true meaning. Laughter opened men's eyes on that which is new, on the future." In this way, over time, laughter helped transform "old truth and authority into a Mardi Gras dummy, a comic monster that the laughing crowd rends to pieces in the marketplace."[51]

What we learn from this analysis about the revolutionary potential of carnival, then, is both positive and negative. Positively, carnival can be seen as providing an embodiment of sorts, however temporary, of something like the kingdom of ends. It offers a vision of the way play can unsettle oppressive hierarchies and create an openness otherwise seldom experienced. Also, it provides a way for an individual to liberate himself or herself from the hold of externally imposed and serious values. Paule Marshall presents a powerful example of this individual liberation in her novel *Praisesong for the Widow*, and Sharon Welch notes the important role of carnival in Marshall's novel *The Chosen Place, The Timeless People* as it helps keep alive the "dangerous memory" of the people of Bournehills: "the memory that [they] were] . . . a people of dignity and self-respect who were violated in slavery, and who are violated in the continued exploitation of capitalist development. And . . . the equally dangerous memory of victory, the three years after the revolt in which they lived as a people without the scourge of white oppression."[52]

At the same time, though, we learn what play cannot be if it is to be truly revolutionary, that is, if it is to disrupt the structures upholding those values. In particular, we see the dangers of a ritualized play, one that is not ongoing and that has not developed its awareness into clear opposition. Such play, while mocking and temporarily unsettling the status quo, is ultimately no challenge to it, indeed is quite likely to strengthen it by serving as a safety valve, providing harmless release even for potentially quite disruptive tensions in the society.

From these accounts of carnival and festival, I conclude, certain conditions must be met if play's revolutionary potential, vis-à-vis the social institutions and structures, is to be realized. First and foremost, it must emerge from clear, critical, and oppositional awareness. Otherwise, it is likely to "become a rather bad joke," and one in support of the very oppression it allegedly mocks, an accusation leveled by Marilyn Frye against much of gay men's "lightheartedness in connection with what is, after all, the paraphernalia of women's oppression."[53] While nonaware play may help to begin the process of developing awareness in the players and liberation from internalized censors, such play seems unlikely to disrupt institutionalized structures of oppression.

It even seems unlikely to liberate the players in any significant way from their own internalization of those institutions and structures. This is why even the most playful approach to sadomasochism in individual relationships seems so fraught with danger. Particularly for women to play erotically, that is, in sexual relationships, even with each other, with violence in a culture that eroticizes violence against women seems more a matter of participation in such violence than opposition to it. Certainly, in such intimate and emotionally charged play, it would be most difficult to maintain the clarity and critical distance required by truly oppositional awareness.[54]

If the activity is to have any chance of unsettling the status quo, other conditions must be met as well. Thus, a second condition is that the playful activity be able to get itself recognized by significant numbers of oppressors as play. Oppressed groups no doubt will have great difficulty with this condition inasmuch as their activity is likely to be characterized from the outset as child- or animal-like and they themselves as somewhat simpleminded. In such circumstances, even open caricature of the serious rules, regulations, and behavior will generally be taken as worshipful imitation rather than as joyful relativizing of the serious.

Third, the play must not serve as a safety valve within the structure of the status quo; in other words, it must not provide an unthreatening venting of tensions that might otherwise erupt and seriously disrupt existing oppressive structures. Given the tendency of the status quo to co-opt all antagonists and challenges, revolutionary play will have difficulty meeting this condition.

Finally, if play is to be revolutionary, it must be ongoing. As long as it has a clearly delineated and anticipated beginning and end separating it from the rest of life, it will not ultimately disrupt and can safely be indulged to break the monotony, to vent discontent, and to show how strong the present system is. Thus, to be effective as a revolutionary strategy, play must catch people off guard.

To clarify the last of these conditions, Kierkegaard's method of indirect discourse may be instructive. Kierkegaard's strategy was to play to the hilt the role of idler and (albeit somewhat transparently) to "hide" behind pseudonyms so his words might catch the reader unaware and affect her or him before rationalizations and other defenses could be constructed. His models for such discourse include the Old Testament prophet Nathan who told King David a story concerning an individual whose behavior paralleled David's "taking" of Bathsheba from her husband, Uriah. When David responded with outrage against the individual in the story, Nathan simply looked at David and said, "Thou art the man."

Although Kierkegaard's behavior as he plays the idler is itself playful and his words supposedly are designed to turn his hearers within
themselves, to make them aware of themselves as individuals and of
their freedom, his use of play remains too much in the arena of individual solutions for it to be useful as a revolutionary model. Although
his method would undercut seriousness, his goal was to turn his audience into lonely individuals, not to undermine an oppressive status
quo. If play is to be revolutionary, it must reverse the model offered
by Kierkegaard. Instead of playing the idler or buffoon, the revolutionary player would probably do better generally playing to the hilt the
role of the ordinary individual of the society so that intermittent and
irreverent mocking of the ordinary has the greatest possible unsettling
effect.

Various mocking strategies have been proposed. Luce Irigaray, according to Rosemarie Tong, suggests exaggeration. Recognizing that
women exist as images in men's eyes, she suggests women "take those
images and reflect them back to men in magnified proportions." By
overdoing these images she hopes to effect their undoing. This strategy is not without its perils since, as she recognizes, "[t]he distinction
between mimicking the patriarchal definition of woman in order to
subvert it and merely fulfilling this definition is not clear."[55] This
distinction seems especially problematic in a society where images,
particularly those of women, offered by Hollywood, by the media, and
by religious fundamentalism frequently are so extreme that further
magnification is difficult to conceive. While feminists would probably
find it jolting to encounter, for example, a real-life *Gone with the Wind*
Mammy or heavy-breathing Marilyn Monroe sex-goddess, it would take
a lot to "magnify" the "proportions" in those images and probably a
lot more to achieve the effect for which Irigaray hopes. A culture
constantly fed such caricatures seems far likelier to respond approvingly to real-life embodiments thereof, even exaggerated ones, if such
are possible.

Consequent upon this difficulty is one to which Bernard R. Boxill
points. He grants, with Orlando Patterson, that the "Sambo" personality in slaves may have been a fraud and a "clowning"—that, as Patterson claims, "Sambo's fawning laziness and dishonesty was his way of
hitting back at the master's system without penalty." If, indeed, such
was the case, then it would have been a way for the slaves to maintain
their self-respect, which, as Boxill argues, can be retained only if they
continually give themselves evidence that they have it. Unfortunately,
though, playing a servile role looks like evidence to the contrary. As
Boxill says:

Unless it is already known to be pretense, apparent servility is evidence of servility. If Sambo gave a perfect imitation of servility, neither he nor his master could have any reason to think he was anything but servile. If his pretense is to provide him with evidence of his self-respect it must, to some discernible extent, betray him. Patterson may be right that the "perfect stroke of rebellion must seem to the master as the ultimate act of submission," but the deception must succeed, not because it is undetectable, but because the master is so blinded by his own arrogance that he cannot see that what is presented as abasement is really thinly disguised affront.

As Boxill recognizes, the powerless may have an immensely difficult time convincing others, and consequently even themselves, that they are clowning.[56]

This does not mean that clowning cannot be an effective way of both acquiring and retaining self-respect. For example, the feminist activist/comedy group Ladies Against Women (LAW) seems to be exploring creatively the possibilities of mocking through playful exaggeration, with the motto "I'd rather be ironing," signs like "My home is his castle" and "Sperm are people, too," and chants like "Hit us again, harder, harder!" The effects of these on women are likely to be generally salutary, but it remains to be seen if such play can significantly unsettle the lampooned views in those who hold them and who exercise power to enforce and to continue to structure reality according to those views.

A thought-provoking suggestion comes from Michèle Le Doeuff. In discussing her childhood passion for Shakespeare—"especially for the characters of the fools"—she confesses that she wished to be either Feste or King Lear's Fool when she grew up, a vocation she gave up when she realized that "life is not as well written as it would have been if Shakespeare had taken charge of it." In philosophy, she later found something similar to the "language of fools," something very close to "their sarcastic and corrosive utterances, their unseasonable taste for truth without pomposity, their corruption of words and their art of impertinence which forces authority, sometimes royal authority, to enter into their irony." This "foolery," she found, was compatible with life as it existed outside of Shakespearean plays, was open even to women, and was completely at odds with the respect for academic hierarchy and the great authors with which academicians had replaced "Socrates' irreverence." Later, she mentions approvingly a statement worn by some French feminists, roughly equivalent to "We do not dare to be ridiculous enough, and it may kill us."[57]

This emphasis on foolery and the ridiculous seems to connect with Le Doeuff's method, a method of exposure and ridicule—"to show that where women are concerned the learned utter, and institutions let them utter, words which fall clearly below their own usual standards of validation."[58] While this strategy is that of a worthwhile and philosophically sound project, relatively few men are likely to feel the bite of her mocking exposure. Few will read her words, and fewer still will feel their sting. The "academicism" to which she points is so firmly entrenched that such irreverence, particularly when it comes from women, is usually ignored or dismissed.

Since women generally are designated socially as creatures of play, the previously delineated conditions that playful activity must meet if it is to be disruptive of the status quo—in particular, the second and third conditions—seem especially difficult for women to meet. Rosemarie Tong cites Dorothy Dinnerstein's recognition that "women have played the part of court jesters, poking fun at the games men play; and women's irreverence has served to release the tension that ripples through the world of enterprise." Because of this release of tension, "things have never seemed bad enough for us to change the course of history."[59] In fact, women's irreverence seems, to many men, nothing more than lightheartedness, a necessary antidote to their own seriousness. Thus, women's irreverence alone is clearly not enough. Only if it is relentlessly unexpected and inappropriate (thereby satisfying the last condition) does it stand any chance at all of unsettling, and then probably only a small one.

Very likely, such play is more useful for developing the morale and vision of the players than it is for changing oppressive institutions and those who seriously uphold them. Laura S. Brown eloquently captures the importance of laughter to the individual even while analogizing it to "whistling in the dark": "As a Jew, I know that my culture has a long history of laughing in the face of the oppressor in order to reduce his power in our souls; if you can find what's funny about the czar, you won't be quite so devastated when he sends his troops to roust you out of house and home."[60] Poignantly, too, her statement captures the lack of effect such laughter had on the oppressor.

Even though the revolutionary potential of play is likely to be more indirect than direct, nonetheless such potential together with its other functions renders it very significant for those who are trying to relate in nonoppressive ways. Sarah Hoagland offers one compelling example of play within community when she discusses the importance of clowns in Anne Cameron's *Daughters of Copper Woman*. Reminiscing about her community "in the days before the invaders came," Granny observes that clowns, ideally without meanness or hostility, were needed and used "to help us all learn the best ways to get along with each other." By simply mimicking the serious gestures of others, clowns enabled people to see themselves as others see them, an important self-recognition apparently made more forceful by the means of presentation. Even a clown would occasionally find another clown in tow: "Sometimes a clown would find another clown taggin' along behind, imitatin', and then the first one knew that maybe somethin' was gettin' out of hand, and maybe the clown was bein' mean or usin' her position as a clown to push people around and sharpen her own axe for her own reasons."[61]

Individually and collectively, the oppressed themselves can benefit greatly from clowning. Mary Daly reminds us that the "reality" around us is man-made and that "[t]he maintenance of such a world indeed requires fools and folly." What she calls the "Be Laughing" of women can crack this reality, unveil its mysteries, and release its hold on the "Lusty Lunatics Laughing Out Loud," enabling them "to See and Act in ways that transcend the rules of fools."[62] Any who have endured the intended stigmatization of the label "lesbian," hurled at them by homophobes, will "laugh out loud" when they read Marilyn Frye's tongue-in-cheek account of efforts to determine the meaning of "lesbian" from dictionary accounts (from which she concludes that "[s]peaking of women having sex with other women is like speaking of ducks who engage in arm wrestling");[63] but, more significantly, they will find themselves internally a bit freer from the pariah connotations of the word. Similarly, I have observed how delighted and even proud women in my classes and generally in my experience are when I casually or not so casually correct anyone who refers to a courageous woman as "having balls" with my own far more politically—and anatomically—correct term "vaginal fortitude."

Moreover, as María Lugones recognizes, play provides a bridge for individuals whose "worlds" are quite different to move toward each other. Access to one another, absolutely necessary for understanding and communication, is barred to the serious, to those who would uphold the rules of the status quo, to those who would conquer. Only those who are open to being fools, who do not worry about competence and self-importance, who reject norms as sacred, and who delight in ambiguity, can understand what it is to be someone quite different and what it is to be ourselves in the other's eyes.[64]

Such "'world'-travelling" is essential for those who oppose oppression in all of its ramifications. On the one hand, it is an unavoidable step in the understanding of oppression. Otherwise, one continues to participate in the structures of dominance and oppression by forcing the reality and experiences of others into limited frameworks, applied with an arrogance like that of the dominant, an arrogance one may resist but at the same time perpetuate. On the other hand, playful "'world'-travelling" continually reveals to us and keeps us open to the complexity of the other with whom we wish to share a world in which each is respected as an end and in which each can appeal to all the others.

Finally, if nothing else, as Anne Tristan and Annie de Pisan observe, the laughter connected with revolutionary activity adds a note of levity and joy and thereby does change the world, making it a little less dismal, a little less sinister, introducing a politics not itself "as sad and sorry an affair as everything else."[65] Such a change, indeed, may be vital if the revolutionaries are to be able to keep before themselves the ideal society toward which they work and to see intimations of their ideal, however small, in their accomplishments. As long as such change is not mistaken for change in the objective structures of oppression and as long as the merriment does not siphon off revolutionary zeal, laughter is an important part of revolution.

CONCLUSION

While play is vital to those who try to free themselves and others from seriousness and from the oppressive structures maintained by such, play may accomplish more than simply helping them avoid burnout and despair. Not only does play offer a way to achieve distance from the seriously held oppressive values of the status quo, but also it enables those who play to glimpse, at least momentarily, a kingdom of ends where the freedom of everyone is acknowledged and where oppressive hierarchies are undone. Even though it has limited potential as a revolutionary strategy, play is nonetheless enormously important.

NOTES

1. Hoagland, *Lesbian Ethics: Toward New Value*, p. 242.

2. Annette Kolodny, "Dancing Through the Minefield: Some Observations on the Theory, Practice, and Politics of a Feminist Literary Criticism," in *Women and Values: Readings in Recent Feminist Philosophy*, p. 252.

3. Jane Caputi and Gordene O. MacKenzie, "Pumping Iron John," in *Women Respond to the Men's Movement: A Feminist Collection*, pp. 70, 79.

4. Soren Kierkegaard, *Sickness Unto Death, Fear and Trembling and Sickness Unto Death*, trans. Walter Lowrie (Garden City, NY: Doubleday, 1941), p. 203.

5. John Barth, *The End of the Road* (New York: Doubleday, 1972).

6. W. T. Stace, *The Concept of Morals* (New York: Macmillan, 1962), p. 50.

7. Stace's actual challenge (*ibid.*, p. 58) is that one who becomes an ethical relativist will inevitably "slip" to "some lower and easier standard." Because words like "slip" and "lower" seem to beg the question in favor of absolutism, I consider only what remains of Stace's criticism after the removal of the question-begging elements.

8. Anderson, p. 149.

9. Jaggar, *Feminist Politics*, pp. 345-46.

10. Sartre, *Being and Nothingness*, pp. 615, 627.

11. Sartre, *Saint Genet*, pp. 612-13, 617.

12. Sartre, *Critique of Dialectical Reason*, pp. 668, 678.

13. For more discussion of the theme of loser wins, see my *Sartre's Ethics of Authenticity*, pp. 96-100.

14. Sartre, *Notebooks for an Ethics*, p. 37.

15. Sartre, *Being and Nothingness*, p. 580.

16. The presumably generic "man" and the considerably less generic "a man" in the following quotation may and even should raise eyebrows or perhaps, as Claudia Card indicated to me after she read this chapter, laughter. In Western culture, it is women and not men who are seen as lighthearted and nonserious entertainers or toys to relieve the seriousness of men. Consequently, this sentence is likely to evoke in many memories of linguistic jokes like that to which Casey Miller and Kate Swift, *Words and Women: New Language in New Times* (Garden City, NY: Anchor Books, 1977), p. 23, refer: "man, being a mammal, breast-feeds his young."

17. *Ibid.*, pp. 580-81.

18. Sartre, *Notebooks for an Ethics*, p. 374.

19. Johan Huizinga, *Homo Ludens: A Study of the Play-Element in Culture* (Boston: Beacon Press, 1950), p. 8.

20. Kant, *Lectures on Ethics*, p. 161.

21. Herbert Marcuse, *Eros and Civilization: A Philosophical Inquiry into Freud* (Boston: Beacon Press, 1955), pp. 187, 190.

22. Huizinga, p. 50.

23. McBride, *Sartre's Political Theory*, p. 8.

24. Sartre, *Notebooks for an Ethics*, p. 17.

25. Maurice Merleau-Ponty, "Sartre and Ultrabolshevism," *Adventures of the Dialectic*, trans. Joseph Bien (Evanston, IL: Northwestern University Press, 1973), p. 195.

26. Sartre, "An Interview (1970)," *Phenomenology and Existentialism*, ed. Robert C. Solomon (Savage, MD: Littlefield Adams Quality Paperbacks, 1991), p. 513.

27. Merleau-Ponty, p. 196.

28. Sartre, "Materialism and Revolution," in *Literary and Philosophical Essays*, trans. Annette Michelson (New York: Collier Books, 1962), p. 237.

29. *Ibid.*, p. 178.

30. Sartre, *Being and Nothingness*, pp. 160-61.

31. de Beauvoir, *The Ethics of Ambiguity*, p. 27.

32. Claudia Card has raised to me the question of whether sadomasochistic "games" would be a playful option. This is a complicated question, first, because the notion of sadomasochism seems to cover so much, and, second, because human freedom is embodied and so intricately connected with facticity, being-for-others, and the past. In a later section, I shall argue that games and festivals involving role-playing may be enormously empowering to those who thereby free themselves from the internalization of the oppression to which they have been subjected. This is particularly true when the normal social roles are reversed and the oppressed can gain an understanding of the social construction and arbitrariness of the oppressor's dominant position. Festivals seem especially promising as a way to empower the oppressed since roles, e.g., of king and subject, may be actually if only temporarily reversed. At the same time, I can imagine the oppressed enacting this role-reversing drama by themselves and achieving the same degree of empowerment.

However, dangers lurk in such role-playing on the part of the oppressed. If individuals who are in fact oppressed continue to play in such dramas the parts they play in their everyday lives, their play may simply disempower them even more, much as the play of little girls often only prepares them for their future roles as subservient wives. Individuals who have been demeaned by those in power are likely not to feel empowered but rather to suffer additional blows to their self-esteem when they are demeaned, even in supposed play, by their peers. Perhaps if roles were alternated frequently or if those in the subservient role are allowed or even encouraged to explore the revolutionary limits of the role, such role-playing would be truly empowering for all the oppressed. If roles are not alternated or expanded, the "play" runs the risk of simply reinforcing the status quo by actually—or only apparently, it may not matter which—instituting hierarchy and oppression within the ranks of the oppressed themselves.

Moreover, even if the roles are alternated, individuals who have been systematically abused by those with power over them are frequently thereby imbued with the oppressors' view of such power as natural, inevitable, and even good. This is even more likely in the case of sadomasochism where the activity continues to eroticize violence against women in the same way it has been eroticized in the society. Such individuals are too likely to enjoy and "get off" on power over another, with the result that what began playfully very quickly turns deadly serious. This clearly does not seem a promising way out of oppression. What is needed is deeroticization of violence, not activity that continues to link pleasure and violence.

Thus, some games seem quite dangerous and potentially antithetical to the joyful embrace of freedom. I suspect this only begins to indicate how difficult it is truly to play in such a serious, oppressive, and violent society.

33. Albert Camus, "The Myth of Sisyphus," *The Myth of Sisyphus and Other Essays*, trans. Justin O'Brien (New York: Vintage Books, 1955), pp. 88-91.

34. Friedrich Nietzsche, *Thus Spoke Zarathustra: A Book for All and None* and "From *The Gay Science*", trans. Walter Kaufmann, *The Portable Nietzsche*, ed. Walter Kaufmann (New York: Viking Press, 1954), pp. 188, 331, 153, 304, 97.

35. Barnes, *An Existentialist Ethics*, pp. 94-95, offers a similar interpretation of unity or coincidence as a "regulating idea or principle." She recognizes that this move is a Kantian one, since it was Kant who proposed in *The Moral Law* the way ideas like that of perfection are to serve in morality as regulative ideas. For Kant, however, such ideas were merely empirically impossible, that is, not in fact achievable in a finite time; and, as I have argued in the chapter on violence, he failed to see or be concerned with ways the utilization of such regulative ideas in morality might contribute to and support violence and injustice.

36. Welch, p. 33.

37. Sartre, *Notebooks for an Ethics*, pp. 172, 435.

38. *Ibid.*, pp. 167, 207, 448.

39. de Beauvoir, *The Ethics of Ambiguity*, p. 10.

40. Sartre, *The Emotions*, trans. Bernard Frechtman (New York: Philosophical Library, 1948), pp. 62-63.

41. See Sartre, "Existentialism is a Humanism."

42. Sartre, "The Last Words of Jean-Paul Sartre, An Interview with Benny Lévy," trans. Adrienne Foulke, *Dissent* (Fall 1980), p. 399.

43. Sartre, *Iron in the Soul*, trans. Gerard Hopkins (Harmondsworth, Middlesex: Penguin Books, 1971), p. 222.

44. *Ibid.*, p. 87.

45. Sartre, *Notebooks for an Ethics*, pp. 48-49.

46. Mikhail Bakhtin, *Problems of Dostoevsky's Poetics*, trans. Caryl Emerson (Minneapolis: University of Minnesota Press, 1984), pp. 107, 122-23.

47. Bakhtin, *Rabelais and His World*, trans. Helene Iswolsky (Bloomington: Indiana University Press, 1984), pp. 264-65.

48. Sartre, *Notebooks for an Ethics*, p. 374.

49. Bakhtin, *Problems of Dostoevsky's Poetics*, trans. Caryl Emerson (Minneapolis: University of Minnesota Press, 1984) p. 127.

50. de Beauvoir, *The Ethics of Ambiguity*, pp. 126-27.

51. Bakhtin, *Rabelais and His World*, trans. Helene Iwolsky (Bloomington: Indiana University Press, 1984), pp. 96, 94, 213.

52. Welch, pp. 62-63.

53. Frye, *The Politics of Reality: Essays in Feminist Theory*, p. 138.

54. For additional discussion of sadomasochism, see endnote 30 in this chapter.

55. Tong, *Feminist Thought* (Boulder, CO: Westview Press, 1989), pp. 228-29.

56. Bernard R. Boxill, "Self-Respect and Protest," in *Philosophy Born of Struggle: Anthology of Afro-American Philosophy from 1917*, ed. Leonard Harris (Dubuque, IA: Kendall/Hunt, 1983), pp. 196-97.

57. Le Doeuff, pp. 9-10, 85.

58. *Ibid.*, p. 37.

59. Tong, *Feminist Thought*, p. 161.

60. Laura S. Brown, "Essential Lies: Dystopian Vision of the Mythopoetic Men's Movement," in *Women Respond to the Men's Movement: A Feminist Collection*, p. 99.

61. Anne Cameron, *Daughters of Copperwoman* (Vancouver, B.C.: Press Gang Publishers, 1981), p. 110.

62. *Websters' First New Intergalactic Wickedary of the English Language*, conjured by Mary Daly in cahoots with Jane Caputi (Boston: Beacon Press, 1987), pp. 262-63.

63. Frye, *The Politics of Reality: Essays in Feminist Theory*, p. 156.

64. Lugones, "Playfulness," pp. 15-17.

65. Anne Tristan and Annie de Pisan, "Tales from the Women's Movement," in *French Feminist Thought: A Reader*, ed. Toril Moi (New York: Basil Blackwell, 1987), p. 67.

Chapter Eight

Conclusion

From the foregoing analyses, we can see how an ethics of freedom adds some important dimensions to feminist theory and simply incorporates and develops others. An ethics of freedom adheres to the feminist ideals of nonoppressive social structures and of reciprocity and respect for freedom in human relationships. It develops these ideals within the context of a philosophy that makes individual freedom central. By focusing on freedom and recognizing its context of violence, this ethics supports the work of those who try to change the status quo and avoids problems endemic to the positions of utilitarianism and Kantian ethics.

Moreover, the emphasis on freedom undermines restrictive and negative views of what it is to be, for example, a woman or a black or a Jew or a homosexual. Thus, it challenges and undermines claims made by essentialist ethics, claims all too often used to buttress the status quo by making whatever happens to exist seem not only natural but also inevitable.

At the same time, feminists must heed Sartre's cautions against premature rejection of natures or essences. Though neither natural nor unchangeable, socially constructed natures or essences are objective structures of racist, sexist, classist, and homophobic societies; and they affect the ways individuals are seen by others and even the ways they see themselves. For those given natures as blacks, as women, etc., under these constructions, to ignore these ways of seeing and being seen is to place themselves in jeopardy. Moreover, such ignoring tends to leave unexamined and unchallenged the ways these "natures" or essences continue to delimit and restrict the options available to these individuals. Unlike some natural features of a human being's existence, however, these natures are not inevitable and inescapable; they can and should be changed. To change them, though, requires not just recognizing them and removing their protective camouflage (whereby they are dubbed "natural") so they can be seen clearly for the socially constructed realities they are. It also requires unmasking the vicious mystifications of manipulated choices as "free" and seeing the manipulations as the oppression they truly are.

Neither can needs serve as the basis of our ethics. They, like natures or essences, are too manipulable by forces of oppression and too easily disguised by ideologies created to mask oppression.

In our efforts to stop such manipulations and restrictions of the freedom of some, we may encounter situations where our only choices are those of reinforcing an oppressive status quo or of violating another's freedom. In anticipating such situations, we do well to heed Sartre's warnings about the ways ethics can be co-opted to reinforce the status quo and to render ineffectual those who work against oppression and for freedom.

Struggling against aggressiveness and violence, often connected with masculinity and so much a part of our society, feminists would no doubt tend to agree with Sartre's rejection of what he calls the maxim of violence—to will any means necessary to achieve an end. Surely feminists must heed his warning that violence not only perpetuates violence in the short run but also that the use of violence to fight the violence of the status quo may corrupt the struggle for a nonviolent society. Thus, feminists would do well to accept and to follow Sartre's admonitions that the means partially embody or exemplify the end and that our ideal be the city of ends—a utopian ideal where everyone is treated as an end, not merely as a means.

While many will resist Sartre's analyses of resistance to social structures of oppression, this, I think, is precisely where feminists have an opportunity to profit most from his ethics. First, as Sartre realizes, the personal is inextricably part of the social, always tainted and corrupted by whatever oppressions help to create the social fabric. Therefore, feminists cannot retreat from an unswerving opposition to oppressive social structures of all sorts. Thus far, most feminists are likely to be in general agreement with Sartre.

Considerably more controversial is his recognition that in situations of oppression, violence is inescapable. No matter how difficult this may be to acknowledge and no matter how unfortunate such situations may be, they unmistakably exist. In our efforts to undermine oppressive social structures, we all too frequently find ourselves, as

Sartre observes, in impossible situations not of our making. As feminists, we are obligated to reject the maxim of violence so often invoked by others and with such devastating consequences. Yet if our nonviolent resistance to violence simply affirms it as permissible and reinforces the oppressive status quo along with the prior violence on which it is based, this is equally unacceptable.

Sartre offers a way out of this dilemma. His way out is morally problematic, as he is quick to acknowledge; but its recognition of ambiguity and even of the questionable nature of ethics itself in an oppressive society is part of its strength. In such impossible situations, violence (that is, violation of others' freedom) may be necessary since any other reactions would acquiesce in and strengthen the oppression. In such cases, engaging in some form of violence is inescapable, and it is important to choose violence against violence, that it, to choose to engage in violence in a way that rejects violence. This means that any use of violence against violence must be limited and clearly recognized as morally unjustifiable. In all other situations, violence must be rejected as a means, no matter how worthy the end.

Whereas love is often presented as an alternative and even as an answer to violence, a feminist ethics must be highly critical as well as politically aware in evaluating the possibilities and realities of love. A critical and political stance will enable us to recognize that an ethics stressing love very likely offers only individual resolutions to what is in fact a social and political problem. If the proposed response to a social and political problem is individual, it is inadequate since individuals and the lives they fashion are far less likely to change the oppressive structures of society than to be molded and corrupted by them. What is required is a political and even revolutionary approach, not an approach delineated, by the very system being challenged, as an acceptable arena for such moral struggle. Unfortunately, in separating the private sphere from the public, society specifies and separates out an arena for individual solutions and thereby guarantees that they will have little if any effect on the public, that is, on the significant structures of the society.

Although a feminist ethics must affirm the dangers inherent in an ethics based on love, it nevertheless can acknowledge as its own ultimate *ideal* the very relations it rejects as a *means* to social change. This turning into an end what some propose as means is done with a very significant proviso, namely, than this ideal cannot be achieved in any meaningful sense in a situation of oppression. With this proviso, a feminist ethics can be developed and an ideal of love put forth without unduly undermining the necessary work of reform and revolution and without offering avoidable support to the status quo it critiques.

A feminist ethics must confront the problem of futility in the struggle for goals, a futility that renders their achievement extremely unlikely and sometimes even impossible. This requires in part being clear about those goals, about the unlikeliness or impossibility of their actualization, and about how they may nevertheless be momentarily reflected in action. It is even more important to see how their momentary reflection in the means is necessary if we are to keep the end in view and if we are to prevent ourselves from adopting the maxim of violence, that the end justifies the means.

To resolve the problem of futility, a feminist ethics must provide a significant place for and analysis of play. Values are chosen and impossible ideals sought by both those who play and those who are serious. Those who are serious, though, do not affirm and do not work for freedom, either their own or others'. Moreover, they use the impossibility of their ideals as justification for any and all activity, thereby ascribing to the maxim of violence. Play allows for the affirmation of freedom and an escape from the problem of futility for those whose actions are guided by ideals surpassing what is practical or perhaps even possible; but it does this without becoming a cover for violence and bad faith. In addition, play itself may offer limited possibilities for revolutionary action.

With such analyses, observations, and arguments, I have outlined an ethics that takes violence seriously both as a reality and as a revolutionary strategy. In this way, I have tried to avoid the unrealistically rosy view of the status quo evinced by too many treatments of ethics and justice. In this way, too, I have tried to ward off invidious comparisons of the effects of racism and sexism, or of their effects compared to those of classism and homophobia, particularly comparisons ignoring the violence supported by all of them as they play their respective roles in a complex network of dominations. A feminist ethics, if I am correct, will forget neither the rapes, beatings, and murders to which women of color have been subjected by virtue of racism nor the rapes, beatings, and murders, most by lovers and alleged friends, to which women of all races have been subjected by virtue of sexism. Nor will it ignore the violence to which men have been subjected by virtue of racism and to which both men and women have been subjected by virtue of classism and homophobia.

A feminist ethics will therefore challenge analyses that ignore or idealize the so-called private sphere, for example, the following, from *Gender Justice* by Kirp et al.: "Racial discrimination could largely ignore the private sphere, focusing on political and economic subordination, while gender discrimination was tempered in the public sphere by the necessity of mutual affecting relationships in the private sphere."[1] Black women and other women of color have been victims of racist violence in the so-called private sphere, and *all* women have been victims of sexist violence in this sphere. Remembering such violence will simply prevent us from ignoring specific forms of violence against women; it need not diminish other forms of racist violence against men and women, other forms of sexist violence against women, and homophobic violence against both men and women. It is simply not necessary to determine which violence does the most harm. In fact, it is impossible even to begin such a debate since there is no way clearly to separate these forms of violence from each other.

At best and at most, what I have presented is a general outline of an ethics. Much remains to be done. I am painfully aware that errors are inevitable, no matter how careful the writer, and must be corrected. While I have tried to listen to many and diverse voices and to guard against the classism, racism, sexism, and homophobia permeating my society and everyone in it, I realize my efforts will be limited in their success. Many of these voices are themselves trying to speak for women unable at the present time to speak for themselves.[2] Thus, they face the same problem that I do, and that compounds my problem. However, not sufficiently sensitive even to those voices or to the predicaments of others, I may have made pronouncements about "women" that fail to apply to all, thereby reinforcing the invisibility of various women in this or other societies. Or perhaps I have discussed other groups and oppressions in a way that strengthens the camouflage already hiding particular oppressions.

Such errors are probably unavoidable, although most lamentable and in dire need of correction when they finally do come to light, and to some extent simply underscore the necessity for feminist criticism to be a truly communal and relentlessly ongoing activity. Although, as Michèle Le Doeuff says, our vantage point in history enables us to recognize Aristotle's "shocking blindness" vis-à-vis slavery, "there is no reason why we should think ourselves any wiser than he was," and thus no reason to believe that we ourselves are not guilty of some error equally egregious.[3]

In addition, feminist imagination must constantly be called upon and pushed to its limit. It is most difficult if not psychologically impossible to work for a better world when even our imaginations are fettered, as they inevitably are, by the limitations of present relationships with others and by the grinding relentlessness of oppressions in our society. When we try to envision loving relationships and an alternative model of society, we more than likely do so in terms of the hierarchies and coercions with which we are all too familiar. We simply have no other models before us. Any different visions of love and friendship, of a truly just society, of fair and nonhierarchical economic relations, etc., must come from imagination and must constantly be subjected to the most critical scrutiny possible, lest we inadvertently allow what exists all around us to taint and corrupt even our visions of alternatives. Thus, we must give our imaginations free rein yet always take the result as nothing more than a proposal, to be accepted, and then most tentatively, only after thorough examination in which as many minds and voices participate as possible. Even with all the effort and precautions we can muster, we must nonetheless acknowledge—and hope—that what comes of our efforts to change society very likely will be far beyond our wildest dreams, possibilities that we simply cannot now imagine.

In addition, much remains to be done in the way of what is known today as applied ethics. It is not enough just to recognize the existence of oppressions and of the violence that both underlies the status quo and constantly surfaces in our extremely violent society. Much is needed from political and social analysts if we are to gain a minimally adequate understanding of what must be resisted and changed. Strategists of all sorts are necessary to devise effective ways to resist and change.

Certainly considerably more thought must be given to when, where, and how violence is to be resisted with violence. Just to recognize violence as sometimes necessary does not resolve troubling and soul-searching questions about what sort of violence is necessary and exactly when and where. In a world already so racked with violence, the thought of adding more, whether by action or inaction, is and should be extremely unsettling. Such a risk must be undertaken with forethought, clarity, and caution.

The possibility of making society even more violent than it is provides an ominous and important counterbalance to Karl Marx's famous and rhetorically effective challenge to the oppressed, that they have nothing to lose but their chains. It must give us pause to realize that some forms of resistance will risk losses other than just the chains of the particular oppression being resisted. Though we might succeed in throwing off some chains, our behavior may place at risk our very goal of a nonoppressive society. Though this possibility rightly gives us pause, we cannot allow our pause to be permanent. We dare not become quiescent since, as we have seen, quiescence, too, would contribute in a different but equally problematic way to the violence in the world and also would place at risk the nonoppressive world we seek since, at the very least, we would be endorsing the status quo and no longer working toward such a world.

NOTES

1. Kirp *et al.*, p. 44
2. Carol Anne Douglas, p. 38, reminds us that many poor and Third World women "have no access to the media, and live in such controlled environments that they cannot get out of their houses." Other feminists must speak for them "until they are in a situation where their voices can be heard."
3. Le Doeuff, p. 7.

Select Bibliography

Adair, Margo. "Will the Real Men's Movement Please Stand Up?" In *Women Respond to the Men's Movement: A Feminist Collection*, ed. by Kay Leigh Hagan, 55–66. San Francisco: HarperSanFrancisco, 1992.

Addelson, Kathryn Pyne. "Moral Revolution." In *Women and Values: Readings in Recent Feminist Philosophy*, ed. Marilyn Pearsall, 291–309. Belmont, CA: Wadsworth Publishing, 1986

Alcoff, Linda. "Cultural Feminism versus Post-Structuralism: The Identity Crisis." *Signs: Journal of Women in Culture and Society* 13, no. 3 (Spring 1988):405–36.

——— and Linda A. Bell. "Lordship, Bondage, and the Dialectic of Work in Traditional Male/Female Relationships." *Cognito* 2, no. 3 (September 1984):79–83.

Allen, Jeffner. *Lesbian Philosophy: Explorations*. Palo Alto, CA: Institute of Lesbian Studies, 1986.

Anderson, Thomas C. *The Foundation and Structure of Sartrean Ethics*. Lawrence: Regents Press of Kansas, 1979.

Andre, Judith. "Power, Oppression and Gender." *Social Theory and Practice* II, no. 1 (Spring 1985):107–22.

Anzaldúa, Gloria. *Borderlands/La Frontera: The New Mestiza*. San Francisco: Spinsters/Aunt Lute, 1987.

Aquinas, Thomas. "From *Summa Theologica*." In *Visions of Women*, ed. by Linda A. Bell, 102–15. Clifton, NJ: Humana Press. 1983.

274   Bibliography

Aristotle. "From *Politics*." In *Visions of Women*, 66–68. *See* Aquinas, 1983.

Baier, Kurt. *The Moral Point of View: A Rational Basis of Ethics*. Ithaca, NY: Cornell University Press, 1958.

Bair, Deidre. *Simone de Beauvoir: A Biography*. New York: Summit Books, 1990.

Bakhtin, Mikhail. *Problems of Dostoevsky's Poetics*. Trans. by Caryl Emerson. Minneapolis: University of Minnesota Press, 1984.

———. *Rabelais and His World*. Trans. by Helene Iswolsky. Bloomington: Indiana University Press, 1984.

Bar On, Bat-Ami. "Why Terrorism Is Morally Problematic." *Feminist Ethics*, ed. Claudia Card, 107–25. Lawrence: University of Kansas Press, 1991.

Barnes, Hazel E. *An Existentialist Ethics*. New York: Vintage Books, 1967.

———. "Sartre and Sexism." *Philosophy and Literature* 14 (1990):340–47.

Barry, Kathleen. *Female Sexual Slavery*. Englewood Cliffs, NJ: Prentice-Hall, 1979.

Barth, John. *The End of the Road*. New York: Doubleday, 1972.

Bartky, Sandra Lee. *Femininity and Domination: Studies in the Phenomenology of Oppression*. New York: Routledge, 1990.

———. "Toward a Phenomenology of Feminist Consciousness." In *Philosophy and Women*, ed. Sharon Bishop and Marjorie Weinzweig, 252–58. Belmont, CA: Wadsworth Publishing, 1979.

Beale, Frances. "Double Jeopardy: To Be Black and Female." In *The Black Woman: An Anthology*, ed. by Toni Cade, 90–100. New York: New American Library, 1970.

Bell, Linda A. *Sartre's Ethics of Authenticity*. Tuscaloosa: University of Alabama Press, 1989.

Blum, Larry, Marcia Homiak, Judy Housman, and Naomi Scheman. "Altruism and Women's Oppression." In *Philosophy and Women*, 190–200. *See* Bartky.

The Boston Women's Health Collective. *The New Our Bodies, Our-

selves: A Book By and For Women. New York: Simon & Schuster, 1984.

Boxhill, Bernard R. "Self-Respect and Protest." In *Philosophy Born of Struggle: Anthology of Afro-American Philosophy from 1917,* ed. by Leonard Harris, 190–98. Dubuque, Iowa: Kendall/Hunt Publishing, 1983.

Brown, Laura S. "Essential Lies: Dystopian Vision of the Mythopoetic Men's Movement." In *Women Respond to the Men's Movement: A Feminist Collection,* 93–100. *See* Adair, 1992.

Butler, Judith. "Variations on Sex and Gender: Beauvoir, Wittig and Foucault." In *Feminism as Critique: On the Politics of Gender,* ed. by Seyla Benhabib and Drucilla Cornell, 128–42. Minneapolis: University of Minnesota Press, 1987.

Cade, Toni [Bambara]. "On the Issue of Roles." In *The Black Woman: An Anthology,* 101–10. *See* Beale, 1970.

Came, Barry with Dan Burke, George Ferzoco, Brenda O'Farrell, and Bruce Wallace. "Montreal Massacre: Railing against feminists, a gunman kills 14 women on a Montreal campus, then shoots himself." *Maclean's* (December 18, 1989):14–17.

Cameron, Anne. *Daughters of Copperwoman.* Vancouver, B.C.: Press Gang Publishers, 1981.

Cameron, Barbara. "Gee, You Don't Seem Like an Indian from the Reservation." In *The Bridge Called My Back: Writings by Radical Women of Color,* ed. by Cherríe Moraga and Gloria Anzaldúa, 46–52. New York: Kitchen Table: Women of Color Press, 1983.

Camus, Albert. *The Just Assassins.* Trans. Stuart Gilbert. *Caligula & Three Other Plays.* New York: Vintage Books, 1958.

———. "The Myth of Sisyphus." *The Myth of Sisyphus and Other Essays,* trans. by Justin O'Brien, 88–91. New York: Vintage Books, 1955.

Canaa, Andrea. "Brownness." In *This Bridge Called My Back: Writings by Radical Women of Color,* 232–37. *See* Cameron, 1983.

Canovan, Margaret. "Rousseau's Two Concepts of Citizenship." In *Women in Western Political Philosophy,* ed. by Ellen Kennedy and Susan Mendus, 78–105. New York: St. Martin's Press, 1987.

Caputi, Jane, and Gordene O. MacKenzie. "Pumping Iron John." In *Women Respond to the Men's Movement: A Feminist Collection,* 69–81. *See* Adair, 1992.

Card, Claudia. "Caring and Evil." *Hypatia* 5, no. 1 (Spring 1990):101–8.

Chesler, Phyllis. "The Men's Auxiliary: Protecting the Rule of the Fathers." In *Women Respond to the Men's Movement: A Feminist Collection*, 133–40. *See* Adair, 1992.

Collins, Margery L., and Christine Pierce. "Holes and Slime: Sexism in Sartre's Psychoanalysis." In *Women and Philosophy: Toward a Theory of Liberation*, ed. by Carol C. Gould and Marx W. Wartofsky, 112–27. New York: G.P. Putnam's Sons, 1980.

Collins, Patricia Hill. *Black Feminist Thought: Knowledge, Consciousness, and the Politics of Empowerment*. New York: Routledge, 1990.

The Combahee River Collective. "A Black Feminist Statement." In *But Some of Us Were Brave: Black Women's Studies*, ed. by Gloria T. Hull, Patricia Bell Scott, and Barbara Smith, 13–22. Old Westbury, NY: Feminist Press, 1982.

Comte, Auguste. "From *The Positive Philosophy*." In *Visions of Women*, 281–82. *See* Aquinas, 1983.

Condorcet, Marquis de, Marie-Jean-Antoine-Nicolas Caritat. "From *Letters from a Dweller in New Heaven to a Citizen of Virginia*." In *Visions of Women*, 214–17. *See* Aquinas, 1983.

———. *On the Admission of Women to the Rights of Citizenship*. In *Visions of Women*, 210–14. *See* Aquinas, 1983.

Contat, Michel, and Michel Rybalka. *The Writings of Jean-Paul Sartre*, vol. I. Trans. by Richard C. McCleary. Evanston, IL: Northwestern University Press, 1974.

"Coping with Femicide." *off our backs* (March 1990):24–27.

Daly, Mary in cahoots with Jane Caputi. *Websters' First New Intergalactic Wickedary of the English Language*. Boston: Beacon Press, 1987.

Davis, Angela Y. *Women, Culture, & Politics*. New York: Vintage Books, 1990.

———. *Women, Race, & Class*. New York: Vintage Books, 1983.

de Beauvoir, Simone. *The Ethics of Ambiguity*. Trans. by Bernard Frechtman. New York: Citadel Press, 1964.

———. "From *The Second Sex*." In *Visions of Women*, 440–48. *See* Aquinas, 1983.

Diderot, Denis. "From the entry "Woman' in the *Encyclopedia* of Diderot and d'Alembert." In *Visions of Women*, 181–90. *See* Aquinas, 1983.

Dill, Bonnie Thornton. "The Dialectics of Black Womanhood." In *Feminism & Methodology*, ed. Sandra Harding, 95–108. Bloomington: Indiana University Press, 1987.

Doerner, William R. "The Man Who Hated Women: A sick obsession ignites the country's worst mass killing." *Time* (December 18, 1989): 30.

Douglas, Carol Anne. *Love and Politics: Radical Feminist and Lesbian Theories*. San Francisco: ism press, 1990.

Dworkin, Andrea. *Intercourse*. New York: Free Press, 1987.

————. *Mercy*. New York: Four Walls Eight Windows, 1991.

Engels, Friedrich. "The Origin of the Family, Private Property, and the State." In *Philosophy and Women*, 172–80. *See* Bartky, 1979.

Faludi, Susan. *Backlash: The Undeclared War Against American Women*. New York: Crown Publishers, 1991.

Fanon, Frantz. *The Wretched of the Earth*. Trans. by Constance Farrington. New York: Grove Weidenfeld, 1968.

Fichte, J. G. "From *The Science of Rights*." In *Visions of Women*, 253–64. *See* Aquinas, 1983.

"14 Women Are Slain By Montreal Gunman" and "Montreal Gunman Kills 14 Women and Himself." *The New York Times* (December 7, 1989): A1, A23.

Fowlkes, Diane L. *White Political Women: Paths from Privilege to Empowerment*. Knoxville: University of Tennessee Press, 1992.

Fraser, Nancy. "What's Critical about Critical Theory? The Case of Haberman and Gender." In *Feminism as Critique: On the Politics of Gender*, 36–56. *See* Butler, 1987.

Freire, Paulo. *Pedagogy of the Oppressed*. Trans. by Myra Bergman Ramos. New York: Continuum, 1990.

Fromm, Erich. *The Art of Loving*. New York: Bantam Books, 1963.

Frye, Marilyn. *The Politics of Reality: Essays in Feminist Theory*. Trumansburg, Crossing Press, 1983.

————. *Willful Virgin: Essays in Feminism*. Freedom, CA: Crossing Press, 1992.

Giddings, Paula. *When and Where I Enter: The Impact of Black Women on Race and Sex in America.* New York: Bantam Books, 1985.

Gilligan, Carol. *In A Different Voice: Psychological Theory and Women's Development.* Cambridge: Harvard University Press, 1982.

Gilman, Charlotte Perkins. "From *His Religion and Hers.*" In *Visions of Women*, 404. See Aquinas, 1983.

————. "From *The Man-Made World.*" In *Visions of Women*, 396–404. See Aquinas, 1983.

————. "From *Women and Economics.*" In *Visions of Women*, 391–94. See Aquinas, 1983."

Ginzberg, Ruth. "Philosophy Is Not a Luxury." In *Feminist Ethics*, 126–45. See Bar On, 1991.

"Grand Jury to review rape case in which woman offered condom." *The Atlanta Journal/The Atlanta Constitution* (October 25, 1992): A14.

Griffin, Susan. "Rape: The All-American Crime." In *Feminism and Philosophy*, ed. by Mary Vetterling-Bragin, Frederich A. Elliston, and Jane English, 313–32. Totowa, NJ: Littlefield, Adams & Co., 1977.

Grimshaw, Jean. *Philosophy and Feminist Thinking.* Minneapolis: University of Minnesota Press, 1986.

Harding, Sandra. "Introduction." In *Feminism & Methodology. See* Dill, 1987.

Hegel, G.W.F. *The Phenomenology of Mind.* Trans. by J. B. Baillie. New York: Macmillan, 1949.

Held, Virginia. "Marx, Sex, and the Transformation of Society." In *Philosophy and Women*, 159–63. See Bartky, 1979.

Helie-Lucas, Marie-Aimée. "Women, Nationalism and Religion in the Algerian Liberation Struggle." In *Opening the Gates: A Century of Arab Feminist Writing*, ed. Margot Badran and Miriam Cooke, 105–14. Bloomington: Indiana University Press, 1990.

Hill, Thomas E., Jr. "Servility and Self-Respect." In *Moral Philosophy: Classic Texts and Contemporary Problems*, ed. Joel Feinberg and Henry West, 484–93. Belmont, CA: Dickenson Publishing Company, 1977.

Hoagland, Sarah Lucia. *Lesbian Ethics: Toward New Value*. Palo Alto, CA: Institute of Lesbian Studies, 1988.

———. "Some Concerns About Nel Noddings' *Caring*." *Hypatia* 5, no. 1 (Spring 1990): 109–14.

Hobbes, Thomas. "From 'Philosophical Elements of a True Citizen.'" In *Visions of Women*, 145–47. *See* Aquinas, 1983.

Holmstrom, Nancy. "Do Women Have a Distinct Nature?" In *Women and Values: Readings in Recent Feminist Philosophy*, 51–61. *See* Addelson, 1986.

hooks, bell [Gloria Watkins]. *Feminist Theory: From Margin to Center*. Boston: South End Press, 1984.

———. *Talking Back*. Boston: South End Press, 1989.

Huizinga, Johan. *Homo Ludens: A Study of the Play-Element in Culture*. Boston: Beacon Press, 1950.

Hume, David. "From 'Of Love and Marriage.'" In *Visions of Women*, 157–59. *See* Aquinas, 1983.

———. "From 'Of the Rise and Progress of the Arts and Sciences.'" In *Visions of Women*, 155–56. *See* Aquinas, 1983.

Hurston, Zora Neale. *Their Eyes Were Watching God*. Chicago: University of Illinois Press, 1978.

Irigaray, Luce. *This Sex Which Is Not One*. Trans. by Catherine Porter with Carolyn Burke. Ithaca, NY: Cornell University Press, 1985.

Jaggar, Alison. "Feminist Ethics: Projects, Problems, Prospects." In *Feminist Ethics*, 78–104. *See* Bar On, 1991.

———. *Feminist Politics and Human Nature*. Totowa, NJ: Rowman & Allanheld, 1983.

James, William. "A Review [of] 1. Women's Suffrage, the Reform Against Nature, by Horace Bushnell, New York, Scribner, 1869, [and] 2. The Subjection of Women, by John Stuart Mill, New York, Appleton, 1869." In *Visions of Women*, 355–64. *See* Aquinas, 1983.

Jerome. "From *Against Jovinianus*." In *Visions of Women*, 83–86. *See* Aquinas, 1983.

Kant, Immanuel. "From *Anthropology from a Pragmatic Point of View*." In *Visions of Women*, 247–52. *See* Aquinas, 1983.

————. "From *Observations on the Feeling of the Beautiful and Sublime.*" In *Visions of Women*, 241–47. *See* Aquinas, 1983.

————. *Lectures on Ethics.* Trans. by Louis Infield. Indianapolis: Hackett Publishing, 1963.

————. *The Moral Law.* Trans. by H. J. Paton. New York: Barnes & Noble, 1963.

————. *Observations on the Feeling of the Beautiful and Sublime.* Trans. John T. Goldthwait. Berkeley: University of California Press, 1960.

————. "On the Supposed Right to Lie from Altruistic Motives." In *Critique of Practical Reason and Other Writings in Moral Philosophy.* Trans. by Lewis White Beck. Chicago: University of Chicago Press, 1949.

————. *Perpetual Peace.* Trans. by Lewis White Beck. New York: Bobbs-Merrill, 1957.

Kelly-Gadol, Joan. "Social Relations of the Sexes: Metholodogical Implications of Women's History." In *Feminism & Methodology*, 15–28. *See* Dill, 1987.

Ketchum, Sara Ann, and Christine Pierce. "Separatism and Sexual Relationships." In *Philosophy and Women*, 163–71. *See* Bartky, 1979.

Kierkegaard, Soren. "From *Journals and Papers.*" In *Visions of Women*, 313–16. *See* Aquinas, 1983.

————. "From *Stages on Life's Way.*" In *Visions of Women*, 302–12. *See* Aquinas, 1983.

————. *Sickness Unto Death.* Trans. by Walter Lowrie. In *Fear and Trembling and Sickness Unto Death.* Garden City, NY: Doubleday, 1941.

Kirp, David L., Mark G. Yudof, and Marlene Strong Franks. *Gender Justice.* Chicago: University of Chicago Press, 1986.

Kojève, Alexandre. *Introduction to the Reading of Hegel.* Trans. by James H. Nichols, Jr. New York: Basic Books, 1969.

Kolodny, Annette. "Dancing Through the Minefield: Some Observations on the Theory, Practice, and Politics of a Feminist Literary Criticism." In *Women and Values: Readings in Recent Feminist Philosophy*, 242–57. *See* Addelson, 1986.

Kuykendall, Eléanor H. "Toward an Ethic of Nurturance: Luce Irigaray on Mothering and Power." In *Mothering: Essays in Feminist Theory*, ed. by Joyce Trebilcot, 263–74. Totowa, NJ: Rowman & Allanheld, 1983.

Le Doeuff, Michèle. *Hipparchia's Choice: An Essay Concerning Women, Philosophy, etc.* Trans. by Trista Selous. Cambridge, MA: Blackwell, 1991.

Lewis, C. S. "From *Mere Christianity.*" In *Visions of Women*, 437–38. *See* Aquinas, 1983.

Lindsey, Kay. "The Black Woman as Woman." In *The Black Woman: An Anthology*, 85–89. *See* Beale, 1970.

Locke, John. "From 'Essay Concerning the True Original, Extent, and End of Civil Government.'" In *Visions of Women*, 150–52. *See* Aquinas, 1983.

Long, Katie. "Cyclorama chief tries to end life of battles." *The Atlanta Constitution* (August 11, 1990): D1, D6.

Lorde, Audre. *Sister Outsider*. Trumansburg, NY: Crossing Press, 1984.

Lugones, María. "On the Logic of Pluralist Feminism." In *Feminist Ethics*, 35–44. *See* Bar On, 1991.

———. "Playfulness, 'World'-Travelling, and Loving Perception." *Hypatia* 2, no 2 (Summer 1987):3–19.

MacKinnon, Catharine A. "Feminism, Marxism, Method, and the State: Toward Feminist Jurisprudence." In *Feminism & Methodology*, 135–56. *See* Dill, 1987.

———. *Feminism Unmodified: Discourses on Life and Law*. Cambridge, MA: Harvard University Press, 1987.

———. *Toward a Feminist Theory of the State*. Cambridge, MA: Harvard University Press, 1989.

Maimonides. "From *The Book of Women.*" In *Visions of Women*, 94–101. *See* Aquinas, 1983.

"Man charged with murder in brother's death" and "Husband, wife die in dispute." *The Atlanta Journal/The Altanta Constitution* (December 6, 1992): E2.

"Man indicted in condom-rape case." *The Atlanta Journal/The Atlanta Constitution* (October 28, 1992): A10.

Manning, Rita C. *Speaking from the Heart: A Feminist Perspective on Ethics*. Lanham, MD: Rowman & Littlefield, 1992.

Marcuse, Herbert. *Eros and Civilization: A Philosophical Inquiry into Freud*. Boston: Beacon Press, 1955.

McBride, William L. *Sartre's Political Theory*. Bloomington: Indiana University Press, 1991.

McMahon, Joseph H. *Humans Being: The World of Jean-Paul Sartre*. Chicago: University of Chicago Press, 1971.

Merleau-Ponty, Maurice. "Sartre and Ultrabolshevism." In *Adventures of the Dialectic*. Trans. by Joseph Bien. Evanston, IL: Northwestern University Press, 1973.

Mernissi, Fatima. *Beyond the Veil: Male-Female Dynamics in Modern Muslim Society*. Bloomington: Indiana University Press, 1987.

Mill, John Stuart. "From *The Subjection of Women*." In *Visions of Women*, 288–98. See Aquinas, 1983.

———. *On Liberty*. New York: Appleton-Century-Crofts, 1947.

———. *Utilitarianism, Readings in Moral Philosophy*, ed. by Andrew Oldenquist. Boston: Houghton Mifflin Co., 1965.

Miller, Casey, and Kate Swift. *Words and Women: New Language in New Times*. Garden City, NY: Anchor Books, 1977.

Montesquieu, Baron de, Charles-Louis de Secondat. "From *The Spirit of Laws*." In *Visions of Women*, 164–70. See Aquinas, 1983.

Moody-Adams, Michele M. "Gender and the Complexity of Moral Voices." In *Feminist Ethics*, 195–212. See Bar On, 1991.

Moraga, Cherríe. "La Guera." In *This Bridge Called My Back: Writings of Radical Women of Color*, 27–34. See Cameron, 1983.

Mott, Lucretia. "From 'Discourse on Woman.'" In *Visions of Women*, 323–27. See Aquinas, 1983.

Moulton, Janice. "Sex and Reference." In *Philosophy and Women*, 103–8. See Bartky, 1979.

Murdoch, Iris. *Sartre, Romantic Rationalist*. New Haven, CT: Yale University Press, 1953.

Musa, Nabawiya. "The Difference Between Men and Women and Their Capacities for Work." Trans. by Ali Badran and Margot Badran. In

Opening the Gates: A Century of Arab Feminist Writing, 263–69. *See* Helie-Lucas, 1990.

Nedelsky, Jennifer. "Reconceiving Autonomy: Sources, Thoughts and Possibilities." *Yale Journal of Law and Feminism* 1, no. 1 (Spring 1989): 7–36.

Nietzsche, Friedrich. "From *Beyond Good and Evil*." In *Visions of Women*, 330–33. *See* Aquinas, 1983.

———. "From *The Gay Science*." Trans. by Walter Kaufmann. In *The Portable Nietzsche*, ed. by Walter Kaufmann, 93–102. New York: Viking Press, 1954.

———. "From *Human, All-too-Human*." In *Visions of Women*, 334–38. *See* Aquinas, 1983.

———. "From *The Joyful Wisdom*." In *Visions of Women*, 339–40. *See* Aquinas, 1983.

———. "From *Thus Spake Zarathustra*." In *Visions of Women*, 341–42. *See* Aquinas, 1983.

———. *Thus Spoke Zarathustra: A Book for All and None*. Trans. by Walter Kaufmann. *The Portable Nietzsche*, ed. by Walter Kaufmann, 103–439. New York: Viking Press, 1954.

Noddings, Nel. *Caring: A Feminine Approach to Ethics & Moral Education*. Berkeley: University of California Press, 1984.

———. "A Response." *Hypatia* 5, no. 1 (Spring 1990): 120–26.

Nussbaum, Martha C. *The Fragility of Goodness*. New York: Cambridge University Press, 1986.

Nye, Andrea. *Feminist Theory and the Philosophies of Man*. New York: Croom Helm, 1988.

O'Neill, Onora. "Kantian Approaches to Some Famine Problems." *Ethics and Public Policy*, ed. by Tom L. Beauchamp and Terry P. Pinkard, 205–19. Englewood Cliffs, NJ: Prentice-Hall, 1983.

Ortega y Gasset, José. "From *Man and People*." In *Visions of Women*, 449–54. *See* Aquinas, 1983.

———. "From *On Love*." In *Visions of Women*, 454–59. *See* Aquinas, 1983.

Parker, Pat. "Revolution: It's Not Neat or Pretty or Quick." In *This*

Bridge Called My Back: Writings by Radical Women of Color, 238–42. *See* Cameron, 1983.

Peterson, Susan Rae. "Coercion and Rape: The State as a Male Protection Racket." In *Feminism and Philosophy*, 360–71. *See* Griffin, 1977.

Plato. *Symposium*. Trans. by W.H.D. Rouse. New York: New American Library, 1956.

Pogrebin, Letty Cottin. *Among Friends: Who We Like, Why We Like Them, and What We Do With Them*. New York: McGraw-Hill, 1987.

Pomerantz, Gary. "Walters family affair: a fatal attraction." *The Atlanta Journal/The Atlanta Constitution* (September 9, 1990): A1, A8.

Randall, Margaret. "'And So She Walked Over and Kissed Him...': Robert Bly's Men's Movement." In *Women Respond to the Men's Movement: A Feminist Collection*, 141–48. *See* Adair, 1992.

Rawls, John. *A Theory of Justice*. Cambridge, MA: Harvard University Press, 1971.

Raymond, Janice G. *A Passion for Friends: Toward a Philosophy of Female Affection*. Boston: Beacon Press, 1986.

Reuters News Service. "Angry Canadians Demand Stricter Gun Laws." *Los Angeles Times* (December 8, 1989): A24.

Rich, Adrienne. *Compulsory Heterosexuality and Lesbian Existence*. Denver: Antelope Publications, 1982.

———. "Women and Honor: Some Notes on Lying." In *Women and Values: Readings in Recent Feminist Philosophy*, 352–57. *See* Addelson, 1986.

Richards, Janet Radcliffe. *The Sceptical Feminist*. Boston: Routledge & Kegan Paul, 1980.

Rousseau, Jean-Jacques. "From *A Discourse on Political Economy*." In *Visions of Women*, 196. *See* Aquinas, 1983.

———. "From *Emile*." In *Visions of Women*, 196–208. *See* Aquinas, 1983.

Ruddick, Sara. "Better Sex." In *Philosophy and Women*, 109–20. *See* Bartky, 1979.

————. "Maternal Thinking." In *Mothering: Essays in Feminist Theory*, 213–30. *See* Kuykendall, 1983.

————. *Maternal Thinking: Toward a Politics of Peace*. New York: Ballantine books, 1989.

————. "Preservative Love and Military Destruction: Some Reflections on Mothering and Peace." In *Mothering: Essays in Feminist Theory*, 231–62. *See* Kuykendall, 1983.

Russell, Bertrand. "From *Marriage and Morals*." In *Visions of Women*, 417–23. *See* Aquinas, 1983.

Santayana, George. "From *The Life of Reason*." In *Visions of Women*, 405–6. *See* Aquinas, 1983.

Sartre, Jean-Paul. *Anti-Semite and Jew*. Trans. by George J. Becker. New York: Schocken Books, 1965.

————. *Being and Nothingness*. Trans. by Hazel E. Barnes. New York: Philosophical Library, 1956.

————. *The Chips Are Down*. Trans. by Louise Varése. New York: Lear, 1948.

————. *Critique of Dialectical Reason*. Trans. by Alan Sheridan-Smith. Atlantic Highlands, NJ: Humanities Press, 1976.

————. *The Devil and the Good Lord*. Trans. by Kitty Black. In *The Devil and and Good Lord and Two Other Plays*, 1–149. New York: Vintage Books, 1960.

————. *Dirty Hands*. Trans. by Lionel Abel. In *No Exit and Three Other Plays by Jean-Paul Sartre*, 129–248. New York: Vintage Books, 1955.

————. *The Emotions*. Trans. by Bernard Frechtman. New York: Philosophical Library, 1948.

————. "Existentialism is a Humanism." In *Existentialism from Dostoevsky to Sartre*, ed. Walter Kaufmann, 287–311. New York: World Publishing, 1956.

————. "An Interview (1970)." In *Phenomenology and Existentialism*, ed. by Robert C. Solomon, 511–18. New York: Harper & Row, 1972.

————. *Iron in the Soul*. Trans. by Gerard Hopkins. Harmondsworth, Middlesex: Penguin Books, 1971.

————. *Kean*. Trans. by Kitty Black. In *The Devil and the Good Lord and Two Other Plays*, 151–279. New York: Vintage Books, 1960.

————. "The Last Words of Jean-Paul Sartre, An Interview with Benny Lévy." Trans. by Adrienne Foulke. *Dissent* (Fall 1980): 397–422.

————. "Materialism and Revolution." In *Literary and Philosophical Essays*, trans. by Annette Michelson, 198–256. New York: Collier Books, 1962.

————. *Men Without Shadows*. Trans. by Kitty Black. London: Hamish Hamilton, 1949.

————. *No Exit*. Trans. by Stuart Gilbert. In *No Exit and Three Other Plays by Jean-Paul Sartre*, 1–47. New York: Vintage Books, 1955.

————. *Notebooks for an Ethics*. Trans. by David Pellauer. Chicago: University of Chicago Press, 1992.

————. "Preface." *The Wretched of the Earth*, 7–26. *See* Fanon, 1968.

————. "The Republic of Silence." *The Atlantic Monthly* (December 1944): 39–40.

————. *Saint Genet*. Trans. by Bernard Frechtman. New York: New American Library, 1964.

————. *Search for a Method*. Trans. by Hazel E. Barnes. New York: Alfred A. Knopf, 1967.

————. "Self-Portrait at Seventy." In *Life/Situations*, trans. by Paul Auster and Lydia Davis, 3–92. New York: Pantheon, 1977.

————. *The War Diaries of Jean-Paul Sartre*. Trans. by Quintin Hoare. New York: Pantheon Books, 1984.

————. *What Is Literature?* Trans. by Bernard Frechtman. New York: Harper & Row, 1965.

————. *The Words*. Trans. by Bernard Frechtman. New York: Fawcett World Library, 1966.

Schopenhauer, Arthur. "From 'On Women.'" In *Visions of Women*, 270–76. *See* Aquinas, 1983.

Singer, Marcus George. *Generalization in Ethics: An Essay in the Logic of Ethics, with the Rudiments of a System of Moral Philosophy*. New York: Alfred A. Knopf, 1961.

Singer, Peter. "All Animals Are Equal." In *Ethics and Public Policy*, 387–402. *See* O'Neill, 1983.

"Slaying, suicide end 'lovers' quarrel,'" *The Atlanta Constitution* (February 18, 1992): D2.

Smith, Barbara, and Beverly Smith. "Across the Kitchen Table: A Sister-to-Sister Dialogue." In *This Bridge Called My Back: Writings by Radical Women of Color*, 113–27. *See* Cameron, 1983.

Smith, Dorothy E. "Women's Perspective as a Radical Critique of Sociologe." In *Feminism & Methodology*, 84–96. *See* Dill, 1987.

Spelman, Elizabeth V. *The Inessential Woman: Problems of Exclusion in Feminist Thought*. Boston: Beacon Press, 1988.

———. "The Virtue of Feeling and the Feeling of Virtue." In *Feminist Ethics*, 213–32. *See* Bar On, 1991.

Spencer, Anna Garlin. "From *Woman's Share in Social Culture*." In *Visions of Women*, 381–90. *See* Aquinas, 1983.

Spivak, Gayatri Chakravorty. *In Other Worlds: Essays in Cultural Politics*. New York: Routledge, 1988.

Stace, W. T. *The Concept of Morals*. New York: Macmillan, 1962.

Stocker, Michael. *Plural and Conflicting Values*. Oxford: Clarendon Press, 1990.

Thomson, Judith Jarvis. "A Defense of Abortion." In *Women and Values: Readings in Recent Feminist Philosophy*, 268–79. *See* Addelson, 1986.

Tong, Rosemarie. *Feminist Thought*. Boulder, CO: Westview Press, 1989.

———. "Sexual Harassment." In *Women and Values: Readings in Recent Feminist Philosophy*, 148–66. *See* Addelson, 1986.

———. *Women, Sex, and the Law*. Totowa, NJ: Rowman & Littlefield, 1984.

Tristan, Anne, and Annie de Pisan. "Tales from the Women's Movement." In *French Feminist Thought: A Reader*, ed. by Toril Moi, 33–69. New York: Basil Blackwell, 1987.

Walker, Alice. "Coming Apart: By Way of Introduction to Lorde, Teish and Gardner." In *You Can't Keep a Good Woman Down: Stories By Alice Walker*, 41–53. New York: Harcourt Brace Jovanovich, 1979.

————. "One Child of One's Own: Meaningful Digression Within the Work(s)—An Excerpt." In *But Some of Us Are Brave*," 37–44. *See* The Combahee River Collective, 1982.

Wasserstrom, Richard A. "Racism and Sexism." In *Philosophy and Women*, 8–20. *See* Bartky, 1979.

Welch, Sharon D. *A Feminist Ethic of Risk*. Minneapolis: Fortress Press, 1990.

Whitbeck, Caroline. "Theories of Sex Difference." In *Women and Values: Readings in Recent Feminist Philosophy*, 34–51. *See* Addelson, 1986.

Wollstonecraft, Mary. "From *Vindication of the Rights of Woman*." In *Visions of Women*, 218–38. *See* Aquinas, 1983.

Woolf, Virginia. *Three Guineas*. New York: Harcourt Brace Jovanovich, 1938.

Young, Iris Marion. "Impartiality and the Civic Public: Some Implications of Feminist Critiqies of Moral and Political Theory." In *Feminism as Critique: On the Politics of Gender*, 57–76. *See* Butler, 1987.

————. *Justice and the Politics of Difference*. Princeton, NJ: Princeton University Press, 1990.

Index

About the Author

Linda A. Bell is a professor of philosophy at Georgia State University in Atlanta, where she continues to devote time and energy, with other like-minded souls, to the development of a women's studies program. In addition to feminist theory, Bell studies, teaches, and publishes in the areas of existentialism, ethics, and continental philosophy. She has published numerous articles, along with two books: the first, an anthology of philosophers' statements about women—*Visions of Women* (Humana Press, 1983)—and the second, a development of an ethics from the writings of Jean-Paul Sartre—*Sartre's Ethics of Authenticity* (University of Alabama Press, 1989).

The present volume combines almost all of her philosophical and feminist interests and concerns. She hopes to think and write more about many of the issues covered in and suggested by this book.